THE HEIDELBERG MYTH

THE HEIDELBERG MYTH

The Nazification and Denazification of a German University

STEVEN P. REMY

HARVARD UNIVERSITY PRESS
Cambridge, Massachusetts, and London, England   2002

Copyright © 2002 by the President and Fellows of Harvard College
All rights reserved
Printed in the United States of America

Library of Congress Cataloging-in-Publication Data

Remy, Steven P.
    The Heidelberg myth : the Nazification and denazification of a German university / Steven P. Remy.
      p. cm.
    Includes bibliographical references and index.
    ISBN 0-674-00933-9 (hardcover : alk. paper)
    1. Universität Heidelberg—History—20th century.   2. Higher education and state—Germany.   3. National socialism and education.   I. Title.

LF2812 .R46 2002
378.43'46—dc21   2002069072

For Beth Kilgore

Contents

Preface *ix*

Introduction: The Swastika in the Ivory Tower *1*

1 Embracing National Socialism *12*

2 The "German Spirit" in Scholarship *50*

3 The National Socialist University at War *85*

4 Constructing the Myth *116*

5 The Limits of Denazification *146*

6 Whitewashing the Ivory Tower *177*

7 A Culture of Forgetting *218*

Conclusion: Complicities and Silences *234*

Appendix A. The Structure of the German University *247*

Appendix B. Dissertations Supervised by Paul Schmitthenner, 1932–1941 *249*

Archival Sources *253*

Notes 255

Index 323

Preface

The catastrophe of National Socialism continues to draw intense interest from scholars and the wider public on both sides of the Atlantic, and confrontations with the Nazi past remain a prominent factor in contemporary German political, economic, and cultural life. In this study of Germany's academic elite and National Socialism, I address myself both to the years of the Nazi dictatorship and to the ways in which this influential elite recalled those years to each other and to the public. What follows also chronicles a systematic and sustained attack on objectivity in research and teaching. That a significant number of scholars representing the birthplace of modern academic freedoms led this attack should serve as a cautionary tale of the often destructive relationship between politics and scholarship.

It has been one of the most pleasurable tasks of this project to thank the individuals and institutions that have assisted me. Above all I thank my wife, Beth Kilgore, and my family, Richard, Delores, and Sharon Remy. Their love, faith, and support made the completion of this study possible. My greatest intellectual debt is to my mentor and friend Jeffrey Herf. As a scholar and a teacher he has inspired me—and will continue to inspire me—by his example. I am also indebted to Steven Merritt Miner, John Lewis Gaddis, and Norman Goda for teaching me much about the craft of history and the historian's profession. Ohio University's Contemporary History Institute and the

Department of History provided a rich environment in which to become an academic historian, and I thank Bruce Steiner, Chester Pach, Lon Hamby, Katherine Jellison, Kara Dunfee, Kathy Cooper, and Sherry Gillogly for their guidance and support. My fellow graduate students (now colleagues) Marc Selverstone, Ray Haberski, Jeff Woods, Jason George, and D. J. Clinton were sources of inspiration, camaraderie, and valued friendship.

Scholars and friends on both sides of the Atlantic were most generous with their comments and suggestions. I am particularly grateful to the late Professor Daniel Penham for his willingness, despite poor health, to speak with me about his experiences as a Counter Intelligence Corps officer in Heidelberg. I also thank Michael Penham, Joyce Monges, Robert Wolfe, James Tent, Jerry Muller, Christian Jansen, Jürgen Kocka, Norbert Frei, Detlev Junker, Michael Grüttner, Barry Katz, Günther Heydemann, Helmut Sonnenfeld, Wolfgang Schwannitz, Florian Jung, and Craig Pepin for their invaluable advice. Volker Sellin and Eike Wolgast at Heidelberg university were most helpful with their suggestions. I also thank Peter Olson, J. D. Marple, the late Melissa Heydenreich, Steve Klinkefus, Carolina Hüttmann, and Steve Sachoff for providing all manner of encouragement and good cheer.

I am grateful to Kathleen McDermott and Nancy Clemente of Harvard University Press for their interest in and close attention to this project. A generous grant from the Deutsche Akademische Austauschdienst made a research trip to Heidelberg possible, and I am indebted to that fine organization. Thanks also to the German-American Center for Visiting Scholars in Washington, D.C., for providing me with an office in the early stages of my research. The completion of this project would have been impossible without the support of the Mershon Center of The Ohio State University and its director, Richard Ned Lebow. Thanks also to Alden Craddock, Matthew Keith, Wynn Kimble, Beth Russell, Pat Glenn, and Ann Powers for making my time at Mershon enjoyable and productive. This study was enriched by conversations at the Mershon Center with Richard Hamilton, Wulf Kansteiner, Michael David-Fox, Alex Stephan, and Alan Beyerchen. I am also grateful for the assistance of numerous archivists and librarians, especially Werner Moritz, Ewald Kessler, and Elisabeth Hunerlach of the Universitätsarchiv Heidelberg, Hans

Müller and Corinna Pfisterer of the Generallandesarchiv Karlsruhe, and Michael Stanske of the Universitätsbibliothek Heidelberg. At the National Archives, I thank Larry MacDonald, John Taylor, and Amy Schwartz. Thanks also to Marti Gansz at the George C. Marshall Research Library and Helen Solanum of the Hoover Institution.

THE HEIDELBERG MYTH

Introduction:
The Swastika in the Ivory Tower

> If one day the situation were reversed and the fate of the vanquished lay in my hands, then I would let all the ordinary folk go and even some of the leaders . . . but I would have all the intellectuals strung up, and the professors three feet higher than the rest; they would be left hanging from the lampposts for as long as was compatible with hygiene.
> —Victor Klemperer, diary entry for August 16, 1936,
>   *I Will Bear Witness: A Diary of the Nazi Years, 1933–1941*

This is a study of academic culture in Germany during and after dictatorship. It focuses on the responses of professors at a single university, Ruprecht Karls Universität in Heidelberg, to National Socialism and examines how they recalled the Nazi dictatorship after 1945. The engagement of Heidelberg's professorate with National Socialism was extensive. They welcomed the Weimar Republic's demise and supported the establishment of the Nazi dictatorship. The willing participation of the academic elite at Heidelberg and other universities was of vital importance to the regime's project of "racial" purification at home, the concomitant war of expansion, and its imperialist economic and cultural offensives in occupied Europe. I argue that what motivated this engagement were complex and varied adaptations to the "German spirit" in scholarship, a concept encompassing aggressive nationalism, racism, anti-Semitism, and the rejection of objectivity in research and teaching. After the war, however, Heidelberg professors constructed elaborate narratives of defense and justification that served to absolve all but a few of connection to National Socialism. Collectively, these narratives formed the Heidelberg myth. The myth contributed to the collective amnesia about the Nazi past that characterized West German society in its formative years, shielded German universities from forthright reckonings with their own pasts, and informed a remarkably resilient consensus among historians regarding the academic elite under Nazi rule. The durability of the

Heidelberg myth in German academic culture testifies to the power of collective memory and the formidable tensions between memory, justice, and democracy in societies emerging from the shadows of dictatorship.[1]

German scholars have long resisted examining their own fields' engagement with National Socialism.[2] Nonetheless, historians began to assess these relationships immediately after the war, forming two opposing poles around which scholarly debate has revolved ever since. The earliest and most influential appraisal was that of the Freiburg historian Gerhard Ritter. In late 1945, Ritter published "The Professor in the 'Third Reich'" ("Der Professor im 'Dritten Reich'") in the journal *Die Gegenwart*.[3] He claimed that the vast majority of professors wanted nothing to do with the regime, its ideology, and its policies. Most, he argued, defended the autonomy of scholarship against ideological interference. Until very recently the consensus among historians has echoed Ritter's recollections. This consensus can be summarized briefly. Two "zero hours"—one in 1933 and one in 1945—bracketed the years of the Third Reich. In 1933, the universities were taken over by a small clique of ideologues and pseudo-scholars who were joined temporarily by a few well-established figures like Martin Heidegger and Carl Schmitt. Germany's once-great universities were henceforth plunged into a new Dark Ages. But the majority who had not been purged rejected National Socialism and struggled to go about their work as before. If they had joined the Nazi Party or the Storm Troopers (Sturmabteilungen, or SA), most had been only nominal members who had joined out of initial enthusiasm or to protect their careers. In any case, scholars like Heidegger and Schmitt became disillusioned and lost influence within the party after the mid-1930s. In 1945, the occupiers—in cooperation with anti- or non-Nazi professors—removed the fanatics and restored the great tradition of the liberal university, at least in the western zones.[4]

Ritter's assessment has been untenable since 1946, when the Latvian-born scholar of Yiddish Max Weinreich published his remarkable and remarkably little-known study, *Hitler's Professors*.[5] Weinreich's indictment of German academic culture was unsparing. Drawing on documents and the publications of professors both famous and obscure, Weinreich concluded that the Holocaust was "not perpetrated solely by a comparative small gang of the Elite Guard or by the Gestapo . . . the actual murderers and those who sent them out and applauded them had accomplices. German scholarship provided the ideas and techniques which led to and justified this unparalleled slaughter."[6] *Hitler's Professors* should have provided a natural starting point for more detailed studies of individual disciplines and institutions by scholars with access to more sources than were available to Weinreich. But most historians on both sides of the Atlantic have ignored *Hitler's Professors* from the time of its publication and it has never been translated into German. Rather, Gerhard Ritter's exculpatory conception of the professorate has remained the most influential.

Beginning in the mid-1960s, leftist West German writers and university students produced a series of works that called attention to the Nazi pasts of numerous prominent scholars, many of them at that time occupying the very highest positions in academe. They were not systematic studies of academic culture under dictatorship, but rather encyclopedic chronicles of compromising statements born out of frustration at a conservative elite's unwillingness to discuss its role in the Third Reich or to reform the academy.[7] Only in the following decades did detailed archival-based studies begin to appear on the regime's policies toward the universities, particular disciplines, individual universities and scientific institutions, students, and prominent individuals (most notably Martin Heidegger, Carl Schmitt, and Hans Freyer). This scholarship greatly expanded our knowledge of the relationship between academic culture and the Third Reich, but the overall assessment of the professorate did not vary substantially from Ritter's thesis. The majority of "ordinary" professors remained an undifferentiated mass, relegated to the shadowy corners of an "ivory tower under siege." Recent research in Germany and the United States, however, is forging a new consensus regarding the extent of academic culture's engagement with National Socialism. That large numbers of reputable scholars put their prestige and talents at the service of the regime can no longer be doubted. Greater attention is also being drawn to continuities in both personnel and research agendas before and after National Socialism, and historians are beginning to recognize that academic culture under the Nazis was more complex than has previously been acknowledged.[8] Yet as recent debates in Germany over the Nazi pasts of several prominent historians have demonstrated, the conception of a professorate that largely maintained its intellectual integrity and stayed out of politics remains well entrenched.[9]

A study that examined the fate of Heidelberg or any other German university from 1933 through the early years of the Federal Republic has not appeared in this growing body of scholarship.[10] A case study offered a way to explore in detail the responses to the Nazis by an influential segment of the German public, thus adding to our knowledge of the impact of National Socialism on German society and the ways in which the Third Reich has been recalled since the end of the war. Carrying the narrative beyond the mythical "zero hour" of 1945 also allows us to disentangle the memory of National Socialism as recalled by Heidelberg professors after 1945 from the contemporary records of their words and deeds in the preceding twelve years. In this study, therefore, I have focused on the everyday history of the Heidelberg professorate—their research, publications, teaching, and their responses to political developments, war, defeat, and occupation. Although the evidence shows that most scholars embraced National Socialism to some degree and opposition was virtually nonexistent, what follows is not an argument for the "collective guilt" of the German professorate. Nor is it an exercise in Enthüllungsgeschichte—the unmasking, for its own sake, of the "brown pasts" of numerous professors. Academic culture in Germany was composed of ordinary individuals who adapted to extraordinary circumstances in a variety of ways, ranging from outright complicity in the regime's crimes to quiet acquiescence to (in the rarest of cases) resistance. This study explores these varied responses in the context of a single institution.

My analysis of the implementation and reception of the Nazi dictatorship at Heidelberg has been informed by three complementary conceptual frameworks. One relates to the nature of the dictatorship itself. The concept of totalitarianism remains valuable to historians of National Socialism in describing the aims and methods of the regime, as well as the "totalitarian temptation"—the yearning, as Karl Dietrich Bracher put it, "for the absolute; that is, for a 'true democracy' . . . that promises a utopian solution to all problems."[11] Adolf Hitler and the Nazi Party sought to control virtually every aspect of life in Germany through the "coordination" of public and private life with the regime's ideological objectives. Universities were to be no exception, and the party aimed to control these influential institutions with the goal of creating, as one party publication put it, a "new type" of student, professor, and scholarship.

But another level of analysis is necessary in order to understand how academics responded to the dictatorship. A large body of scholarship has shown the responses to Hitler, the Nazi Party, and the regime's policies among various segments of the German public to have been extremely complex, involving varying degrees of active or passive accommodation, outright opposition, or some combination thereof. Historians have also revealed that local conditions and actors were often crucial in shaping events in a "polycratic" dictatorship. Further, as Ian Kershaw has argued, the nature of Hitler's leadership alongside the "fragmentation of government" made initiatives on the part of the public not only possible but also crucial to the regime's survival. The various forms that these initiatives took at one of Germany's most famous and prestigious universities are a major focus of this study.[12]

Second, I have paid close attention to continuities and discontinuities in Heidelberg's academic culture. Beginning and ending the story in 1933 and 1945, respectively, tends to reinforce a particular conception of Germany's past: namely one that holds the twelve years of Nazi rule to have represented an aberrant disruption in German history. Both breaks and continuities marked the transitions from the Weimar Republic to the Third Reich and from the Third Reich to the Federal Republic of Germany. With the important exception of Jewish and leftist scholars fired from 1933 to 1937, there was considerable continuity of personnel from the Weimar Republic to the Third Reich. The debates among professors over the purposes and forms of the university and the nature of scholarly inquiry that erupted in the late nineteenth century did not simply end in 1933 but continued in modified forms into the Third Reich. Research in a number of areas was adapted to new ideological circumstances, but this adaptation was not simply imposed by the state on unwilling university faculties. In many cases it drew upon scholarly developments predating 1933. Continuity in personnel also characterizes the transition from the Third Reich to the Federal Republic, while research agendas and previously published material were revised to accommodate changed political circumstances. Furthermore, Nazi-era scientific advances and methodological innovations in a variety of fields influenced work undertaken in postwar laboratories and seminar rooms. Scholarship in Germany did not come to a standstill between 1933 and 1945.

Finally, I have considered the relationship between politics, ideology, and scholarship. Before and after 1945, it became commonplace for contemporary observers and historians to proclaim that there was no coherent policy toward academic culture under the Nazis, let alone such a thing as "Nazi scholarship."[13] But a clear policy existed from the beginning of the Third Reich and was embraced widely if unevenly at all universities: universities and scientific institutes were to be purged of Jews and "Marxists" and their work was to serve the "Volk." Beyond this, was there such a thing as "National Socialist scholarship"? Developments at Heidelberg and other German universities shed light on the social and institutional contexts in which the production and legitimization of knowledge takes place. Historians, sociologists, and scientists themselves have long debated this problem. I contend here that there is no such thing as "normal" or "abnormal" science. What becomes accepted as valid scholarly knowledge is contingent upon certification by a community that has agreed to respect a set of principles of experimentation and verification. The power of the knowledge scholars produce comes from its implementation into technology, which may be put to both constructive and destructive purposes.[14] But these communities and the individuals that constitute them are influenced by a welter of cultural, political, and economic factors that can affect how research is conducted and the kinds of outcomes that will be considered legitimate or not legitimate. This was no less the case in Germany between 1933 and 1945 than in other times and places.

Academic culture in the Third Reich would seem to be an ideal site for exploring the contingent nature of how scholarly knowledge is gained. Yet relatively few historians have taken up this challenge.[15] For the historian of universities in Nazi Germany it is necessary to understand the evolution of the regime's paradigm of scholarship on its own terms and to investigate its relationship to academic culture. This paradigm became known as the "German spirit." This concept was not simply a Nazi Party propaganda tool that was ignored within the ivory tower and ridiculed from abroad. Its sources in Germany's cultural and political life predate 1933 and its principal advocates were university professors and right-wing intellectuals.[16] It encompassed streams of völkisch nationalism, anti-Semitism, and biological and cultural racism and entailed an antipositivist conception of scholarship that placed all research and teaching in the service of the "people's community," defined in racist terms.[17] Many of its proponents considered race a determinative factor in human history and rejected the concept of "value-free" scholarship, contending that the "racial" identity of the scholar himself determined how accurately he could examine and evaluate the world.

This is not to argue that a rhetorically or substantively "pure" National Socialist scholarship ever came into being. Scholars quarreled among themselves over its meaning and applications and party figures complained that the "German spirit" had inspired the work of too few professors.[18] In a little-known 1934 study, fourteen of the "greatest German researchers" were asked the deceptively simple question "What is race?" and provided fourteen different answers.[19] Yet the evidence from Heidelberg indicates that the "German spirit" made significant if uneven inroads into academic culture, pervading the study of physics, biology, medicine, history, law, theology, literature, and language. As we will see in the second half of this book, the notion that the "German spirit" represented an abuse of scholarship imposed by the Nazi Party on the universities and embraced by a small minority of ideological fanatics formed the basis of the exculpatory postwar Heidelberg myth.

The narrative that follows proceeds chronologically. In Chapter 1 I explain how the "coordination" of Heidelberg from 1933 to 1936 was decreed from above and implemented from below. In the second chapter I explore the increasingly important place that racist concepts and the orientation of scholarship toward the regime's expansionist aims—the "German spirit"—occupied in research and teaching between 1936 and 1939, and in Chapter 3 I show how these developments continued into the war years. The immediate postwar period, when the university's leadership constructed the Heidelberg myth, is the subject of Chapter 4. In Chapter 5, I focus on the professorate's response to the American policy of denazification. Chapter 6 analyzes the importance of the civilian tribunal process (the Spruchkammer) at Heidelberg for the memory of National Socialism. Finally, I survey the university in the early years of the Federal Republic and consider the implications of the return of former Nazis to the faculties for scholarship, political renewal, and the memory of the Nazi past.

A brief summary of Heidelberg's fate during the Weimar Republic will help place what follows into context. The tide of illiberal currents that capsized the Weimar Republic flowed from Germany's intellectual and academic elites. The pervasiveness of antiliberal traditions in the universities can be attributed largely to the unwillingness of the professorate to come to terms with the nation's rapid modernization and the dislocations brought about by World War I. By the late nineteenth century, the distinguished German university professor had come to occupy a position of authority and influence unrivaled in the rest of Europe or in the United States. Not only had their institutions produced some of the world's greatest scientific achievements, but the "Mandarin elite," as Fritz Ringer labeled them, controlled access to the powerful civil service through the administering of qualifying examinations and in general laid claim to representing the propertied and educated classes. Overwhelmingly male and the products of upper- and middle-class backgrounds, they became deeply skeptical of modern democratic mass politics in general and opposed radical social reform in particular. Anti-Semitism was also pervasive in academia, though the virulent racist strain that had emerged in Germany and elsewhere in the late nineteenth century was relatively rare before 1933. By the outbreak of World War I, the German professorate had become steadfast supporters of the German Empire, the "intellectual bodyguard of the Hohenzollerns" according to a contemporary French observer, and often outspoken champions of expansionist military and foreign policies.

Yet most professors considered themselves "apolitical" in that they believed they served an ideal that transcended ordinary politics: the cultivation of the whole person to serve the higher ends of a true "culture state." Germany's rapid modernization and the resulting social changes, however, had shaken the Mandarins' self-confidence in their position as the principal bearers and transmitters of Germany's cultural capital. German universities had expanded rapidly and scientific and technological advances had led to seemingly ever increasing disciplinary specialization and the emergence of technical schools, which in the minds of many professors threatened their own status and influence. The tensions created by these developments sparked rancorous debates over institutional reform, the purpose of the university in the modern world, and whether scholarly inquiry itself could ever be wholly free of the values of the scholar. Perceived national humiliation in 1918 and the economic crises of the Weimar years further alienated professors (particularly a growing number of young scholars facing dim career prospects) from the existing political and economic order, hence fueling the resolve of many to subvert this order and replace it with one that would reestablish their cultural hegemony over a revitalized German nation.[20]

Writing shortly before his death in 1949, the Heidelberg legal scholar and Weimar-era Minister of Justice Gustav Radbruch likened his university's pre–World War I intellectual climate to Noah's Ark—every "new form" of intellectual seemed to be represented there.[21] Marianne Weber echoed these sentiments in her rose-tinted recollections of Heidelberg in the Weimar Republic. The university, she wrote in 1949, "had been a haven of intellectual freedom . . . no one suffered for his political or philosophical beliefs."[22] In the Weimar years, Heidelberg was indeed home to an unusually broad political spectrum among its professorate, earning it a national reputation as a "stronghold of liberalism" and the republic's "model university." This liberal and tolerant atmosphere formed an important part of what was known as the "Heidelberg spirit," an atmosphere further enriched by the university's worldwide renown, the relatively large number of prominent scholars working in all the faculties, an abundance of foreign students, and a variety of informal academic and artistic circles. The liberal Baden government accommodated professors with a wide range of political views and was comparatively tolerant of Jewish instructors and students. A significant number of Heidelberg professors—principally in the philosophy and law faculties—supported Germany's republican experiment. Heidelberg had also become a vibrant center of the young discipline of sociology, above all due to the presence and legacy of Max Weber and the efforts of his younger brother, Alfred. Alfred Weber, along with Emil Lederer, ensured that a range of views on politics and scholarship was represented at the Institute for Social and Political Sciences (Insosta), whose instructors and students included a galaxy of young luminaries.[23]

The sociologist Karl Mannheim, writing from the pained perspective of exile from his native Hungary, noted in the early 1920s that Heidelberg "is cosmopolitan despite its tradition, because they have been accustomed here for centuries to strangers."[24] Many Americans in particular had become familiar with Heidelberg as tourists or by reading Mark Twain or seeing *The Student Prince*. Scholars, students, and writers from the United States found the university inviting and hospitable. With its reputation, legendary fraternities, and charm, it represented to many the quintessential "German university." Moreover, a number of influential Americans studied at Heidelberg and later formed important cultural conduits between Germany and the United States. The sociologist Talcott Parsons, for instance, would become instrumental in introducing Max Weber to American scholars. One of the most prominent postwar American "cultural diplomats," Shepard Stone, also studied at Heidelberg (albeit very briefly) and would use his contacts there and at other universities very effectively in conducting what Volker Berghahn has referred to as America's "cultural Cold War" in postwar Western Europe.[25] In the mid-1920s, the American ambassador to Germany, Jacob Gould Schurman, himself a one-time Heidelberg student, was instrumental in raising $500,000 to build several new university buildings.[26]

But there were limits to this liberal and international spirit. Though Heidelberg was generally hospitable to Jewish scholars, informal restrictions on their advancement existed there as at other universities. Hence the philosopher Ernst Hoffmann declined to supervise Paul Oskar Kristeller's Habilitation (doctoral dissertation; see Appendix A) in 1928 because a prior commitment to mentor another Jewish student meant that Hoffmann "could not possibly support two Jewish candidates at the same time."[27] As the map of the professorate's political activities and publications drawn by Christian Jansen indicates, conservative nationalists dominated most faculties, and younger, junior-level instructors in particular demonstrated clear antirepublican convictions throughout much of the 1920s.[28] As Germany's economic and political fortunes seemed to be shattering beyond repair by the early 1930s, the strength of liberal forces across the faculties waned while conservative, antirepublican, and anti-Semitic sentiment increased in strength.[29] That the boundaries of tolerance at Heidelberg had reached their outermost limits by 1932 is revealed in the case of the statistician Emil Gumbel. At German universities throughout the 1920s, a number of prominent Jewish, socialist, and pacifist professors were denied promotion, harassed by right-wing colleagues and students, and driven outright from their institutions.[30] As a socialist, committed pacifist, and a Jew, Gumbel was the ultimate "outsider" to Germany's conservative nationalist academic culture. His well-known chronicles of political violence committed by both the left and the right that exposed the judicial system's leniency toward the latter earned him the enduring enmity of the radical right. After years of public controversy at Heidelberg, Gumbel was hounded from the university in a campaign led by conservative professors, local right-wing agitators, and radical students.[31] On July 2, 1932, in the wake of the Gumbel affair, the Frankfurt magazine *Deutsche Republik* announced that "'liberal' Heidelberg has thus opened the era of the Third Reich in the sphere of academia!"[32]

That the ground at Heidelberg and other universities was well prepared for the Nazi seizure of power supports the claim made in 1932 by the right-wing political theorist Edgar Julius Jung that National Socialism's intellectual preconditions were being formed outside National Socialism itself.[33] Commentary by professors at Heidelberg and elsewhere on the health of Germany's political and academic cultures had by this time become distinctly gloomy and fatalistic, and few offered practical remedies as calls for revolution from the radical left and right intensified.[34] Though pro-democratic professors remained a strong presence until the end of the Weimar Republic, the lines dividing left and right had become unclear by the early 1930s, as prominent liberals departed and "antiliberal democrats" alongside conservative nationalists advocated authoritarianism to address the nation's chronic political instability and to create a true "democracy" based on a unified "people's community." Not surprisingly, interest in the fascist regime in Italy grew among professors and students.[35] Although many viewed Hitler's appointment as Chancellor in January 1933 as just another change in government, their enthusiasm grew as the Nazi Party launched its so-called national revolution. It is to the responses among Heidelberg's professorate to the Nazi consolidation of power that I turn in the next chapter.

CHAPTER ONE

Embracing National Socialism

National Socialism has become Germany's destiny; it must fulfill its mission.
—Willy Andreas, commencement address, Heidelberg University, May 1933

The final years of the Weimar Republic were dominated by increasingly unstable political coalitions and a turn to authoritarian rule. On Janaury 29, 1933, President Paul von Hindenburg appointed Adolf Hitler Chancellor in a new coalition government of National Socialists and conservative nationalists. The new Chancellor, however, set out immediately to consolidate total power for himself and the National Socialist German Workers' Party (Nationalsozialistische Deutsche Arbeiterpartei, or NSDAP) by subordinating public life to the regime's authority in a process known as Gleichschaltung (coordination). Hitler's objective was not to destroy established institutions but to ensure their complete loyalty to the party's goals in general and to himself in particular.[1] As part of the civil service, the universities were to be "coordinated" with the new regime. In this chapter I examine the responses of Heidelberg's professorate to National Socialism during the first years of Nazi rule. Nazi-controlled state governments purged "unwanted elements" from the faculties and student bodies and curtailed institutional self-governance at all universities. But Heidelberg's "nazification" was accomplished both from above by decree and from within the university through a process of "self-coordination," the extent of which varied from faculty to faculty.[2]

As was often the case in the governance of Nazi Germany, there was no single ministry or national organization responsible for the nation's universities, but several. The party attempted to control university professors primarily through the Reich Education Ministry (Reichserziehungsministerium, or REM), the National Socialist University Instructors League (Nationalsozialistische Deutscher Dozentenbund, or NSDDB), and the Security Service (Sicherheitsdienst, or SD). Though the influence of the REM and its head Bernhard Rust could be considerable, its effectiveness was hindered by bureaucratic conflict with other ministries.[3] The Dozentenbund, aimed at shaping the political commitment of younger instructors, was neither particularly effective nor popular, and the power of individual Dozentenbund leaders varied widely. At Heidelberg, just over half the professorate ultimately became members, and the local Dozentenbundführer from 1935 to 1945 was an undistinguished professor of dentistry who wielded little authority within the university.[4] The extent of the SD's power over Germany's universities remains unclear. At Heidelberg there was no shortage of informers among the professorate. Although the local records of the SD were apparently destroyed, American intelligence reports and postwar denazification trial records identified fifteen professors as informants.[5]

Of greater significance for Heidelberg were the actions of the Baden state government, Nazi students, and professors themselves. The first measures aimed at the university's "coordination" were implemented from Karlsruhe by the new Minister of Culture, Otto Wacker, and his adviser on university matters, Eugen Fehrle. On the advice of the Freiburg philosopher Martin Heidegger, in January 1933 Wacker decreed new constitutions for Freiburg and Heidelberg that imposed the "Führer principle" on both institutions.[6] It was the first of Germany's states to take this step; Prussia promulgated a similar decree in October. The new constitution curtailed though did not eliminate Heidelberg's autonomy of self-governance. The Rector was designated the "Führer" of the university and was to be named by the Minister of Culture. His tenure was indefinite, though the Minister could replace him at any time. All powers formerly residing with the Great and Small Senates were given to the Rector. A "Senate" consisting of the Rector, his deputy (Chancellor), the faculty chairmen, and five others selected by the Rector from the ranks of the full, junior, and honorary professors and the unsalaried lecturers (Privatdozenten) would continue to exist but could no longer make decisions binding on the institution. The faculty chairmen were to be appointed by the Rector from the body of full professors, were responsible directly to him, and served at his pleasure. Although faculties retained the authority to bestow advanced degrees and to submit calls for new faculty members, their recommendations were subject to review by the Ministry in Karlsruhe and the REM and NSDDB.[7]

Meanwhile, the regime was taking further steps to reconstruct the faculties. On April 21, 1933, Bernhard Rust decreed that the rectors and faculty chairmen at Prussia's universities who had been serving before February 1, 1933, were to step aside and new elections were to be held to fill those posts. The same demand was subsequently presented to non-Prussian universities. Many of the men elected to replace their colleagues were National Socialists or Nazi sympathizers. At Heidelberg, however, the new elections did not produce drastic changes. The chairmen of the theology, medical, and philosophy faculties were reelected. But those of the law and natural sciences faculties were Jews and had resigned or had been dismissed, so new chairmen were elected. All were either at that time pro-Nazis or quickly fell into line behind the regime.[8] In the wake of Rust's election decree, the conservative nationalist historian Willy Andreas offered to resign as Rector. Both the Small and Great Senates, however, decided by vote that he should serve out the remainder of his term. But Nazi students in particular did not consider Andreas radical enough to lead the university in the new state. A turning point may have come following a speech at Heidelberg by Martin Heidegger on June 30. Heidegger claimed the national revolution was not yet taking place at the universities. A young history instructor, Gerd Tellenbach, recalled that one student became so agitated by Heidegger's speech that he remarked that Andreas should be rewarded for his lack of vision with a bullet in the head. This student's sentiments were no doubt shared widely among his contemporaries, and attacks on Andreas's rectorship in the Nazi press ran for months.[9] Nonetheless, Andreas served out the remainder of his term.

His successor was the undistinguished legal scholar Wilhelm Groh, who would serve as Rector until 1936. The Great Senate's election of Groh on July 8, 1933, was to be the last free election to this position until 1945.[10] Pro-Nazi professors and students had envisioned Groh as Rector months before his election. Some who voted for him probably hoped that he would be acceptable to the new government and not an agent of radical change. If so, they were disappointed very quickly. Upon becoming Rector Groh circulated a memorandum aimed at distancing himself from his predecessor. German universities, he argued, had failed in their duty to educate "the people," had not served to unify the nation, and "frequently . . . absorbed foreign ideas which were incompatible with the German character and the German nature." The National Socialist "revolution," however, had reversed this development, but without the help of people such as Andreas.[11] In a speech to the entire teaching body in the early summer of 1935, he demanded that those professors who were not prepared to advance the revolution in the universities be removed, and here he meant above all "the Jews and those married to Jews."[12] During his tenure as Rector Groh packed the university's leadership with Nazis or Nazi sympathizers.[13] To the "Führer principle" of the new constitution he added an invention of his own—the "Führer's staff" of hand-picked advisers, all radical Nazis.[14] The move was undoubtedly meant to bolster Groh's standing within the party and solidify his control over the university by keeping decision-making in a tight circle around him. Aside from this administrative innovation, Groh made no original contributions to scholarly debates on law in the new state. He was, as Helmut Seier suggested, an effective "power tactician" skilled at ingratiating himself with the regime.[15]

The first years of the Third Reich also marked the apogee of Nazi student radicalism and influence. At Heidelberg, Nazi student leaders such as Franz Alfred Six, Richard Oeschle, Fritz Kubach, Goetz von Chelius, and above all Gustav Adolf Scheel were determined to purge the university of "non-Aryans" and "Marxists" and educate male "political soldiers" for the Third Reich.[16] Scheel's influence on Groh and on the university's day-to-day affairs in this period was considerable. "Not the Rector," the aging historian Otto Brandt complained to Hermann Oncken in August 1934, "but a wild student leader governs, in whose antechamber professors wait uncomplaining for over an hour until they will be graciously allowed in!"[17] Scheel and his cohorts attacked "non-Aryan" professors in the local press, arranged for disruptions and boycotts of their lectures, and accompanied police and SA detachments on numerous house searches. Nazi students played an active role in the faculty purges and the "auto-da-fé" of books on the university's main square.[18] They also attempted to create a university within the university by organizing lectures by visitors such as Martin Heidegger and Helmut Nicolai and by Heidelberg students and professors on "the intellectual foundations of National Socialism" (Franz Alfred Six), "the worker and labor organization in Germany" (Ernst Schuster), "doctors, the diseased, and the people" (Heinrich Kunstmann), "folklore and homeland" (Eugen Fehrle), and "the law of German labor" (Wilhelm Groh).[19]

Of particular importance for the university were the purges and reconstruction of its faculties in the wake of the "Law for the Restoration of the Professional Civil Service." Two days before the regime promulgated the national law on April 7, 1933, the government of Baden decreed that all civil servants "of the Jewish race" in Baden "regardless of confessional affiliation" were to be dismissed immediately. Civil servants who could not "guarantee that they have always unreservedly supported the national state" were also to be dismissed.[20] In 1933 and 1934, at least sixteen hundred scholars (out of a total of about five thousand university teachers), were dismissed. By late 1938, Germany (including Austria) had lost 39 percent of its university teachers. Berlin and Frankfurt were the hardest hit proportionately and in absolute numbers, losing over 32 percent of their instructors. Heidelberg was a close third, with over 28 percent lost between 1933 and 1938. The overwhelming majority were fired on "racial" grounds.[21] Most of those dismissed in the 1930s left Germany for other European countries or the United States. Of the purged Heidelberg professors, thirty-one left Germany, most never to return. Nearly all went to other western European countries, Turkey, or the United States, though many could not or chose not to remain in the first place they landed. The evidence regarding Heidelberg's professors compiled by Dorothee Mussgnug indicates that all who left attempted to maintain careers in their fields of specialization, but met with varying degrees of success.[22]

The personal, professional, and financial problems facing those who chose or were forced to leave Germany were enormous. Although some received assistance from American or British foundations and ad hoc emergency organizations created to assist persecuted German scholars, most were on their own. The mathematician Arthur Rosenthal remained in Heidelberg after his dismissal while seeking, without success, a teaching position abroad. In the aftermath of the Reichskristallnacht in November 1938 he was taken into "protective custody" and interned in Dachau for four weeks. After his release he was offered an unpaid one-year position at Princeton University. With ten Reichsmarks in his pocket, the fifty-two-year-old Rosenthal arrived in the Netherlands in July 1939 and left for the United States the following March, but not before losing his entire personal library in a German air raid on Rotterdam harbor. After leaving Europe, Rosenthal had to turn his attention to rescuing his nearly seventy-five-year-old mother, then interned in a concentration camp. After five months of effort, he managed to secure her release and passage to the United States. Thereafter, his professional situation improved. Until 1941, he lectured at the University of Michigan and a year later began teaching at the University of New Mexico.[23]

Jewish scholars responded to the regime's measures in a variety of ways. Many Jewish and non-Jewish professors alike believed that Hitler's regime would not last. The Leipzig philosopher Hans-Georg Gadamer, for instance, recalled that "none of us knew how far the anti-Semitism of Hitler went, how seriously to take it, and to what extent it was just a selling point, an instrument towards the seizure of power rather than the real policy of the Nazis. My Jewish friends almost entirely took the view that it was not serious."[24] The philosopher Karl Löwith continued to teach at Marburg as long as he could, though he knew his dismissal was imminent. In his memoirs, he admitted that he had deceived himself "for years" by believing that "anti-Jewish measures would be moderated."[25] Many others held themselves to be loyal and patriotic Germans first, Jews second or—in the case of the Heidelberg legal scholar Walter Jellinek—not at all.[26] The Dresden philologist Victor Klemperer considered the Nazi regime distinctly "un-German" not only because it was barbarous but also because it attempted to overturn the traditions of the "Rechtsstaat" (the state based on the rule of law). Many no doubt shared the prediction of the Breslau legal scholar Ludwig Waldecker in December 1933 that "a great state such as Prussia will not tolerate illegality or perversions of the law." Another Jewish jurist at Breslau, Ernst Cohn, advised Jellinek to adapt to the new regime and avoid confrontation.[27] Karl Löwith also recalled an atmosphere of uncertainty and a desire among Jewish scholars "to wait and see how things would develop, and to avoid any personal exposure."[28] Certainly, the absence of solidarity on the part of their non-Jewish colleagues came as a hard blow to many. "I naturally ask myself," the scholar of Romance languages Leo Spitzer wrote Löwith in April 1933, "whether I could and should not do something martyr-like—but it is now up to the 'others.' I recently heard the Matthew Passion, which is highly relevant in its description of the loneliness of the persecuted. By that I do not mean to say that there are no good souls and sympathetic natures here, as anywhere else. But there exists a fundamental lack of understanding and solidarity between those who are secure and those who are not."[29]

The situation at Heidelberg supports Spitzer's assessment: the dominant response of the professorate to the loss of their Jewish colleagues was almost total silence. In this respect Heidelberg was not exceptional among German universities. Only the Medical Faculty appealed to the Ministry of Culture in Karlsruhe on behalf of Jewish scholars. The statement, dated April 5, 1933, and signed by its chairman, Richard Siebeck, was unusual in that such statements were rare in Germany and because it went so far as to hint at criticism of regime-sponsored violence—"the danger . . . that all sense of responsibility is being pushed aside by emotional or impulsive violence." Siebeck and his colleagues wrote that the faculty serves the "eternal science" of medicine and that "the universities are committed to national traditions and the state" and that German academics are obliged to teach in a "German" manner. But they also pointed out that Jews had made substantial contributions to medicine and that it would be Germany's great loss if they were removed from the universities. The central plea, however, was for the protection of legality and the integrity of the civil service. If civil servants were going to be purged from the university, the statement concluded, only those with competence in the relevant field could rightfully make such decisions.[30] The memorandum reveals the ambiguities in the relationship between non-Jewish and Jewish scholars in German universities. Powerful currents of resentment toward Jews in academia predated 1933. Yet, as Fritz Stern has suggested, many non-Jewish scientists, business leaders, and politicians benefited from and recognized the contributions of individual Jewish scholars to German scientific achievement. The Medical Faculty's memorandum reflects this recognition, as well as the widely accepted notion of Jews as somehow separate from "Germans."[31]

In her unpublished memoirs, the Heidelberg botanist Gerta von Ubisch recalled the silence of her colleagues in the face of the purges. Von Ubisch, the first woman in Baden to complete a Habilitation and receive the state's permission to teach at a university, was fired in

1935 on "racial" grounds. The full text of her remarkable memoirs has remained unpublished and largely unread in the archives of Heidelberg University's library for nearly fifty years:

> One asked oneself, how was it possible that the universities did not speak out against this law; that they did not unanimously speak up for their colleagues. If all university professors, doctors, jurists had done this, if all had gone on strike, this law could have never been carried out. There are a number of reasons this did not happen. One was that the timing of the law was skillfully chosen. Over the Easter holiday, in which very many instructors, who had not been warned, were traveling . . . those returning were presented with a *fait accompli*. Second, the law, with the limitations demanded by Hindenburg, did not affect so many full professors, since nearly all had been in one or another position in the war or claimed to have been in essential work . . . It affected nearly all young teachers who had not taken part in the war. Because of caste-conceit and the sharp borders that existed between full professors and non-full professors, the firsts were not very interested in the lasts . . . The third reason . . . was that, in their heart of hearts many Germans were anti-Semites and each one had one more or less large circle of Jews that he knew well and that he accepted as exceptions, while he rejected the Jews *in principle*. There were many among the university professors who found that there were too many Jews among the instructors.[32]

The "fearfulness" of the situation began to become clear to the majority of unaffected professors only when, for instance, their own children employed as civil servants were fired, or when they saw their participation in faculty meetings and committees restricted, or when their classes were boycotted or disrupted by Nazi students. Many if not most Heidelberg professors, in other words, rejected Jews in the abstract or as a group. In some cases, they proved willing to defend Jewish colleagues out of ties of friendship or professional affiliation or concern for the disruptive impact of large-scale dismissals. But collective indignation, let alone opposition, was absent in Heidelberg as it was at every other German university.

Of greater concern to most was the intrusion of the state into the university's affairs and the hardships that the purges would inflict on the functioning of seminars and institutes. In a supposedly confidential memorandum Willy Andreas prepared for Otto Wacker in September 1933, the historian expressed approval of the "national revolution" and many of the regime's measures but defended the university's autonomy. He argued that there were certain "traditional elements" of the old constitution that if kept would assist in building the university in the new state. Self-government, for instance, was not only a fundamental part of the specifically "German" university tradition that predated the liberal era but also one that had roots in ancient Germanic tribal voting practices. Andreas also requested that the state formally affirm its willingness to uphold the freedom of research and teaching, not least for the effect such an affirmation would have abroad. Further, he questioned the naming of the Rector by the Ministry, quoting Tacitus's admonition that "the leader commands more through his example than through might." Despite these reservations, however, Andreas was glad to see the power of the Senate curtailed and the authority of the faculty chairmen increased.[33] A similar argument is found in the Senate's formal response to the purges, which claimed that the university "is deeply affected" by the purges and requested that the Ministry act to protect it. Professors, the statement pointed out, are called to their positions by "competent university authorities" and in many cases have tenured positions and could not be dismissed on the grounds laid out in the new law. Further, implementation of the decree would result in the loss of irreplaceable scholars. The university would thus not be able to "fulfill its duty to the State and the German people."[34] There was some initial justification for these fears, particularly in faculties hit hardest by the purges. In the winter semester of 1935 and 1936, for instance, not a single full professor was available to teach a course in mathematics.[35]

Legitimate fear of the SA and Nazi students during the tumultuous months of 1933 and 1934 most certainly influenced these sentiments. Some professors who had not been fired yet were barely tolerated by the Nazis were subjected to a range of humiliations, such as boycotts, disruptions of their classes, and house searches. Some were eventually restricted from travel to scholarly conferences abroad, prevented from publishing, or denied access to the university's library. Others had their pensions reduced. For some, maintaining a semblance of normal academic activity could be extremely difficult. Ludwig Wesch, an acolyte of the physicist and long-time Nazi supporter Philip Lenard, made life miserable for the physicist Walter Bothe by conducting exercises with SS troops for hours on the roof of the Physics Institute directly over Bothe's office.[36] The weekly afternoon gatherings at Alfred and Marianne Weber's residence were suspended by the hosts themselves, if only temporarily. When the meetings resumed, the atmosphere had chilled considerably. "The discussion of contemporary issues," Marianne recalled, "had to be avoided. Students could be invited only after very painstaking selection. The group tried to avoid notice, but even then it was under observation. Members who thought that their academic posts were endangered and who felt under pressure to join the Storm-Troopers in order to give evidence of their devotion to the new state, ceased to participate."[37]

As at all other German universities, there were no acts of collective protest by professors against the Nazi Party's policies and actions. When Alfred Weber resisted the SA's attempts to fly the swastika over public buildings, including his own institute, following the March 1933 elections, a furious campaign erupted against him in the Nazi press.[38] The *Volksgemeinschaft* asked, "Did you protest in a newspaper, Herr Weber, when red pirate flags were hoisted over public buildings in 1918? Did you protest in a newspaper, Herr Weber, when the German scientist Professor Lenard was manhandled by Marxist rabble?" The notoriously mercurial Weber responded in the *Heidelberger Tageblatt* that in 1918 he had had no time to protest flag hoisting of any kind because he had been totally preoccupied with "forming Free Corps units against the Spartacist uprising." Weber's action was not an expression of opposition to National Socialism per se, though it took a great deal of courage to stand up to the SA, but rather a protest against extra-legal measures. Weber's public defense of himself strikes one as all the more courageous given that he received no support from either Rector Andreas or the Senate. Contrary to his claims in 1945 and after that he had been fired on political grounds, Weber resigned from the university voluntarily, four months before he would have reached his official retirement age.[39]

Individual scholars who refused to join the party or put their scholarship at the service of the Nazis often retreated into "inner immigration"; that is, they turned their attention to subjects of interest to them but not, they hoped, to the new authorities, or developed a form of writing unique to dictatorship in which criticism of the regime was cloaked in analogy, metaphor, or satire. Following his discharge on political grounds, Gustav Radbruch immersed himself in a biography of the nineteenth-century criminologist Anselm Feuerbach, making rapid enough progress to have the book published in Vienna a year after his dismissal.[40] Gerhard Anschütz retreated to his study and wrote his memoirs. Karl Jaspers recalled the period between his firing in

1937 and the early years of the war as a "time for reflection," since he received a pension and enjoyed the relative luxury of having time in which to read, think, and write.[41] Alfred Weber similarly recalled that the years of the Third Reich represented the "first period of my life in which I could be really productive without the encroachment of daily work."[42] Marianne Weber's salon remained the only forum where such scholars could discuss their research without fearing denunciations from jealous Nazi colleagues or Nazi students.[43]

Adolf Hitler detested intellectuals and university professors, and the calumny and insults heaped upon the academic elite by various Nazi Party satraps are legendary. Party officials believed they had good reason to distrust Germany's professorate. Although the NSDAP had scored substantial victories among students before 1933, professors were another matter. Perhaps a dozen full professors across Germany joined the party before Hitler was named Chancellor, and prominent non–party member supporters such as Philipp Lenard were rarities. Hence party criticism of professors was widespread in 1933 and 1934. "Cocooned in the dubious Sleeping Beauty idyll of an academic autonomy," one party publication declared in 1933, "the world of scholarship no longer had an ear for the roaring stream of life and so, when it forcibly intruded, academics felt it as a hostile disturbance."[44]

Such criticism was overstated. The dominant response of professors who had not been fired was enthusiasm for the new regime and a willingness to adapt to it. In advance of the March 1933 elections, three hundred professors signed a call for support of the NSDAP and Adolf Hitler. A month later and two weeks after hundreds of its constituents' professors had been fired, the Association of German Universities issued a statement (on its own initiative) that heaped praise on the "new German Reich." Also in April the German Recotors Conference established a special committee to prepare for the "close integration [of the universities] with the Volksgemeinschaft." In November, seven hundred of a total of about two thousand full professors nationwide signed an avowal to "Adolf Hitler and to the National Socialist state."[45] Associations representing various academic disciplines also pledged their support and hundreds of individual professors joined the Nazi Party.[46] By September 1935, sixty-one instructors and staff at Heidelberg had become party members, and forty-one had joined the SA. Thirty-four more would become party members in 1937.[47]

But support for the new regime went beyond the signing of declarations, and party membership in a dictatorship is not by itself a reliable indicator of ideological conviction. At Heidelberg a significant number of professors from all levels of the university hierarchy and from all age groups supported the new regime in a flood of publications, speeches, and private correspondence. Most professors expressed joy over the demise of the Weimar Republic, which was invariably described as "weak," "foreign," and "un-German." Most who commented on the events of the spring of 1933 viewed them as part of a "national revolution" that embodied a mixture of continuity with Germany's past and the radical, youth-oriented element of the National Socialist "movement." Professors also praised various Nazi Party policies while justifying or at least ignoring the party's anti-intellectualism and sponsorship of violence against its opponents. Many would have agreed with the Heidelberg theologian Andreas Duhm when he characterized the events of the spring of 1933 by paraphrasing Robespierre's defense of revolutionary violence: "In a revolution, heads fall, and a young movement is cruel."[48] Anti-Jewish statements and references to race and the "racial superiority" of the "Germans" proliferated. The year 1933, then, did not represent a "crisis," as many professors claimed after 1945; rather it witnessed a "national uprising" that promised to link the pre-republic past to a glorious future.[49]

In 1933 and 1934, for instance, Willy Andreas lauded Hitler and the "national revolution" as promising to provide the way out of the morass of the Weimar Republic. "National Socialism," he thundered in his May 1933 graduation address, "has become Germany's destiny; it must fulfill its mission . . . More courageously and decisively than before we shall place ourselves in the unleashed stream of the nation."[50] Praise for Adolf Hitler himself was not uncommon, nor was a general acclaim of the "return" of a single "great leader" and national unifier worthy of Bismarck's and Hindenburg's legacies. Hence Andreas portrayed Hitler as Hindenburg's true successor: "Hindenburg and Hitler have joined together in the struggle for the highest dignity of the nation. With the transfer of the chancellorship to Adolf Hitler, the venerable head of state himself opened the door to the Third Reich for the National Socialist movement."[51] Walter Jellinek argued that "since 1919, the aim of [Hitler's] gigantic will has been to recreate the solidarity of the front in his defeated homeland."[52] In a similar fashion, Otto Erdmannsdörfer, the Prorector, celebrated

Hitler's efforts at building the National Socialist "movement of national uprising," which has brought Germany out of the "misery" and weakness of "party-political" and "class divisions."[53] The jurist Heinz Hildebrandt wrote that the "Führer state" was "building trust and belief" in the "mission of the German race" and "the genius of the Führer."[54] In the effort to unify Germany, the physician Philipp Broemser, appropriately enough, concluded that Hitler would act as a surgeon, who in the "most extreme crisis" would cut the "boil" out of the German public's body "before deadly blood poisoning occurred."[55]

Willy Andreas and others did not limit themselves to speeches and publications. In a March 27, 1933, letter to Joseph Goebbels, Andreas offered to counter anti-German "propaganda" in the foreign press through his contacts with American students and government officials. The offer is a good illustration, as Philipp Gassert has pointed out, of both the party's and the German elite's sensitivity to foreign perceptions of events in Germany.[56] The sociologist Arnold Bergsträsser, who had engaged in propagandizing for the regime in France, also justified its economic measures to British economists in late 1933. Bergsträsser blamed democracy for failing to produce "that social and political unity which is necessary in order to overcome a crisis like the world crisis of 1929" and argued that "National-Socialism wants to establish a real unity between State and society. This is the deeper meaning of the rejection of Liberalism. The main idea is not to allow the existence of any sphere apart from the State."[57]

In a letter to Eugen Fehrle in May 1934, the theologian Martin Dibelius offered to propagate a positive view of the regime's measures at theological conferences in England. In conversations with British colleagues, Dibelius noted that there were often opportunities to "point out the character of the German revolution and the new German state formation and to take positions against the false and completely ignorant representations in various newspapers." Recalling the political pessimism of the last years of the republic, Dibelius relayed "the wonder of German unity, which most of us had held as late as Christmas of 1932 to have been impossible." Further, the regime had "energetically and sincerely" taken steps to alleviate the plight of German workers. The regime's "cleansing of moral life, particularly in the big cities," occasioned little comment from his hosts, and Dibelius noted that this kind of measure was hardly unknown in British history. Regarding single-party rule in Germany, he explained that the new regime aimed at "the widest possible integration of the most organizations and people in a national corporation, which the state sustains." Finally, "endeavor[ing] to present the sources of contemporary German anti-Semitism as objectively as possible," Dibelius dragged out a number of anti-Semitic shibboleths common to German academics: "the overflowing of Jews in certain professions, the immigration of Eastern Jews [Ostjuden] after the war, the well-known great cases of corruption." Officials in Karlsruhe were impressed enough to request that Dibelius continue his "activities" at future conferences.[58]

Professors also used their expertise in their own disciplines to express support for the regime. Members of the law faculty were particularly vociferous. In detailed summaries of German public law published in the journals *Reich und Länder* in 1933 and the *Annuaire de L'Insitut International de Droit Public* in 1934 and 1935, Walter Jellinek justified every major legal step taken by the regime and praised it for overcoming Germany's political, class, regional, and religious divisions. But political unity was not enough, and the new state also had to take measures to preserve its "physical and moral health." Hence the July 1933 "Law for the Prevention of Genetically Diseased Offspring," which provided the basis for forced sterilization of those deemed by medical experts to pose genetic threats to the Volk, was justifiable. Like many of his colleagues Jellinek regarded the events of 1933 as part of a "revolution." The political measures taken by the regime were not fundamentally "antidemocratic" but "antiliberal:" "It is the completely antiliberal conception of the new state that justifies the suppression of the individual. It *wishes* to be antiliberal . . . The individual is nothing at all without the state; he owes all his dignity of being human only to his subordination to the state." This understanding of rights has to come through education, and the key to this education in the new Reich would be not the Gymnasia and the universities, but the Propaganda Ministry, the Hitler Youth, the SA, and the SS.[59]

In his 1934 piece in the French journal, Jellinek also argued that the enormous political power concentrated in Hitler's hands did not mean that a single individual could determine Germany's fate. Indeed, the form of the state would limit arbitrary power: "The division of the functions of the state between a multiplicity of ministers and the necessity of collegial deliberation of all the schemes of law is a limit of appreciable psychological importance for the functioning of legislation. On the other hand, considerable psychological and historical obstacles oppose attempts to endanger independent tribunals. The time of arbitrary arrests of absolutism is definitely closed ... It must not be forgotten that a voluntary restriction of supreme power resides in the German word 'Führer,' the ideological content of which can hardly be translated into a foreign language." Jellinek's assessment of how a "totalitarian" state was supposed to operate foreshadowed postwar assessments of the "polycratic" dictatorship by German historians. That is, the multiplicity of ministries and overlapping jurisdictions constrained Hitler's personal power.[60]

Jellinek's colleagues, particularly Reinhard Höhn, Heinz Hildebrandt, and Georg Dahm provided similar justifications. Höhn, who would soon become one of the most influential intellectuals in the SS, took ideas he had absorbed as a member of the conservative Jungdeutsche Orden (Young German Order) in the 1920s and Nazi Party rhetoric and translated them into a rejection of the divisive individualism that supposedly pervaded liberal constitutional orders. In its place, a unified "people's community" would be constructed.[61] Heinz Hildebrandt, a Privatdozent, proclaimed that the decisive break with the Weimar Republic entailed the end of the "people's alienation from justice." The new state would "reunite German law with the German people's soul."[62] Dahm, a student of Gustav Radbruch who in his mentor's words had "immigrated to the new gods" and joined the NSDAP in May 1933, demanded that German judges in the new state coordinate their legal judgments with the National Socialist political order.[63] As Ingo Müller has shown, comparable statements erupted out of law faculties across Germany, providing rhetorical support for the regime and legal justification for its actions.[64]

Sociologists also were among the supporters of the regime's policies. Carl Brinkmann proclaimed that the "national uprising" would lead to to the "breakthrough to our social awareness of the great truths of the nation and the race." For the nation's economic life, this would mean "abandoning acceptance of automization and to understand the state at all times as responsible not only for the motor, but for the entire machine."[65] For Arnold Bergsträsser, the party's conception of a unified state and society informed its economic policies, which sought to subordinate "private interest" to the "common good" and justified large-scale state intervention in the economy. Bergsträsser rejected out of hand Franz Neumann's Marxist analysis of the German economy as "the dictatorship of monopolised industry and of the big estate owners" by pointing to "the temper of the middle classes and the social reasons for their policy, the land reform and the part played by the small holders, and not least the practical increase of State power by its influence on the banking system and by the enlargement of public works." In the eyes of Bergsträsser and other pro-Nazi professors, in short, National Socialism was not reactionary but revolutionary. Yet Bergsträsser also claimed that the steps being taken by the German government comported with capitalism's "inevitable" evolution: "I am convinced ... that the transformation of Liberal capitalism into a system of integrated political and economic bodies, and the increasing influence of the State on economic life, was a general and necessary development of the twentieth Century."[66]

Scholars whose fields were far removed from the practical realms of politics and economics also drew on their own fields' vocabulary to justify their support of the regime. The Germanist Hermann Güntert, writing in the introduction to his *Origins of the Germans* (*Der Ursprung der Germanen*) on the occasion of a "new national Germany" in March 1933, argued that National Socialism's ascent to power had given the study of the German language new meaning, and that "only when the German people is conscious of its essence and its character and thus learns to consider and evaluate foreign culture and foreign spirits with self-confidence and pride will it be able to win the pitiless and ruthless struggle for the existence of the people." Although the text of his book had already been written, Güntert concluded that "I would not know how better to conclude my book" than to cite Hitler's "great cultural-political" speech at Nuremberg in September 1933, in which he had celebrated the historic "creative racial" core of the Germans as the source of their strength in overcoming the problems of the present.[67] The historian Kurt von Raumer placed the significance of the "national revolution" in the context of Germany's historic national disunity. The "idea of the German people," he wrote in the journal *Wort und Tat*, "is the empire." The "national revolution" of 1933 is a true "German revolution" that "will only be realized by us from the grounds of our traditions and from the powers of our race."[68]

Anti-Semitism appeared in a variety of forms in this outpouring of praise. In general, such statements presented the Jews as scapegoats for Germany's problems, past and present. Thus Walter Jellinek considered the regime's anti-Semitic purges "necessary" for solving a number of problems, such as the supposed overpopulation of the universities. Kurt von Raumer blamed the failure of the 1848 revolution on, among other things, "the disproportionately strong participation of Jewry." Jews were held to be "foreign bodies" that had polluted Germany's cultural life—hence Martin Dibelius's and Andreas Duhm's references to the supposedly pernicious effects of "Eastern Jews" in postwar Germany, or Otto Mann's claim that the "Jewish press" distorted "objective" reporting. Hermann Güntert blamed "West European" and "Jewish thinking" and "Jewish literature" for distorting Germany's "will to live" and diluting its intellectual heritage.[69] Also striking is the frequency with which "race" is mentioned, particularly the "German race." As a category in the natural sciences and in the humanities, race was by no means novel to academic culture in Germany and elsewhere, but after 1933 it appears with greater frequency in the publications, speeches, and course titles of Heidelberg professors.[70]

Assessing the responses of those professors who were either soon to be dismissed or who were not dismissed but were anti-Nazi or at least non-Nazi is more difficult. Gerhard Anschütz, the distinguished legal scholar and one of the Weimar Republic's staunchest defenders, resigned before he could be fired. In his view, a career as a scholar of constitutional law demanded political engagement. "The task of the constitutional scholar," he wrote to the Baden Ministry of Culture on March 31, 1933, is "to impart knowledge of German constitutional law, but also to educate students in the sense and spirit of the prevailing system of government." Since this required "a high degree of inner connectedness with the state system," which he did not possess, he requested that the Ministry allow him to retire.[71] Hans von Eckardt, the director of the Institute for the Study of Journalism, communicated his dismay at his firing to Willy Andreas by calling attention to his service at the front in World War I and his loyalty to the crown and advocacy of continuing the war. In his postwar career, von Eckardt claimed that he remained a committed nationalist who became estranged from the German Democratic Party (Deutsche Demokratische Partei, or DDP) and clashed repeatedly with leftists in Heidelberg. Under their influence, he argued, socialist students shunned him and his institute.

Conversely, von Eckardt claimed that Franz Alfred Six, one of the university's Nazi student leaders, himself had found cooperation between the institute and representatives of the Nazi-dominated student government highly satisfactory.[72] These arguments were to no avail and von Eckardt was dismissed, most likely because of Six's determination (von Eckardt's claims notwithstanding) to get rid of him.[73]

A revealing assessment of the events of early 1933 from the perspective of Heidelberg's academic aristocracy is Eugen Täubler's "Heidelberger Gespräch" ("A Heidelberg Dialogue"). Written around 1944, it recounts a meeting at Marianne Weber's house in March 1933. Using pseudonyms to designate himself, Marianne Weber, Alfred Weber, Karl Hampe, Karl Jaspers, and Herbert Sultan, Täubler recalled an atmosphere of considerable unease and uncertainty. Ranging over Plato's ideas on the state and the examples of the Roman Empire and Charlemagne, the group struggled without much success to comprehend the events of the previous three months. Täubler leaves the unmistakable impression that the participants felt that all values and previous certainties had been shaken and called into question. The uneasy atmosphere suggests that the "inner immigration" into which many present went represented more than a form of staying out of trouble with the authorities. It provided a way to come to terms with Germany's fate that did not involve leaving Germany or "immigrating to the new gods."[74]

Täubler's troubled reflections on the uncertain present and future were the exception among Heidelberg's professorate in 1933 and 1934. Most of those who spoke out in this period voiced unequivocal support for the dictatorship. Such statements reflected a mixture of conviction and opportunism. The "national revolution" had in the eyes of its supporters delivered Germany from the widely hated republic. Certainly, however, some professors seized the chance to ingratiate themselves with the regime. For younger scholars accustomed to years of professional hardship and sympathetic in any case to the radical right, the opportunity to advance into hundreds of newly vacant positions must have provided strong incentive to at least appear cooperative. In addition, those who were reluctant to express sympathy for the party's program before the Nazi victory in 1933 now felt free to do so. A comment attributed to Carl Brinkmann is telling in this respect. According to the former Insosta student Hans Gerth, by the summer of 1933 Brinkmann was opening his lectures with the words "finally, we can speak freely."[75] Another factor is continuity with Weimar-era political affiliations. Paul Schmitthenner, Ernst Wahle, Friedrich Endemann, Robert Jelke, Philipp Lenard, and Hans Nieland had all belonged to the German National People's Party (Deutschnationale Volkspartei, or DNVP) and, like many others, made the transition to the NSDAP before or after 1933 without difficulty. Similarly, Eugen Fehrle had belonged to the German People's Party (Deutsche Volkspartei, or DVP) before 1933, as had Walter Jellinek (though the latter, defined as Jewish by the regime, would never have been able to join the Nazi Party). Similarly, Willy Hellpach abandoned his liberal faith for belief in fascism's and then National Socialism's ability to create a "true democracy."[76]

Finally, individual Germans could interpret National Socialist ideology in a variety of ways. It lacked, as Franz Neumann pointed out in his 1944 study of the dictatorship, a "theory of society as we understand it" and was "constantly shifting" around a core of "certain magical beliefs—leadership adoration, the supremacy of the master race."[77] This lack of "categorical and dogmatic pronouncements" left the door open to diverse interpretations of just what the new leader and state expected of its citizens. Millions of Germans hence engaged in a process of "working toward the Führer," as Ian Kershaw characterized it in his biography of Adolf Hitler.[78] University professors at Heidelberg and elsewhere were no exception. The result was not only cut-throat competition among party leaders and massive corruption and inefficiency, but also the accelerating self-radicalization of the entire society. Whatever the motives of their authors, the statements helped legitimize the regime within Germany and abroad. They contributed to the social consensus "backing Hitler" (to borrow a term from Robert Gellately) and served to separate "true Germans" from "others," the latter development a precondition for widespread discrimination, political and economic disenfranchisement, and ultimately genocide.[79]

The role of the university in the Third Reich was a contested issue left unresolved at the top levels of the Nazi Party. Party leaders developed no unified plan to create "a new type" of professor, student, and scholarship. Reflecting its general distrust of the universities, the party created or planned new institutes (which nonetheless filled their rosters with university professors)—such as Walter Frank's Institute for the History of the New Germany and Heinrich Himmler's "Ancestral Heritgage" project (Ahnenerbe). But the future of the universities was debated most extensively among professors themselves. These debates were largely a continuation of arguments over the structure and purpose of the German university that had erupted in the Wilhelmine and Weimar eras.[80]

The most influential figures in this period were Ernst Krieck, Alfred Bäumler, Adolf Rein, Hans Freyer, and Martin Heidegger. Krieck, a professor of pedagogy at a teachers college in Frankfurt and in 1933 the Rector of Frankfurt University, was the most radical. In a barrage of speeches and articles in his own journal, *Volk im Werden,* Krieck called for a revolutionary overhaul of the university through a "leveling" of its hierarchical structure and the total focus of its research and teaching on the ideological goals of the state.[81] Alfred Bäumler, Krieck's principal rival, held similar views. Adolf Rein and Hans Freyer advocated not the overturning of the existing system but the grafting of "political education" onto the university's traditional structure.[82] The views of the Freiburg philosopher Martin Heidegger, however, were the most influential in Baden in 1933 and 1934.[83] For Heidegger, the university had to renew itself by attending to the most fundamental principles of knowledge, truth, and science, as first articulated by the philosophers of ancient Greece. Grounded in this "essence," university students and teachers were obliged to serve the German people and state with intense devotion. Although the university was to "give itself its own laws," it would remain linked closely to the "Volk" that it served.[84]

Heidegger's ideas resonated widely and positively in Nazi and non-Nazi circles.[85] One prominent German admirer was Karl Jaspers. Although he was dismayed by Heidegger's rapid conversion to National Socialism, he considered the speech "the only lasting document of today's academic will."[86] Jaspers then drew up his own "theses" concerning university reform in late July and early August 1933, ostensibly for Heidelberg colleagues, though Jaspers considered sending his proposals to the Minister of Culture in Karlsruhe.[87] He believed the situation facing German universities in 1933 to be "one of unique possibility as well as danger." On the one hand, "decisive direction by a man with unlimited power over the universities" (the Minister of Culture) could actually achieve some needed institutional reform. On the other hand, this "deciding authority" may not be capable of protecting and fostering German science, which must ultimately be free from outside interference if human knowledge is to expand. The "deciding authority," therefore, must be advised by those "who have experience in the German university." "I cannot but approve of the new constitution," he wrote to Heidegger, but ". . . if the constitution is to be effective in the long run, then whoever has such authority would also have to be liable for errors . . . I wish this aristocratic principle complete success." Jaspers also warned that the university is not "not the place for political battle" and that "the palpable intrusion of subaltern minds at the university, who see a chance for themselves or would like to create one, who make up programs in a style in keeping with the times without having achieved anything decisive, would be a danger only if this very noticeable type would actually succeed. As far as I can tell, however, this is not the case."[88]

Jaspers's "theses" represent the last stand of the Mandarins against the philosophers of the new state—Heidegger, Krieck, Freyer, and others. Given what had occurred in Germany by the summer of 1933—the first steps toward dictatorship *via* the Enabling Act, the rampages of Brownshirts and Nazi students, boycotts and book burnings, the purges of Jews and leftists from the civil service—the political naiveté of Jaspers's "theses" is striking. His praise of Baden's new constitution revealed an acute case of wishful thinking. In believing that its "aristocratic principles" might redress old problems, he badly misjudged the new regime's destructive dynamism. Like some of his colleagues, Jaspers defended the university's autonomy of self-governance while praising the abolition of the troublesome Senate. But the most radical and influential university reformers at that time wanted not to tinker with a fundamentally sound but hobbled system, but to renew or overturn it completely. In 1933 it appeared that the time of the traditional Mandarins such as Jaspers or Willy Andreas had passed.[89]

Or so it would have seemed in 1933 and 1934. As Michael Grüttner has emphasized, the influence of the "philosopers" of National Socialism did not last beyond the mid-1930s. All of them fell into disfavor with various party figures and ministries. Postwar apologias to the contrary, Heidegger's, Freyer's, and others' disaffection with National Socialism was not the principal source of their decline. Personal conflicts were certainly part of the problem. Ernst Krieck, for instance, considered himself the single most important "philosopher" of National Socialist pedagogy and exhausted himself in years of quarreling with various real and imagined rivals.[90] But there are deeper causes. The decline in the philosophers' influence can be attributed primarily to the passing of the Machtergreifung (seizure of power) and Gleichschaltung and to the party's impatience with those professors forged in the traditional Mandarin cast. Party figures concerned with university affairs favored the merger of racial determinism, instinct, and action with a respect for practicality and technical innovation over the abstract philosophizing of what they considered to be an elite group of opportunists. The future, in short, belonged not only to those scholars who owed their academic appointments solely to party membership, but, more significant for the fate of scholarship in Nazi Germany, to those whose research and teaching proved useful to the regime.

Debate over the future of the university was not limited to the likes of Heidegger and Krieck. Heidelberg professors representing all disciplines also envisioned a transformation in the form and purpose of the university. The essays by a variety of instructors representing different faculties, ranks, and generations published in the May 18, 1933, edition of *Der Heidelberger Student* are exemplary. The common theme was that research and teaching must serve the German "Volksgemeinschaft" and not some abstract notion of "objective truth" or knowledge for its own sake. The Medical Faculty instructor (and soon to be full professor) Johannes Stein thus proposed that "knowledge must serve life and teaching must guide action," while Paul Schmitthenner argued that the universities must become "political universities" in the sense that "politics in the highest and last sense" meant service to the unified German people. Self-government and freedom of research would be upheld, but only to the extent that the university's work served the state and people. The authors did not make clear exactly how that was to be accomplished.[91]

Aggressive national chauvinism and völkisch concepts pervaded other statements on the purposes of the university. Willy Andreas declared that the "time of high-flown homeless intellectualism" was past and that "knowledge shall become action, intellect faith, will, and deed," while the young medievalist Gerd Tellenbach demanded that "German science must become fighting science." The philosopher Hermann Glockner called for the construction of a "German corporate body" within the universities that would teach "German" history, regional studies, folklore, archaeology, "nordic cultural regions," language, literature, music, religion, law, philosophy, and other subjects. For Glockner, only true "Germans" had the responsibility and ability to teach "German" subjects.[92] Individual disciplines would contribute to this transformation of academic culture. In times of change, the philosopher Otto Regenbogen wrote in 1934, the lessons of antiquity had much to contribute to the formation of the "German spirit" among young people, particularly the promotion of the "unity" between the people and the state. Citing Adolf Hitler's claim that "the newspaper is the means of the people's self-education," Wilhelm Waldkirch produced a three-volume scholarly treatise on the newspaper in the new state, which he, like Hitler, envisioned becoming "the standard organ of political instruction" to "advance the decisive reconstruction of the empire."[93]

At the end of 1935 Hans Hermann Adler, the new director of the Institute for the Study of Journalism, summarized the outlook of many of his colleagues in a survey of developments at Heidelberg since 1933 published in the journal *Hochschule und Ausland*.[94] In recent decades, he wrote, the university had revealed a "strong affinity" for "cosmopolitanism," which found support in the Weimar Republic. The result had been the disunity of scholarship and the detachment of scholars and students from their duty to the German people. In the wake of the National Socialist revolution, however, Heidelberg's professorate had proven willing to reverse this situation. Thus the members of the Medical Faculty were now prepared to devote their expertise to the tasks expected of them by the new state, particularly in the realm of "racial-hygienic, population- and socio-political and hereditary-pathological tasks." The Physics Institute, renamed after Philipp Lenard in late 1935 (see Chapter 2), was a point of pride, because Lenard was a Nobel laureate and a longtime supporter of Adolf Hitler. The merger of the former Insosta with the Mannheim Technical School would produce an army of technical specialists, one that would serve the goals of the "total state." The Law Faculty had reoriented itself to serve the "fundamental reconstruction of German legal study," and the Philosophy Faculty was now dominated by another longtime National Socialist, Ernst Krieck.[95] By the end of 1935, in short, Heidelberg was well on its way to becoming the "National Socialist university."

Carl Brinkmann's views merit particular attention. In *Der Heidel-*

berger Student he argued that socialism and liberalism were responsible for infecting intellectual life with the idea that the destiny of a people is dictated by impersonal forces outside their control (namely, class conflict) and the notion that society is inexorably moving toward a "classless society" and a form of common world citizenship.[96] For Brinkmann it was the "national uprising's greatest gift to science" that this pernicious idea was being refuted. But he did not regard the "old ideals" of "suppositionless" research and the goal of education for "true humanity" as no longer valid at the university. Further, he cautioned, "we do not want to disdain what the exchange of commerce and technology, science and culture between peoples offers us, and what [can be] adopted by us." Above all, research and teaching were obliged to serve the state and people. Brinkmann's tempering of ideological fervor with a relatively hardheaded concern for the usefulness of scholarly achievements captures the viewpoint of many professors who put their talents at the regime's disposal. Unlike, for instance, the "German physicists" who produced acceptable ideology but poor physics, it was scholars who shared Brinkmann's outlook who made the most substantial contributions to the regime's policies. Taken together, however, these statements reveal that Heidelberg's professorate was prepared to embrace the "German spirit" in scholarship, and that willingness was to intensify in the second half of the 1930s.

While professors proclaimed their support for the "national revolution" and their willingness to create a "political university," the practical matter of reconstructing the faculties in the wake of the ongoing purges had to be confronted. Who replaced the dismissed professors? From 1933 to 1939 vacant chairs were filled by political appointees who made little if any contribution to their fields and by a number of talented scholars who embraced Nazi ideology and oriented their research and teaching to its goals. This development was not dictated from above, nor was it necessarily related to Nazi Party membership. Appointments were shaped to a great extent by state governments, rectors, and individual faculties and professors.

The experience of the Theology Faculty at Heidelberg from 1933 to 1945 illustrates the wide range of possible responses to National Socialism among university professors. The university's smallest faculty, it suffered the least disruption in the first three years of Nazi rule and most of its members never joined the NSDAP.[97] The faculty also remained largely outside the conflicts between the Confessional Church and the Nazi-sponsored "German Christians."[98] The university's course catalogs from 1933 to 1945 reveal hardly any lectures or seminars that reflect the racist ideology or aggressive nationalism that would be offered by every other faculty. Yet a number of the faculty's professors melded Nazi ideology with their scholarship. It was the only faculty to offer overtly anti-Semitic courses in 1944 and 1945: "The Jewish Question as World-Historical Problem" and "The Jewish Question in the Seventeenth and Eighteenth Centuries" (both taught by Ernst Kiefer).[99] A young Privatdozent for practical theology, Andreas Duhm, was an outspoken anti-Semite, though he remained a marginal figure on the faculty.[100] The chairman in 1933, Robert Jelke, applied for membership in the NSDAP in 1933 and became a member in 1937. But his penchant for denunciation and intrigue generated such instability within the faculty that even Nazi students were relieved to see him replaced by Theodor Odenwald, who would serve as chairman from 1935 to the end of the war.[101] Before 1933, Odenwald had demonstrated pro-democratic sympathies (in September 1931 he was mentioned as a possible candidate for the Weimar Circle of pro-Republic academics). Although he did not join the NSDAP until 1939, he became a member of the "German Christians" in 1933.[102] As Susannah Heschel has shown, Odenwald (along with the retired theologian Georg Beer and the scholar of Islam Rudi Paret) participated in the Institute for the Study and Eradication of Jewish Influence in German Church Life, created in 1939 by Protestant church figures in Thuringia and devoted to reconciling Nazi anti-Semitism with Christianity.[103] The relationship of their colleague Renatus Hupfeld to National Socialism and the German Christians was more ambivalent. He wrote approvingly of the Nazi Party and Nazi students in 1932, and of the "national revolution" the following year. While sympathetic to some of the objectives of the "German Christians," Hupfeld did not become a member or reveal himself to be a rabid anti-Semite. He was eventually welcomed into what was left of Marianne Weber's circle of anti- and non-Nazi scholars.[104]

Martin Dibelius and Gustav Hoelscher formed the durable non-Nazi core of the faculty. It may seem surprising that Dibelius—as one of the university's most prominent Weimar-era democrats—was not fired on political grounds. Although he had, along with Hupfeld, Otto

Frommel, and Heinz-Dietrich Wendland, signed a petition in 1934 calling for the resignation of "Reich Bishop" Ludwig Müller (the former army chaplain appointed by Hitler in 1933 as bishop of the German Protestant Church), Dibelius did not stage any local public protest that would have enraged Nazi students. Opinions among Nazis at Heidelberg varied on Dibelius. Richard Oeschle, a leading Nazi student, vouched for his former teacher's political reliability in a letter to Eugen Fehrle.[105] In May 1939, Dozentenbundführer Karl Schmidhuber reported to Rector Paul Schmitthenner that he had "no doubts" about Dibelius's political reliability.[106] In addition to these votes of confidence, Dibelius's scholarly stature in Germany and abroad was enormous and this fact may also have deterred Karlsruhe from dismissing him. Theodor Odenwald, a former pupil, also protected him.

Dibelius's activities in the first years of the Third Reich exemplify the complex and multifaceted nature of political adaptation among scholars. As noted previously, he engaged willingly in informal propagandizing for the new regime during trips to scholarly conferences abroad. For the Foreign Office, Dibelius remained useful. An REM official responsible for the foreign activities of German scholars pointed out to superiors in 1937 that Dibelius—though hardly a National Socialist—belonged to the group of theologians who because of their nationalism and disillusionment with the Weimar Republic had recognized that "Germany was National Socialist and must remain National Socialist." Because of these convictions, it was this official's understanding that Dibelius had had "great success" (particularly in England) as an advocate for Germany. Indeed, as it was no secret that he had signed a petition against the naming of Ludwig Müller as "Reich Bishop," his opinions probably carried that much more weight with his foreign colleagues.[107]

Gustav Hoelscher, a well-regarded Old Testament scholar, lost his position at Bonn University in 1934 ostensibly on political grounds, but in reality because the state Education Ministry and an opportunistic junior faculty member wished to pack the faculty there with fellow "German Christians." Hoelscher was not initially wanted at Heidelberg, either. The Education Ministry, the Senate, some faculty members, and Nazi students all wished to have a party member from Tübingen, but at the last minute the Ministry in Karlsruhe called its second choice, Hoelscher. Robert Jelke considered Hoelscher a theologian without any religious faith, a member of the anti-Nazi Confessional Church, and a man whose attitudes toward Jews were friendly. Further, Nazi students, with the blessing of Rector Groh, launched a boycott of Hoelscher's lectures. The boycott had to be lifted by order of the Education Ministry, which may have considered this kind of step against a prestigious and relatively harmless scholar to be an embarrassment. Hoelscher was welcomed within the faculty by Dibelius and Hupfeld, and like them became a regular participant in Marianne Weber's circle.[108]

The faculties and the seminars constituting the Philosophy Faculty—history, philology, Insosta, and chairs in geography, art history, and Egyptology—were hit particularly hard by both purges and retirements. Eugen Täubler, Richard Alewyn, Leonardo Olschki, August Grisebach, Ernst Hoffmann, and Karl Jaspers were fired on "racial" grounds between 1933 and 1937. Further, Heinrich Rickert, Karl Hampe, Johannes Hoops, Hermann Ranke, and Friedrich Panzer all retired on the grounds of old age.[109] In philosophy itself, Groh appointed the pro-Nazi Hermann Güntert faculty chairman, and he held that post until 1937. Upon Heinrich Rickert's retirement, Ernst Krieck was called to Heidelberg after a tumultuous year as Rector of Frankfurt university. Appropriate to Krieck's speciality, Rickert's chair was renamed "the chair for pedagogy and philosophy." When Karl Jaspers and Ernst Hoffmann finally lost their positions, the REM changed Hoffmann's chair to one for art history (filled by the pro-Nazi Hubert Schrade), while Jasper's chair became the professorship for military policy and military sciences (occupied by Paul Schmitthenner).[110]

On the eve of the Nazi seizure of power, conservative nationalists, most notably Willy Andreas and Paul Schmitthenner, dominated the History Seminar. Andreas stuck to traditional diplomatic and military subjects that reflected his ideological outlook—"Germany and the Great Powers," "People, Leadership, and State in the Course of German History," and similar titles.[111] Paul Schmitthenner's interests ran along similar lines. He engineered the creation of the Seminar for the History of Warfare, which I will discuss in more detail in Chapter 2. Such seminars were also created at the universities in Rostock, Jena, Berlin, Hamburg, and Munich. Schmitthenner had been lecturing on war and politics at Heidelberg since 1928. He had also been active in the DNVP before joining the Nazi Party in August 1934. In the spring of 1933, he joined the new Nazi-dominated state government. By September, Schmitthenner had been made a state minister without portfolio. The bulk of his attention, however, was consumed with the university and the creation of the Military Sciences Seminar, which drew historians and colleagues from other faculties and specialists from outside Heidelberg.[112]

A significant if temporary addition to the History Faculty was Günther Franz, who replaced the distinguished medievalist Karl Hampe. Franz, a specialist in early modern agrarian history and the Thirty Years' War, had joined the SA and the NSDAP in 1933 (he would leave the former for the SS in October 1935 and serve as a high-ranking officer in the Race and Settlement Main Office and in the SD) and was an outspoken anti-Semite who played an important role in purging the history profession of Jewish scholars. Though Franz stayed only three semesters before leaving for Jena, he provided the impetus for the creation of the Institut für Fränkisch-Pfälzische Geschichte und Landeskunde (Institute for Frankish-Pfalz History and Regional Studies), an interdisciplinary center for Westforschung (research on Western Europe) in Baden, which I will discuss in the following chapter.[113]

Like Schmitthenner's seminar, another largely political creation was Eugen Fehrle's chair for folklore, which Fehrle, Hermann Güntert, and Otto Wacker set out to create in the summer of 1933. Fehrle was appointed full professor in 1934 and his chair was created in May 1936.[114] He also served as chairman of the Philosophy Faculty in 1942 and 1943 and the Prorektor from 1943 to 1945, and collected numerous other titles in and outside Heidelberg, mostly related to folklore. For his efforts in the "reorganization" of Heidelberg, Fehrle was made an honorary Senator in July 1942.[115] In 1939, he joined the SS and became a regiment adviser for ideological instruction. His ascent was due largely to his ideological fervor and talents as a self-promoter (the SS did not consider his scholarship to be "epoch-making"). The rapid ascent of a scholar who before 1933 might have never attained a full professorship was also due to the prominence the regime—in particular the SS under Heinrich Himmler—placed on the study of Germanic folklore, which supposedly located the "pure Aryan soul" in Germany's distant past. Before 1933, there were chairs for folklore at only three universities (Hamburg, Dresden, and the German University in Prague). From 1933 to 1935, full professorships were created at Heidelberg, Berlin, Leipzig, and Tübingen.[116]

The Institute for Social and Political Sciences (Insosta) and the small Institute for the Study of Journalism saw their ranks decimated by the purges. Insosta's remaining liberal scholars were dismissed in 1933 and five student assistants lost their positions. Hans von Eckardt, the director of the Journalism Institute, was dismissed on political grounds and replaced by Hans Hermann Adler, who had Groh's and the Nazi students' support.[117] Insosta itself ceased to exist. Beginning in the summer of 1933, the Baden state government merged the small Commercial College of Mannhein with Heidelberg's Philosophy Faculty, a move it had been considering for fiscal reasons for several years. Alfred Weber recalled the merger as an outright attempt by the Nazis to destroy the social sciences at Heidelberg: "[Insosta] with its library of more than 40,000 volumes lay as a beached wreck rotting as sacrifices on the shore. In place of social studies, the apparently unpolitical concept of commerical management was introduced into the university. Yet [the staff of the commercial school] was headed by known party members who introduced a genuine National Socialist propaganda campaign in the following years."[118] Carl Brinkmann, however, advocated the merger, claiming that the move would promote a kind of unity of scholarly endeavors. He was probably motivated by a combination of opportunism and a desire to see the social sciences oriented more toward his kind of empirically oriented research, a trend that would be strengthened by the incorporation of instructors from a technical college. The merger was completed by the fall of 1933 and Insosta was renamed the Faculty for Political Science and Economics.[119]

The changes at Insosta illuminate how politics and scholarship became closely entwined in the early years of the Third Reich. Although many of Germany's best sociologists had lost their positions, sociology was hardly dead as an academic discipline at Heidelberg or at other universities, as Alfred Weber and others claimed. As Carsten Klingemann has shown, the purges and the demands of the regime brought empirically oriented sociology—particularly research that dealt with demography, economics, industry, and rural and urban sociology—to the fore. Throughout the Third Reich there was substantial participation of such empirically oriented sociologists in various government-sponsored projects. Their influence would extend far beyond 1945, and represents one of the strongest continuities in German academic culture between the Third Reich and the postwar period.[120] Courses offered by the new faculty were interdisciplinary and of remarkably broad scope. They combined the study of political theory, history, economics, "racial sciences," sociology of an empiricist bent, business affairs (advertising, market and finances research, banking, and so forth) and extensive foreign language instruction. By the winter semester of 1935 and 1936 the faculty was holding lectures on "the ancient Germans" (Ernst Wahle), "the history of German farmers" (Günther Franz), "people and state" (Reinhard Höhn), "people and economy" (Arnold Bergsträsser), "the American New Deal" (Herbert Sultan), "agricultural economics" (Carl Brinkmann), and "the history of education" (Ernst Krieck). The following year, Carl Schneider was delivering lectures on "people and race."[121]

The two leading figures at what was left of the original institute were Arnold Bergsträsser and Carl Brinkmann. Bergsträsser was fired on "racial" grounds in 1936, but not before playing a key role in the new faculty's first three years.[122] Within the new faculty he promoted numerous Nazi students who completed dissertations with titles such as "Political Propaganda of the NSDAP in the Struggle for Power" (Franz Alfred Six, 1934) and went on to other universities or to high-ranking positions in the SS, the Propaganda Ministry, and various Reich education offices. Brinkmann was never a party member, but he did belong to the Dozentenbund and Jursistenbund (Nazi University Instructors' League and Jurists' League, respectively) and later claimed to have been dragooned into the SS. He was an influential member of the German Sociological Society (Deutsche Gesellschaft für Soziologie, or DGS) and made numerous scholarly contributions (in economics and sociology) to organs of the Academy of German Law (to which he also belonged) and helped found Heidelberg's Institute for Spatial Economics (Institut für Grossraumwirtschaft). Like Bergsträsser, he also supervised the work of several Nazi students who would go on to prominent academic careers in the Third Reich and the Federal Republic.[123]

Of the instructors brought over from Mannheim, Walter Thoms and Ernst Schuster became the most influential. Thoms joined the NSDAP in December 1932 and had taught industrial economics at Mannheim as a Privatdozent since August 1933. At Heidelberg he was promoted to full professor in 1940, served as the chairman of the faculty from 1939 to 1945, and in 1942 became the director of the Institut für Grossraumwirtschaft.[124] As we will see, Thoms was determined to infuse the study of industrial economics with the "worldview of National Socialism."[125] Schuster, a veteran and a member of the Social Democratic Party of Germany (Sozialdemokratische Partei Deutschlands, or SPD) until 1925, joined the Nazi Party on May 1, 1933, and the Juristenbund in August 1934.[126] Schuster emerged as one of Heidelberg's leading specialists on Grossraumforschung (research on large territories), devoted to the exploitation of European countries under German rule and the construction of a "new economic" order in Europe. Officially, he represented the Reich Working Group for Regional Research (Reichsarbeitsgemeinschaft für Raumforschung) at Heidelberg and was also a member of the university's Institut für Grossraumwirtschaft.

Finally, the addition of Wolfgang Panzer to the Philosophy Faculty is worth mentioning. In 1935, Panzer, enjoying Wilhelm Groh's support, replaced Johann Sölch, who had accepted an appointment in Vienna. Before assuming this position, Panzer had served as an adviser for university affairs in the REM (he had joined the NSDAP in 1934), where he acted ruthlessly against Jewish geographers. At Heidelberg, as we will see, he cofounded the Institut für Fränkisch-Pfälzische Geschichte und Landeskunde and also became a director of the Western German Research Society (Westdeutsche Forschungsgemeinschaft).[127]

Heidelberg's Law Faculty provides another example of change and continuity, not only from the Weimar Republic to the Third Reich, but, as we will see in later chapters, from the Third Reich to the Federal Republic of Germany. About one third of Germany's legal scholars were dismissed from the universities after 1933 (120 of 378 teaching in 1932), most of them on "racial" grounds.[128] Younger scholars well disposed toward National Socialism and influenced very strongly by Carl Schmitt filled the vacuum. This generation would become a dominant presence in postwar West German academic legal circles. Heidelberg's Law Faculty fits this pattern closely.[129] From 1933 to 1937, 8 professors were dismissed, including Gustav Radbruch, Gerhard Anschütz, Ernst Levy, and Walter Jellinek. The twin pillars of support for the republic and a law-based state on the faculty had been Anschütz and Radbruch, but the antirepublican right—Friedrich Endemann, Wilhelm Groh, Heinrich Mitteis, Walter Jellinek, Georg Dahm, Reinhard Höhn, Heinz Hildebrandt, and Friedrich Wilhelm von Rauchhaupt—dominated the faculty.[130] Among the conservative professors, there was a general uniformity in views regarding the law in the new state. The most important theme linking conservative and Nazi scholars—Hildebrandt, Dahm, Höhn, and later Carl Bilfinger, Herbert Krüger, Ernst Forsthoff, and even scholars of Roman law such as Georg Dulckeit—was an embrace of "German common law" and rejection of the concept of individual rights protected by law.[131] The acceptance of this conception of the law entailed excluding "non-Germans" from civic life, a critical step in creating and implementing the steady stream of anti-Semitic laws that began to appear in the spring of 1933.[132]

Throughout Germany, a relatively large number of physicians joined the Nazi Party or became enthusiastic supporters. Many medical scientists developed and disseminated Nazi race theories in their classrooms and were both designers and perpetrators of some of the regime's most heinous crimes, principally "euthanasia" and experiments performed on concentration camp and death camp inmates. During the Third Reich Heidelberg's Medical Faculty would ultimately contain a higher percentage of NSDAP members than any other.[133] In 1933, the head of the university's Psychiatric Clinic, Karl Wilmanns, was dismissed for allegedly mocking Hitler and Goering. He was replaced by Carl Schneider, who had been serving as head doctor at an asylum in Bethel (near Bielefeld). Although he had joined the NSDAP in 1932 and was supported by Philipp Lenard, he was appointed primarily because of his scientific qualifications.[134] He had published extensively on psychiatry in the 1920s, and in 1930 produced a well-regarded study on schizophrenia. In the summer semester of 1934, he replaced Philipp Broemser as the chairman of the Medical Faculty and would remain in this position until 1937. He also became the head of Baden's Racial Policy Office. Since the director and three instructors in the Psychiatric Clinic had been dismissed, Schneider had the opportunity to surround himself with devoted assistants. A number of them went on to distinguished careers in both West and East Germany, unimpeded by the past association with their mentor or their own complicity in medical crimes.[135]

The Nazis' sterilization and "euthanasia" programs were a direct outgrowth of scientific and popular interest in "racial hygiene" (or eugenics), a branch of hereditary science that had emerged in England in the nineteenth century. By the first decades of the twentieth century, racial hygiene had become well established in Germany's academic culture. German eugenicists were divided between those who favored "positive" eugenics (meaning the use of laws, government incentives, education, and propaganda to encourage only the "genetically fit" to procreate) and "negative" eugenics (sterilization and "euthanasia"). By the late 1920s and early 1930s, advocates of negative eugenics had gained the upper hand, and a voluntary Reich sterilization law was proposed in 1932. In 1933, advocates of sterilization found themselves embraced by the new regime and became the principal drafters of the "Law for the Prevention of Genetically Diseased Offspring" of July. The law stated that those deemed by duly appointed physicians to be suffering from a loosely defined set of "illnesses" (ranging from epilepsy to "congenital feeblemindedness" to "chronic alcoholism") could be sterilized against their will or the will of their caretakers.[136] From 1934 to 1936, 168,953 men and women were sterilized (437 died from the surgery). From 1936 to the outbreak of the war, perhaps 300,000 more were sterilized, and perhaps 75,000 more during the war.[137]

Carl Schneider's interest in sterilization predated his arrival at Heidelberg. To begin with, he was a student of Oswald Bumke, a renowned geneticist and an advocate of sterilization in the 1920s (and, after 1933, of "euthanasia"). Just before assuming his duties at the Psychiatry Clinic, Schneider addressed a conference in Goslar on the "impact of population policy and hereditary biological measures on the care of dromomaniacs [Wandererfürsorge]," a reference to the new sterilization law. Schneider renounced his earlier skepticism of sterilization and hailed the new law on the grounds that the mentally ill or "abnormal" could not belong to the new state in any legal sense—they were by definition "antisocial." Further, he argued that it would become the civic responsibility of the psychiatrist to provide proof of the health of every patient.[138] Schneider wasted no time after arriving at Heidelberg in beseeching Karlsruhe for funds to expand the Psychiatric Clinic to the point where it would become the first clinic to implement "care" of the mentally ill in line with the "new times." At this point, despite his praise of the July decree on "hereditary diseases," he was seeking ways of rehabilitating the mentally ill, principally through work therapy. There is evidence, however, that by 1934 he was advocating to his students inhumane treatment of the mentally ill in the Bethel asylum. Further, along with Theodor Pakheiser and (after 1936) Ernst Rodenwaldt, Schneider would teach a number of courses on "race and racial hygiene."[139]

Schneider's influence on the rebuilding of the Medical Faculty was enormous. On his and Johannes Stein's recommendations, the well-known gynecologist Hans Runge was called to Heidelberg from Greifswald to replace Erich von Eymer (who had departed to Munich). A Nazi Party member since April 1933, Runge would engage in sterilization procedures at Greifswald and at the Heidelberg's Women's Clinic and oversee dissertations dealing with the sterilization of women.[140] At the Heidelberg clinic, 285 sterilizations were carried out from March 1934 to September 1935, all of them as required by the "hereditary protection" law.[141] Schneider, Stein, and Scheel also secured the promotion of the violently anti-Semitic former Medical Faculty student of orthopedics, Otto Dittmar, to an assistant professor position. Stein himself, on Schneider's and Wilhelm Groh's recommendations, was promoted to the chair for internal medicine.[142] It is also likely that Schneider played a role in the calling of Johann Duken to fill Ernst Moro's chair in pediatrics. A war veteran, Free Corps volunteer, and member of the Stahlhelm (the Weimar-era right-wing paramilitary organization) from 1919 to 1932, Duken joined the Nazi Party, the SA, and the SS in 1933. The following year, he became an assistant in the Racial Policy office in Berlin and an Obersturmführer of the SD of the SS.[143] He was not, however, invited to Heidelberg solely on political grounds, since he was by 1933 a well-known professor of pediatrics.

Following Philipp Broemser's departure to Munich, Schneider recommended that Johann Daniel Achelis be called to fill the chair in physiology. Like Duken, Achelis was a veteran and former Free Corps volunteer. Following a brief period of study at Heidelberg, he lectured on the history of medicine at Leipzig University and entered the right-wing circle around Hans Freyer. From March 1933 to September 1934, Achelis served as an adviser on university matters to the Prussian Ministry of Education. In that position, he oversaw the dismissals of numerous professors and worked to replace them with convinced National Socialists, particularly those close to his friend Freyer. While not a highly distinguished scholar, he was invited to Heidelberg as a full professor largely because of his ministerial activities.[144]

A more significant addition to the Medical Faculty in 1935 was Ernst Rodenwaldt, who replaced the retired Emil Gottschlich. Rodenwaldt was a renowned specialist in tropical diseases and had also established himself as a prominent theorist of "racial hygiene." As Annegret Ehmann has pointed out recently, he belonged to a circle of prominent academics who had served in the German Empire's colonial possessions (in Rodenwaldt's case, Togo and later the Dutch East Indies) and whose theories of "racially mixed peoples" (Mischlinge) were to influence the formation of Nazi race policies.[145] He belonged to the NSDAP for several months in 1932, but renounced his membership for reasons that remain unclear. His departure, however, in no way impeded his career. Carl Schneider wrote in 1936 that "his position on eugenics and racial hygiene is good and well known, sufficient to allow his call to a Racial Hygiene Institute in Munich or a newly created Hereditary Institute in Berlin. In general I hold him to be politically reliable."[146] The Heidelberg Dozentenschaft (Instructors' League) concurred, noting that "politically he manifests a positive attitude toward National Socialism."[147] Even the radical Studentenschaft (Students' League) recognized his value as a scientist and skill as a lecturer, even if he "was not perhaps rooted so deeply in the worldview of National Socialism."[148] In the late 1930s and early 1940s, Rodenwaldt lectured on "racial hygiene" and published numerous articles denouncing the "mixing" of races in colonial possessions and supporting the Nuremberg race laws of 1935.[149]

The Natural Sciences Faculty was convulsed by the purges. Though Philipp Lenard had been retired since 1931, he exerted considerable influence on the reconstruction of the faculty at Heidelberg and elsewhere.[150] At his request, the party appointed him a "Head Assessor" to advise on the purges, and he intervened repeatedly on behalf of favored instructors, most of them young and all of them party members.[151] To a greater extent than in the Medical Faculty, new appointments were made primarily on political grounds, and it was more than a symbolic gesture that Heidelberg's Physics Institute was renamed the Philipp Lenard Institute in December 1935, an act that established Heidelberg as one of two bastions (the other became Munich) of "Aryan physics."[152] Lenard further maligned and obstructed those scientists he considered unworthy, particularly if they had demonstrated any support for Albert Einstein's theory of relativity. Lenard was supported by his colleagues, particularly August Becker, Ludwig Wesch, Otto Erdmannsdörfer, and the noted astronomer Heinrich Vogt (whose appointment to the Heidelberg faculty in 1933 Lenard had helped secure), and revered by Nazi students. As Mark Walker has pointed out, however, the "coordination" of physics institutes at Heidelberg and other universities drove many scientists who were more interested in research than "German physics" into quasi-private bodies such as the Kaiser Wilhelm Society, private firms, and the military.[153]

The Mathematics Faculty was an unusual case in that both chairs were occupied by Jewish scholars in 1933—Arthur Rosenthal and Heinrich Liebmann—who could not be fired immediately. Both received temporary reprieves, Rosenthal because he had fought at the front in World War I and Liebmann because he had been a civil servant before August 1914. Regardless of the letter of the law, for the Ministry in Karlsruhe, Otto Erdmannsdörfer (and later Heinrich Vogt), Wilhelm Groh, and Nazi students, this situation was intolerable and over the next several years Rosenthal and Liebmann were hounded out of their positions. Rosenthal resigned as faculty chairman in April 1933, and in the fall of 1934 was barred, as all Jewish professors were, from state testing committees. Heinrich Vogt bragged to a secretary at the observatory that "I have made sure that [Rosenthal] gets no more students," and in the spring of 1935, Nazi students, with Groh's full support, initiated boycotts of Rosenthal's and Liebmann's lectures and arranged for other mathematics courses to be taught at the same time as both professors were lecturing.[154]

Under this relentless pressure both men retired from the university, Rosenthal in May and Liebmann in June of 1935, several months before they would have been dismissed in the wake of the Nuremberg race laws. Their positions were filled by Herbert Seifert and Udo Wegner. These appointments were not made on purely political grounds. As Erdmannsdörfer noted shortly after the war, "I can only deny that the faculty had been influenced in their appointments to the chairs in mathematics by political or party-political viewpoints. They were proposed solely on the grounds of their scholarly achievements."[155] Seifert, with no party connections and seemingly little interest in politics, had already earned a reputation as a gifted scholar. Udo Wegner, conversely, had been teaching at the Technical College in Darmstadt since 1932 and before then had found only unsteady employment as a mathematician. Although he did not become a party member until 1937, he had demonstrated affinity for the Nazis at Darmstadt and had joined the SA in 1933. As the chemist Karl Freudenberg speculated after the war, a combination of Wegner's youth, professional insecurity, and party affiliation most likely accounted for his appointment to Heidelberg, Erdmannsdörfer's postwar claim notwithstanding. He was not only acceptable politically, but pliable.[156]

The Nazi takeover of Heidelberg from 1933 to 1936 was accomplished by imposition from above and accommodation and acquiescence from below. Despite the open disdain and distrust of the universities among the Nazi Party's leadership, professors of different age groups, faculties, and positions greeted the seizure of power and the Gleichschaltung with great enthusiasm, thus contributing to the regime's legitimacy in Germany and abroad. This enthusiasm was no doubt driven in part by opportunism. But much of the National Socialist message appealed to professors' conservative nationalist sentiments, their disgust with liberalism and the Weimar Republic, and their anti-Semitism. Most professors were silent, however, as their colleagues were robbed of their rights and livelihoods. Only measures leading to unprecedented state incursions into the university's affairs led professors to express any objections. Finally, the reconstruction of the faculties in the wake of the purges brought in not only young instructors with more ideological zeal than scholarly ability, but also highly talented scholars willing to put their abilities at the service of the state.

Heidelberg's experience suggests a more differentiated typology of university professors than has been presented in previous scholarship. Older, well-established "orthodox Mandarins" were initially receptive to the regime and its policies to widely varying degrees, but in most cases their enthusiasm went unrewarded. Defending their institution's traditional structure and autonomy, they were of little practical value to resentful party functionaries after 1933. Similarly, there was only a temporary and marginal place in Nazi Germany for "philosophers" of National Socialism such as Ernst Krieck. Like his more accomplished counterparts at other universities who theorized about the nature of National Socialism, Krieck was marginalized within the party by the mid-1930s but remained devoted to National Socialism as he interpreted it. A third group encompasses those who owed their rapid advance in the academic hierarchy primarily to their ideological commitment. At Heidelberg, this development was most pronounced in the appointments to the Physics Institute and was the handiwork of

Philipp Lenard. But other good examples include Krieck, Wilhelm Groh, and Eugen Fehrle. Almost without exception, these professors lost their positions after 1945 and never reentered academia. Finally, there is the group of scholars who had emerged from the mainstream of their various disciplines, including Carl Schneider, Ernst Rodenwaldt, Carl Brinkmann, Wolfgang Panzer, Paul Schmitthenner, Heinrich Vogt, Johann Duken, and many others. Most, but certainly not all, were relatively young—born after 1890. It is this group of scholars whose talents ultimately proved of greatest practical value to the state. Unlike their counterparts mentioned above, most of them retained or returned to academic positions after 1945. As we will see in the following chapter, their roles in the Third Reich illuminate not only the impact of politics on academic culture, but also the role of ideology in shaping the "German spirit" in scholarship.

CHAPTER TWO

The "German Spirit" in Scholarship

> National Socialism has recognized the fact that to construct a system of knowledge without presuppositions and without certain value judgements at its foundation is totally impossible.
> —Bernhard Rust, "National Socialism and the Pursuit of Learning," June 1936

The most striking sight greeting a visitor to Heidelberg's university square in the summer of 1936 was an enormous bronze eagle perched above the front portal of the main classroom building. Five years earlier, the construction of this building was completed with funds raised by Jacob Gould Schurman, then the U.S. ambassador to Germany and once a student at the university. On the recommendation of the renowned Heidelberg Germanist Friedrich Gundolf, the dedication inscribed on the building's façade read: "Dem Lebendigen Geist"—to the eternal spirit. Above the dedication sat a bronze statue of Athena holding a genius. In 1935, the Athena was relegated to an out-of-sight side of the building. A year later a bronze eagle sculpted by Otto Schliesser in the kitsch grandeur of Nazi-approved art was placed over the main entrance, its head quite deliberately facing westward toward France. Another Heidelberg professor, the conservative nationalist scholar of Germanic languages and literature Friedrich Panzer, provided a new dedication to be inscribed over the original: "Dem Deutschen Geist"—to the German spirit. This inscription, along with the eagle, would be removed by order of American occupation authorities nine years later. The Athena and the original dedication were then returned, where they remain to this day.[1]

The occasion for this transformation of the Universitätsplatz was the celebration of the university's five hundred and fiftieth anniversary, deemed by Hitler himself to be of "national" significance. Aimed primarily at defining, justifying, and celebrating "German scholarship and culture," the three-day affair in June 1936 was unique in the experience of universities in Nazi Germany. Historians have paid little attention to this event, and the few accounts that do treat it have dismissed it as a crass propaganda stunt engineered by Joseph Goebbels and Bernhard Rust to bolster the image of the Third Reich at home and abroad.[2] Hitler and officials in Berlin, Karlsruhe, and Heidelberg indeed saw the potential for a substantial propaganda windfall at a time when it was expedient for Germany to appear as a "normal" European nation to the rest of the world. But historians have not investigated the extent to which professors embraced the ideal of "the German spirit" in scholarship. What was particularly "National Socialist" about research and teaching at Heidelberg from 1935 to 1939 is the subject of this chapter.

The celebration at Heidelberg took place at a pivotal point in the history of Nazi Germany. By the summer of 1936, Adolf Hitler's personal power in Germany was secure and unopposed. The economy was recovering, and full employment would be achieved that year. The years 1935 and 1936 had witnessed a string of foreign policy successes that further bolstered Hitler's support at home and raised his stature abroad. It was thus the face of a proud and stable nation willing (if largely on its own terms) to be a peaceful member of the international community that was to be presented to the world at Heidelberg and at the upcoming Berlin Olympiad. Yet around the same time, the regime was accelerating and intensifying the persecution of German Jewry and beginning its preparations for war. The first Nuremberg race laws, promulgated in September 1935, and the decrees that followed relegated German Jews to a form of subordinate and degrading "citizenship." Those who were unable or unwilling to leave Germany were subjected over the next several years to a rising tide of abuse and isolation culminating in a regime-sponsored pogrom and the internment of thousands in concentration camps. Concurrently, the regime was preparing for war via the Four-Year Plan, announced by Hitler in September 1936. That plan, as Saul Friedländer has illustrated recently, was linked to intensifying state-sponsored anti-Semitism as Hitler and other party leaders placed the Jews at the center of Bolshevism, which they held to be behind the plans for another world war.[3]

German academic culture contributed to these developments by embracing the "German spirit" in scholarship and placing research and teaching in the service of the regime's objectives. The emergence of the "National Socialist" university was thus driven to a great extent from within Heidelberg's walls. The renaming of the Physics Institute after Philipp Lenard in late 1935 and the anniversary celebration the following summer provided highly visible platforms from which both the regime and individual professors could define the relationship between scholarship and National Socialism and the proper role of the universities in the Third Reich. But in the wake of what were largely "administrative" measures—purges, new constitutions, and new courses—came what Reinhard Heydrich referred to as "the spiritualization of the struggle." In the context of the universities this meant above all defining "German scholarship." In a vision of academic culture shared widely if unevenly by professors across the disciplines, the "National Socialist university" was free of not only Jewish instructors and students, but of the "Jewish spirit" as well. In particular, the university would dispense with "Marxist-Jewish" hyper-specialization and embrace interdisciplinary research and teaching considered to be of practical value to the "Volksgemeinschaft." Further, race would be considered a determinative factor in shaping humanity's past and present and the "race" of the scholar himself would determine the quality of work he produced. By 1939, then, there was remarkable congruence between the regime's conception of scholarship in Germany and that which emerged at Heidelberg.

One of the most significant attempts to define the "German spirit" in science was made on the occasion of the renaming of Heidelberg's Physics Institute after Philipp Lenard in December 1935.[4] The ceremony drew an array of party figures, Heidelberg professors, proponents of "Aryan physics" from other universities and institutions, Nazi students, and representatives of several major industrial concerns (the event and the institute itself were partly funded by Siemens Halske A.G. Berlin, I. G. Farbenindustrie, and other firms). The bulk of the agenda was dedicated to defining "German natural sciences" and what distinguished them from "Jewish science." Lenard and his allies held that scientific discovery comes through observation and experimentation and not excessive theorizing and reliance on abstract mathematical constructions. It was the latter attribute that the Aryan physicists ascribed specifically to the Jews and the adherents of relativity theory. Further, according to the Aryan physicists, non-Jewish scientists could also be guilty of "thinking" like Jews if they adopted relativity theory. Johannes Stark would level this very accusation at Werner Heisenberg less than two years later.[5]

The speeches were not limited to physics. In the view of the non-physicist participants, the "German spirit" must pervade all research and teaching in the natural sciences, and the sciences must be unified in the service of the Volk. Ernst Krieck argued that in the nineteenth century science had been separated from philosophy and had been shattered into a "heap" of disconnected specialties that ultimately did not serve the people.[6] For the biologist August Seybold, the natural sciences in Germany stood at a crossroads: they could take either a "west-European-American" path or a "German" path. The former would continue the trend of multiplying the disciplines until all scientific knowledge "sinks" into a form of "technics" rather than "true natural research."[7] Johannes Stein, at that time director of the university's Ludolf-Krehl Clinic, similarly argued that "in nature, all pathological events are ranked. And every medical effort intervenes in this event of nature, in inventive and transformative forms for curing and benefit, but also to act on and destroy defects." Like Krieck and Seybold, Stein bemoaned scientific hyper-specialization, which threatened to "stunt and smother" "the life" of the "Volk." It was Hitler himself who had demanded that medical scientists, like all German scholars, must "develop the healthy embryos to promote and combine the natural powers which nature itself has designed for the life of the people."[8] The speakers were not, however, of completely one mind on the proper approach to science, particularly the proper role of technology. Hans Rukop, the director of Telefunken G.m.b.H. in Berlin, warned that scientific research could not be dictated from above to the extent that the Aryan physicists desired. He said only that both "scholarly" and "technical" physicists served the German "Volk," and that this was really the most important task.[9]

The event was significant, then, because the speeches represented an important attempt by party officials and professors alike to define the "German spirit" in science. But it was also significanct in the political realm. As Alan Beyerchen has shown, the affair marked the beginning of the Aryan physicists' attempts to purge physics in Germany of "Jewish influences" and to control appointments to university chairs and research institutions. Heidelberg itself had already become a stronghold of Aryan physics. After December 1935, the Aryan physicists' crusade made inroads into other quarters. In 1936, a journal devoted to "Aryan mathematics," *Deutsche Mathematik,* began publication. A year later, proponents of Aryan physics took editorial control of the prestigious *Zeitschrift für die gesamte Naturwissenschaft.* They also obtained chairs at five other universities and technical schools. Their crowning achievement was the denial of a chair in physics at Munich University to Werner Heisenberg. This particular campaign was led by Johannes Stark, who had labeled Heisenberg a "white Jew" in the SS organ *Das Schwarze Korps.* Although Heisenberg himself may not have been Jewish, Stark charged, he was guilty of "thinking" like a Jew and advocating "Jewish science."[10]

The "Aryan physicists," as we will see in Chapter 3, ultimately lost the battle for domination of Germany's physics community. Despite the determination of its devotees and some formidable party connections, they were often inept as political tacticians and not numerous enough to overcome the resistance of the majority of German physicists, who had correctly evaluated the importance of Einstein's discoveries for physics and who wished to avoid political interference with their work. Above all they failed because Aryan physics ultimately could not produce the results demanded by the regime during the war.[11] The preponderant power of the Aryan physicists at Heidelberg, however, did not mean that no valuable research took place there. As we will see in the following chapter, important war-related projects were undertaken there in this period. The greatest successes were scored by Walther Bothe, whose research in nuclear physics (though not conducted in the Lenard Institute) made possible the creation of Germany's first cyclotron.[12]

Meanwhile, the planning of the university's anniversary celebration had been under way for nearly a year. But it was not until the end of 1935 that the event took on national and international significance, because Hitler had declared that the celebration was to be of "national" significance.[13] Its primary objective was to trumpet to Germany and to as much of the world as possible the achievements and promise of "German science and culture" and to demonstrate the close connection between the university and the "Volk."[14] But the propaganda goals of the regime and the university had begun to backfire months before the event itself. Prominent British academics and the British journal *Nature* had become persistent critics of developments at Heidelberg after 1933. In May 1933, representatives of Oxford, Cambridge, and London universities warned Hitler that the purges would damage the prestige of German universities in the eyes of the world.[15] In December 1935 the editors of *Nature* had warned that the regime's policies were closing the door on international cooperation in the sciences via the creation of the Science Congress Center (Wissenschaftliche Kongres[s]-Zentrale), which *Nature*'s editors claimed was simply a vehicle to disseminate propaganda and control which German scientists attended conferences.[16] In January 1936 *Nature* published a translated summary from the German press of the proceedings at the Lenard Institute in Heidelberg, which called attention to the centrality of race and anti-Semitism in most of the addresses.[17] This report was followed one month later by an article condemning the upcoming anniversary celebration as a shameful propaganda stunt.[18]

Nature's missives on the ceremony did not go unnoticed at Heidelberg. The university's archives contain numerous clippings from German and foreign papers (including *Nature*) regarding the controversies surrounding the renaming of the Physics Institute and the anniversary celebration, revealing that Wilhelm Groh and others were acutely sensitive to foreign opinion. As Klaus Hentschel has pointed out, editorials in the foreign press critical of developments in Germany could be used for different purposes—"in support of efforts to uphold good relations with foreign countries . . . or as evidence of alleged anti-German sentiment."[19] But they were also interpreted as a kind of validation of "German science." In response to the January 18 editorial in *Nature* August Becker remarked to Groh that "it appears to me that nothing could have been a better verification of the necessity of our Heidelberg event than these remarks."[20] Similarly, Ernst Krieck viewed the anniversary celebration as "a great demonstration of the German will to science." The foreign press could never do enough to vilify "German science and universities." Indeed, echoing Becker, he declared that such attempts at vilification only "justified the great scale of the celebration."[21] August Seybold, however, took a more defensive position, suggesting that the Rector pressure the Reich Education Ministry to prohibit all German scientists and institutions from receiving *Nature* and imposing "the highest penalties" on any instructor caught with a subscription.[22] Seybold got half of his wish granted at the end of 1937, when the Ministry forbade subscriptions to *Nature* in Germany.²³

German and foreign universities were invited to send representatives to the celebration in Heidelberg, and a number of foreign scholars and dignitaries were selected to receive honorary degrees. But at about the same time *Nature* was publishing its critiques British universities and scientific associations began to decline their invitations. Birmingham's and Oxford's decisions may have been influenced by a letter to the London *Times* by Herbert Dunelm, the bishop of Durham, published on February 4. "The racial fanaticism which has swept over Germany," Dunelm wrote, "has not left the universities unaffected, and in Heidelberg its influence has been specially great . . . The University in Germany has to face the new doctrine of German science, as the Church has to face that of German religion."²⁴ The letter sparked a month-long debate in the pages of the *Times*. Critics of the bishop's position suggested that isolating German scholars, who were held to be the passive victims of the dictatorship, would do them and the cause of academic freedom no good while person-to-person contact between English scholars and their German counterparts might help undermine the regime's university policies.²⁵

In a letter to the London *Times* published on February 16, Birmingham's principal, Charles Grant Robertson, defended his institution's decision to decline Heidelberg's invitation, which had been made unanimously by Birmingham's Senate. An individual British professor lecturing at a German university was one thing, he argued, but the dispatch of a designated representative to Heidelberg could only indicate approval of the regime and its policies by British scholars.²⁶ The correspondence that followed in British newspapers and journals provides a view of elite opinion on the state of German universities after three years of National Socialist rule. The views expressed in Britain would form part of the conventional wisdom about German academic culture that persists in part to the present. This opinion held the regime to be intensely anti-intellectual and to have a strong animosity toward fundamental academic freedoms and traditions of objective, "value-free," and "international" scholarship. Nearly every commentator viewed Germany's universities as passive victims of a regime bent on controlling every aspect of their existences, and held that the vast majority of professors who had not been purged nonetheless rejected National Socialism. Harold Stannard of the British Athenaeum no doubt raised more than a few eyebrows when he pointed out that "the members of German University *Senates*" are responsible for the dismissals of their Jewish colleagues.[27] In any case, the decisions of Birmingham and Oxford led Wilhelm Groh to announce the withdrawal of the invitation to all British universities (except Cambridge, which had accepted) on March 2.

The spectacle that finally took place at Heidelberg from June 27 to June 30 went unrivaled in the history of German universities in the Third Reich. The celebration included ceremonies, tours, and the bestowal of honorary degrees on distinguished foreign guests. A gala event was held in the Great Hall of Heidelberg's castle, where Joseph Goebbels delivered a perfunctory address, a congratulatory telegram from the absent Führer was read, and Bernhard Rust spoke on "National Socialism and the pursuit of learning."[28] The final ceremony took place the morning of June 30, with speeches by Ernst Krieck on "objectivity of science as a problem" and Johannes Stein on "medicine and the people."[29] In form and content the event was a party affair. The common ceremonial trappings of public party functions—banners, flags, SA detachments, and the military cast of much of the proceedings—linked the party with the university. All of it sought to demonstrate, as Wilhelm Groh noted to assembled guests in the castle's Great Hall, that "we feel the greatest joy that the old confrontation between politics and science has become irrelevant. For us, there is no tension between the intellectual work of the nation and its political way of life."[30] Groh's audience that evening certainly reflected this view. In addition to Goebbels and Bernhard Rust, it included Hans Frank, the president of the German Academy of Law and the future governor of occupied Poland, Franz Seldte, the co-founder of the Stahlhelm and the Minister of Labor, an array of military officials, the Reich student leader Albert Derichsweiler, the rectors of most other German universities, and the leadership of the Baden state government.[31]

In a 1937 report on the celebration, Ernst Krieck, by then Heidelberg's Rector, boasted that the event had showcased to the world the oldest German university and the triumph of German science.[32] Across the Atlantic in New York, Thomas Mann simultaneously proclaimed that "the regime itself has declared that there is—for the time being—no home for the living spirit in Germany's universities."[33] As propaganda, the results of the celebration were decidedly mixed and far less successful than the summer games that began in Berlin a little over a month later. The decision of British universities in particular not to attend and the international press attention the ensuing controversy attracted was a hard blow. A few universities in other European countries also declined the invitations, including the University of Leyden in the Netherlands, the University of Oslo, and the University of Basel. The decision of Jacob Gould Schurman, the former ambassador of the United States, not to attend was yet another embarrassment.

But many other universities sent representatives. The largest national delegation was from the United States.[34] Attendance, as Helmut Heiber noted, was considerable in a world with about sixty independent nations, fifty of them with universities.[35] In addition, as Robert Proctor has pointed out, some foreign observers—particularly medical scientists—admired developments in Germany's post-1933 academic culture.[36] Writing in 1937, the young instructor in the Journalism Institute, Wilhelm Classen, pointed out that numerous prominent French, Czechoslovak, and Polish intellectuals had also rejected—wittingly or unwittingly—the notion of "objective reality" that could be evaluated by "objective scholarship."[37] Viewed in this way, Krieck's boast may not be too much of an exaggeration.

If the celebration was not an unalloyed propaganda victory, both party figures and professors succeeded in defining "German scholarship." The most important speech on National Socialism and science at Heidelberg was Bernhard Rust's "National Socialism and the Pursuit of Learning." Rust's address was reprinted and commented upon widely in the German and foreign presses.[38] His thesis was that the national and racial background of individual scholars shapes all scholarship. In Rust's view, there is no such thing as purely "objective science." Beginning in 1933, the state moved against the two groups in academia responsible for repressing national consciousness and propagating a false conception of scholarship: the "Marxists" and the Jews. Rust explained that Jews were purged from the universities because as members of an "alien race" they were incapable of knowing "the order of nature and the order of events which form the object of [their] study." German universities, then, were being "radically remade, in line with the great transformation that has taken place in the inner life of the German people"—the collective realization of "the essential unity" of the "German people." The result of this "transformation" was not only that "the field of knowledge is no longer split up into an indefinite number of more or less unrelated subjects" but that "it has recovered its vitality and acquired a new sense of loyalty and obligation"—"loyalty and obligation" to the state and to the German "Volk." Given the scholars' own "racial purity" and the proper orientation of their research and teaching toward the state and people, Rust added that they would be free to conduct research as they saw fit.[39]

Several aspects of this speech are worth comment. First, its content was shaped partly to counter foreign criticism that academic freedom and the international spirit of science had been banished from Germany. Second, Rust's ideas had been circulating in Nazi circles for years and can be traced back to previous debates over the extent to which scholarship could and should strive to be "value free," with the Nazi Party and its supporters among the professorate rejecting the ideal of value neutrality.[40] Third, Rust's speech was also in part a response to the more extreme views of the Aryan physicists. Rust considered them to be intent on excessive ideological interference in the course of scientific research. He believed instead that scientists would make the correct choices on their own if (1) they themselves were not Jewish; (2) they were working in an environment free of Jews and "Jewish influences"; and (3) they were serving the interests of the state and the people. But the difference with the Aryan physicists was really one of degree. For both the Aryan physicists and Bernhard Rust and their respective allies in the government and academia, anti-Semitism and the organic connection between "Wissenschaft" and the "Volk" that it served remained the twin pillars of scholarship in the Third Reich. The matter became particularly urgent, however, with the announcement of the Four-Year Plan just three months after the celebration at Heidelberg. Rust and other leading party figures understood that universities and research institutes would have to make an important contribution to the plan. In March 1937 Rust announced the creation of the Reich Research Council but emphasized that the plan's demands would not smother independent research at the universities.[41] As far as Nazi students were concerned, Rust warned them to leave professors alone.[42]

How did these ideas play themselves out in research and teaching at Heidelberg? The evidence suggests that they were more widely held there than has been acknowledged. Following Rust most closely was Ernst Krieck. As his biographer Gerhard Müller noted, the celebration at Heidelberg represented the "highpoint of Ernst Krieck's public reputation in the Third Reich."[43] In his own address on scholarship, Krieck rejected what he considered a vestige of Enlightenment-era faith in "insights and truths which are not conditioned by race or nationality or by the time in which they appear, but are always and everywhere the same." Although he declared that German scholars should continue to communicate with their foreign counterparts and that "German science requires of all its scholars and devotees not only strict fidelity to truth" and "precision of technique," the purposes and relevance of the results of scientific inquiry, he said, are determined by the racial background of the scholar himself. "Science," he argued, "is limited as to its concepts and methods by the language and the racial characteristics of the people concerned." It was preposterous, Krieck asserted, to claim that "pure reason" had been the driving force behind the Western world's scholarly achievements. "It can be fully demonstrated," he argued, "that not one single science has been developed by the mechanism of pure reason"; rather, "every worthwhile achievement in the sphere of the natural sciences, no less than in the sciences of culture, has been intimately bound up with the fundamental racial characteristics of the people concerned."[44]

That the various faculties at Heidelberg were approaching their subjects along these lines is revealed in a special edition of the *Volksgemeinschaft* published on June 30.[45] In general, they concurred with one commentator's statement that Heidelberg was both Germany's "oldest" and "youngest" university: the faculties were building on great past traditions and forging ahead boldly after dispensing with useless ones.[46] In outlining the tasks of German folklorists, Eugen Fehrle drew on the work of his mentor Albrecht Dietrich. Dietrich sought to reveal the essence of a people that transcended historical circumstances and social contexts. Fehrle viewed it as his own mission to build on Dietrich's interest in comparing different cultures by narrowing the focus to the German "Volk" and fusing it with racist conceptions he had been developing since at least the mid-1920s. In the *Volksgemeinschaft* he boasted that "the primary task of the chair of folklore is to explore German folk traditions, in its eternal stock, in its nature, which lies in our blood."[47] The chairman of the Philosophy

Faculty, Hermann Güntert, argued that language was one of the fundamental sources of the "Volk" that formed a vital link with its forefathers. Hence language instruction was crucial to its future survival. Not surprisingly, Güntert dismissed attempts in recent years to create an "international language" (Esperanto) as "delusional" and destructive of the culture of a people.[48]

The youngest of the university's faculties, the State and Economic Sciences Faculty, was, according to its chairman, Eduard Bötticher, also the most advanced and in the widest sense the most "political," primarily because all individual disciplines that rightly belonged in the realm of "state and economic sciences" were now "set to a unified goal and united in a 'political faculty' in the widest possible sense." These included those taught at the former Technical College in Mannheim, especially business management, the largest institute for translators in Germany, and the Institute for the Study of Journalism at Heidelberg itself. Further, representatives from physics, chemistry, and law shared joint appointments with the State and Economic Sciences Faculty. Again, the goal was to transcend teaching political and economic sciences for their own sake and put them in service of the state's economy and the "welfare of the *Volksgemeinschaft*."[49]

Paul Schmitthenner also reached for the title of representing the "youngest discipline" of the university through his chair for "history with particular provisions for history of warfare and military sciences." For Schmitthenner, who would become Rector in 1938, the university was "a place of military-political education." The Germans are "a people of work and peace" who do not want war, but "we know well that war could fatefully break out around us. Therefore, we must prepare to defend our freedom and our honor." For Schmitthenner, the nature of modern war was "total war," which demanded a new kind of total preparation. He pointed out that military science in the National Socialist sense was more than just another book-bound academic specialty. "There is no single military science," he said, but rather "a greater number of different military sciences, in part intellectual, in part natural sciences, in part technical." The study of "military sciences" was thus obliged to expand beyond the confines of individual battles, tactics, and leadership. "In contrast to this old style of the history of warfare," he added, the new style "will thereby serve the 'Volk' as a part of National Socialist science, [and] it will produce a connection between science and politics and pursue its scientific research on the strictest methodological basis toward new goals, making the results useful to our people in the present and in the future." Teaching tactics, strategy, and leadership was "a matter for the army." Schmitthenner was interested instead in "the education of people who think in military-political terms, who join an inner soldierly attitude with scientific methods, basic knowledge, and military-scientific understanding."[50]

Not surprisingly the Lenard Institute was hailed by Ludwig Wesch in a fawning, anti-Semitic tribute. If one wanted to trace the history of the "new physics," and that person was "honest and no Jew," he would find that the great scientific advances of recent years were attributable to Philipp Lenard. But what of the institute's research? Lenard and his acolytes had succeeded in purging all remnants of theoretical physics (meaning "Jewish influence") from the institute, allowing "intellectual justification and experimental research to join together." The institute thus picked up on experiments conducted by Lenard in the 1890s on the effect of electricity on electrons and also focused on the more practical areas of short-wave, ultra-shortwave, ultrasound, phosphors, and television broadcasting.[51] The institute's work would remain occupied primarily with these areas until the end of the war, as Wesch's extensive postwar report to American investigators makes clear.[52]

As we have seen, Johannes Stein had already lamented hyper-specialization in the sciences—a complaint that he repeated in a speech at the June celebration. Here he also defended Germany's sterilization laws and the responsibility of German doctors to secure the "racial health" of the "Volk:" "New, great tasks are today placed before the German doctor, which have never been demanded of him before. We cannot yet estimate the greatness and impact of the successful intervention into the life of the Volk, an intervention which kills the pathological and unworthy in embryo, shackles and vanquishes destructive forces, and promotes and develops all Volks-building forces."[53] Similarly, Carl Schneider called for the "inner connection between the German doctor and the German people": "The fundamental question of educational reform [in medical schools] is aimed at newly winning the real inner unity of all medical acts, at the overcoming of false fragmentation . . . at the education of the coming generation of doctors for the preservation and increase of German hereditary health and education for the struggle against all possibilities for degeneration."

Schneider then identified Hitler as the "teacher and adviser of every single German in all questions of the people's health."[54]

A source from the university's archives opens a window onto the general orientation of the faculties by the summer of 1936. At the June celebration forty-three honorary degrees were conferred upon visiting dignitaries by Rector Groh.[55] The recommendations from the different faculties made to Groh as to which people should receive honorary degrees offer insight into the relationship between dictatorship, propaganda, and scholarship.[56] Karl Engisch, chairman of the Law Faculty, aligned his recommendations with those provided by the Academy of German Law. The primary criteria appeared to be a friendly attitude toward Germany or participation in the academy's work. Not surprisingly, no British legal scholars were awarded honorary degrees.[57] Only two foreign theologians received honorary degrees.[58] The chemist Karl Freundenberg recommended Gustaf Komppa, a well-known Finnish chemist, because of Komppa's accomplishments (which Freudenberg linked to "German-ness") and prestige and also his presumed racial "fitness": "in his scientific existence, Komppa is rooted completely in Deutschtum . . . By appearances, Komppa is of Finnish blood. His children also appear to be. I consider it most unlikely that he has Jewish elements."[59]

Hermann Güntert's nominations on behalf of the Philosophy Faculty were based on demonstrated friendliness toward Germany, important political connections with various Reich ministries (especially the SS), and scholarship that celebrated the German "Volk" and culture. According to Güntert, the political scientist and Rector of the Herder Institute at the university in Riga, Wilhelm Klumberg, had undertaken in recent years to make that university "a German bulwark." G. A. S. Snijder, a classical archaeologist in Amsterdam, was "a genuine friend of National Socialism and himself active in a National Socialist spirit in Holland." In a similar vein, Güntert recommended the Swedish folklorist Sigurd Erixson, who had already been invited to study folk history in Germany by Walther Darre, the Nazi Agricultural Minister. The Danish publisher Ejnar Munksgaard was a "genuine admirer of Hitler" and published numerous books in German every year in Denmark. A particularly notable choice was Heinrich Ritter von Srbik, professor of history in Vienna and one of the German-speaking world's best-known pan-Germanists.[60]

Representing the State and Economic Sciences Faculty, Carl Brinkmann recommended Douglas B. Copland, the prominent Australian economist and an advocate of freeing his country's currency, foreign trade, and credit policies from "one-sided dependency" on London's financial markets. Like the concerns of other faculty members, Brinkmann's were not simply academic, but geopolitical and racist. His recommendation of the Croatian agrarian economist and former Yugoslav state minister Otto von Franges is revealing in this respect. Not only had Franges, as a guest of the Reich Minister of Agriculture, participated several times in harvest and farm festivals, but

> as a former Yugoslav state minister and extremely influential agrarian-political researcher and university instructor . . . he is not simply a symbolic figure for the friendly relationship between Germany and its native states, but moreover for the idea of an expansive east European region [Grossraum], meaning close mutual order based on the division of labor of Germany with its entire agrarian and recently industrialized eastern outer regions from the fringe states to the Balkans. That he is not of old stock [Altserbe], but rather a Croat, could only heighten the effectiveness of our honor in view of the intellectual leading role and friendly stance toward Germany of the Croats as well as in view of the reconciliation of national antagonisms.[61]

Brinkmann also endorsed three German-Americans, Henry Janssen, Ferdinand Thun, and Frank Knight. Brinkmann did not consider Janssen and Thun prominent scholars, but he did think they were important conduits between Germany and the United States who had donated "great sums" toward promoting "German science and culture," including donations for the construction of the new university building in Heidelberg. They had held to their positions, Brinkmann added, "despite opposition within their own families and spiteful Jewish attacks."[62] Knight was different, however, in that he was a highly regarded scholar (and "a farmer's son from Iowa," no less). He had studied in Austria and Germany, including at Heidelberg, where he had come into close contact with Max Weber and other liberal theorists (though remaining "critically opposed to all of them") and had produced a number of significant studies on "theories of Austria's liberal production and distribution systems."[63] Most of those recommended by Güntert and Brinkmann (though not Copland and Knight) were awarded honorary degrees.

The Medical Faculty's recommendations, made by Ernst Rodenwaldt, Carl Schneider, and the leadership of the Anatomical Institute focused above all on "racial sciences" and the potential propaganda value of honorary degrees for the university and for Germany. Rodenwaldt's first candidate was the Dutch chemist Barend C. P. Jansen, who had done path-breaking research on the nutritional value of vitamin B1 in Batavia (Indonesia) in the 1920s. Jansen's discoveries had had great practical benefits for the Dutch colonial administration, Rodenwaldt claimed, because they had improved the nutrition of military personnel, prisoners, and residents of youth homes. Consequently, Jansen's nutritional hygiene discoveries "had become the model for all colonial nations and would also be for us Germans, should we again win colonies." Rodenwaldt also recommended Herman Lundborg, director of the Racial-Biological Institute in Uppsala, Sweden, whom Rodenwaldt counted "among the premier racial hygienists of science" and described as a "friend to Germany." Along similar lines, Rodenwaldt recommended Harry Hamilton Laughlin, director of the Eugenics Records Office in Cold Springs Harbor, New York, from 1910 to 1940 and one of the most influential advocates of sterilization in the United States. As with his recommendations of Jansen and Lundborg, Rodenwaldt saw an award to Laughlin as having significant propaganda value in America, where, he noted, "racial hygiene questions are propagated in the same way as they are by us, but where many questions of the German racial laws are greeted with mistrust."[64]

Carl Schneider was particularly interested in courting Laughlin. In May Schneider notified the American of the university's intention to grant him an honorary degree. Laughlin, though he could not attend the celebration, accepted the honor because "it will come from a nation which for many centuries nurtured the human seed-stock which later founded my own country and thus gave basic character to our present lives and institutions." Shortly before the celebration, Laughlin donated eight of his own books and twenty-one reprints to Heidelberg's library, including "The Legal Status of Eugenical Sterilization," "Eugenical Sterilization in the United States," "Analysis of America's Modern Melting Pot," and "Biological Aspects of Immigration."[65] As Stefan Kühl has shown, this exchange highlights the particularly strong mutual influences and interest in eugenics research between Nazi Germany and the United States.[66] Finally, the acting director of the Anatomical Institute (writing for August Hirt) was particularly insistent on the importance of the potential recipient's political credentials vis-à-vis Germany. He recommended another prominent racial hygienist, the Swiss professor of medicine Otto Nägeli, a distinguished scientist and pro-German. "It is no doubt superfluous," he argued, "if I account for the scientific importance of the outstanding researcher. What is decisive from my standpoint is . . . his friendly position toward Germany during the war, after the war, and above all also after the seizure of power in Germany."[67]

Another development that reveals the increasing receptiveness to the "German spirit" in scholarship among Heidelberg professors from 1936 to 1939 was the creation of several special institutes and seminars that focused on the military preparedness of German society, the status of the Reich's western borders, and the formation of an organic bond between the university, scholarship, and the "Volksgemeinschaft." As a reflection of the importance the regime placed on military sciences and the determination of Paul Schmitthenner, the first such special seminar to be created at Heidelberg was that for the history of warfare in the fall of 1933. In February 1936, Schmitthenner described the position to the Ministry of Culture as "representing a new creation in so far as it utilizes, on strictly scientific basis and with strictly scientific methods, the military-historical and military-political results of the latest research as tools for National Socialist and political education." Further, the chair would at the same time serve as a "frontier professorship of particularly high value" because it would strengthen the "mental consolidation" and the "absorption" of National Socialism in Germany's southwest.[68] By early 1936, however, Karlsruhe still had not approved the creation of the chair, or provided Schmitthenner much in the way of a budget. Part of the problem had been restrictions on the creation of such military-related professorships and institutes imposed by the Versailles treaty. As such restrictions disappeared and Germany's economic situation improved substantially, funds for the institute increased. By 1941, its annual budget had reached 2,000 Reichsmarks, nearly half the History Seminar's total budget.[69] Despite the initial lack of funds from Karlsruhe, Schmitthenner could boast of an increasing number of students in the seminar—twenty-five in the winter semester of 1933–34 to fifty-six in the winter semester of 1935–36—drawn from a variety of faculties (journalism, medicine, law, and others).[70]

Schmitthenner himself taught most of the seminar's courses, with an occasional lecture contributed by Ernst Krieck on "the National

Socialist worldview." Schmitthenner's offerings included mainstream topics such as "German history from 1918 to 1933" (summer 1935) to more inventive themes such as "the mental-spiritual struggle in the world war" (winter 1935–36), "the nature and essence of the German soldier" (summer 1936), "total war" (winter 1936–37), "masters of war art," (winter 1937–38), "History of German colonial wars" (summer 1938), "cultural history of war" (1938–39), and similar topics.[71] Further, a list of dissertations completed or nearly completed under his supervision sheds considerable light on the orientation and priorities of the seminar (for these, see Appendix B).

Another significant addition after 1936 was the Institute for Frankish-Pfalz Regional and Folk Research. The institute was created in 1939 on a recommendation made two years earlier by Günther Franz, who had already begun to orient research in the History Seminar toward the westward expansion of Germany's borders. The institute was part of a national network devoted to regional research, in this case "Westforschung" (research on western Europe). Before and after 1933, "Westforschung" was overshadowed by "Ostforschung" (research on the east)—the former never received the same level of funding or official favor from the regime as did the latter.[72] Nonetheless "Westforschung" institutes like Heidelberg's contributed to the surge of interest in the expansion of Germany's borders that can be observed throughout academic culture in this period and provide a good example of the increasing interdisciplinary orientation of much scholarship in the Third Reich.

"Westforschung" at Heidelberg and elsewhere was a form of regional and local history with historiographical roots in Germany going back to the nineteenth century and Franco-German antagonism.[73] As Peter Schöttler has argued, World War I and its aftermath proved to be a catalyst for a new kind of aggressive, nationalist "Westforscher." After 1918, the regions of primary interest were the Rhineland, Alsace-Lorraine, Eupen-Malmedy, and the Saarland. Hermann Aubin at the University of Bonn established the leading center of the new Westforschung, and a string of similar institutes would appear in the 1920s and 1930s, including Heidelberg's. They were characterized not only by their advocacy of territorial revision in Germany's favor, but by their broad scope of research interests—interests that went beyond the study of diplomacy and military campaigns to encompass language, culture, folklore, and other subjects. Collectively, they belonged to the Western German Research Association (Westdeutsche Forschungsgemeinschaft, or WFG), which had been created from the old Rhine Research Association (Rheinische Forschungsgemeinschaft) in 1931. After 1933, of course, the status and future of Germany's western borders remained of considerable interest to the regime and many university professors from a range of disciplines.[74]

In late June 1937, Wolfgang Panzer and the historian Fritz Ernst described the necessity for the institute to the Baden Ministry of Culture. Their hope was to build on regional research undertaken by Franz. They began by noting that "in recent years it has been often stated that the new university must be tied to the homeland and region" and that similar institutes had already been created in Freiburg and Frankfurt on the model of Aubin's institute. The geographical gap to be addressed by the proposed institute at Heidelberg was the Rhein-Frankisch, or "Old-Pfalz," territory. Heidelberg was the "natural middle point" for research on this area. History and geography would form the institute's core disciplines, but the directors envisioned incorporating other fields, notably early history, Germanistik (German language and culture), folklore, mineralogy, geology, anthropology, "racial sciences," botany, and zoology.[75] Just over two years later, in a clear expression of how academic culture was prepared to contribute to Germany's war of expansion, Fritz Ernst explained the institute's purpose in the local edition of the *Volksgemeinschaft:* "The world war has brought an entirely new impulse to the scholarly study of regional history . . . old problems are to be newly tackled: the division of the Reich in individual states has been rescinded, the way is now free for the great historical territory."[76] The research of the institute's historians and geographers would contribute to this territorial expansion, particularly, Ernst pointed out, by study of the history of population settlements. Numerous other Heidelberg professors engaged in Westforschung, including Walter Peter Fuchs, Kurt von Raumer, Ernst Wahle, Friedrich Panzer, and Eugen Fehrle.

Of Wolfgang Panzer's anti-Semitism and commitment to the regime's expansionist aims there can be no doubt. In a December 1935 speech in Danzig on "geography in the service of national-political education," which was published the following year in *Zeitschrift für Erdkunde,* Panzer praised Hitler for restoring Germany's pride and providing individual Germans with the tools to rebuild the nation and people. For the nation's scholars, this "people's service" would serve both as a teacher and a "protector of pure scholarship for the highest goals." For geographers, the task was to study not just rivers, mountains, and cities, but "the region and its people" as an organic whole. Panzer further defined "Germany's living space" (Lebensraum): the "flatland" extended from the "threshold of the Artois" in the west and stretched eastward "far into the Russian steppes"; the "low mountain ranges" encompassed part of western France; and the Alpine region ranged from the Mediterranean through the Carpathian mountains and deep into Eurasia. As Panzer himself acknowledged, this vision of Germany's rightful "living space" was hardly original, but the drive toward its realization had been given new life by Hitler and the "national revolution."[77]

Panzer's counterpart in the new institute, Fritz Ernst, presents a more complex case. Ernst's career typifies the complex, shaded response to National Socialism among some academics. Ernst replaced Günther Franz in 1937. He was a student of Johannes Haller, a well-known scholar of Franco-German relations and one of the few full professors to support Hitler publicly before 1933. Ernst himself was reportedly an enthusiastic member of the student SA in Tübingen from December 1933 to the beginning of 1935.[78] At Heidelberg he declined two requests, in 1937 and 1938, by Richard von Kienle, the party's "trusted man" in the History Seminar, to join the NSDAP, though von Kienle later prevailed successfully upon Ernst to join the Dozentenbund.[79] No doubt partly as a result of Ernst's disinclination to join the party, some regional officials did not consider him reliable politically. In January 1941, the Gau student leader for Baden, Richard Scherberger, listed Ernst among those professors whose contribution to the building of the National Socialist university was "highly debatable." "He is indeed an excellent lecturer," Scherberger reported, "but is a representative of the old school and will always stand in the way of a new orientation in German philosophy."[80]

Ernst's defenders have pointed to this document as evidence that he was not compromised by National Socialism.[81] As we will see, professors themselves employed a similar strategy in the denazification process. Ernst's career, however, was hardly derailed because of his resistance to party membership. He remained a co-director of the Frankish-Pfalz Institute, began a scholarly journal *(Die Welt als Geschichte)* in 1936, published until 1943, and continued to teach until the end of the war. His experience therefore casts doubt on the postwar claims made by other members of his generation that membership in the party or one of its affiliated organizations was necessary for a young scholar to pursue an academic career.[82] Ernst's case was not singular. Statistics collected by the Reich Education Ministry in 1939 reveal that less than half of new appointees to university positions since 1937 belonged to the party.[83]

Scherberger's report says more about the outlook of what was left of the radical Nazi student movement than it does about Ernst's engagement with National Socialism. For Scherberger, the paragons of the Nazi professorate at Heidelberg were Paul Schmitthenner, Eugen Fehrle, Heinrich Vogt, and especially Ernst Krieck.[84] By holding Ernst's career and outlook to the standards of the largely ignored Krieck in particular, Scherberger reveals his own mind-set to have been out of sync with the dominant currents of research and teaching at Heidelberg by roughly five years. Ernst was an ardent conservative nationalist whose scholarly endeavors justified and supported Germany's imperialist ambitions.[85] He and Wolfgang Panzer took advantage of an opportunity to establish an institute for Westforschung at Heidelberg because through such an institute both believed they could pursue their ideological and professional interests. Clearly, however, Ernst sought to keep a distance from party ideologues like Scherberger and resisted Eugen Fehrle's attempts to influence the institute ideologically.[86]

In a similar manner, developments in the Social and Economic Sciences Faculty (formerly Insosta) reflected the increasingly close connection between regime and research, between the emphasis on interdisciplinary approaches and practical applications and interest in territorial expansion.[87] The faculty focused on agrarian economics, population settlements, and "spatial" research (Raumforschung). Until the end of 1935, the Rockefeller Foundation had provided a substantial amount of funds. The faculty's work was later supported by the newly created Reich Working Group for Spatial Research and the Reich Office for Regional Administration (Reichsarbeitsgemeinschaft für Raumforschung, or RAG, and the Reichsstelle für Raumordnung, or RfR). The research was to serve the planned territorial and population expansion of the Reich.[88] The dissertations undertaken by students of the Social and Economic Sciences Faculty reflected this agenda. As Carsten Klingemann has argued, projects undertaken by students of the former Insosta represented a step away from traditional approaches to sociology in Germany and toward the empirically based social research that would become a prominent feature in postwar West German sociology and economics. This is not a surprising development given the political and ideological conditions under which its proponents received their training.[89]

Klingemann has characterized the development of sociological research in the Third Reich as one that produced "social scientific experts—no ideologues."[90] He argues that academic sociology provided the regime, a modern "technocracy," with experts to help it achieve its aims. But Klingemann also claims that these sociologists lacked any ideological motivation; they were simply "experts." For their part, "the 'normal' aspects of social technocracy made the crimes possible; the Weltanschauung enabled them to become monstrosities. The participation of the sociologists was one of the normal elements."[91] As further evidence, Klingemann notes that those sociologists devoted to the Nazi Weltanschauung got nowhere during (and after) the Third Reich. Yet there was indeed a connection between Nazi ideology and research, especially that of a practical nature. It was an ideology—a belief in an aggressive expansion of territory and population driven by racist considerations—that justified and legitimized the kind of empirically based projects that came to prominence in the social sciences at Heidelberg and other universities. The regime saw to it that research that furthered the implementation of this ideology received its support. The connection, in short, between "expert" and "ideology" was not clear cut in the case of sociologists any more than it was in the other faculties.

The most committed ideologue in the Social and Economic Sciences Faculty was Walter Thoms. Thoms belonged firmly to the socialist wing of the Nazi Party, and his ideas owed a great deal to those of Werner Sombart.[92] For Thoms, economic life in Germany rested on two pillars, race and space, and the ultimate goal was always "das Recht auf Arbeit"—the right to work. Economic systems were related "racially" to the people who created and managed them. Hence "capitalist thought is Jewish thought . . . Capitalism is always liberal, individualistic, egotistic, materialistic, international. Capitalist thought is the weapon for the realization of the Jews' pretensions to world domination." To the contrary, the "national socialist economy" is an "expression of the order of the life of the people" that above all seeks to put all of its people to work and eschews selfish profit-seeking and capital accumulation.⁹³ In the war's early years, when German territorial expansion was rapid and secure, Thoms projected this vision to the hoped-for German-dominated "new Europe:" "The European regional economy will carry the character of the German Volks-economy, because it has been born from the same laws of configuration, that is, it will be socialist."⁹⁴

A third institute created in this period was Ernst Krieck's "Folk and Cultural-Political Institute" (Volks- und kulturpolitischen Institut). Riding the crest of his visibility and influence in and beyond Heidelberg, Krieck envisioned it as an attempt to put into practice the ideas expressed by himself and Bernhard Rust at the anniversary celebrations.⁹⁵ The principal goal was to unite politics and scholarship and to overcome the borders between individual disciplines. In effect Krieck was attempting to institute at Heidelberg a permanent Dozentenakademie (one of the Dozentenbund's ideological "training camps" for its members). The institute's research and teaching agenda would be aimed at "domestic cultural policy" and "foreign cultural policy."⁹⁶ The effort was ultimately unsuccessful; Krieck simply did not have the influence or the connections to affect a fundamental transformation of the university's structure.

What of "racial sciences" at Heidelberg in this period? Unlike other universities, Heidelberg did not see the establishment of a special institute devoted to the study of race or "racial hygiene."⁹⁷ Yet, as we have seen, hundreds of forced sterilizations were carried out in the women's clinic under the direction of Hans Runge and there was considerable interest among two of the most influential professors in the Medical Faculty, Carl Schneider and Ernst Rodenwaldt, in "racial hygiene" and sterilization. Schneider offered lectures on race to general audiences up to 1936. Thereafter they were delivered by Rodenwaldt, August Seybold, and the zoologist Paul Krüger. Schneider's interest in sterilization research and practice in the United States was made clear in his correspondence with Harry Laughlin, discussed above. And, like other professors of medicine, by 1936 Schneider was thinking along the lines of medicine as the practice of maintaining both the health of individuals and the health of the Volksgemeinschaft, defined in racist terms.⁹⁸ As we will see in the next chapter, Schneider became one of the leading directors of the regime's program to systematically murder the mentally ill and handicapped. The Nazis' "euthanasia" program ultimately resulted in the deaths of tens of thousands of people, and, as Henry Friedlander has shown recently, provided much of the experience and some of the personnel for the "Final Solution."[99]

Ernst Rodenwaldt's teaching and research also remained oriented toward "racial sciences." Like Schneider, he continued to hold lectures on topics dealing with race. And, again like Schneider, he was particularly interested in eugenics research and sterilization practice in the United States. Along with many other German medical scientists, Rodenwaldt had developed an interest in racial issues before 1933. Although it is true that his pre-1933 publications did not contain the kind of racist mysticism popular among many Nazi ideologues (a point Rodenwaldt's lawyers would make repeatedly in his defense after the war), they nonetheless helped form the foundations of the "racial state," not least because the author was a reputable scientist. Rodenwaldt and others pursued research into the means of "racial purification" after 1933 because they believed it constituted good science and good politics. The regime, hardly hostile to science, supported their endeavors. The argument employed after the war by scientists and historians alike that men like Rodenwaldt advocated sterilization or sprinkled their writing with facile references to "race" in order to save their careers or "camouflage" their true anti-Nazi sentiments distorts the historical record.

Along with Eugen Fischer, Ernst Rüdin, Friedrich (Fritz) Lenz, and other prominent "race researchers," Rodenwaldt became a co-editor of the journal *Archiv für Rassen- und Gesellschaftsbiologie (einschliesslich Rassen- und Gesellschaftshygiene)*. His publications in this and other journals in this period, particularly "How the Germans Can Protect the Purity of Their Blood in Countries with Colored Populations" (1936), "The Repercussions of Racial Mixing in Europe's Colonial Lands" (1938), "The Various Racial Elements of Balinese Castes" (1938), and "National Socialist Racial Awareness as the Basis for the Colonial Activities of the New Europe" (1939), reveal his ongoing interest in the racial characteristics of populations in tropical climates and their significance for European (and especially German) colonial administration.[100] These and other works illustrate the close connection between politics and science that pervaded his research. In the case of the tropical locales with which Rodenwaldt was familiar, for instance, he argued in 1939 that Germany must not make the same mistake as the Dutch and French in allowing "natives" and colonists to "mix" with each other. It was imperative in his view to extend domestic laws "protecting" the German "race" to the colonial possessions Germany was sure to acquire in the near future. Rodenwaldt based this conclusion both on the "demands" of the German public and on what he considered to be a solid scientific basis explored in his numerous publications on "racial hygiene."[101]

The case of the psychiatrist Viktor von Weizsäcker is more ambiguous. A student of Ludolf von Krehl at Heidelberg, von Weizsäcker served as a medical officer on both the eastern and western fronts in World War I. He became a full professor at Heidelberg in 1930 and taught there until accepting a position at Breslau in 1941. It is clear that as early as 1933 and probably earlier von Weizäcker was thinking about the "extermination" of the mentally ill.[102] Like many of his colleagues, he considered the mentally ill to be "inferior" and hence candidates for "exclusion" from the Volksgemeinschaft. His apologists have failed to come to terms with his subsequent involvement in the "euthanasia" project, in which he conducted research on the brains of victims in his Breslau clinic.[103]

But racist conceptions were not limited to medical scientists. The case of the historian of antiquity Fritz Schachermeyr is illustrative. Schachermeyr arrived in Heidelberg in 1936 and taught there until 1941. He had been active in Nazi student groups in Jena since 1931, as a Gauführer in Thuringia in 1933 and 1934, and then in Austrian Nazi Party circles.[104] While at Heidelberg, Schachermeyr drew on the racist conceptions of both Hans F. K. Günther and Ludwig Clauss to describe the relationship between race and culture in ancient Crete and its implications for the image of the "western race" and the "European spirit." Schachermeyr sought to modify the significance some race theorists attributed to the representations of the ideal "western racial types" in the art of Crete by identifying the presence of supposedly inferior Asiatic elements.[105] His work on Crete, Carthage, and political leadership in ancient Greece reveals that the "racial sciences" formed an integral part of his overall understanding of the past and its relationship to the present and did not simply provide a source of stock phrases inserted to appease party fanatics.[106]

The theologian Gerhard Rosenkranz provides another example. In 1936, Rosenkranz published a book on the importance of race and ethnicity for Protestant missionary work in China.[107] Rosenkranz hoped his study would contribute not only to a better understanding of the work of evangelical missions in that country, but also to a more differentiated notion of how race affected the complex interactions between peoples and religions as they crossed national and linguistic boundaries. His specific concern was that a useful understanding of "the notion of race, blood, and soil, a community of people and the faithful," was being prevented by "zealous contemporary discussions of worldviews." Indeed, Rosenkranz noted that no one in Germany seemed to be certain what was meant by "race," and settled on Friedrich Lenz's definition: "subdivisions of the human race, which have been distinguished through particular hereditary factors."[108] As with Schachermeyr, the concept of race formed the foundations of Rosenkranz's exploration of the successes and failures of evangelical missionary activity in China.

The "German spirit" also pervaded the study of languages and literature. The most influential figure among Heidelberg linguists was Hermann Güntert. For Güntert and many other scholars, Indo-Germanic linguistic traditions were tied "racially" to the German people.[109] As early as 1929 Güntert had considered race a determinative factor in the emergence of languages. In outlining the future tasks of comparative language study in the journal *Wörter und Sachen*, he suggested that "if one compares [to the Indo-Germanic languages] a language of completely different construction, for example a Bantu language, just in terms of its structure, the massive differences in predisposition and ways of thinking between the different races and peoples become clear . . . Here is the point at which biological laws of heredity will eventually become a problem for language research."[110] Güntert held to this line of thinking throughout the Third Reich. In 1938 he assumed the co-editorship of the journal *Wörter und Sachen* with Walther Wüst, the curator of the SS's Ancestral Heritage (Ahnenerbe) project. In his introduction to the journal's new series, Güntert stated that "language alone never forms a true element of the people's community, because every language is the expression of the character of a people, and that is dependent upon many deeper effects, from the depths of unconscious sources, biological powers, from race, genetic make-up [Erbmasse], from natural predisposition, temper, living space, from common history."[111] He based his 1943 *History of the Germanic Peoples* (*Geschichte der germanischen Völkerschaften*) on the assumption that

> racially—and that means in the quality of their natural hereditary substance—the "barbarians" were superior to "classical" peoples [the

Greeks and Romans] in the purity of their nobility and type, insofar as those of Indo-Germanic stock who had been pulled to the south had naturally mixed with tribally, linguistically, and racially foreign peoples . . . For awareness of this—a true Copernican revolution for history of our spirit—we can thank biological racial research, which has conclusively proven that . . . according to their linguistic kinship, "Indo-Germanic"–named peoples were at the core a Nordic race of peoples. This absolutely certain evidence is therefore of portentous importance because it determined that linguistic kinship is not racial kinship: the Romans of the republic and later of the empire spoke Latin . . . but racially the Romans of the imperial era had become almost an entirely different people; everywhere Jews had easily learned and spoke the languages of the peoples in whose ranks they had parasitically attached themselves, but they did not give up nor were able to give up their race and racial characteristics in the human substance passed along hereditarily."[112]

A variation on this theme is Richard von Kienle's work. Von Kienle, also a specialist on Indo-Germanic languages, became a director one of the Ahnenerbe's many scholarly departments.[113] Before leaving Heidelberg for Hamburg in 1941, he wrote an Ahnenerbe study on the formation of the "Germanic community." Von Kienle surveyed ancient Germanic tribal traditions to discern the elements of "Sippe," "Bund," and "Stamm" (kin, bands, and stock) that distinguished "Germanic" from "non-Germanic" peoples and hence the superior political, legal, and military order of the German peoples, which was being reconstructed in the Third Reich after centuries of struggle and disunity. His study, however, is pervaded not by overt racist conceptions, but by a general claim that the "blood-bound form of community" was the essential starting point for an investigation into the culture of any people.[114] The book shows that the "German spirit" could encompass a variety of interpretations that were open to criticism or approval by broadly like-minded scholars.

Every one of the university's professors of Romance languages and literature wrote works that appropriated the "German spirit" in scholarship. Even before the war, as Frank-Rutger Hausmann has illustrated, Germany's leading professors of Romance philology sought to locate German influences in Europe's Romance-language nations and highlight the alleged superiority of German culture. This task would become particularly important in the war years, when Romance-language scholars played leading roles in German scientific institutes in occupied or German-allied countries.[115] Heidelberg's leading Romanist was Walter Mönch.116 Mönch personified the "political soldier" envisioned by Nazi Party ideologues: he was a young, talented, ambitious, and politically committed scholar. He arrived at Heidelberg from Berlin in 1938 and became director of the Dolmetscher (Translator's) Institute. He joined the NSDAP in 1937 and the same year became head of the Dozentenbund's Office of Foreign Affairs (Auslandsamt). At the outbreak of the war in 1939, he served as a translator for the Wehrmacht in France. From 1940 to 1944, he lectured at the Belgian university in Lüttich and in 1943 assumed the directorship of the German Scientific Institute in Brussels.117

Mönch's embrace of the "German spirit" is evident in a number of works he wrote on French literature and Franco-German relations. A revealing example is found in his 1938 study of sixteenth-century French literature.118 Mönch's assessment of the essayist Michel de Montaigne is:

> In peculiar contrast to his contemporaries—he was by birth half-Aryan ... [he] is not a little conceited over the purported old aristocratic origins of his "race," as he put it, or his "house" ... In reality he came from a merchant family, which had become rich through the flourishing herring trade. His father's nation is not England, but probably Portugal ... The father's influence on the son had been extraordinarily deep; and as lovingly as Michel had spoken of his father, he took little account of the heritage of his mother, Antoinette de Louppes. She probably came from a Jewish family persecuted in the Inquisition, had fled Spain or Portugal and sought a new life for itself in southern France ... However, certain characteristics of his personality, his thought, and his worldview clearly appear that remind one of his mother's racial foreignness: the easy changeability and ability to adapt his own essence; the lack of heroic passion and preparedness for the religious and national-political interests of the Fatherland alongside the cosmopolitan-accented attitude of his thought and his portrait of humanity.119

Mönch attributed these conflicting aspects of Montaigne's personality to the writer's divided "racial" heritage. "Like his character," Mönch concluded, "his literary achievement vacillates in history's opinion. The racial brokenness of this thinker is, in his life as in his work, noticeable ... He did not make history, but rather observed it as a skeptic from on high ... Montaigne is regarded in France as the first French literary figure of importance, one who ushered in a series of moralists who would become a typical apparition of French literature in the following centuries."120

Mönch's international political agenda is revealed in an article he published in 1938 in the journal *Geist der Zeit* on the French nationalist writer Alphonse de Chateaubriant.[121] Mönch singled out Chateaubriant as one of the few French intellectuals who understood the significance of National Socialism "for the remaking of European humanity and civilization." He not only knew Germany and Germans from all walks of life, but was aware of the "unity of the German racial soul" and the significance of Hitler himself for the nation's fate. What's more, Chateaubriant also recognized that France and Germany shared a common European fate and that France's future lay in embracing its former enemy and repulsing Bolshevism's advances. Mönch saw the future in similar terms, citing with approval Chateaubriant's statement that "the Rhine is no border which one runs up against, but rather a strategic line at which men find each other.'"[122] As we will see in the following chapter, Mönch would carry this interest in reconciling Germany with French-speaking lands in the new German-dominated Europe with him to Lüttich and Brussels.

A more extreme example was Edgar Glässer, first an assistant to Mönch and later a full professor. In numerous publications, Glässer sought to prove that language reflects humanity's "biological, racial" make-up. Like Mönch, Glässer believed that race was a determinative factor in history. In a 1938 article titled "On the Race and Style of Alphonse de Lamartine," Glässer remarked that the French author's "true Nordic" features reveal themselves in his physical appearance and in his prose. His "ideal of a people's community," Glässer wrote, "was based not on the state, but rather on ancestry."[123] In his 1939 book *An Introduction to Racial Language Research: A Critical-Historical Exploration* (*Einführung in die rassenkundliche Sprachforschung: kritische-historische Untersuchungen*), Glässer attempted to show that language was "the representative form of the racial soul": "In the spirit of language the creative voice of the blood is not to be ignored, everything else is delusion."[124] As for the "Jewish question," Glässer concluded that the Jew could only attempt to assimilate in terms of language. "But the impact of this fictive assimilation on both the growing spiritual life and the growing forms of language," he warned, "is in fact so fatal that a growing community that wishes to possess the freedom to assess itself must always be able to recognize the symptoms of sickness in its intellectual life and in its culture of Jewish dominance over language."[125]

As these examples illustrate, the "German spirit" was not a monolithic construction; it could be interpreted and incorporated into scholarship in different ways—professors could select certain elements of the "German spirit" and ignore others if they chose. One of the results of this diversity of views within the National Socialist university was that scholars could and did differ with each other and were often critical of each other's work. The book review sections of contemporary scholarly journals in every field record such disagreements and criticism. Hence, for instance, Walter Mönch rejected Edgar Glässer's racist conceptions while himself embracing another variant of racism. During the Third Reich, the matter was one of degree. It would only be in the postwar era when all shades of gray were repainted in black and white that the extreme racist conceptions of an Edgar Glässer would be considered solely representative of nazified scholarship.

Further evidence that the period 1936–1939 was a turning point for Heidelberg in the context of wider changes in German academic culture is Ernst Krieck's brief term as Rector and Paul Schmitthenner's assumption of this post, which he would hold until the end of the war. In early 1937 Wilhelm Groh left for a position in the Reich Education Ministry in Berlin.[126] When Krieck arrived at Heidelberg in 1934 from Frankfurt, he was well received by Groh and Nazi students and became a member of the inner leadership circle around the Rector. A year later he was appointed Dozentenbundführer for the Gau of Baden. As we have seen, his visibility inside and outside Heidelberg reached a high point in the summer of 1936. Krieck's primary concern, to judge from his proposed "Cultural-Political Institute," his numerous publications, and his engagement in the special indoctrination "camps" for young university instructors, was revolutionary reform of academic culture from within.[127]

But Krieck was Rector for only a short time, from April 1937 to October 1938. Given his largely self-proclaimed status as the premier "philosopher" of National Socialism, he had already entangled himself in ideological and personal disputes with Alfred Rosenberg, Alfred Bäumler, and Wilhelm Hartnacke. Most important, after 1936 Bernhard Rust had no use for him. In light of the announcement of the Four-Year Plan and the Reich Education Minister's determination to have German universities contribute to its realization, it is not difficult to see why Rust disdained Krieck and favored his replacement, Paul Schmitthenner. From Rust's standpoint, there was little practical value in Krieck's work, despite his popularity among some ideologues and Nazi students. In November 1938, Rust named Paul Schmitthenner the new Rector of Heidelberg.

From ideological, political, and practical standpoints, it was an ideal choice. Schmitthenner described himself as a "soldier, politician, and scholar" who had "like few in Germany joined scholarly, political, and soldierly practice and theory in one person."[128] Although he pledged that Krieck's "course will go on unbroken" and did not alter the leadership of the faculties or Senate membership, by temperament and background he was far more acceptable to most faculty members than Krieck.[129] Within a few years, Schmitthenner had become the most powerful figure in southwest Germany's academic culture. Upon Otto Wacker's death in 1940, he managed to get himself appointed Culture Minister of Baden while still serving as Rector of Heidelberg (hence becoming his own boss), and shortly thereafter was appointed by Gauleiter Robert Wagner to head educational affairs in occupied Alsace.[130]

As part of the regime's accelerating persecution of Germany's Jews, the last purges were initiated in 1937, the bulk of them having occurred between 1933 and 1936. Once vacated positions were filled, the composition of the faculties did not change substantially. This does not mean that the final peacetime years at Heidelberg were uneventful and monotonous, interrupted only by the spectacle of the anniversary celebration in June 1936. In particular, the rising tide of anti-Semitism in Germany had a direct impact on the university. The promulgation of the "German Civil Servants Law" of January 21, 1937, completed the purges in academia. The key provision was that not only civil servants but also their spouses were required to be "citizens" (Reichsbürgers), as opposed to "subjects" (Staatsbürger). As a result of the new decree, from 1937 to 1940 seven highly distinguished professors (Karl Jaspers, August Grisebach, Hermann Ranke, Otto Regenbogen, Karl Geiler, Hermann Höpke, and Heinrich Zimmer) were fired because of their marriages to "non-Aryans."[131]

The details of Karl Jaspers's case and the impact of his firing on him personally are particularly revealing. Shortly before the law was enacted, Wilhelm Groh, then serving in the Reich Education Ministry in

Berlin, notified the Ministry of Culture in Karlsruhe that "Frau Jaspers is a Jewess."[132] Although Jaspers's dismissal was seemingly ensured, the Ministry was not oblivious to the prominence of his reputation abroad and the uproar his firing was bound to provoke, and delayed his dismissal.[133] Rector Ernst Krieck, however, saw no reason why Jaspers should be granted exceptional status: "Jaspers is married to a full Jewess . . . In the period following the war he stood far to the left politically. This attitude was complemented by an outspoken professorial and scholarly aristocratism. Jaspers is a representative of the so-called philosophy of existentialism, with connections to Kierkegaard and Nietzsche. His cheeky little volume "The Spiritual Situation of Our Times" had once been widely read, including by National Socialist students. Existential philosophy has strong connections to evangelical theology—the so-called critical orientation. As a representative of existential philosophy, Jaspers is also well known abroad."[134] In Krieck's view, Jaspers did not understand National Socialism and existentialism was irrelevant and useless to the "movement." A report by the Ministry of Culture concurring that there were no reasons to make an exception for Jaspers drew almost word for word on Krieck's report, adding that he had made no political contributions to National Socialism after 1933 and emphasizing that he not served with particular distinction or been wounded in World War I.[135]

With the consent of the Reich Education Ministry Jaspers was dismissed by Baden's Ministry of Culture in June 1937.[136] In July, Jaspers wrote the Ministry in Karlsruhe and the REM and asked that his status be changed to "retired" because of poor health and his long and distinguished service to the university and the study of philosophy in general.[137] Krieck, after helping make possible Jaspers's removal, recommended on the grounds of his former colleague's poor health and the minor uproar that his firing had occasioned in the foreign press that his "dismissal" should be officially designated a "retirement" with "the state of his health given to the press as the overriding reason" for his "retirement."[138] Karlsruhe assented, and recommended—"in view of Professor Jaspers's reputation in Germany and abroad"—that he be given the status of a "retired" professor and thus granted a pension.[139] Hence, Jaspers's fame and the regime's continued sensitivity to foreign criticism saved him temporarily from complete loss of income.

Jaspers's marginalization within his own faculty had begun before his formal dismissal. In an autobiographical statement written shortly after the war, he recalled that though he had continued to teach until 1937 without the disruptions he had heard were forthcoming, "the hinderances were considerable. No more [requests] from me were authorized. The assistant in the Philosophy Seminar no longer acknowledges me. I had to relinquish administrative authority in the seminar after 1935."[140] Yet in terms of his life as a scholar after his firing, Jaspers recalled the period between 1937 and the early years of the war as a "time for reflection." He continued to write, though after 1938 he was prohibited from publishing his work in Germany.[141] But he was increasingly isolated from contact with other scholars—an aspect of tyranny particularly detrimental to intellectuals. In a telling passage in his "Philosophical Autobiography," Jaspers recalled that "until the spring of 1939, I had the good fortune of friendship with Heinrich Zimmer, the Indologist, who, under the pressure of those days, had to emigrate with his family, first to England, and afterwards to the USA. Those were the last broadly-conceived and penetrating intellectual conversations I had with a man in Heidelberg."[142] The events of these years also forced him to meditate on what it meant to be a German. "The consciousness of being German became a question," he recalled: "What is German? Who is German? When, in 1933, my wife, who, as a German Jewess, was betrayed by Germany, rejected Germany which she loved more perhaps than I did myself, I replied definitely and insolently . . . Think me to be Germany."[143] Here there are striking parallels between the responses of Jaspers and those of Victor Klemperer, though their legal statuses were exactly reversed and Klemperer had been thrown out of his job in 1935. Klemperer, like Jaspers, considered himself to have remained an individual fortress of the "real Germany," the values and cultural heritage of which he held to be besieged by barbarism.[144]

A major turning point in the persecution of German Jewry occurred a year after Jaspers's firing. Using as a pretext the assassination in November of a Paris-based German diplomat by a young Jew, Herschel Grynszpan, the regime unleashed a nationwide pogrom. The flood of decrees that ensued stripped German Jews of nearly all prospects of economic, cultural, or religious existence. The pogrom in Heidelberg proceeded the way many others did across Germany. Jewish holy places and businesses and residences owned and occupied by Jews were destroyed while bystanders watched without protest. Perhaps a hundred and fifty Heidelberg Jews were taken into "protective custody" and deported to Dachau. One week later, Torah rolls and other sacred items stolen from the synagogues were burned on the Universitätsplatz, where five years earlier the student SA had burned "Jewish-Marxist" literature.[145] The extent of Heidelberg professors' and students' involvement in the pogrom is unclear, but it is certain they were involved.[146] As Marion Kaplan argued recently, the pogrom revealed the German public's attitude toward Jews as "a mixture of rampant viciousness, studied ignorance, and occasional kindness."[147] Substantial opposition was nonexistent, and the response of the churches and the universities was once again nearly total silence.

Articulated reactions were probably limited to intimates, trusted colleagues, or private diaries. The event did not spark the creation at Heidelberg of an opposition circle of conservative professors, as the pogrom at Freiburg did there.[148] One telling incident involving Paul Schmitthenner stands out. As anti-Semitism across Germany intensified after the passage of the Nuremberg race laws of 1935, Joseph Goebbels decreed that after October 1935 war memorials were not to list the names of Jewish soldiers. But the decree apparently went unenforced until Schmitthenner wrote to the Baden Ministry of Culture on November 10, 1938. "In view of the struggle of world Jewry against the Third Reich," the new Rector declared, "it is intolerable that the names of members of the Jewish race remain on plaques of the war dead . . . I consider the removal of the Jewish names necessary."[149] The Ministry forwarded the letter to Bernhard Rust, who in turn managed to bring it to Hitler's attention. Hitler subsequently decreed that "on already existing memorials and plaques the names of Jews will not be removed." All new memorials, however, could bear no Jewish names. Schmitthenner was less successful than his predecessor, Krieck, who a month earlier had successfully petitioned the Ministry of Culture to have the names of American donors, some of whom were Jewish, removed from the new university building.[150]

On November 21, 1938, just two weeks after the pogrom, Paul Schmitthenner boasted in a speech honoring the university's five hundredth and fifty-second anniversary that "we are no longer the university of the liberal age."[151] He was speaking not just of a change in personnel or the addition of a few new courses but of the fundamental transformation of Germany's academic culture. No longer would the nation's universities serve what he and many others considered an abstraction—scholarship and knowledge as such—rather they would serve the German people and their historic mission. With Heidelberg's rosters now filled with "true National Socialists," he noted that at this provincial university research and teaching were already being oriented in the new direction. For him, the humanities would play a major role in this transformation alongside the hard sciences enlisted in the Four-Year Plan. Schmitthenner was voicing a widely held vision of the university in the Third Reich. Both party figures and professors from all disciplines embraced the "German spirit" in scholarship. This "spirit" was fundamentally opposed to traditions of research and teaching held throughout the Western world in that it (1) rejected "objectivity"; (2) declared that scholarship did not serve an intangible notion of truth for truth's sake, insisting instead that German academic culture was to serve the German "Volk"; and (3) opposed hyper-specialization—the "'heap' of disconnected specialties," as Ernst Krieck put it in late 1935. At the heart of the entire conception was race. The individual scholar's race determined how that scholar looked at the world, and as representatives of an "inferior race" Jews were incapable of examining the natural world honestly and accurately. The Nazis were not the first to attack the positivist tradition or to argue that scholars carry their values with them when they conduct research. Nor would they be the last. Their key contribution was to place race at the core of their assault on objectivity. As we will see in the next chapter, these developments intensified during the war years.

As sociologists of scientific knowledge have long understood, the boundaries between scholarly communities and the wider political, economic, cultural, and national contexts in which they operate are highly porous, and individual scholars do not operate independently of these contexts. The history of German academic culture in the Third Reich reflects these dynamics. The regime curtailed the autonomy of the university, purged it of "unwanted elements," and demanded that its remaining members serve the "Volksgemeinschaft" to which they belonged. The regime's ideologies and policies favored and legitimized certain avenues of research and teaching—particularly those related to "purifying" the German "race" and preparing for a war of expansion—and attempted to exclude others. The case of Heidelberg reveals that this conception of scholarship was widely if unevenly adopted by professors from across the disciplines.

CHAPTER THREE

The National Socialist University at War

> German science ... must gather all powers together in order to fulfill the determined tasks of our völkisch renewal, it must become "fighting science."
> —Gerd Tellenbach, "Der Führer," July 5, 1936

Shortly after his election as Rector of Heidelberg in the fall of 1933, Wilhelm Groh declared that the university should provide the "shock troops" for National Socialism. After the outbreak of the war in September 1939, Rector Paul Schmitthenner announced that Heidelberg would become "der Waffenschmied der Wehrmacht des Reiches"— the armorer of the Reich's army.[1] Schmitthenner was addressing students in early 1940 and was no doubt intoxicated by Germany's unbroken string of military victories. His statement, however, should not be dismissed as empty nationalist bombast. For years he had oriented his teaching and research toward military preparedness. His example was far from singular at Heidelberg. In this chapter, I explore the ways in which professors at Heidelberg put their scholarship at the service of war. We have seen that the regime had met with broad acceptance from within academic culture, which contributed to preparations for territorial expansion and the construction of a new "racial order." I argue here that developments after 1939 should be seen as a continuation and intensification of those of the previous three years. The argument that the universities suffered from state neglect after the "Gleichschaltung" and that subsequently conditions for research and teaching declined steadily cannot be sustained. Scholars from all disciplines contributed their prestige and expertise to the war through publications and lectures, through planning the exploitation and resettlement of conquered territories, through developing weapons and weapons-related technologies, and through medical experiments and the murder of innocent human beings. In contrast, individual or organized resistance by professors and students to the war was rare, and in the case of the former, nonexistent.[2]

World War II in Europe was Hitler's long-planned war of territorial expansion and "racial purification." It became the most destructive conflict in human history, the crimes committed by the Germans and their collaborators against combatant and noncombatant populations alike—material plunder, enslavement, deportations, and genocide—being without precedent in scale and barbarity. During the war, the regime expected, funded, and received extensive support from universities and scientific research institutions. In a revealing comment in early November 1945, the chemist Karl Freudenberg noted "we should like . . . to retain one thing from the Nazi period: the copious financial means."[3] To cite just a few important examples: the Reich Education Ministry saw its budget double between 1935 and 1938 from 11 to 22 million Reichsmarks, and then it grew to 97 million by 1942; the Interior Ministry devoted 43 million Reichsmarks to research in 1935—by 1942 the figure had reached 131 million; the SS budgeted 2 million Reichsmarks for Volkstumsforschung (research on Germanic peoples and culture) alone.[4] Ute Deichmann has revealed in detail the extensive financial support the regime provided to hundreds of university-based biologists.[5] And as Kristie Macrakis has shown, the Kaiser Wilhelm Society saw its budget increase from 5.6 million Reichsmarks in 1933 to 14.3 million by 1944, and it conducted a variety of important war-related research projects.[6] The army, air force, and navy all sponsored research branches, drawing personnel from the major scientific institutes and universities.[7] Further, the Foreign Office established a network of scholarly institutes (Deutsche Wissenschaftliches Institute) in allied or conquered territories in order to help solidify German rule.[8]

Unlike most other universities, Heidelberg was not touched physically by the war. A small university town with no major port, railway connections, or industry, it was never bombed from the air and the city itself did not become a battleground. Its case thus presents something of an anomaly—a university where research and teaching continued virtually uninterrupted into early 1945. The war also resulted in no significant structural changes at the university, and there was considerable continuity in personnel between 1939 and 1945. Two additions to the faculties after 1939, however, are worth close consideration, both for the light their cases shed on the complexities of adaptation to National Socialism among academics and in regard to their importance to Heidelberg after the war. In 1943, the legal scholar Ernst Forsthoff and the surgeon Karl Heinrich Bauer came to Heidelberg from Vienna and Breslau, respectively.

Forsthoff was a student of Carl Schmitt's, and, like several other Schmitt protégés, he became an influential figure in the Third Reich and then in conservative West German legal circles and served as mentor to a generation of postwar scholars.[9] Like numerous scholars of his generation, Forsthoff was a veteran of the youth movement, became a frequent contributor to several antidemocratic right-wing journals, and supported the National Socialists before 1933. His most influential scholarly contribution in 1933 was a short book, *The Total State (Der Totale Staat)*, the basic ideas of which he had developed prior to 1933. His basic argument was that an all-encompassing "total state" would triumph over a divided and weak liberal democracy. The Nazis, in his view, embodied the ideals expressed in the book, and Forsthoff praised the new regime's policies, including the exclusion of Jewish citizens from the civil service.[10] In the winter of 1933, he applied for membership in the SA, but withdrew his application the following year. In 1938, he joined both the NSDAP and the Dozentenbund, though he no longer paid dues to the former after 1941. Having been drafted into an infantry regiment in 1936 and discharged two years later, he was recalled a month before the invasion of Poland and served in that campaign before being discharged in October 1940 and allowed to return to teaching.[11]

Much like Fritz Ernst, Forsthoff earned the enmity of some Nazi students while teaching at the University of Vienna. He was too independent-minded for their liking, having opposed the regime's policies on religion and the proposed conversion of several churches into party museums. Further, in 1938 and 1941 he published two essays that argued for limits on the authority of the "total state." But to conclude that he was thoroughly out of favor with the party (as Forsthoff himself did after the war) or even that he experienced a process of "deradicalization" before the end of the war is debatable. There is the matter of a notorious annotated collection of documents published in 1935, 1938, and 1943, *German History in Documents since 1918*

(*Deutsche Geschichte in Dokumenten seit 1918*), in which Forsthoff justifies every major public policy of the regime up to 1938. It suggests that he, like other disillusioned if not necessarily "deradicalized" conservatives, considered this period to have represented the "total state's" most promising and fruitful years.[12] The fact that the books were published at all, however, reveals that the regime attached some value to them. After the war, Forsthoff credited the offer of a post at Heidelberg following the tumult of Vienna to the efforts of Dozentenführer Karl Schmidhuber.[13] Finally, the party considered him trustworthy enough to deliver lectures to the army in Nancy in October 1943 and again in Lyon in January 1944.[14]

Another notable addition in 1943 was the surgeon Karl Heinrich Bauer.[15] Like Forsthoff, Bauer was an extremely talented scholar. Unlike Forsthoff, who was barred briefly from teaching after the war, Bauer was never suspended from his position. Indeed, he became the most influential German figure in the university's immediate postwar period, overseeing its reopening in 1945 and serving as the first postwar Rector. Like Forsthoff's, Bauer's postwar academic career was a stellar one. Indeed, his research on cancer places him among Germany's greatest surgeons. To this day he is recalled in academic and nonacademic circles alike as an anti-Nazi. After the war, Bauer himself boasted that (to cite but one of many examples) "through my entire career, I rejected Nazism from the outset, externally and internally."[16] He also presented himself, successfully as we will see, as a victim of Nazi persecution.

These claims are demonstrably false. Like many physicians in Germany and elsewhere, Bauer had a strong interest in "racial hygiene." His 1924 book on the subject, *Rassenhygiene,* belongs solidly in the tradition of many similar works that lent scientific and broad public respectability to the ranking of "races" (with Germans at the top) and the search for ways to "purify" a given race.[17] Bauer's work was also unremarkable in this field in that it considered "every ethnic group a hopeless racial mix," looked favorably on voluntary sterilization of women, and rejected the "nonsense of certain racial fanatics demanding spartan methods" (that is, euthanasia and legally mandated sterilizations). But it is worth pointing out that in an eerily prescient passage Bauer advocates a war of "racial" expansion. According to Bauer, a healthy and growing people "with good biological-racial strength" would naturally be forced to expand and settle beyond its narrow borders, particularly in regions occupied by peoples who were "internally rotten and worn out."[18]

The relatively moderate tone of *Rassenhygiene* notwithstanding, Bauer became an outspoken supporter of the Nazis' sterilization law in 1933 and himself performed sterilizations.[19] He justified the law in publications and speeches as necessary to protect the Volk and published, with Felix von Mikulicz-Radecki, a standard guide to surgical sterilization as required by the new law—*The Practice of Sterilization Operations (Die Praxis der Sterilisierungsoperationen).*[20] He was also a member of the Prussian State Health Council after 1933 (he had joined it in 1926). Further, a Breslau colleague recalled after the war that though Bauer was never a member of the local Hereditary Health Court, "he executed sterilizations which were suggested by the [court]." Johann Daniel Achelis, a Medical Faculty colleague at Heidelberg and a radical Nazi, also stated after the war that "it can be positively assumed that Bauer had carried out sterilizations by order of the [Breslau] Hereditary Health Court. Bauer too knew about the murders of insane persons at that time."[21]

Yet, again unlike Forsthoff, Bauer was never a member of the Nazi Party, because he was married to a "non-Aryan," Ingeborg Fuchs. In an assessment of Bauer's scientific abilities and political reliability dated January 1, 1941, the Rector of Breslau University pointed out that "Professor Bauer is married to a grade 2 *Mischlinge,* and because of that it has been ordered by [Reich Education Minister Bernhard Rust] that Professor Bauer should not be placed in the political foreground."[22] As Bauer himself noted a year later, Rust knew of his marriage to a "non-Aryan" before he approved of his promotion to full professor at Breslau in 1933.[23] Contrary to Bauer's postwar claims, however, he did not suffer "persecution" under the Nazis because of his marriage to Fuchs. Although he could not join the party, he served it and the Wehrmacht in numerous other ways, and his career flourished. First, as noted, he was a specialist in sterilizations. Second, he gave numerous speeches in Germany and abroad and operated on prominent Bulgarian and German military figures (in one instance at the personal request of Hermann Goering). Third, in 1942 Hitler granted Bauer a special "racial dispensation" allowing him to serve as a staff surgeon in the Wehrmacht reserve. This dispensation was granted not only because of Bauer's abilities, but because one of Hitler's personal physicians, Karl Brandt, as well as several generals that

Bauer had operated on, intervened on his behalf. In any case, his services earned him first- and second-class War Merit crosses.[24] Further, he served as one of the many academic "cultural ambassadors" active in German scientific institutes abroad (in Bulgaria and possibly also in Hungary and Sweden).[25] In addition to all of this, he was not prevented from publishing, becoming, for instance, the co-editor (with his former teacher Rudolf Stich) of a standard multivolume surgical reference work.[26]

In December 1942 Bernhard Rust appointed Bauer to head Germany's finest university surgical clinic.[27] Any objections to Bauer's transfer to Heidelberg within the faculty, Rector's office, or Ministry of Culture were quashed by his "racial dispensation."[28] Not surprisingly, Bauer taught courses at Heidelberg on "military surgery." Part of his lectures in 1943 and 1944, as numerous former students recalled after the war, involved identifying cases of self-inflicted wounds among soldiers and referring them to military courts. Bauer himself also admitted to American investigators that he had served as an expert witness in at least one court-martial involving self-inflicted wounds.[29] A conviction in such cases usually resulted in execution.

How did professors at Heidelberg respond to the war? A series of lectures delivered and published between November 1939 and November 1941 provide insight into both attitudes about the war and the ways in which scholarship was intended to support it. Taken together, these lectures—the "War Lectures" (Kriegsvorträge)—reveal widespread enthusiasm and the extent to which the "German spirit" had penetrated academic discourse. Since this period witnessed Hitler's greatest military victories, the lectures reflected considerable optimism. Speakers repeatedly described the war as the mission and destiny of the German people, and much invective was directed at France and England. Ernst Krieck referred to England as "the vampire of the people, the exploitative initiator of all disorder, all strife, and all injustice in the world for three hundred years" and blamed England and France together for eviscerating what should have become a great German empire in the Thirty Years' War.[30] Everyone assumed final victory, and consequently there are repeated references to a German-dominated postwar order in Europe. Most speakers also repeated the familiar theme of the need for a close connection between the "Volksgemeinschaft" and academic culture. As Paul Schmitthenner put it in January 1940: "We understand that the fulfillment of our people, for us so tragically late, has come for Europe at the right time—at the moment of its greatest racial-spiritual weakness. We are filling this European breach." It was the mission of the German people to correct the "mistakes" of the French Revolution and the "British-Imperialist revolution" in order to "recreate Europe through a German revolution through power and blood and wisdom in the service of the world."[31]

Several speakers took up problems of economic and legal organization. Ernst Schuster, speaking on "the military spirit" in German economic life, argued that planning and organization had to be accompanied by the "activation of human capabilities." These capabilities were those of the soldier—the "will to create order," "decisiveness," "insight into the people's community of destiny," "the qualities of courage, wisdom, clarity, pride." "Certainly," Schuster concluded, "we need new inventions, new machines, new manpower, new raw materials; we must rebuild, change, divert, calculate, construct organizations. But with all these we will only be prepared if we unite as members of the people's economy, as a community of labor . . . We are fortunate in that the leader of the German people has given us clear goals."[32] Herbert Krüger spoke in similar terms on the "psychological powers of the people's community" behind the front lines, the most important power being "the confidence that binds the leader and the people with and among each other." This organic bond would ensure victory: "Here a deed of psychological armament for the great world-political conflict has been performed, on which military rearmament stands on an equal plane. Our enemies err if they believe they will be able, as in the [first] world war, to first achieve psychological and then military victory. Today, not only the military but also the psychological inferiority lie on the other side. So sharp are our weapons, so strong is the confidence in our leader. With both joined, victory this time will not elude us."[33]

The scholar of Roman law Gerhard Dulckeit took up the broad theme "law in the past and the present."[34] The highest historical stage of legal evolution, he argued, was being realized in the Third Reich: "In the construction of the people in family and kin (genetic make-up), economy and judicature, state and culture, the concept of law and along with it human life reaches its highest and richest truth and reality."[35] That is, the law of a given people emerges from its own inner "character" (intellectual and physical) and its history and customs. But what about the law in wartime? Dulckeit rejected out of hand adherence or subordination to "international law," which he considered an "empty utopia" and an "instrument of power in the hands of the capitalist-Jewish world powers."[36] For Dulckeit, the war in Europe was more than a matter of battlefield encounters—it also involved a struggle between two hostile legal and political orders, one "national" and representative of a true "people's community," the other based on the "imaginary prehistoric natural state of the individual person" of the Enlightenment era. There remains for any people, he claimed, "only one single highest commandment regarding its behavior: its honor and its moral right to life." On this basis the Third Reich had overthrown the "Versailles diktat," because it robbed the German Empire of its "living space and means of supporting the life of its people," and was now fighting a new war to maintain its "honor and its own laws."[37]

The "selective embrace" of modernity, as Jeffrey Herf described it, that characterized the "reactionary modernist" paradigm of right-wing intellectual and scientific culture before and after 1933 is evident in most of these addresses and particularly so in the assessment of "the awareness of nature and military power" by the physicist August Becker.[38] How was it, Becker asked, that Germany could have achieved such tremendous technological achievements, achievements that inspired awe among Germans and fear among their enemies? His answer was the "typical German yearning for nature, the tenacity and thoroughness in the constant mining for new truths, the always deepening awareness of natural revelations" that allowed the German researcher to translate the "fixedness of bands of molecules [into Germany's] helmets, protective bunkers, and tanks, the potential energy of explosives and fuel [into] its bombs, mines, gunnery, vehicles, and airplanes, the potential energy of compressed gasses and vapors [into] torpedo tubes and steam-driven engines, kinetic energy [into] flying missiles, the wavelike spread of sound, light, and the electromagnetic powers [into] the different types of remote sensing, remote guidance, and transmission."[39] Becker likened this process to creating a work of art. After all, he reasoned, when one looks upon a work of art, one normally does not focus on the "raw materials"—the paint or the canvas—but the painting itself. Becker was hardly alone in equating cultural characteristics supposedly "essential" to Germans with technological advance. His characterization of German technical prowess was echoed at Heidelberg by Joseph Goebbels two years later, in 1943: "The steely romanticism of our time manifests itself in exhilarating achievements, in a restless service to a great cause, in a sense of duty that will be raised to an unalterable principle . . . The empire of droning motors, heaven-storming technical inventions, grandiose industrial creations, vast, nearly untapped regions which we must settle for our people—that is the empire of our romanticism."[40]

Following the German invasion of Poland on September 9, 1939, the Armed Forces High Command (Oberkommando der Wehrmacht, or OKW) ordered that most universities close their doors temporarily, those doors to be reopened pending the progress of the various campaigns. Aware that the outbreak of war would result in the curtailing of activities at Germany's universities, the chairmen of most of the faculties pressed the Rector to do what he could to prevent the interruption of their work. But at Heidelberg only the Dolmetscher Institute, the Physics and Chemistry Institutes, and the State and Economic Sciences Faculty continued to function during the brief suspension, while the chairman of the Medical Faculty, Hans Runge, was authorized to offer lectures—called Frontkursen—to the Wehrmacht and medical students inducted from Heidelberg and its environs.[41] On October 11, in any case, OKW approved the reopening of Heidelberg for the coming semester (beginning in January 1940).[42]

The arguments put forth by the various chairmen reveal not only enthusiasm for the war and preparedness to support it, but evidence that war-related research in some faculties had been well under way before the outbreak of hostilities. Karl Bilfinger, chairman of the Law Faculty, proposed that teaching and research continue in "international law (basic courses, politics of international law, misdemeanor law, neutrality law, and law of war), as well as military law, also criminal law."[43] As for the Philosophy Faculty, Hubert Schrade wrote that "intellectual military preparedness encompasses all cultural realms, [and] it also demands the preservation of the entire Philosophy Faculty."[44] Similarly, Paul Böckmann argued that the work of the German Language and Literature Seminar was necessary to "strengthen the nation's intellectual and spiritual powers of resistance." In case of a long war, he added, Germanists would be needed to "strengthen the fighting spirit" of coming generations.[45] Conversely, the Anglicist Harro Jensen argued that it would be important to cultivate a stock of students familiar with "the great enemy" England, and to spread what they had learned beyond the university's walls.[46]

Walter Thoms could make a similar case for the State and Economic Sciences Faculty. Thoms first singled out the Dolmetscher Institute and the instruction it provided in French, English, Italian,

Spanish, and Russian, and the special courses offered to Wehrmacht officers "with particular consideration [given] to military language" in the same five languages. Further, the Institute for the Study of Journalism collected enemy "propaganda," the analysis of which would be of considerable future importance. On the justification that "the economic strength of a people in the current war is just as important as its military strength," Thoms recommended that the faculty's other institutes—especially the Institute for National Economics and Statistics, the Industrial Economics Institute, and the Raw Materials and Merchandise Institute—continue their work uninterrupted.[47]

The Medical and Natural Sciences Faculties considered themselves particularly important for the conduct of the war. In a letter to the Reich Education Ministry, Hans Runge argued that the Medical Faculty—its professors of hygiene, pathology, pharmacology, physiology, and anatomy—were obliged to both the German people and the military. The Pharmacological Institute, directed by Fritz Eichholtz, for instance, had already been developing drugs to resist poison gases and conducting other war-related medical research in conjunction with the Kaiser Wilhelm Insititute.[48] The university's clinics, he proposed, could be converted into reserve hospitals for the army. Further, "the maintenance of the Forensic Medicine Institute is of fundamental importance in view of emergency medical services as well as medical-legal demands."[49]

The Philipp Lenard, Chemistry, and Geology Institutes were engaged in war-related research before the outbreak of the war. The Lenard Institute's projects, as summarized for Paul Schmitthenner by August Becker in October 1939, reveal a close connection between the institute, the military, and several private concerns:

a. Infra-red questions in cooperation with army weapons research

b. Phosphorescence analysis in connection with Telefunken A. G. Berlin

c. Questions of navigational lights, at the instigation of the explosive and pyrotechnic factory Cleeboom

d. Questions related to phosphor in cooperation with I. G. Frankfurt Höchst

e. Geiger-counter analysis, soon to be put at the disposal of army weapons research

f. Hygrometric studies, which will shortly be put at the disposal of army weapons research

g. Meteorological questions of electrical atmospheric disturbances, which are important for aeronautics[50]

Further, Karl Freudenberg, the director of the Chemistry Institute, and his assistants had long been working closely on Four Year Plan projects.[51] Finally, The Geology Institute had three assistants and its director, Julius Wilser, working as geologists for the Wehrmacht.[52]

Heidelberg professors made other tangible contributions to the war effort. War-related topics were taught extensively. As we have seen, from the time of the Machtergreifung professors from across the faculties taught courses on subjects related to geopolitics, war, and race. This trend continued and intensified after 1939. Paul Schmitthenner, for instance, continued to teach almost exclusively on war-related subjects, as did his assistant Wilhelm Ganser ("The Military and Military Thought of the Great Powers: Russia, Japan, Italy"; "Introduction to the Study of Military History and the Study of Military Policy"; and—with Schmitthenner—"War-historical and Military-Political Problems"). Ernst Rodenwaldt continued to teach courses on "Volk and race," and added "Heredity and the Study of Race" (taught along with August Seybold and Paul Krüger). The Medical Faculty offered the most war-related courses: "Military Law and the Law of War" (Friedrich von Rauchhaupt); "Selected Portions from Special Pathological Anatomy with Special Consideration for Military Pathology" (Alexander Schmincke); "Military Psychology" (Carl Schneider); "Surgical Clinic with Regard to Accident and War Surgery" (Martin Kirschner); "Military Medicine" (Richard Siebeck); "Military Pharmacology and Military Toxicology" (Fritz Eichholtz); "Work, Sport, and Military Physiology" (Johann Daniel Achelis); "Military-Chemical Physiology—Chemistry of Chemical Weapons" and "Military Neurology: War Injuries to the Nervous System" (Waldemar Kutscher); "Hygiene with Military Hygiene" (Rodenwaldt); and "Surgery Clinic—Especially Accident and Military Surgery" (Karl Heinrich Bauer).[53]

Geopolitics and particular geographical regions drew close attention, especially England, France, and Japan. Wolfgang Panzer taught the courses "France and the British Isles" and "Geography and Geopolitics of the World's Oceans." In 1941 and 1942, Wilhelm Classen offered a series of courses on regional geopolitics, particularly relating to Asia and Japan: "East Asia as Living Space" (Lebensraum), "Living Space and Regional Principles [Grossraumprinzip] in Political Discussion of Foreign Lands," and "The Japanese Claim to the New Order in East Asia." In the winter semester of 1943 and 1944, a series of lectures on "Japan and Germany" included "The Island of Formosa: The Southern Shaft of the Japanese Empire before the War" (Panzer), "Japanese Spirit and Japanese Religion" (Gerhard Rosenkranz), "Japan's Rise as a World Power" (Willy Andreas), "The Young Great Power of Japan and the European Colonial Powers, 1867–1932" (Fritz Ernst), and "Japan in the Current War" (Schmitthenner).[54]

All other faculties made some contribution. Natural Sciences offered "Geology of the Western Theaters of War" (Ernst Becksmann) and "The Geological Structure of Europe, Its Theaters of War, and Its War- and Economic-related Deposits" (Julius Wilser). Carl Brinkmann offered "Foreign People's Economics," while the Journalism Institute offered "Organizational Questions of Newspaper Publishing during the Wartime Economy" (Walter Mehls) and "The Newspaper in Total War," and "The Nature of Journalism Abroad" (both from Hans Hermann Adler). Unnamed members of the Law Faculty were responsible for "Law in War." The Dolmetscher Institute began to provide training in Polish, and created courses to teach Wehrmacht officers how to speak Spanish, Italian, Russian, French, and English.[55] The Theology Faculty provided "War and Religion in the History of German Piety" (Günther Moldaenke). Finally, along with the heavily ideological smorgasbord offered by Ernst Krieck and Eugen Fehrle, Willy Wagenknecht taught a course called "The World View of Bolshevism."[56]

Lectures and publications on the war were also provided beyond the walls of Heidelberg. Professors were enlisted after 1942, for instance, to present lectures to young academics stationed in France.[57] Another important development was the "Aktion Ritterbusch" project. In early 1940, Paul Ritterbusch, a legal scholar and Rector of Kiel University, assembled publications and lectures on war-related issues solicited from four to five hundred university professors representing twelve disciplines. Collectively, the endeavor produced 67 books and brochures, including 24 edited collections containing 299 different contributions. The project was funded by the German Research Society (Deutsche Forschungsgemeinschaft, or DFG) and addressed the west from 1940 to 1941, and then the east from 1942 to 1945.[58] At least eighteen Heidelberg instructors participated (or were slated to participate) in the project: Paul Schmitthenner, Friedrich Panzer, Paul Böckmann, Hermann Gundert, Reinhard Herbig, Harro Jensen, Ernst Rodenwaldt, Carl Brinkmann, Johannes Hoops, Walter Thoms, Hermann Glockner, Hubert Schrade, Edgar Glässer, Mario von Wandruszka, Walter Mönch, Gerhard Hess, and possibly Martin Dibelius. The German Institute for Foreign Policy Research (Deutsches Institut für Aussenpolitische Forschung) solicited scholarly studies of a variety of foreign policy issues (particularly related to Great Britain) by university professors and high-level party figures, issuing such titles as *England against Arabia*, *The Empire against Europe*, and *Great Britain: Hinterland of World Jewry*. From Heidelberg, series authors included Martin Dibelius, *British Christianity and British World Power* (1940); Carl Brinkmann, *Economic Liberalism as a System of the British Worldview* (1940) and *English Economic Imperialism* (1940); Carl Bilfinger on various aspects of American foreign policy; and Eugen Fehrle, *The German People in Alsace*.[59]

The analyses proffered were steeped to varying degrees in the "German spirit." At this early stage of the war, the principal target of the Heidelberg contributors to the series was, as in the War Lectures, Great Britain. Both Carl Brinkmann and Martin Dibelius highlighted what they considered the shallowness and hypocrisy of two principal British institutions: the Empire and the Church of England. Hence Brinkmann called attention to the pretense of the British government's longstanding claim that its Empire fostered "liberty" by attempting to show how imperial policies had stunted the economic development of Ireland, India, Egypt, and other places. Brinkmann suggested that the English national character, with no honor or calling higher than exploitive profit-making, was essentially weak and corrupt.[60] As for England and its church, Dibelius argued that "this Christian people acts in a markedly un-Christian manner, cloaking its entire political life along with all its most profane expressions of power with Christian motives." The explanation lay in the "absence of fundamental belief, derived from an immense insular-puritanical Old Testament–based illusion, upon which rests the equating of the English people with God's people." This "illusion" resulted in political acts—whether those of "political necessity or political blindness"—that were "interpreted theologically or juridically" and justified as the "enforcement of God's commands or holy law." The Englishman,

Dibelius concluded, "borrows the veil of religion in order to conceal his objectives, but forgets that in doing so he strives to join two incompatible things and that God's Empire is not the British Empire."[61]

Eugen Fehrle stayed closer to home in his study of the ethnic German population in Alsace. Alsatians were not "suspended," Fehrle argued, "between German and French essences, as determined by race, manner, and speech, and thus vacillating between both cultures and ways of life"; rather "the population of Alsace is thoroughly German." The region's "Germanness" was evident in the architecture of its houses and towns, the customs and rites of its residents, and not least in the history of its political and literary past. "It may be suggested—especially abroad"—he concluded, "that we have conquered a foreign land . . . This applies only to a small portion of the Alsatian population, above all to immigrant Frenchmen and Jews and to a few weak and misled Alsatians. We do not have a 'vanquished' people to win over; rather we have thousands of German brothers who have always seen Alsace as their clandestine German home."[62]

Professors of Romance languages at Heidelberg and other universities became particularly active in the service of Germany's wartime cultural imperialism.[63] In 1940, Walter Mönch began holding lectures at the university in Lüttich, Belgium. Shortly thereafter he became the director of the German Scientific Institute in Brussels. His detailed reports on his activities in Lüttich shed light on the goals and methods of wartime German cultural imperialism.[64] Mönch's purpose was to help solidify German rule in Belgium by promoting awareness of German culture and fostering cooperation with pro-Nazi Belgian elites. To do this, he attempted to foster what the *Brüsseler Zeitung* referred to at the time as "the deep unity of both countries in the sense of a higher European order."[65] This was particularly true for French-speaking Walloonia, where Lüttich was located. In Mönch's view, the Walloons sat "between the Romantic and Germanic worlds." In his report on the 1941–42 academic year, he described his strategy of forging closer cultural ties:

> It appears to me that . . . classicism—Goethe—Romanticism, and their respective relations to the most developed contemporary French literature, philosophy, and intellectual history not only touch on important themes, but through these will also push through a cultural-political outcome: namely, first the enlightenment of (in most cases completely ignorant) Belgian students or, as the case may be, instructors, as to the

mighty German cultural achievements in Europe over the past two hundred years; and second the gradual incorporation of the Walloons into the German intellectual world, in which they will still be able to gradually feel at home in the preservation of their Romantic character. They must be made to understand that the new Europe will emerge not from the hateful rejection of one or another cultural circle but in the synthesis of the Germanic and Romantic worlds, in which they themselves—as Walloons—can take up a not unimportant place if they understand correctly the needs of the hour.[66]

Hence Mönch's lectures in Lüttich aimed at these "cultural-political" goals: "The Germanic and Romantic Worlds," "German and French Romanticism," "Goethe and the French World," and a planned lecture on "German and French classicism."[67] For Mönch, then, there was no distinction between scholarly work and what he referred to as "cultural-political activities" on behalf of closer German-Belgian ties. Only after 1945 would he claim to have engaged exclusively in the former activity.[68]

The publications of numerous Heidelberg humanities professors illustrate how historical parallels and analogies could justify and support Nazi ideology and war aims. As Volker Losemann has pointed out, for instance, the academic study of ancient history was of great interest to Hitler and a large number of scholars catered to this interest by linking the study of antiquity with the goals of National Socialism.[69] German scholars had in any case long drawn parallels between Rome and Carthage and Germany and Great Britain. In 1943 a two-volume collection of essays relating the lessons of classical antiquity to Germany's war effort was published, the second volume of which was devoted to the struggle between Rome and Carthage. Contributors to this collection—which included some of Germany's most prominent scholars of the ancient world—portrayed the conflict as one between the "racially superior" Germanic peoples and the inferior "Semitic" peoples.[70] Hence this assessment of Punic artwork by the Heidelberg classical archaeologist Reinhard Herbig:

> They [the Punic peoples] mixed a true mish-mash of artistic styles and traded profitably with this formless mush with the unbiased buyers who had granted them access to their lands. If anywhere, let the Punic peoples' disrespect for foreign peoples' character be understood here. They presented [their art] exclusively as commodities of more or less higher value and arrived at better results and heftier prices by ruthlessly mixing

and corrupting [the artwork]. The small amount that flowed from their own essence was a genotype from ancient Phoenician indigenous peoples, in any case long a mixed result of numerous oriental styles of the great eastern cultures of the Nile and of Mesopotamia, from Syria, Persia, and Asia Minor.[71]

Herbig's text was not overtly anti-Semitic. But the characteristics described above were those anti-Semites had long attributed to Jews—profit-obsessed, dishonest, without worthy native cultural traditions, parasitic—and the analogy could not have been lost on many readers.

Another revealing example is Fritz Ernst's 1936 study of Great Britain's rule over India. Interest in the British imperial experience was not limited to nationalist academics like Ernst—Hitler himself was fascinated by the way in which the British ruled India with a few officers and bureaucrats, and he referred to the Ukraine as "that new Indian Empire."[72] Ernst warns that "if the world war brought a great period to a close, one which saw the ever-stronger spread of the white peoples, if in our time this spread has come to a halt and if the wave of other races should rise up against the white, then it is time to once again look back at the role that the relations between England and India have played in the centuries of white world domination. As white outposts in Asia, the English have greatly accelerated the development of the Asians. From English-ruled India, they have affected all sides."[73] Ernst hoped to continue to explore the British experience in India through a biography of Robert Clive, the British East India Company official who was instrumental in solidifying Britain's rule in the late eighteenth century. The parallels with Germany's own geopolitical interests were not lost on Ernst.[74] Another example is his contribution to a 1940 festschrift in honor of his mentor Johannes Haller, in which Ernst addresses the disunity of German Volk since the Middle Ages and the failure of eastern expansion and permanent settlement. The article is a thinly veiled endorsement of the current war and expansion to the east as a means of unifying all Germans.[75]

History itself could be "Germanized" in the service of the war or National Socialism. An example of this is a collection of essays by some of Heidelberg's specialists on "Westforschung" titled *Germany's Fate in Alsace (Deutsches Schicksal im Elsass)*, published in 1941.[76] Since "the Führer has entrusted the Reichstatthalter in Baden with carrying out the reintegration of Alsace into the Reich," Paul Schmitthenner and Friedrich Panzer noted in the foreword, the university sponsored a series of lectures, later published in *Germany's Fate in Alsace,* by Schmitthenner, Panzer, Eugen Fehrle, Walther Köhler, Paul Böckmann, Herbert Rudolph, and Friedrich Metz (from Freiburg) on Germany's historic presence in the region. Their essays ranged over the history of German influences and their alleged dominant political and cultural presences. Hence Walther Köhler argued that Alsace's greatest Humanist-era and Reformation-era figures were German and its population had wished to remain so in the face of French encroachment. "'Valiant Germans, preserve in honor the name of antiquity!' the Strasbourg town clerk, Sebastian Brandt, called out to his Alsatian home and to the German Fatherland. To be an Alsatian meant for the Humanists on the left side of the Rhine to be a German."[77] Paul Böckmann, in an essay on "Germany's fate in the Alsatian literary evolution in the modern era," suggested that "perhaps the most important moment in the evolution of German literature took place in Strasbourg," when in 1770 Goethe met Herder and experienced a "new immediacy in the desire to express himself" with "the reversal in poetic demeanor [going] hand in hand with a new German national consciousness." In his subsequent travels around the region "Goethe felt himself awe-struck by the German manner of this borderland and experienced with new eyes German landscapes, German people, German artwork." The implications of this awakening went beyond Goethe's own literary production, since "all of us have, consciously or unconsciously, found sustenance in this happy emergence, so much so that through this event the name Strasbourg obtained its particular and solemn ring. If Goethe could have become so deeply and essentially reawakened there, then this Alsace belongs especially to us, and it must be a German land as such, unlike any other." Böckmann concluded by thanking "the National Socialist renewal of German life and the glorious struggle of our army" for "returning" Alsace to Germany.[78]

As we saw in Chapter 2, several institutes were created in the mid- and late-1930s that focused on military preparation and territorial expansion. One of the most significant created after the outbreak of the war was devoted to regional economic research—the Institut für Grossraumwirtschaft (research on the economies of large territories). Three factors account for the creation of Heidelberg's institute. Paramount was the regime's plans to create a self-sufficient German-dominated European "Grossraum."[79] Another was the parallel growth of interest among German economists and sociologists in new Europe-wide trade relations. Debate over "regional economics" and its potential benefits and drawbacks for German trade predated the Third Reich, but became a matter of great practical urgency after the outbreak of the war. In 1939, a group of economists and sociologists led by Werner Daitz created the Society for European Economic Planning and Regional Economics (Gesellschaft für europäische Wirtschaftsplanung und Grossraumwirtschaft, or GWG), which was subsumed under Alfred Rosenberg's domain. University-based economists were not too far behind. In October 1941, the Society of German Economists devoted a meeting in Weimar to "European regional economics." A third factor was the German army's invasion of the Soviet Union in June 1941. Rapid initial success sent various ministries scrambling to find ways to manage and exploit huge swaths of territory now under German rule. As Klaus Brintzinger has pointed out, this factor most likely accounts for the institute's relatively quick and "unbureaucratic" creation.[80]

Finally, there were the efforts of Walter Thoms, the driving force behind the institute at Heidelberg. Thoms was not seeking to create an entirely new area of research for the State and Economic Sciences Faculty. Rather, he wished to expand the work of its members, because "the development of European regional economics under German leadership demands that more or less all German economists devote themselves to a great extent to the problems of regional economics."[81] Further, he envisioned the institute as training future generations in "practical economic policy"[82] and cooperating with other German and non-German economists working in the same field.[83] These points were stressed by the institute's titular head, Fritz Landfried, a state secretary in the Reich Ministry of Finance: the university and the Ministry would cooperate in the "reconstruction of Europe's economic order."[84] During the first meeting of the institute's leadership in early January 1942, Landfried proclaimed that the task of the institute was to form a "bridge between scholarship and practice." The Ministry wanted the institute not to simply parrot its positions, but to provide it with practical help and to cooperate with it in training future generations of students who "from the beginning will be initiated into the necessity of practical economic policy."[85]

Planning and negotiations between Thoms and the Ministry of Finance took place in the summer and fall of 1941. The institute would be devoted to "research on the structures of the future European regional economy," as the official announcement published in the *Völkischer Beobachter* put it.[86] Thoms himself described the institute's tasks in its first annual report: "This war is a military conflict with an old, declining world. It is the struggle against capitalism and will end with the victory of a Völkisch-based socialism. The liberal-capitalist economy has broken down; regional economies will emerge all over the world. The European region-wide economy has arisen. At this time the great military and ideological conflict has charged economic sciences with a task—to cooperate in this struggle for the reorganization of the Völkisch way of life."[87] Thoms's view of a divided world remained unaltered in the face of Germany's rapidly disintegrating military fortunes. His Seminar for Regional Economics, held in July 1944, addressed the theme "Völkischer socialism and European social policies"; Thoms declared that "the social order stands in close connection with the economic order—both belong together and cannot be separate from each other. The National Socialist revolution initiated the formation of a new order of life. This second world war has become the struggle for its achievement." In the period before and after the World War I, the "individualistic-capitalist" system dominated the belligerent nations' economies and societies, though after the war Russia was consumed with this system's mirror image: collectivism. Outside Russia, the "individualistic-capitalist" system proved incapable of solving the "social question." It was only in Germany following the National Socialist revolution that "Völkische socialism" was established. The success of this revolution formed the basis of the war by Germany's enemies. Hence, "two worldviews for the formation of a living order stood in diametrical opposition to each other in the military and spiritual struggle: the German 'Völkisch' idea of the living order and the Jewish-international conception, represented through the Jewish-Bolshevist and the Jewish-plutocratic 'system.'"[88]

The institute was connected to and received much of its funding—60,000 Reichsmarks annually—from the Reich Ministry of Finance, and the Reich Education Ministry gave its approval to the project in February 1942.[89] Thoms directed its work until the end of the war (after 1942 alongside Carl Brinkmann's replacement at Heidelberg, Horst Jecht). Along with Thoms, Brinkmann, and Jecht, the institute's membership included economists from the State and Economic Sciences Faculty, most notably Ernst Schuster and Eugen Sieber, as well as Paul Schmitthenner and representatives from the Reich Ministry of Finance, the Party Chancellery, the Reich Ministry of Education, and Baden's Ministry of Culture. The work of the institute was divided into five sections, with Brinkmann's responsible for "methodological problems, trade policy, regional problems of the eastern and mid–South American regions, and agricultural policy" and Schuster's for "basic questions of regional economics," "regional order" and economic planning, "regional sociology," "regional social policy," industrial policy, and "regional relations with other parts of the world." Thoms's section dealt with employment reserves, social policy, and foreign trade; Carl Sandig's section was also responsible for trade issues, and Eugen Sieber's for money and credit policies.[90] The institute continued its work until early 1945, and it was formally disbanded by the university, probably on the orders of American occupation officials, in March 1946.[91]

The institute produced a number of published and unpublished studies, conducted seminars, and hosted a conference at Heidelberg in late 1942 on the economic reconstruction of territory under German occupation. Fritz Landfried opened the conference with an address titled "The Common Destiny of Continental Europe in Total War." Ministry of Finance officials and Heidelberg professors then delivered several variations on this theme: "The Economic Reorganization of the Eastern Regions" (Dr. Ter-Nedden, Berlin), "British Trade Policy and Continental Europe" (Dr. Imhoff, Berlin), "The Unity of the Mediterranean" (Biagio Pace, director of the Centro di studi e d'azione per l'ordnine nuovo), "The Economics of Electricity in Continental Europe" (Dr. E. Barth, Berlin), "The Development of German-Dutch Economic Relations" (Dr. von Boeckh, The Hague), "Regional [European] Cooperation" (Ernst Schuster, Heidelberg), "German Capital for the Construction of the European Regional Economy" (Ernst Sieber, Heidelberg), "Main Features of Bolshevist Management" (Walter Thoms, Heidelberg),[92] "The Baltic Sea and Grossraum" (C. Axel von Gadolin, Helsinki), "German Agricultural Machinery and Its Importance for Europe's Food Economy" (E. M. Hofweber, Firma Heinrich Lanz, Mannheim), and "Problems of Chemistry in European Regional Economics" (Carl Wurster, I. G. Farbenindustrie AC, Ludwigshafen). Finally, Carl Bilfinger addressed a closed session consisting of instructors from the State and Economic

Sciences, Law, and Philosophy faculties on "regional frontiers and worldwide communications."[93]

The institute also produced several unpublished, "in-house" studies of various regions of Europe and other parts of the world. In 1944, it published the first study in a projected series on "Grossraumwirtschaft": Konstantin Bobtschev's *The European Regional Economy and Bulgaria (Die Europäische Grossraumwirtschaft und Bulgarien)*.[94] Bobtschev, a Bulgarian economics professor, argued that the path to European economic stability and growth lay in the "European regional economy," and not autarky, which tended to bring benefits to a small number of powerful states. In Bobtschev's view, "Grossraumwirtschaft" meant the organization of neighboring independent states united in overcoming economic instability and the harmful effects of national economic insularity. As "thanks to Germany's victorious struggle against the dictated Paris peace treaty," Bulgaria's territory had been enlarged. Its economy remained overwhelmingly agricultural, though there was a small and growing industrialized sector. With the proper organization, he argued, Bulgaria was in a position to be a productive and not disruptive factor in a future European-wide economy. The basis for this judgment was the nation's trade relations with Germany, which accounted for two thirds of Bulgaria's trade, and Bobtschev expected his country to remain closely tied to Germany: "Bulgarians recognize very well Germany's significance: Germany—the great and loyal wartime comrade in the first war, the victor on all fronts in this war, the liberator of the quintessentially Bulgarian regions of Macadonia and Thrace." Bobtschev then provided a raft of statistics on his nation's ethnic composition, population growth, agriculture and industry, and foreign trade.[95]

How important were the institute's activities to the regime's occupation and exploitation of conquered territories? In its relatively short lifespan, the institute did not produce an extensive body of publications and reports, and it did not foster the extensive international contacts envisioned by its founders. The related activities of its members remain obscure. In the summer of 1944, for instance, Walter Thoms agreed to serve as an adviser on "the problem of Bolshevist economic and social policy" to an unidentified section of Alfred Rosenberg's Ministry for the Occupied Eastern Territories. In the summer of 1942, he had gone to the Ukraine to study the matter and also planned to assist in assembling a library of "Bolshevist economic literature" that the governor-general of Poland, Hans Frank, had informed him was being established in Cracow.[96] In what was probably the final formal meeting of the institute in January 1945, Fritz Landfried suggested that a study be undertaken that addressed "how we have shaped the economies in the occupied regions." It's unlikely such a study was ever produced before the collapse of the Third Reich a few months later.[97] Without question, however, the massive economic and cultural plunder in German-occupied Europe, though it varied from region to region, could not have been undertaken without expertise provided by Germany's willing academic elite.

The Institut für Grossraumwirtschaft was not the only institution at Heidelberg for research supporting Germany's expansion. Ernst Schuster was also the director of the Institute for Political Economy and Statistics (Insitut für Volkswirtschaftslehre und Statistik) and head of the Heidelberg Committee on Regional Research (Arbeitsgemeinschaft für Raumforschung), a branch of the Reich Research Council (Reichsforschungsrat). In these capacities, he was responsible for "a whole range of war-related research assignments" and had at his disposal a small army of assistants. For the Reichsforschungsrat he was involved in research on conurbation, regional price and wage differentiation in Germany and in Europe, and "Western Europe and its integration in the ranges of Europe." For the army's high command, his institute was assigned to prepare courses for soldiers in the basics of political economic theories. The Reich Ministry of Finance also told Schuster to undertake a "critical overview of foreign refutations of German economic policies" and an "overview of scientific activities of émigré German professors of economics."[98]

Several other institutes were created or at least proposed in this period. One of the largest was the Dolmetscher Institut.[99] It also gave language instruction to army officers, beginning in 1938, and it provided translators to industry, the press, Ausland institutes, the Foreign Office, and the SS.[100] Less is known about the Institute for Air Defense Research (Institut für Luftfahrtforschung), which was technically part of the air force and was directed from Munich by Adolf Bäumker, a central figure in aviation research. Two sister institutes were created, one at Vienna and the other at Heidelberg. Heidelberg's institute was directed by Udo Wegner and granted a start-up budget of 260,000 Reichsmarks and an annual budget of 130,000 Reichsmarks. It was plagued by bureaucratic conflict over lines of authority and did not contribute anything of scientific or military value to the war effort.[101]

What of the "Aryan physicists" during the war? As we have seen, Philipp Lenard and his acolytes established Heidelberg as one of two centers of Aryan physics. During the war, as Alan Beyerchen has shown, the movement to purge Germany of "Jewish physics" collapsed, primarily because the "Aryan physicists" failed to maintain the backing of powerful party figures, and because of the demands of the war and the resistance of Germany's best physicists.[102] In 1941, with the assistance of Reich Minister of the Post Wilhelm Ohnesorge (a former Lenard student), the Institute for International Post and News Broadcasting (Institut für Weltpost- und Weltnachrichtenwesen) was created at Heidelberg. The purpose was to facilitate the construction of a European-wide regional economy and to strengthen the projection of German influence worldwide after the expected victory. Ludwig Wesch became the institute's director and along with Udo Wegner, Carl Bilfinger, Kurt Timm, and Johann Friedrich Gladenbeck taught courses related to the institute's work: "Information in World Trade," "Legal and Political-Scientific Problems of Communications," "Tariffs," "International Organizations and Communcations," "Transmitters and Receivers of Radio and Communications Technology," and similar subjects. The extent and value of the research conducted is unclear, though by the end of the war the institute had amassed a considerable amount of valuable technical equipment.[103] Further, as we will see in Chapter 6, Wesch's research on phosphors was considered particularly valuable to American occupation officials interested in harvesting German scientific advances.[104]

The most direct link between the university and the regime's crimes was found in the psychiatry clinic. Its director, Carl Schneider, played a central role in the "euthanasia" program (or "Operation T-4," so named after the address of its Berlin headquarters), which was launched in October 1939 when Hitler decreed that upon medical examination, handicapped adults and children could be subject to "mercy killing." The program was placed under the jurisdiction of the Ministry of the Interior, though the SS would later become involved. The primary motive behind the program was to "purify" the German people and German society by ridding them of the "incurably ill," who were considered incapable of contributing to the construction of the "racial" utopia. This drive drew upon the "eugenics" movement developed in and outside Germany long before the Nazis came to power. The first concrete steps were taken in 1933 through the legal and physical removal of Jews from German society and forced sterilization of the mentally ill and "social undesirables." Systematic murder was the next step. But the program had another purpose—medical research, which was conducted extensively on living subjects or on corpses in university clinics, in specially designed research centers, and eventually in concentration camps.

Both the mass murder and premortem and postmortem research on the victims was planned, directed, and implemented by biomedical scientists and university professors. Special questionnaires were sent to mental hospitals and after being filled out were evaluated by selected panels of T-4 physicians. These panels then decided whether a given patient was to live or die. Those selected to die were transported to killing centers, where they were gassed or given lethal injections. By the summer of 1941, over seventy thousand people had been murdered. But widespread public awareness of the program and opposition to the manner in which the killings were being carried out led the regime to shift course—the program was never halted, but it was thereafter conducted in greater secrecy and mainly in the occupied eastern territories, where thousands more were killed. As Henry Friedlander and others have shown, the "euthanasia" program provided the model, the experience, the methods, and some of the personnel for the "final solution" to the "Jewish question in Europe."[105]

Schneider began his official involvement in the program as one of ten to fifteen physicians recruited by the Reich Chancellery to plan and advise the program. He also became Operation T-4's leading researcher. Schneider's objective was to obtain a steady supply of patients to examine and experiment upon both before and after they were murdered. He forged his clinic at Heidelberg into one of two major research centers; the other was at the Brandenburg-Görden hospital and was directed by Hans Heinze. In particular, Schneider was interested in studying victims' brains. With funds from T-4 and the Interior Ministry, he expanded his experimental facilities first to a nearby state hospital in Wiesloch, and then to another at Eichberg. The facility at Eichberg was already functioning as a killing center for children, and it provided Schneider and his assistants and students with a steady supply of human "subjects" and highly coveted brains. Under Schneider's tutelage, moreover, his Heidelberg clinic also became an important training center for other T-4 specialists, notably Friedrich Mennecke.[106]

Schneider drew a number of assistants to his clinic who participated in various experiments. After the war, all of them denied knowledge of their mentor's activities, avoided prosecution for their own roles in the program, and went on to illustrious careers in the postwar Germanys.[107] A research prospectus drawn up by Schneider at his Heidelberg clinic in January 1941 reveals the following plan to explore the effects of electrical shock and insulin-induced shock:

> By Dr. Suckow, 1. The development of motility through experiments on idiots; 2. special factors in insulin and shock therapy in various mental illnesses.
> By Dr. Schmorl, 1. Experiments on the differences between induced and spontaneous seizures in humans; 2. hydrogen experiments on patients with convulsive disorders, including idiots.
> By Dr. Schmieder, 1. Constitutional types in exogeneous convulsive disorders, including head injuries suffered in combat; 2. prevention of vertebral fractures in cases of convulsive shock.
> By Dr. Rauch, brain histopathology in idiots. Physical dysplasias, particularly in the context of experiments with idiots.
> By Dr. Wendt, a collection of material on functional endocrine disturbances in developmentally induced physical dysplasias, particularly in the context of experiments with idiots.[108]

Schneider also relied on several doctoral students to assist him with experiments, one of whom was his daughter-in-law, Monika Schneider (nee Jörgen). Research for her dissertation, ultimately titled "Metabolic Endurance Tests in Feeble-Minded Children," involved "a series of experiments with children [aged three to thirteen] who were generally idiotic but physically healthy." The results of her experiments became particularly valuable when these and other children were later murdered and their corpses made available for comparative study by Monika Schneider's father-in-law and other clinic students.[109]

Carl Schneider's role in the "euthanasia" program illustrates both the close relationship between ideology and science and the connections between the regime and academic culture in the Third Reich. As we have seen, the German biomedical science community and the medical profession had widely embraced the ideas and practices that would form the basis for regime-sponsored medical crimes, most notably eugenics, "racial hygiene," sterilization, and "euthanasia." Further, these groups predominantly conservative political orientation and their willingness to view the German public as a "Volksgemeinschaft," defined in racist terms, led to a nearly seamless congruence between their outlook and interests and those of the regime, which supported them with "legal" cover, facilities, manpower, and money. Finally, it is clear that Schneider also hoped to use his involvement as a means to keep psychiatry a viable "science." As he wrote around 1941: "As long as people have psychological functions, there will have to be a science within medicine concerned with the links between physical illness and psychological processes, and the alleviation of all kinds of disturbances in this area. Indeed, such a science will become all the more indispensable, the more seriously we intend to transform the slogan of the totality of life into a real understanding of the biology of this totality in health and illness. This science may be called psychiatry or something else; it may eventually be defined as something other than medicine, given the changing classification of the sciences."[110]

Despite looming defeat and increasing physical and material hardships, no significant organized opposition to Hitler and the party in Germany ever arose.[111] There is little evidence of opposition by university professors or students at Heidelberg or elsewhere (with the glaring exception of the "White Rose" group in Munich). Martin Dibelius probably had contacts with members of various opposition figures such as the Heidelberg pastor Hermann Maas.[112] Alfred Weber was one of the very few Heidelberg professors who could claim after the war that he was thoroughly and consistently anti-Nazi and that he acted on this conviction. As his biographer, Eberhard Demm, has shown, Weber remained firmly opposed to the Nazis throughout the Third Reich and resisted even modest, superficial kinds of compromises with the regime. He refused, for instance, an invitation from the German Institute for Foreign Policy Research to contribute an article to its annual review of European affairs in 1943, and a year later turned down a personal request from Hans Frank to write a memorial article on Max Weber. He (along with Karl Jaspers) hoped for an early allied victory after the war broke out and in 1943 established contact with members of several resistance groups and with the resistance figures Carlo Mierendorff, Emil Henk, and Theodor Haubach.[113]

Weber's example was exceptional. But more significant was the continued existence of Marianne Weber's circle, which served as a link for non- and anti-Nazi scholars and intellectuals to the pre-Nazi period. During the Weimar Republic, Weber's salon brought together mainly liberal- or conservative-nationalist scholars to discuss scholarship and current affairs. The circle ceased to meet temporarily during the turbulent early months of the Nazi regime and Weber feared the authorities would put an end to them once they resumed. Still, her salon could draw a regular audience of thirty people (perhaps seventy belonged to the circle).[114] The guests included professors who had left the university voluntarily or had been dismissed, such as Alfred Weber, Ernst Hoffmann, Hans von Eckardt, Otto Regenbogen, Karl Jaspers, and those still teaching, particularly the theologians Gustav Hoelscher, Martin Dibelius, and Renatus Hupfeld, along with local writers whose works were out of favor with the regime.[115]

It should not be surprising that the regime did not break up the circle. With the exception of Alfred Weber, its participants did not engage in the kind of "opposition" that would have drawn the attention of the Gestapo, namely organized political resistance, advocacy of communism or socialism, public expressions of defeatism during the war, or—above all—the protection of Jews.[116] From the point of view of local party officials and powerful figures in the university, the circle simply posed no threat. Most of the individuals meeting at Weber's house were nationalists of a conservative bent in any case. In general, the gatherings of an aging academic aristocracy to dwell on narrow and recondite subject matter could hardly have seemed subversive. None of the participants themselves, of course, was Jewish, and Karl Jaspers, himself married to a "non-Aryan," spoke to the circle only once before withdrawing to the seclusion of his apartment.

In contrast to the circle's earlier days, when very often sociologists dominated the discussions, "literary historians and historians of art as well as philosophers and theologians now had the floor."[117] The subjects of their talks may, on the surface, have seemed arcane and unpolitical, but this was not really the case. As Marianne admitted shortly after the war to the American occupation officer Edward Hartshorne "meanings of the political sort were allowed to leak out but never openly avowed."[118] The Weber circle provided its members both with an opportunity to discuss their scholarly interests and with an opportunity to level subtle, indirect criticism at the regime and its barbarous war. In 1943, for instance, Hans von Eckardt lectured on the legacy of Russian literature for that nation's intellegentsia. "The great works of

Russian literature from Pushkin to Turgenev, Gorki and Tolstoi to Dostoievsky," von Eckardt argued,

> shared in the responsibility for the annihilation of the Russian intellectual in the conflagration of the Russian revolution. Transfigured by poetry and organisationally ineffectual, their passionate love of the people, of the peasants and the proletariat, of all simple souls, including the backward, the feeble-minded and criminals, aroused an exaggerated self-consciousness in the lower classes. Above all, the erosive self-criticism and self-revelation of the faults and weaknesses of the upper classes which were presented in the great literary works destroyed the respect of the masses for the educated, and above all, for a spiritual and intellectual existence. As a result, the Bolsheviks could calumniate this whole stratum as parasites and vermin and then destroy them. The audience was profoundly and enduringly impressed. As humane, socially minded human beings, they were reinforced in their belief that they must not renounce their ideals and their conviction of the autonomous value of intellectual activity in favour of the masses and of a less differentiated form of culture.[119]

Von Eckardt limited his talk, of course, to Russia and Russian intellectuals. But certain parallels with the situation in Germany after 1933 could not possibly have been lost on anyone present. Gustav Hoelscher, in another example, held forth on his specialty, the Old Testament. Yet as Hoelscher must have been well aware, a large number of German theologians had gone to considerable lengths (through the "German Christian" movement and the Institute for the Study and Eradication of Jewish Influence on German Religious Life) to invalidate the Old Testament as part of its campaign to "dejudaize" Christianity. Otto Regenbogen, Marianne Weber recalled, spoke on "the apparently remote topic of 'The Speeches in the Historical Work of Thucydides' of which he presented parts in new translation. When he portrayed the portrait of that age and its intellectual background, he was saying something to us which seemed exceptionally close to our present-day experiences ... His listeners grasped once more that our species confronts unsolved conflicts of value which form polar human types, conflicts of power and interest which are never enduringly resolved and which become so enshrouded in grandiose ideals that human beings can never enjoy ultimate peace with their fellowmen and can never bring their world into order."[120] The Weber circle in the Third Reich should, then, be seen as embodying a collective form of what some historians have labeled "Resistenz"—a form of resistance that involved refusing the state's total claim on truth and an unwillingness to accept Nazi ideology while falling short of public opposition to Hitler and the regime's policies.[121]

The Weber circle's activities also represented a form of resistance and indirect criticism common to intellectuals under dictatorship—what Leo Strauss referred to in his classic study *Persecution and the Art of Writing* as "writing between the lines."[122] Strauss argued that no dictatorship was really capable of repressing independent thinking completely, though the written word was subject to censorship and overt criticism of the regime was out of the question. But "a man of independent thought can utter his views in public and remain unharmed, provided he moves with circumspection. He can even utter them in print without incurring any danger, provided he is capable of writing between the lines."[123] Through the use of metaphor, satire, or allegory, some journalists and intellectuals were able to express their own dissatisfaction with the regime and level criticism at it—criticism that would be understood by careful readers. The Weber circle was unusual in that its members could indulge themselves and each other openly with a form of "speaking between the lines."

A systematic study of "writing between the lines" in German academic culture during the Third Reich remains to be written.[124] One example from the historian Fritz Ernst illustrates the ambiguities and shifting contours of ideological engagement with the regime. As we have seen, Ernst was a conservative nationalist who, though he never joined the NSDAP, nonetheless supported Germany's territorial expansion. But by 1943 his attitude had changed, as is demonstrated in a telling passage in an article ostensibly about Karl the Bold of Burgundy (1433–1477): "What he lacked was balance, a consistent maturity . . . He allowed a glut of hate and ambition to consume him, without drawing lasting strength from it . . . So never did he have inner freedom. He wanted to rule and would never be free of mistrust; he planned great things, but he was only inflexible . . . That towards his end his pathological characteristics revealed themselves more frequently and more crassly is without doubt. He no longer had the flexibility to learn from his defeats. Despite elementary military mistakes he held himself to be a great field commander. His final plans were the most fantastic. He no longer had any inner order."[125] It is worth stressing that Ernst's criticism was of the quality of leadership (after all, Karl had "the greatest war machine of the time"), not of ends, and this places him in the company of a growing number of like-minded conservative opponents of Hitler.

There is ample evidence that many professors continued to believe in the scientific, "racial," and political value of their work and in the possibility of some kind of miraculous victory even as Allied armies advanced into the Reich itself. Until very late in the war, Carl Schneider fought tirelessly to secure brains for research at his clinic. He fled Heidelberg on a bicycle shortly before the Americans arrived.[126] In January, the Institut für Grossraumwirtschaft held a series of lectures on—astonishingly, it may seem, given the looming collapse obvious to all but the most self-deluded—the organization of the European regional economy and Japan's "new order" in East Asia. At this final meeting, Fritz Landfried warned neutral nations that "whether they wished to see it or not, Europe has no other choice than to follow the path that Germany has mapped out or be devoured as a colony of the United States or Bolshevism."[127] Behind closed doors, the institute's directors speculated among themselves what would happen if (!) the "Anglo-Americans" came.[128] On January 30 (traditionally a day of official celebration in observance of the Nazi seizure of power), Karl Heinrich Bauer "praised the glory and tradition of the Reich" through the loudspeakers at the surgical clinic, adding that "our beloved Führer was saved from a ruthless attempt on his life by a divine providence," that Germany's soldiers should continue to fight, and that students working in the clinic should remember that "millions of Germans are lucky to defend their country with weapons in hand and we are condemned to set the thigh-bones of old hags."[129] On March 7, in his last official message to the faculties, Paul Schmitthenner trumpeted that "the chances of an all-encompassing decisive battle in the coming months are absolutely favorable . . . The real material means and strength, which we still possess, suffice to achieve the victory to the fullest measure." In order to help secure the victory, he added, teachers should educate their students to hate their enemy remorselessly.[130] Shortly thereafter, he appointed the aging and long-retired Anglicist Johannes Hoops as Rector and fled Heidelberg.

Undoubtedly the end of the war came as a great relief for those who once approved of the regime and then became disillusioned, the members of Marianne Weber's salon (most of whom would be called on very shortly by American occupation authorities to begin rebuilding the institution), and above all Karl and Gertrude Jaspers. Near the war's end, they learned that Gertrude was scheduled to be deported from Heidelberg on April 14.[131] Karl Jaspers sought out Paul Schmitthenner, Karl Engisch, Eugen Fehrle, Ernst Krieck, and perhaps others to intervene with the Gestapo and SS on their behalf. It is clear that the first three indeed tried to help the Jaspers, while Krieck declined.[132] The matter became irrelevant on April 1, when American troops captured Heidelberg. As Jaspers himself would declare on several occasions after the war, it was the Americans alone who saved him and his wife.

CHAPTER FOUR

Constructing the Myth

> There are . . . still only two more or less intact organizations that are qualified for leadership: the churches and the universities.
> —Karl Heinrich Bauer, Military Government Questionnaire,
>   (Fragebogen), July 1945

The year 1945 did not represent a "zero hour" in German academic culture.¹ Rather, it marked the beginning of a series of partial and modified restorations. In the universities, this meant the restoration of the pre-1933 university structure and—after a relatively brief disruption—the return of hundreds of compromised scholars to teaching positions. But only a few purged by the Nazis after 1933 were able or willing to return to their former positions. In the following four chapters, I trace the course of these restorations and the implications for the memory of National Socialism in postwar West Germany.² In this chapter I focus on the crucial first months of the occupation. Immediately after American troops occupied the city and closed the university, a small group of professors began meeting to plan the institution's reopening. This group consisted primarily of older scholars intent on restoring the university's pre-1933 structure and resuming instruction as quickly as possible. Unwilling and unable to reform the universities by fiat, American officials allocated the bulk of the responsibility for rebuilding Heidelberg to the professors. Although denazification generated considerable conflict between occupiers and the occupied, the entire university reopened in January 1946, eight months after the collapse of the Third Reich.³

Developments in the first months of the occupation laid the groundwork for the Heidelberg myth. The myth served to absolve all but a very few of complicity with the Nazis. It also comported with what was widely though not universally accepted outside Germany about the fate of the universities under National Socialism. It was fleshed out by Heidelberg professors in 1945 and has been repeated in nearly every memoir account by non-Nazis and former Nazis alike and in official histories published by the university, and it has informed most scholarly accounts. The Heidelberg myth was composed of the following elements: First, before 1933, the university was a bastion of democracy and tolerance. Second, in 1933, the new regime smashed its autonomy of self-governance and disposed of academic freedom, and it also rid the university of the professors who had been supporters of democracy. Third, the regime, intent on making Heidelberg a "model National Socialist university," installed a small number of ideological fanatics of dubious scholarly qualifications to keep the university "nazified." The vast majority of professors (even if they had joined the party) wanted nothing to do with the regime, its ideology, or the "German spirit" in scholarship. They became "opponents" of National Socialism by maintaining standards of "objectivity" in their research and teaching and were thus persecuted by the party, jealous colleagues, and Nazi students.

As a result, therefore, Heidelberg—as Fritz Ernst put it in 1960—"had the reputation of being the most radical university in the sense of the NSDAP."[4] But thanks to the heroic efforts of anti-Nazi professors and the assistance of clear-sighted American officials, the great traditions of pre-1933 Heidelberg were restored after 1945. The Third Reich, in this view, represented a radical aberration in Heidelberg's history, one imposed almost entirely from outside its walls and bracketed by two "zero hours," one in 1933 and another in 1945. There was some truth to this narrative, but the Heidelberg myth obscured and attempted to excuse a great deal—namely, the extensive engagement of the professorate with National Socialism. As we have seen, what constituted this engagement were complex and varied adaptations to the "German spirit," a concept encompassing "voelkisch" nationalism, racism, anti-Semitism, and the rejection of "objectivity" in scholarship. The myth, however, involved the construction of an ideal type of "Nazi professor": a single-minded, fanatical man without any legitimate scholarly accomplishments who alone embraced this supposed perversion of research and teaching.

On April 1, 1945, elements of the United States Seventh Army occupied the city of Heidelberg and immediately ordered the university closed.[5] The following day, the local detachment of the army's Counter Intelligence Corps (CIC) began to arrest and interrogate targeted professors. Paul Schmitthenner, Eugen Fehrle, and Carl Schneider were initially nowhere to be found. The CIC located and arrested Karl Schmidhuber, Udo Wegner, Walter Thoms, Ernst Krieck, Johann Duken, Theodor Odenwald, and two younger instructors, Alex Ritzert and Karl Roelcke, on the grounds that they were SD informants or SS officers.[6] Dozens of other instructors and assistants, of course, had been drafted into the Wehrmacht and were unaccounted for.[7] Paul Schmitthenner and his wife, as it turned out, had taken refuge in a castle at Wiesberg. When the Wehrmacht garrison there surrendered to the Americans, Schmitthenner was arrested and spent the following two and a half years in seven different internment camps.[8] Carl Schneider was also soon found and arrested. A year later, while in prison, he committed suicide. Philipp Lenard had hidden himself in a town outside Heidelberg. When no one came for him, he turned himself in. Uncertain about what to do with the eighty-year-old professor, the Americans contacted Samuel Goudsmit, the Dutch-born émigré officer charged with assessing Germany's progress on atomic weapons research. Goudsmit's advice was: "'Ignore him!' . . . This, for a Nazi, was a greater punishment than being tried in Nuremberg." In a bizarre coincidence, the physicist Walter Bothe was mistakenly arrested by the CIC and then forced to share a cell with his former nemesis and Lenard protégé, Ludwig Wesch.[9]

Almost immediately after the occupation of Heidelberg, CIC agents located Emil Henk, whom they knew to have been a resistance figure. Henk convinced the young American officers that it was necessary to begin reconstructing the university as quickly as possible, despite the fact that Dwight Eisenhower had ordered all universities in the American zone, where Heidelberg lay, to be closed indefinitely. The CIC agents, suitably impressed, arranged on Henk's recommendation for Karl Jaspers, Gustav Radbruch, Otto Regenbogen, Elsa Jaffe, and Alexander Mitscherlich to meet at Henk's home.[10] This group then began gathering at Jaspers's apartment and elected more members—Karl Heinrich Bauer, Martin Dibelius, Renatus Hupfeld, Fritz Ernst, Alfred Weber, Ernst Engelking, Kurt Oehme, Wolfgang Gentner, and Walter Jellinek. It became known as the Committee of Thirteen and formed the core of the university's postwar leadership. Its members undertook the reconstruction of the faculties, drafted a new constitution, constituted the first postwar Senate and rectorship, and negotiated with American authorities for the reopening of the university. Their influence extended beyond the immediate postwar months: Bauer, Dibelius, Radbruch, and Regenbogen would serve as the first postwar chairmen of their respective faculties, and Bauer would be elected the first postwar Rector. They would also wield considerable influence over which faculty members would be retained and which would be dismissed.[11]

The emergence of this group under the auspices of the CIC was part of a striking phenomenon of German society immediately after the collapse of the Third Reich. Among the population in the early months of the occupation, officials noted a combination of apathy and despair alongside a readiness to organize at the local level.[12] Numerous small groups did indeed spring up across occupied Germany to, as one former officer put it, "jump into the breach" left vacant by the dissolution of the machinery of the dictatorship.[13] Although historians have devoted much attention to the activities of leftist (or "Antifas") groups, a strong conservative element was also present. "With the Nazis gone," as an Office of Strategic Services (OSS) report put it in May, "these elements occupy the most important positions in German society . . . The Left puts the emphasis on rooting out all traces of Nazism as the prerequisite to a new start; the Right concentrates on attempting to conserve whatever is potentially valuable from the shambles left by the Hitler regime."[14] The readiness of this group of Heidelberg professors to organize and set to work on reconstructing the university fits this pattern closely in that they represented just such a well-entrenched elite seeking to "conserve whatever is potentially valuable."

Most members of the Committee of Thirteen shared important characteristics, though were not quite as homogenous a group as has been assumed. Most were old, having been born in the 1870s and 1880s. With the exception of Ernst, Mitscherlich, and Gentner, they had experienced their formative years as students and scholars in Wilhelmine and Weimar Germany. Jaspers, Weber, Dibelius, Regenbogen, Oehme, and Jellinek were longtime colleagues at Heidelberg and represented the university's exclusive aristocratic academic culture. Their attitudes toward the liberal democratic values that American officials simply assumed they embraced varied from skepticism and pessimism (Jaspers) to outright hostility (Bauer, Jellinek, Ernst). Only Weber, Radbruch, and Dibelius could be counted as active and steadfast supporters of the Weimar Republic. Further, their experiences in the Third Reich varied considerably. None of them had belonged to the Nazi Party, but only Weber, Radbruch, and Jaspers could be considered genuinely and consistently anti-Nazi. The rest had continued to teach throughout the twelve years of the Third Reich, and had compromised themselves to varying degrees with National Socialism.

In the spring and summer the committee was consumed with immediate, practical problems and with drawing up teaching plans for the reconstituted faculties. Perhaps most important in this early stage was the writing of a new constitution. By June, Karl Jaspers, Gustav Radbruch, and Walter Jellinek had produced a draft. As state institutions, German universities had traditionally received their constitutions from their respective state governments. Owing to the collapse of state authority and the initiative of the Committee of Thirteen, a constitution was created from within the university itself for the first time since the Middle Ages. It proposed to reinstate the university's pre-1933 structure and add further protections from state encroachment and "outside influences." Its authors noted at the outset that the "highest basic law of the university is the freedom of teaching and of learning." They aimed to establish "an organic order of spiritual protection and learning . . . against the incursion of fanatical masses of students and instructors in the determination of university questions."[15] Jaspers and the others hoped to limit the number of students admitted in order to create a "geistesaristokratische Ordnung"—an "aristocratic intellectual order." In a private conversation with the OSS officer and historian Felix Gilbert, Jaspers inquired whether the American authorities would approve of this terminology, to which Gilbert responded that they most certainly would not.[16]

Although "aristocracy of the spirit" does not appear in the draft constitution, the aristocratic spirit of the document's authors pervades the text. Virtually all administrative powers were returned to the full professors. Indeed, "the self-administration of the whole university" was now the responsibility of the Small Senate, which would again be drawn almost exclusively from the ranks of the full professors. The powers of the Rector, the junior instructors, and the students would be strictly limited. The new constitution was adopted quickly by the first German governments in Baden and belatedly approved by American occupation authorities. It remained largely unmodified until the 1960s.[17]

Notably without influence in the drafting of the new constitution were the younger members of the Committee of Thirteen—Mitscherlich, Ernst, and Gentner. In a perceptive report on developments at Heidelberg written for the OSS in November 1945, Felix Gilbert summarized the split:

> The older men who made their careers and reputations in the pre-Hitler era, have been inclined to look back upon that period as the ideal, or at least the reality, by which the new University's development must be gauged. The younger generation in the teaching staff has tended to reject both the Weimar Republic, which furnished them no benefits and which they held partially responsible for the rise of Hitler, and the Nazi regime, which they dismiss as a bad government gone intellectually, as well as physically, bankrupt. These younger men cannot be said to have any positive ideas on the development of the University, partly because of the sterility of the past twelve years, during which they came to scholarly maturity. Instead they are oriented toward the future . . . Thus while both groups have participated in the drafting of the university constitution, it is primarily the work of older elements, whose interest lies mainly in forms and the reestablishment of the external structure of the old tradition . . . This is part of the basic disagreement between the older group, which ascribes the unhealthy developments in the University to the physical incursion of the outside world into the sphere of academic life, and the younger group which views the University's degeneration as part of the general degeneration of German life . . . [Fritz] Ernst has explicitly stated that the constitution is insignificant and that the fate of the University lies elsewhere.[18]

If the younger members of the group had little by way of their own program to propose, they no doubt viewed the quick reopening of the university as a priority that demanded unity on the German side. In any case, they were outmatched in number and authority by the older professors. As Mitscherlich recalled in his memoirs: "Many held the opinion—the mistaken opinion—that what had struck us in January 1933 and after was a great misfortune. Everything that stemmed from the period before 1933 now appeared worthy of restoration."[19] When in early August Wolfgang Gentner proposed to the committee that the office of the Prorector be occupied by a non-Ordinarius, Karl Heinrich Bauer flatly rejected the idea because it went "against all tradition."[20]

The new constitution's drafters thus revealed some basic assumptions about the National Socialist past—above all that the university was solely a victim of the Nazi Party and Nazi students. Any reforms instituted by the regime that might have been considered "progressive" in the post-1945 political context—principally loosening the grip of the full professors by including junior scholars and even students in the institution's governance—were tainted thoroughly by association and unwanted by the postwar leadership in any case. This view, held by older full professors, was summarized well by Karl Freudenberg in November 1945: "Vocationalism interjected in the Nazi period shall be abolished. Thus the faculty outwardly returns to the status of 1933—not to reestablish the old forms, but to do away with intruded damages . . . Along with reorganization, self-management is reestablished on the basis of equal rights for all colleagues . . . The 'leader principle' must be extirpated to its last roots."[21] Substantial reform of German universities would have to wait for over twenty years, when the grip of the full professors was weakened and junior faculty, students, and employees were given a greater say in institutional governance.[22]

Further evidence of the restorative impulses among older professors was Alfred Weber's determination to dissolve the State and Economic Sciences Faculty and reestablish sociology (Nationalökonomie) within the Philosophy Faculty. Weber's well-known activism on behalf of Germany's postwar political reconstruction along democratic lines did not include such reconstruction within the ivory tower itself. He held that much of the State and Economic Sciences Faculty and their work was hopelessly compromised with National Socialism, and in any case he did not consider the Philosophy Faculty to be a proper home for trade-school training in business.[23] On August 29, 1945, the Small Senate voted to dissolve the State and Economic Sciences Faculty, a move that sparked a strong negative reaction among local business and trade union leaders and the faculty's former students. Something of a compromise was reached when the Mannheim Technical School was reopened and took over the courses formerly taught at Heidelberg.[24] Weber and others on the Committee of Thirteen, particularly Otto Regenbogen and Karl Jaspers, also hoped to draw future university students primarily from the ranks of the exclusive, humanist-oriented Gymnasia. Not only would this strategy limit the quantity of university students, but it would, in theory, improve their quality. They believed that the state's failure to maintain higher university entrance standards had produced the "university proletariat" that had proven so susceptible to National Socialism.[25]

On the German side, Karl Heinrich Bauer was the driving force behind the reopening of the university. During the initial months of the occupation, he managed to avoid dismissal for several reasons. Bauer had never belonged to the Nazi Party and American authorities did not yet know enough about his past to recommend his dismissal.[26] Another reason was his initiative in organizing the Committee of Thirteen, which impressed both Bauer's colleagues and American officials. Bauer's energy seemed boundless. The detailed diary of his activities from August 1945 to March 1946 held in the university's archives supports Karl Jaspers's recollection that the surgeon "radiated a zest for action."[27] The Americans, intent on reopening university medical facilities as soon as possible for the training of new doctors, saw the energetic Bauer as the natural point man. Furthermore, Bauer's skillful use of the language of democratic reform impressed American officials. And finally, he falsified his Fragebogen (Military Government Questionnaire) by omitting or at least glossing over many of his activities over the past twelve years.

Bauer's views on the future form of the university did not differ substantially from those of Jaspers or Weber. In his Fragebogen, Bauer stated that Germany's traditional classes of leaders had been decimated or discredited by the Nazis and the war, and that left only two "more or less intact" institutions capable of providing Germany with a new leadership class: the churches and the universities.[28] Although he larded his public statements and regular reports to the Military Government with references to the need for democracy in Germany, he favored the "aristocratic intellectual order" sought by Jaspers, Weber, and others. In a letter to Jaspers in early June, he argued that "German democracy is only thinkable with the corrective of an aristocracy . . . There remains only *one* aristocracy, that of intellectual achievement."[29] In Bauer's conception, future students would be predominantly male and fewer in numbers.

Bauer also concurred with his fellow committee members that "there was no longer any place" for the exclusive student fraternities (the Americans had banned these organizations in any case) and student political organizations.[30] His sentiments regarding organized student political activity reflected a view held by his colleagues at the time and later.[31] Not only were the disruptions of the pre-1933 era still present in the minds of the university's new leadership, but so were the presumed effects of twelve years of dictatorship. In the immediate postwar years, this inclination to restrict political activity was probably sound. American officials noted a strong strain of unregenerate militancy among many students at Heidelberg and elsewhere, and the lectures on collective guilt and war crimes given by Karl Jaspers at Heidelberg and Pastor Martin Niemöller at Erlangen met with notably hostile responses.[32] After a visit to Heidelberg, the American journalist Shepard Stone recorded similar impressions in an article published in the *New York Times*. Karl Jaspers confided to him during his visit that a year earlier his lectures on German guilt had met with "deep hostility" and noted that "even today many students are stubborn chauvinists," though "gradually more and more of them are willing to listen."[33] Nonetheless, hostility among professors to student political action was deep and enduring.[34]

The new constitution, limits on student participation in university affairs, and the excision of the State and Economic Sciences Faculty all testify to a powerful restorative consensus among Heidelberg's elite. This concern went beyond simply reclaiming former prerogatives. A deeper impulse was an instinctive distrust of the revolutionary and destructive potential of the "masses," a view captured succinctly by Karl Jaspers in an October 28, 1945, letter to Hannah Arendt: "Here we have to see now what we can rebuild out of chaos. I am optimistic, provided world history does not just roll over us and destroy us. We still have young people eager to learn, few of them—but then, the masses have always been obtuse and tied to the clichés of their times."[35] Jaspers, Weber, Dibelius, Bauer, and others had experienced firsthand the rampages of Nazi students, the state's encroachment on the university, and the broadening of its leadership to include non-full professors and students. Their solution in 1945 was retrenchment. By restoring the university's autonomy and exclusive governance by the full professors and limiting the number of students, a true intellectual aristocracy would be created, one grounded in humanism and devoted to the free pursuit of knowledge uncorrupted by politics. This conception not only precluded structural reform, but reinforced a central pillar of the Heidelberg myth. It was the state's encroachment on the university's autonomy along with legions of Nazi students drawn from the ranks of an "academic proletariat" that had caused the disaster at Heidelberg in 1933.

The university in whatever form, of course, could not be reopened without the approval of the occupation authorities. During the war, the Allies had agreed that Germany would be forced to accept unconditional surrender, complete occupation, and joint rule until it could be demilitarized, "denazified," and democratized. What was to be American policy toward Germany's universities? Addressing this question requires consideration of what American officials knew about German academic culture during the Third Reich.[36] That the universities were largely passive victims of a totalitarian onslaught from outside their own walls was the dominant assumption of most of the British and some American critics of Heidelberg's five hundred and fiftieth anniversary celebration in 1936. In the late 1930s and early 1940s, British, American, and German émigré scholars produced numerous books on the alleged destruction of German academic culture.[37] Frieda Wunderlich captured the outlook of many émigrés in the journal *Social Research* in 1937: "All safeguards protecting academic liberty against administrative interference have been broken down . . . research too is doomed to disappear or to go to the catacombs," though "only some of the teachers have been won over, very few in the universities."[38] Up to 1938, a few American journalists and diplomats filed accounts of what was happening to Germany's academic culture, emphasizing the regime's assault on the universities.[39] The U.S. ambassador to Germany himself, William Dodd, wrote President Franklin Roosevelt in August 1937: "There is . . . all but universal conviction that the German universities have been practically destroyed . . . Among the professors and dozenten of the German universities there are less than half as many able men as there were before [World War I] . . . The rest are, in general, a bad lot, stupid, incompetent and often dishonest."[40] This view was generally carried through into the war years when information was even harder to come by. An OSS report, for instance, noted in early 1943 that "the Universities have . . . been radically interfered with and 'gleichgeschaltet.' Like all other stages of education in Germany, the universities and technological institutes have been made to serve the aims of the Nazi Party system."[41] Little was known, in short, about what had taken place *within* the walls of the universities themselves.

This assessment was modified shortly after CIC agents and occupation authorities began their initial investigations. Just over a week after Heidelberg was occupied, CIC officers prepared a detailed report on the situation at the university. Much of the information had come from interrogations of "pro- and anti-Nazi faculty members." The agents noted that "the Nazis deprived the university of its traditional autonomy, self-government, and academic freedom. They closely observed and controlled activities at the University." Further, they amassed a considerable amount of information—most of it accurate—about the activities of Paul Schmitthenner and other leading Nazis. The agents also identified a group of twenty-one men they believed could form "a nucleus of anti-Nazi professors" to begin reconstruction work.[42] Finally, a SHAEF (Supreme Headquarters Allied Expeditionary Force Europe) report (possibly drawing on the results of the CIC's investigation) dated May 5, 1945, and submitted to the U.S. secretary of state by Robert Murphy concluded the following about Heidelberg: "Professors in general were pro-Nazi; students were 'mildly and moderately Nazi.' Anti-Nazism was limited to German communists, generally older people, the nobility and 'elements associated with the University.'"[43]

What was to happen once the occupation was under way? Planning for the "reeducation" of the Germans began in a variety of governmental, academic, and émigré circles in the United States during the war.[44] U.S. State and War Department officials generally agreed that (in addition to the dismissal of compromised instructors): (1) Nazi and pro-Nazi materials had to be removed from the schools and universities; (2) anti-Nazi Germans must carry the bulk of the responsibility for reforming their own nation's educational system; and (3) as the declaration signed by the Allies at Potsdam put it, "German education shall be so controlled as completely to eliminate Nazi and militarist doctrines and to make possible the successful development of democratic ideas."[45] In the planning stages, the definition of a "Nazi" was unclear, and occupation planners and the OSS had incomplete information on compromised and reliable individuals at the various universities.[46] Thus a fundamental contradiction existed between the desire for sweeping "reeducation" and the intention to let the Germans themselves "carry the bulk of the responsibility" for educational reform.

As Uta Gerhardt has shown, American officials, drawing on analyses of individual and collective behavior under dictatorships developed by psychiatrists and sociologists in the 1930s and 1940s, aimed at changing the "German character" itself in order to exorcise the antidemocratic demons that plagued it and German society.[47] Some German émigré scholars were more skeptical. Werner Richter, a Weimar-era Prussian Minister of Education and also an émigré, warned at the end of the war that German scholars would not cooperate with American reeducation schemes: "Constructive work can be certain of success only if the victors are moved by mercy instead of by force in cultural and spiritual matters and if sufficient confidence is extended to those Germans who are willing to devote themselves with all their energies to the democratic reconstruction of the educational system."[48] In discussions with the OSS's Foreign Nationalities Branch, Thomas Mann, Lion Feuchtwanger, Emil Ludwig, Alfred Döblin, and Bruno Frank all said they did not believe the Germans could be "taught" democratic principles. "Educating the German is almost hopeless," Döblin argued, "because the majority of the professional classes are [sic] Nazis. The spiritual forces of the Germans are in the universities and schools which are reactionary."[49] The émigré political theorist Franz Neumann concurred, noting in 1946 that "to attempt to re-educate Germans by military government action is to attempt the impossible."[50] For Neumann, the universities would remain bastions of conservatism and hence breeding grounds for extremism as long as they continued to draw their students and professors from the nation's "traditional ruling groups" and refused to open their ranks to "outsiders," such as "practicing lawyers and recognized writers." Although the victors could not themselves "reeducate" the Germans, Neumann recommended that they break up systemic barriers to genuine democratic renewal within the schools and universities.[51]

Immediate and practical problems took center stage in the occupation's early months. Educational reform was not a high priority for General Lucius Clay, first deputy military governor and then military governor of the American occupation zone, who remarked at the time that "you cannot teach education on an empty stomach."[52] In the face of chaotic conditions, a general desire to hand responsibility to the Germans, and the importance the Americans placed on developing local, "grass roots" democracy, many officers evidently agreed with Clay. That this was the case in Heidelberg is made clear in the CIC's first report on the university: "A fundamental reorganization [of the university] is necessary. But legal forms should be closely followed and the hand of the Allied military not blatantly present. This is necessary in order that the University will be respected by the German people as their own institution based on academic freedom."[53] The CIC officers recommended that the new German government "select a nucleus of anti-Nazi professors (with 'aid and counsel' of the Allied education board)," which would then propose a new constitution and select instructors "untainted" by National Socialism. Further, professors should be given wide latitude in rebuilding their faculties.[54] Eventually, they should be put into contact with their counterparts in British and American universities. As it turned out, this was in broad outline the policy the Americans pursued. The bulk of the responsibility for reopening the university and—beginning in 1946—for "denazifying" the faculties would fall to the Germans themselves. The American role would be primarily negative. The first "positive" educational reform programs sponsored by the United States would have to wait until 1947 to be put into action.[55]

The relatively quick reopening of Heidelberg and other universities in the American zone was driven not by lofty ideals regarding education for democracy but by perceived practical necessity: the need to train German medical doctors as quickly as possible to avert what Lucius Clay and other high-ranking officials believed to be a looming public health catastrophe.[56] Their desire to see medical instruction resumed as quickly as possible also comported with a determination to work around restrictive occupation directives and the army's reluctance to take on extensive responsibility for administering occupied Germany. In early July 1945, General Morrison Stayer, the head of the Military Government's Public Health and Welfare Division, embarked on a tour of the U.S. zone's surviving medical facilities. He brought with him a thirty-three-year old civil affairs officer, Edward Hartshorne, who soon became responsible for overseeing the reopening of all seven universities in the American zone. Hartshorne was unusually well qualified for this job. He was fluent in German and had written *The German Universities and National Socialism* in 1937, at the time the most detailed study of the subject available anywhere. In the fall of 1941, he went to work for the OSS as an analyst of German affairs but later transferred to the Psychological Warfare Branch of the Office of War Information. After entering Germany in April 1945 he jumped at a chance to become involved in university affairs and transferred to the nascent Military Government's newly created Education and Religious Affairs Division.[57] His visit with Stayer in early July set in motion the chain of events that would lead to Heidelberg's reopening.[58]

In line with American policy, Hartshorne believed that the Germans should bear the bulk of the responsibility for reforming and reopening their universities. "Since the German university faculties," he wrote in the Military Government's *Weekly Bulletin* in 1946, "have a tradition of self-government stretching back to the Middle Ages it was hoped that out of the wreckage of defeat each university would be able to put forward a 'citizens' committee' of the sort capable of taking charge and not merely working under M[ilitary] G[overnment] directives but of doing the job—our job—to all intents and purposes for us, and better than we could have done it ourselves."[59] On merely practical grounds a more hands-on role for himself would have been impossible because Hartshorne was virtually the only person on the American side responsible for overseeing the reopening of the seven universities in the American zone until OMGUS (Office of the Military Government of the United States) could get around to appointing full-time "University Officers." German professors would undoubtedly have resisted extensive American interference in any case. Many felt both responsible and capable for shaping the future of their own institutions. When Hartshorne and some American colleagues presented their ideas for university reform to Karl Jaspers, the philosopher replied, "we should merely 'hold the mirror up' and let the Germans draw their own conclusions."[60] Hartshorne's solution, born of belief and necessity, was to create a series of "University Planning Committees" in the U.S. zone modeled on Heidelberg's Committee of Thirteen. Privately, however, Hartshorne quickly developed doubts about the ability of the professorate to rehabilitate itself and the universities. By mid-July, having begun his study of professors' Fragebogen, he noted in his diary that "[the questionnaires] would form a basis for a post mortem on the German academic profession under National Socialism. The adjustment of the entire profession would come very clearly from these data."[61]

His keen interest in the future of the universities notwithstanding, high-ranking officials remained uninterested in an active role in university reform for officers like Hartshorne. On September 20, after meeting with General Stayer, he recorded in his diary: "the working plan shall be 'denazification without reform.'"[62] In a critique of Stayer's position, Hartshorne arranged for an essay titled "Our Responsibility for German Universities" to be published in the American journal *Forum* under the name of his father-in-law, the Harvard historian Sidney Fay.[63] Here Hartshorne argued that German universities had been "at their best in the Bismarckian and Wilhelmian era" and had suffered grievous losses under dictatorship and war. Hartshorne had faith that the "pre-1914 staff"—Friedrich Meinecke, Hermann Oncken, Max Planck, Jaspers, Weber, Radbruch, and Dibelius—could contribute to "educational reconstruction," but he knew that none of them had many productive years left. On the other hand, Hartshorne had less confidence in the younger generation, which he viewed as riddled with compromised and subpar scholars. The most realistic solution, he concluded, was to encourage American academics "to work with and service the men we leave or place in charge of German higher education" and thus to "reeducate" German colleagues by example.[64]

At Heidelberg in July, the Americans found all of the university's clinics fully intact, if lacking supplies and some instructors. They asked Karl Heinrich Bauer to draw up a plan for reopening (which he had already done). Although Hartshorne noted in his diary that "the faculty would be purged . . . No one was to be protected," the determination of American authorities to reopen medical facilities as soon as possible meant that exceptions to the strict denazification directives then in effect might have to be made. While thousands of Germans were being arrested and thrown out of their jobs, Stayer informed Hartshorne and other officers at a July 10 meeting in Erlangen that "most doctors must be retained despite formal Nazi affiliation, although Nazi MDs who committed atrocities will be deprived of their licenses. Euthanasia and sterilization, provided not practiced for political reasons, not to be construed as 'atrocities.'"[65] At this point, Hartshorne and a fellow officer, John Muccio, could see the potential pitfalls in a hasty reopening. Muccio reported to Lucius Clay's top political adviser, Robert Murphy, on July 10 that "the reopening of such a school would immediately have a great deal of publicity, and it was all-important, therefore, that the institution be completely denazified, not only [on] account of its importance at the institution itself, but on account of the great psychological effect it would have on the Germans generally as an indication of whether we really mean business or not in eradicating Nazism."[66] This view was shared by Alfred Weber, who suggested to Hartshorne that if the university was opened too quickly, "people would say: 'See, it doesn't matter; one can change one's opinions every few years, but the university goes on just the same.'"[67] Despite the urgency of Stayer's orders, Hartshorne was determined to carry out a thorough screening process.[68]

* * *

No aspect of the American occupation of Germany then or since has been as controversial among Americans and Germans as denazification.[69] U.S. policy was initially the most severe. Occupation guidelines dictated that "all members of the Nazi Party who have been more than nominal participants in its activities, all active supporters of Nazism or militarism and all other persons hostile to Allied purposes will be removed and excluded from public office and positions of importance in quasi-public and private enterprises such as (1) civic, economic, and labor organizations, (2) corporations ... (3) industry, ... (4) education, and (5) the press."[70] After several months of waffling, U.S. authorities decreed that anyone who had joined the party before May 1, 1937 (or had joined after that date and had been a zealous Nazi), would be placed in a "mandatory removal" category. By the fall of 1945, tens of thousands of Germans in the American zone were incarcerated, dismissed from their jobs, and denied employment.[71] This situation immediately brought local officials face to face with the fundamental dilemma posed by sweeping denazification: who would be left to run Germany?[72] Although some officers were notoriously lax, most did their best to follow the directives. German-Jewish émigrés serving in the Counter Intelligence Corps were among the most ardent proponents of thorough purges. Among Germans, the arrests and purges initially met with widespread approval but soon became enormously unpopular.[73]

Against this backdrop, Hartshorne began the initial screening process at Heidelberg, which lasted until the middle of August. Hartshorne, the CIC, and the Military Government's Special Branch (denazification) investigators would study a special Fragebogen designed by Hartshorne especially for university instructors and compare the information with university, Nazi Party, and Military Government records. Instructors would be grouped into "mandatory removal," "conditional removal," "unconditional acceptance," or "conditional acceptance" categories. Those who had joined the party before 1937 and were thus dismissed could submit a petition for reinstatement as long as they could prove that they had been "nominal Nazis." Hartshorne also agreed to give the faculties "the first chance at exclusion." American authorities would exercise only "veto" power over the professors' choices, a decision that, as he reported later in the Military Government's *Weekly Bulletin*, "gave the universities the initiative in the matter, allowing them to simply omit Nazi names from their lists of proposals."[74] His thinking on this was evidently influenced by his extensive contact with the Marburg philosopher Julius Ebbinghaus. At Marburg, Hartshorne noted in his diary, Ebbinghaus distinguished between those of his colleagues who would carry out a thorough purge themselves and those who would only go so far as the Americans demanded, believing that dismissal by the occupier rather than by one's own colleagues conferred a kind of "honor."[75]

At Heidelberg, Karl Freudenberg had expressed his views on dismissals a month earlier in a letter to Johannes Hoops. Noting that the American authorities had stripped Paul Schmitthenner of his ministerial titles, "it would be an ignominy," he wrote to Hoops, "if the dismissal of this man as professor did not spring from the initiative of the university, but rather was carried out without such by the Americans."[76] Over the next several months, the Senate petitioned the Military Government and the newly elected Baden state government to dismiss a number of individuals. On July 24 and 26, Hoops submitted an initial total of only thirteen professors: Paul Schmitthenner, Eugen Fehrle, Ernst Krieck, Otto Söllner, Erwin Kiefer, Carl Schneider, Johann Duken, Georg Mollier, Hermann Schlüter, Ernst Horstmann, Rudolf Abendroth, Ludwig Wesch, and Hans Himmel. Hoops closed with the request that the Military Government, whatever its final decisions, issue a notice to the press that "this motion with regard to the above-mentioned persons was made by the university."[77]

Even before he wrote Hoops regarding faculty-initiated dismissals, Freudenberg had drawn up his own list of names to be struck from the Natural Sciences Faculty roster. Not surprisingly, he named Ludwig Wesch and Hans Himmel. "Wesch," he wrote "owed his ascendance from assistant to full professor exclusively to his party-political connections. His advancement resulted without the knowledge of the faculty . . . Wesch, because of his connections to the SD and SS, was generally feared. He favored National Socialists to fill vacant positions and influenced instruction in the most unfavorable sense in order to cut off the advancement of science by fighting quantum theory and other modern developments in physics. A single scientific achievement by him is unknown . . . Wesch is an example of organized mediocrity and inferiority, a typical representative of Nazi 'science' from whom a better part of the faculty had remained distant." He had much the same to say about Himmel, who had been a "spearhead of National Socialism" at Heidelberg and contributed nothing of any significance to his field.[78] In mid-September, Otto Regenbogen, the acting chairman of the Philosophy Faculty, submitted to the Rector the names of Schmitthenner, Fehrle, and Krieck, because they "were fundamentally important for the destruction of the old scientific spirit of the university" (though the Senate had voted to exclude them on July 18 in any case). Also included were several students of these professors: Wilhelm Classen, Wilhelm Ganser, and Waltraud Eckhard.[79]

In a request to the new Mannheim district government in October, Otto Regenbogen elaborated on the reasons the Senate had decided to exclude Schmitthenner, Fehrle, Krieck, and their students from the Philosophy Faculty's rosters. Schmitthenner, he reported, not only was a high-ranking SS officer, but had strived to bind the university closely to the party, had promoted academically unqualified students on ideological grounds, and had allowed his own "scholarly sense to die away under political influences and as a teacher [had] permitted, without scholarly thoroughness, the history of warfare to be put to the service of intellectual preparation for warfare." Fehrle—also an SS officer and also an SD informant—was charged with responsibility for the purges until 1935. With Schmitthenner and Krieck, Fehrle had tyrannized the Philosophy Faculty. As a scholar he was of no importance and owed his advancement to his party connections. Regenbogen was forced to admit that Krieck's early scholarship was of some importance (hence his 1923 honorary doctorate from Heidelberg), but his fanatical commitment to National Socialism nullified his earlier contributions to pedagogical sciences.[80]

Recommendations for dismissal from the Theology Faculty were determined largely by Martin Dibelius and Gustav Hoelscher. They recommended that Theodor Odenwald be removed, because over the years of the Third Reich he had become "more and more alienated from theology for reasons of politics." In the case of Robert Jelke, their objections were more personal than political, since he had repeatedly denounced Dibelius and behaved so erratically that even Nazi student leaders felt compelled to discipline him.[81] They were also determined to remove Andreas Duhm, Otto Söllner, and Erwin Kiefer, above all because they had belonged to the "German Christians" and infused their teaching with politics and, in the case of Kiefer, anti-Semitic diatribes. Further, Dibelius and Hoelscher did not consider them to be scholars of any repute.[82] Contrary to the situation with other faculties, particularly medicine, there was congruence between Dibelius's and Holescher's recommendations and the Military Government's decisions, though several cases, as we will see in the following chapter, generated considerable conflict.[83]

Karl Heinrich Bauer was the most vocal and active opponent of the purges at Heidelberg. He sought to protect former Nazi Party members and limit the extent of the dismissals. It would be his attitude toward the screening process that would create the most conflict between Bauer and other Germans, Edward Hartshorne, and later CIC agents and Special Branch investigators. In early July, with the hope that "the action of denazification will be run through and completed as soon as possible," Bauer (along with Curt Oehme and Ernst Engelking) proposed that only seven instructors from the Medical Faculty be removed from its rosters: Carl Schneider, Johann Duken, Hugo Kleine, Georg Mollier, Hermann Schlüter, Ernst Horstmann, and Rudolf Abendroth. Since there were many more former party members on the faculty than were listed here, Bauer and the others argued that "for those who were in the party only as fellow travelers, but in no way as active party-adherents, it is proposed to leave them in place. That should not mean that their party membership be excused. But on the other hand, since the maturation of young scientists deteriorated significantly during the Nazi era, it would be a great drawback to eliminate them because the *niveau* of the faculty could not be guaranteed after purging merited scientists only because of their membership."[84] Ernst Engelking was even more explicit. The central problem facing the future course of medical instruction at Heidelberg, he reported in November, "arise[s] from the fact that a part of the research and clinical men, and indeed also excellent men, have entertained the most close connections with National Socialism. By this they cannot be engaged in the frame of the university *at present* . . . At present there is a great lack of suitable personalities for research and lecturing in all branches of medicine at Heidelberg."[85] Bauer had confessed the same in his diary on August 23: "It is admittedly difficult to find non-Nazi surgeons, etc."[86] Despite these concerns, there is little evidence that he, Engelking, or members of other faculties attempted to recruit demonstrably non-Nazi scholars from other universities, despite Hartshorne's and other American officials' repeated insistence that such replacements were available.[87]

Taken together, these arguments formed a central part of the distorted and exculpatory version of Heidelberg's past that more than any other individual Bauer was responsible for propagating.[88] In several memoranda to the Military Government, Bauer articulated a concise formulation of the Heidelberg myth. His remarkable statements are worth quoting at length:

> Among the universities, Heidelberg—founded in 1386—is the oldest. It was world famous as a bastion of democratic freedoms. By 1933, not a single full professor was a member of the NSDAP! As a result, the scorn and hatred of the Nazis against Heidelberg was that much greater. SS agents imposed from the outside dismissed all representatives of the democratic worldview from their chairs and placed radical elements in their places. But these extremists failed, fled, and the remainder will—so far as they have not been arrested—be excluded by us ourselves. Nazism was never in a position to conquer the core of the spiritual fortress of Heidelberg. The venerable old idea of the university presses powerfully toward a new life. The deposed professors have been reinstated, new calls are being prepared, a new program motivates the spirits and the purged university is yearning fully to enable the spiritual reeducation of the German people for preparation of a new future.[89]

Bauer elaborated on this narrative to American officials in Heidelberg four months later:

> Shortly after the [occupation] recognized anti-Nazis assumed the leadership of the university; the professors dismissed under Hitler were at once reinstated, and those twenty-two professors who at no time had had anything to do with Nazism became the source of regeneration for the university. A "Committee of Thirteen" established by the CIC prepared to reconstruct the university from outside and within. A new university statute was drawn up, and ancient academic self-government, which has always been purely democratic, was reintroduced . . . The provisional staff of teachers is capable at once of resuming education in all faculties . . . The members of the new staff of teachers are fully conscious of the fact that purification of the university from all destructive Nazi elements is the absolute demand of the moment. On its own initiative the university petitioned the German government to dismiss from the staff of teachers a great number of Nazis and also informed the Military Government of their names. The university finds itself in a difficult situation because of the fact that General Stayer made the then chairman of the Medical Faculty and now acting Rector [Bauer] personally responsible for the reestablishment of the high scientific level of the year 1913. Military Government, therefore, will understand that the university appeals to higher headquarters for those who, according to their own strong convictions, have never been Nazis in their hearts and who, at the same time, are scientifically high-ranking scholars and are capable of helping to give new value to the reputation of Heidelberg throughout the world.[90]

Bauer's narratives are among the most concise and influential summaries of the Heidelberg myth. The number of "genuine Nazis" on the faculty had been few, they had been imposed on the university by the regime, and they were not scholars of merit. Bauer's analysis drew an implicit connection between "scholarly accomplishment" and political affiliation, bolstering the myth that those who were competent scholars were not Nazis. From here, it was a short step to the argument that commitment to "traditional," "nonpolitical" scientific values became a form of political resistance in the Third Reich. It is also striking that Bauer limited his summary of the Nazi purges in 1933 to include only "representatives of the democratic worldview," making no mention of the Jews. As we have seen, outspoken democrats constituted a relatively small minority of those dismissed at Heidelberg and elsewhere. The vast majority of those purged were German Jews, the Nazis' primary targets.

Bauer used this conception of Heidelberg's past to bolster his arguments for retaining compromised instructors for the Medical Faculty. This put him on a collision course with the Americans—at least while Edward Hartshorne was present and U.S. policy remained broadly punitive. Hartshorne intended to follow his directives to the letter. Yet he also realized that engagement with National Socialism was more than a matter of party membership. Hence his interest in the university's own personnel files and local party records, which he believed would reveal the extent of each professor's engagement with National Socialism.[91] He also remained suspicious of claims of ignorance when it came to membership in party-affiliated organizations. When he and his investigators questioned the physician Curt Oehme (a Committee of Thirteen member) about his monthly donations to the SS, Oehme claimed ignorance. "I told him," Hartshorne noted, that "he had 'supported persecution of Jews,' and gave him a little lecture on the 'politische Unklugheit' [political imprudence] of Germans. He seemed quite subdued (He will not be forbidden to teach). It seems that almost all the characters that have survived these painful times in Germany are vollkommen zermürbt [totally demoralized]. Lacked a sense of chronology and a sense for history and society."[92] Despite Fritz Ernst's prominent role on the Committee of Thirteen and pleas by Bauer, Hartshorne doubted he would be able to serve as Prorector, most probably because he had been denounced by Willy Andreas and had belonged to the SA.[93] In addition, Hartshorne excluded compromised professors from elections to the new Senate, including some who had not belonged to the party, such as Andreas, who, like Oehme, seemed to be suffering from selective amnesia. "Andreas is very worried over his exclusion from the Rektoral election," Hartshorne wrote in his diary on September 12; "I showed him compliments paid him by the Gauamtsleitung, but he was very hard to convince. He couldn't think what the 'Septemberkrise, 1938' was! (Nazi documents said he had behaved very well then.)"[94]

Before the end of July, Hartshorne was losing patience with Bauer's resistance to the screening process and with the unwillingness of professors to cooperate with his investigations. His diary entry of July 24 records: "One of our sleuths came in today and made a good point. Since a considerable number of the university teachers managed to come through without compromising themselves, it is no defense (in general) for the others to say: 'We had to.' . . . Support of Achelis by Bauer and other members of the Medical Faculty is disheartening. Will raid his house tomorrow and settle this case once and for all! The proclivity of 'Einwandfrei' Germans to rush to the support of their colleagues who were fools enough to compromise themselves with the Nazi cause is surely one of the most startling and depressing aspects of post-Nazi German academic society."[95] His exasperation with the situation at Heidelberg must have been heightened by what he witnessed at other universities in the American zone. At Marburg, for instance, he noted in August that "the professors themselves . . . wish to have a slate of university officials without any [former party members]."[96] The time pressures and enormous scale of the thorough screening Hartshorne was determined to carry out led him to conclude that "the investigation of all these men in a thorough manner is going to take too long for the opening of more than the Medical and Theological faculties this fall. So much the better."[97]

When the first screening was completed just in time for the partial resumption of instruction by the Medical Faculty, scheduled for August 15, the Americans had rejected forty-three members out of a total of seventy-nine active instructors—54 percent—for reinstatement.[98] The results of the investigation were accurate, if in some cases incomplete. The CIC rejected Johann Daniel Achelis not only because of his party membership, but because they had discovered that he was "appointed Director of Universities in the Prussian Ministry of Education for the purpose of purging the Universities of Jewish teachers." Even though Carl Schneider was in the "unconditionally rejected" category, there was no mention of his leading role in the "euthanasia" program. Similarly, Viktor von Weizäcker's role in the program went unnoticed (the CIC remarked that he "is known not to have participated in any Party functions or activities"). On Hans Runge, the director of the Women's Clinic and "unconditionally rejected" for reinstatement, the CIC reported: "Highly popular, world famous Dr. On file are numerous testimonies by Jews and anti-Nazis stating he saved them from concentration camps at great risk to himself. However, in spite of his excellent character, conduct, and mentality, it would be incorrect to say that he had never been more than a nominal Nazi. His party files are unfortunately missing."[99]

Bauer took the news of the dismissals badly, claiming to Hartshorne that "our exclusion was going to ruin the university, introducing a lowering of objective scholarship and standards comparable with 1933." Hartshorne was unmoved. "I told [Bauer and Hoops] of a pool of available personnel elsewhere in the U.S. zone and the impossibility of retention of Nazi figures in view of the world attitude towards German guilt."[100] On August 17, Bauer reported to the Senate that the "faculty would be decimated to a far greater extent than expected." With the Senate's agreement, he intended to press the Americans to restrict the severity of the purge.[101] Over the next several months Bauer and others petitioned the Military Government to retain numerous compromised faculty members.

In stark contrast to Bauer and others, Alfred Weber and Hans von Eckardt insisted from the outset on an extensive purge. Weber was determined to see his newly constituted Nationalökonomie Seminar free of former Nazis. Weber was one of the few Heidelberg professors to oppose the retention of professors who had not been singled out by the Senate for dismissal.[102] Hans von Eckardt was similarly inclined. In the American-licensed newspaper *Die Neue Zeitung* he pronounced that the Germans themselves were not pursuing denazification vigorously enough. Church officials, schoolteachers, and university professors were inexplicably devoting their energies to denouncing the "injustice" of denazification measures, rather than condemning the Nazis as the "murderers of millions of Jews and the desecrators of the honest name of the Christian German nation." Without using his name, he denounced Gustav Radbruch for supporting the retention of two former Nazi party members on the Law Faculty, Karl Engisch and Eugen Ulmer.[103]

Despite the growing tensions over dismissals, the partial reopening of the Medical Faculty took place on August 15 with a ten-week refresher course being offered to about five hundred ex-Wehrmacht physicians. Bauer and Jaspers delivered the inaugural addresses. Bauer's short speech was an unremarkable rehash of statements culled from his memoranda and newspaper essays of the previous months.[104] More striking was Jaspers's address, the content of which provided a preview of his better-known essay "The Question of German Guilt."[105] Although at the outset he stated that the reopening marked "a new beginning after the ruin which had overtaken the university for twelve years," he claimed that "secretly the core of the university remained intact" and added that "the rebirth of our university could never mean that we merely want to continue where we left off in 1933." What had happened to the universities, and what had to change?

In Jaspers's mind, the trouble began in the latter half of the nineteenth century, when the "unity of the sciences" was shattered, presumably, though Jaspers does not say so explicitly, by rapid modernization and scientific advances. As a result, "the sciences were dispersed; in every separate science, ambitious to represent the whole of science, pseudo-science intruded; disintegration followed, culminating in the phantasmagorias of the National Socialist period. On the other hand, science proved unable to integrate into the whole the new factual forces of the epoch, particularly technics, and to penetrate them spiritually."[106] In Jaspers's view, the result had simply been the grafting of politics onto scholarly research. Consequently, great crimes had been committed, particularly by physicians.[107] He hoped that the occupiers would approve the restoration of "our former constitution and self-government," but he did not consider this a sufficient condition for "regeneration." Regeneration would occur through the restoration of basic academic freedom—the unpoliticized search for "truth"—and "respect for human existence." Not surprisingly, he argued that the entire university had to be functioning if it was to serve the ideals of truth and humaneness. With nineteenth-century ideals restored the university could "expand into all the major concerns of humanity in our time. It would make up for what has been missed in the course of nearly a century." The ultimate goal was to allow each individual scholar to tend to his own specialty while living "in the awareness and perspective of the whole."[108]

Edward Hartshorne was moved by Jaspers's speech but many students and some professors received it with hostility.[109] This unfriendly atmosphere intensified over the following months. "Never before 1937 did I experience so little of a kindly attitude toward me in the auditorium as I do now," he wrote Hannah Arendt in September 1946; "publicly I'm left in peace. But behind my back people slander me: the Communists call me a forward guard of National Socialism; the sullen losers, a traitor to my country."[110] Jaspers's address was indeed courageous. Almost alone among German university professors in the summer of 1945, he confronted the question of German guilt in a public forum, even speaking out on some of the specific crimes of the German medical community. Yet, taken as a whole, the speech added another brick to the construction of the Heidelberg myth. By the end of the nineteenth century, in his conception, the university lay in a fractured, weakened state. Politics intruded in the form of "pseudo-scientists" backed by state power. Together, they "forced" physicians to commit crimes. Had the search for truth unhindered by ideological blinders and "humaneness" fostered by exposure to philosophy and theology "stood fast," then "National Socialism would not have invaded medicine."[111]

A few months later, Jaspers produced a thoughtful and little-known critique of German academic culture under National Socialism, "Science in the Hitler State" ("Die Wissenschaft im Hitlerstaat"). In a remarkable admission, he noted that "science as such could only be ruined by scientists." But he went on to reinforce the Heidelberg myth by arguing that "only very few notable men of recognized intellectual stature connected themselves to National Socialism" and those that did were motivated primarily by opportunism. Claiming that the party's control over the universities was by no means total, honest scholars could continue their work relatively unimpeded. In judging his colleagues in the postwar context of denazification, he tried to strike a balance: "One must keep in mind the entire personality and its achievements and not simply isolate and judge derailments. But one must also not forget the charges as a whole. And one must guard against self-righteousness, which is all too prone to personal vendettas and is the justification of reckless denazification without prudence." Here Jaspers's expressed the dominant view among Heidelberg's professors toward denazification: that supposedly "isolated" instances of support for the regime should not be seen as polluting a scholar's entire career. Denazification, in this view, aimed at doing just this.[112]

Following the widely publicized resumption of medical instruction, pressure on occupation officials to authorize the reopening of the entire university intensified.[113] On August 26, Bauer requested that the entire university be opened as quickly as possible in order to help save a generation of young people: "In the new university they will face teachers threatened, maltreated, and persecuted for their point of view during the Nazi era . . . Professional training schools cannot produce this purification. The new German students need the life that comes out of the unity of all studies."[114] On November 1, the entire Medical Faculty was reopened. The Theology Faculty followed in December. On January 15, 1946, amid even wider publicity than had attended events the previous summer, the entire university reopened. But, as we will see in the following chapter, the months leading up to and immediately following the January reopening were marked by intensifying conflict between occupier and occupied over denazification.

Following the resumption of instruction in the Medical School in mid-August, Edward Hartshorne spent little time at Heidelberg. In the fall, the university was assigned its first full-time Military Government "University Officer" and Hartshorne thereafter devoted most of his efforts to denazification at Marburg, which he considered the "most promising" of the U.S. zone universities. Following press reports in the spring of 1946 that Munich University remained a hothouse of Nazi sentiment, Walter Dorn recommended to Lucius Clay that Hartshorne be assigned to Bavaria to sort things out. Hartshorne would never have the chance to oversee an investigation. On August 28, while driving with his wife to Nuremberg, he was shot by a German civilian and died two days later. His killer, allegedly a black marketeer, was himself shot dead by army police shortly thereafter. An investigation found no evidence of political motives in Hartshorne's murder.[115] The Military Government and the universities had lost an eloquent champion of a thorough but just purge.

Most German academics dismissed after 1933 left Germany. Very few (4 percent of the total) returned. Some had died or become American or British citizens and did not consider themselves "exiles" in the sense that they were prepared to return to Germany immediately after the collapse of the National Socialist state. Neither the universities nor the postwar state and national governments ever made a systematic effort to bring the victims of the purges in academia back to Germany.[116] In the first years of the occupation, then, an opportunity to take a decisive step to right a great injustice was not taken by the professors themselves or the first postwar German governments. Despite the promulgation of reparations laws in the late 1940s and early 1950s, those few who fought for compensation, a pension, or a teaching position often encountered insurmountable legal barriers and the academic elite's unwillingness to demand that they receive invitations to return to their former positions. The era of partial restorations in academic culture inaugurated in 1945 did not for the most part include restoring instructors who had lost their positions after 1933.

The record at Heidelberg is ambiguous. There is no evidence that a systematic attempt to bring purged scholars back to the university was ever considered by its postwar leadership or by the Baden Education Ministry. "For two years," Emil Gumbel wrote to Max Seydewitz in May 1947, "I have had earnest thoughts about my return to Germany. I had expected that the German universities would have undone individually or collectively the dismissals of those fired on political or on so-called racial grounds and then informed us when our positions would again be available to us. This has universally not taken place."[117] At Heidelberg, sixty-five instructors had been fired by the Nazis after 1933. Twenty-one died in the intervening twelve years of the Third Reich. Of the surviving forty-four, thirty lived in exile abroad and fourteen remained in Germany. Twelve of the latter group lived in Heidelberg or elsewhere in the American occupation zone, one (August Grisebach) in Potsdam in the Soviet zone, and one (Leonard Perels) had been interned in France. Eleven of the twelve managed to return to their former academic positions (or, in the case of Gerhard Anschütz, retained emeritus status). One of them, Karl Wilmanns, died in August 1945 before he could rejoin the Medical Faculty. The remaining ten instructors restored to active teaching positions were Walter Jellinek, Gustav Radbruch, Karl Geiler, Hermann Hoepke, Ernst Hoffmann, Karl Jaspers, Otto Regenbogen, Marie Baum, Hans von Eckardt, and Hermann Ranke. Only six of the purged Heidelberg professors living abroad returned to Germany, three to Heidelberg and three to other universities.[118]

These numbers do not tell the full story, as Dorothee Mussgnug pointed out in her study of the persecuted Heidelberg instructors. Jaspers, Radbruch, Jellinek, and other members of the Committee of Thirteen were restored almost immediately to their former positions and formed the backbone of the university's postwar leadership. They lived in or around Heidelberg, knew each other well, and were in most cases known and trusted by the Americans. But many others encountered considerable difficulties in recovering their positions, and a few refused to come back to Germany. Since his dismissal by the Nazis, for instance, Leonardo Olschki never again published anything in German or attempted to regain a connection with Heidelberg after the war. In a sad irony, he would be dismissed from the University of California at Berkeley in 1950—by that institution's chancellor and Board of Regents—for refusing to sign a "loyalty oath." He declined an offer of reinstatement two years later.[119] Without question, part of the problem was the reluctance of the university Senate or individual faculties to adopt a blanket policy toward bringing back purged instructors. The case of the art historian August Grisebach is illustrative. In 1945, Grisebach's chair was occupied by Walter Paatz, not a party member, but a member of the Dozentenschaft and Dozentenbund.[120] Acting on a general principle that all purged instructors should automatically receive an offer to return to their former positions, however, would force others out. In this case, Paatz would lose his job. Was this justifiable legally or ethically? The Philosophy Faculty decided against restoring Grisebach on the grounds that "not the person (Herr Paatz), [but] rather the state carries the responsibility for National Socialist injustice."[121]

The return of other scholars was hampered by intra-faculty machinations or byzantine financial and bureaucratic constraints imposed by state education ministries. Arthur Rosenthal's return to his former chair, for instance, was sabotaged outright in 1945 by Herbert Seifert, who at that time was struggling to obtain the position for his mentor, Wilhelm Threlfall.[122] Seifert dismissed Rosenthal as a subpar mathematician and Threlfall was subsequently offered the post at Heidelberg. Although Rosenthal was finally offered the chair following Threlfall's sudden death in 1949, he rejected the offer. He had become an American citizen in the intervening years, but more important, he noted, "because the overwhelming majority of current German students were up until four years ago educated in the Nazi-*Geist* and had stood under the exclusive influence of the most intensive Nazi propaganda, I cannot imagine how I, as a Jew, could possibly have frictionless cooperation with this generation of students . . . during the last period of my activity at Heidelberg University and particularly after, too many terrible things occurred that I cannot forget and that make my return impossible."[123] Many others must have shared similar reservations about their former colleagues who had retained their positions in Third Reich or were suspended only briefly by the occupiers after the war.

The ordeal of Gerta von Ubisch merits particular attention. Following her dismissal on "racial" grounds, the fifty-year-old von Ubisch left Germany and taught briefly in the Netherlands and Switzerland. As with many dismissed scholars, finding permanent employment proved extremely difficult. She managed to secure a position conducting genetic research at an independent institute in São Paulo, Brazil. When the war in Europe ended, she tried to return to Germany via Norway, but securing a visa proved difficult and she was forced to wait an additional seven years before finally returning to Heidelberg, destitute and nearly seventy years old. The Rector of Heidelberg along with Walter Jellinek supported her application to the Ministry of Culture for a pension but the ministry concluded that since she had been "only" a Privatdozent in 1933 and thus not technically a civil servant she was unqualified for a pension. When she appealed, the presiding judge claimed that she in fact left Heidelberg "voluntarily" in 1933. To compound this humiliation and blatant injustice, she was forced to accept what was a pittance and was never granted legal standing as a retired university professor. Although her situation improved somewhat following the passage of a new compensation law in Baden-Württemberg in 1955, the experience left her embittered.[124] "Twenty years is a long time," she wrote the Rector in 1956, "but it should not be so long that all crimes of the Nazis should be forgotten. I never would have thought that I would ever attend a hearing—and it would seem not as the plaintiff but the defendant—in which the Nazis methods would be denied. The Ministry of Culture must be criticized for the fact that it sent as the representative of the government, and thus as my opponent, [an official] who was so young that he was ignorant of the provisions of the infamous Aryan-paragraph—or believed he could ignore them."[125] In her unpublished memoirs, she compared her situation with that of the widow of Reinhard Heydrich: "No non-German will understand . . . that his widow, with retroactive power from 1950—or perhaps earlier—had been granted the widow's pension of a high officer, presumably because there are no laws regarding the nonpayment of a pension to a widow of a mass-murderer in a high government position."[126]

Exceptional among Heidelberg professors was yet again Alfred Weber, who did more than any other instructor there to retrieve persecuted colleagues for his newly reconstituted faculty, particularly Hans von Eckardt, Herbert Sultan, and Marie Baum. In June 1946, von Eckardt, with considerable help from Weber, resumed his directorship of the Institute for the Study of Journalism. The Baden government opposed Marie Baum's immediate reinstatement, but she was nonetheless awarded "honorary membership" in 1949.[127]

The first months of the occupation were crucial for the future of Heidelberg. Most significant, the foundations were laid for a *mythos Heidelberg* that presented the university as a victim of an anti-intellectual political offensive that, though backed by Nazi students, came from outside its walls. Most professors, according to the myth, respected the autonomy of science and did not compromise themselves with the regime. In 1945 and to a great extent ever since the myth precluded any extensive examination of the engagement with National Socialism among the ranks of the professors and justified a return to the pre-1933 university structure. Hence professors closed ranks over the autonomy of the university and the necessity of curtailing student political activity. The Americans, for their part, left decisions regarding the structure of the university almost entirely in German hands. They did so out of a belief that this was the best way to foster democratic values in German society and because reform by fiat would have been resisted fiercely by the professorate.

The first wave of systematic purges did not take place until the fall of 1945. Charged with overseeing the reopening of the Medical School, Edward Hartshorne and a small team of intelligence officers set out to "screen" the proposed faculties. The scope of the screening was determined by the most expansive criteria in all of occupied Germany. The professors, who had been granted the option to screen their own faculties, singled out only a handful of the most fanatical Nazis. Unwilling to confront the extent of their own or their colleagues' complicity with National Socialism, they selected with very few exceptions those who owed their positions to party membership. Thus was a link made between ideological fervor and a lack of scholarly qualifications, providing a springboard for the argument that high scientific ability was a form of political resistance. Those who had been party members and good scholars, as well as "reputable" individuals, could not be considered "Nazis." The Heidelberg myth was thus firmly entrenched when denazification in the American zone intensified in the fall of 1945.

CHAPTER FIVE

The Limits of Denazification

> Hardly had the last echoes of gunfire died way in the distance when with a hurry and flurry completely unjustified by the situation at the time, the doors of the medical school were thrown open last September without consideration for the fact that Heidelberg University, as well as all of the German Universities, had been, over a period of twelve years, Nazified to the core.
> —Daniel F. Penham, CIC Special Agent, February 1946

The American policy of denazification reached its greatest scope between the fall of 1945 and the fall of 1946. This brief surge was attributable largely to the atmosphere created by what some historians have called the "Nuremberg interregnum," denoting the period from the end of the war in Europe to the conclusion of the Nuremberg war crimes trials in September 1946. In this period, much of the world's attention was focused on the crimes of the Nazis and public support in the United States for denazification was very high.[1] Universities in the American occupation zone were the particular targets of intensive denazification investigations. In early 1946, Heidelberg was the scene of a sharp conflict between professors and occupation officials over denazification. It was ignited by Daniel Penham, a young German-Jewish émigré CIC officer. Penham considered Heidelberg to be "Nazified to the core" and was determined to carry out an unsparing purge. The evidence he amassed compelled him to conclude that an exhaustive investigation of the professorate and student body was necessary. Yet professors at Heidelberg put up intense resistance to Penham's investigation by denouncing him as insane, sabotaging his efforts outright, and by pleading with other American officials to intervene on their behalf. The duel between Penham and the professors hardened their opposition to confronting the extent of their engagement with National Socialism and further bolstered the Heidelberg myth.

Contemporary documents, memoirs, and scholarly accounts have almost without exception assessed the period of Penham's investigations as a bizarre and disruptive interlude and Penham himself as—literally—a madman.[2] He was, according to Fritz Ernst's recollections in 1950, "undoubtedly a severely schizoid psychopath."[3] Karl Heinrich Bauer declared that Penham had died in an insane asylum following his return to the United States.[4] This view may also have been widespread among students.[5] Nearly every scholarly account that deals with the events of late 1945 and early 1946 uncritically parrots these facile assessments. Hence James Mumper, who likened Penham to Torquemada, claimed he acted with "extraordinary zeal" and possessed "an ungovernable temper." Similarly, Renato de Rosa referred to the atmosphere "created" by Penham as "inquisitorial," while Dorothee Mussgnug concluded that he used "questionable means" in conducting his investigations.[6] Another recent account notes that Penham made the reopening of Heidelberg "extraordinarily difficult" because he "screamed and shouted abuse at professors and students alike, seeing in virtually everyone he encountered an unregenerate Nazi, even in Rector Bauer."[7]

Penham was neither a renegade agent nor a madman. He was representative of a vocal minority among occupation officers that considered German society to be "nazified to the core." That he was intent on conducting a thorough investigation of the university to ensure that it was purged of Nazis and pro-Nazis alike is clear. His methods were considered "unorthodox" for several reasons, presumed "mental instability" not being one of them. The targets of his investigation, for one thing, were certainly unaccustomed to being treated in any manner that fell short of servile. Second, most were unwilling to confront the university's undisputed role in supporting National Socialism, preferring instead, as we have seen, to construct a myth of victimization. More important, there can be little doubt that in the atmosphere of immediate postwar Germany a young, uniformed, German-Jewish émigré with the authority to incarcerate elicited powerful fears among the professors.

Penham's arrival in Heidelberg coincided with an intensification of denazification throughout the American zone. A perceptive American official's fears, noted in Chapter 4, that a public relations disaster might result if reopening was allowed before the faculty could be investigated thoroughly were already being validated by developments elsewhere in the U.S. zone. In Aachen, the first German town occupied by the Americans for any length of time, journalists claimed that officials did not consider denazification a high priority.[8] In June, the liberal American news magazine *The New Republic* reported that the American-appointed Minister President of Bavaria, the conservative anti-Nazi Fritz Schäffer, had appointed former Nazis to high-level positions in his government. In September, a *New York Times* reporter argued that by tolerating former Nazis in "some of the best jobs in commerce and industry" American occupation officials demonstrated a greater concern with economic recovery than with denazification. To make matters much worse, General George S. Patton, commander of the U.S. Third Army and the military governor of Bavaria, revealed his impatience with denazification to American reporters by likening Nazi Party membership with political party patronage at home. As a result of the Schäffer affair, Patton's remarks, and the resulting uproar in the American press, General Clay ordered an intensification of denazification throughout the American zone ("Law Number 8").[9] The following month, a wave of purges rolled over the American zone. By the end of March 1946, hundreds of thousands of individuals from the public and private sectors had been dismissed from their positions.[10] Universities in the American zone were targeted by yet another wave of purges in the summer of 1946, occasioned by Military Government and press reports of incomplete denazification.[11]

As denazification intensified in the American zone in late 1945, criticism on the American and German sides grew exponentially. Reservations about the policy expressed by some American officers immediately after the onset of the occupation grew in late 1945 and in 1946. Intensified denazification, as William Griffith, an officer stationed in Bavaria, recalled, was "opposed by the military government denazification staff . . . It brought unnecessary interference with German economic recovery, concentration on small fry and statistics, and consequent neglect of general political objectives. Few positive steps were taken, then or later, to appoint sincere anti-Nazis to high German positions."[12] Although Griffith regarded Law Number 8 as far too expansive and harmful to Germany's economic reconstruction, he believed overall that a large number of dismissals were justified and necessary. The principal problem, in Griffith's and other occupation officers' assessments, lay in the willingness—or unwillingness—of local Military Government officials to carry out their orders.¹³ These men understood that for denazification to be just and effective, extensive investigations and trials would have to be conducted, and that was not a viable option. One officer recalled estimating that formal trials for every incriminated person might go one for thirty years.¹⁴

The policy's staunch defenders were few. Although a minority, they were very often émigré officers serving in the army, OSS, or CIC. Their view of Germany's Nazi past was uncompromising, as was their conception of the way in which the victors should shape the future. The émigré scholar Karl Loewenstein, an editor of *Social Research,* dismissed the idea that the vast majority of Germans had rejected National Socialism and welcomed the arrival of the allies. "Acts of spontaneous vengeance," he pointed out, "would have been a healthy sign; they were expected and would have been condoned by the American Military Government, but they just did not occur." He also rejected the near universal claim that everyone was forced to support the party in some way, or face penury or worse:

> There were Germans in official positions who resisted pressure and refused to join the party; they chose to resign and be pensioned off rather than continue in service under the regime. They were few—too few, I concede—but they existed. And the Germans knew that a person who resigned was neither put in a concentration camp nor even required to forfeit his pension; he just walked out . . . I admit that it is a fundamental right of a man not to be a hero. But the fact that a person of integrity loaned his name, for selfish and opportunistic reasons, to a party which he now professes to have despised all the time contributed to entrenching the regime . . . Had there been mass resignations of university professors, civil servants, judges, in 1933, or even in 1937 . . . perhaps the regime would not have lasted, or at least we would have found more people whom we could trust implicitly.¹⁵

How was it possible, then, for occupation officers to distinguish between Nazi and non-Nazi without recourse to a "general criterion" such as party membership? The answer was to conduct thorough investigations, something, Loewenstein regretted, most American officials were unwilling and unable to carry out.

Moses Moskowitz shared Loewenstein's skepticism regarding the German public. A Polish-born émigré, Moskowitz was a member of the staff of the foreign affairs division of the American Jewish Committee (AJC) and a Military Government officer. Of particular concern to Moskowitz was the place of anti-Semitism in National Socialism. As an occupation officer, he had interviewed hundreds of Germans and come to an unsettling conclusion: "Most Germans produce one excuse or another to explain away their former association with the Nazi activities . . . after to talking to hundreds of former Nazis, one comes to the conclusion that this disclaimer of Nazi belief and conviction is not deception prompted by fear or expediency. It is sincere—and in some ways this makes the phenomenon more frightening . . . Opportunism there undoubtedly was. But people who adhere to a tenet of faith that expresses their innermost feelings, and in the name of which six million human beings have been slaughtered, do not readily disavow their belief in a moment of adversity." Moskowitz could cite only one individual who had "arisen in Germany to exhort his people to repentance and expiation for the mass graves of Jews dotting half the European continent"—Karl Jaspers. The vast majority, however, not only believed in their own innocence, but have "convince[d] themselves that they, too, have been victims of Nazism." For Moskowitz, this explained perhaps more than any other factor the "enigma of German irresponsibility." After all, why should one feel guilty if one believes that he too is a victim of a criminal regime? If the Germans themselves would not "make amends for the crimes of Nazism," then sweeping and punitive denazification was necessary. "The Germans," Moskowitz concluded, "know very well that the extermination of Jews was a large-scale enterprise and that an untold number of people were directly engaged in it. Until they are identified, every German is suspected of having been one of them."[16]

Stefan Heym, a journalist and émigré officer, hoped to go even further. In an editorial sent to the *New York Times* (but never published), Heym argued that Germany had never undergone a true social revolution that would have paved the way to a healthy democracy. If the Germans themselves could not make such a revolution, then it was incumbent on the victorious allies to do it for them. For Heym, therefore, more than an extensive purge was necessary. What was needed was fundamental social and economic restructuring, including a "complete transformation of the German educational system, whereby the actual nature of the system must be changed."[17] This outlook, which Heym shared with a few other émigrés working as analysts for the OSS (most notably Franz Neumann), was exactly what Military Governor Lucius Clay was determined to avoid, preferring instead to foster democracy "from the ground up rather than from the top down."[18]

Among Germans, occupation officials observed an initial surge of support for dismissals. But in the summer and fall of 1945, criticism of denazification on the German side increased considerably. The results of extensive public opinion surveys conducted in the U.S. zone by the Military Government and analyzed by Richard and Anna Merritt are revealing. They indicate that although a majority supported denazification in principle, they opposed it in practice, most often because they felt that too many "small fish" were being netted while the bigger ones were getting away.[19] The OMGUS surveys also revealed that the policy's most vociferous critics belonged to the well-educated and upper social-economic groups. And many did not hesitate to voice their criticisms privately to Military Government officials or publicly in recently licensed newspapers and journals.[20] Western Germany's nascent political leadership was well aware of this emerging groundswell of public discontent. Throughout the spring and summer of 1946, Konrad Adenauer, the leader of the conservative Christian Democratic Union [CDU], called repeatedly for an end to sweeping denazification on the grounds that large numbers of party members who were hardly fanatical Nazis, let alone guilty of criminal acts, were being persecuted unjustly and driven back into the arms of reaction.[21] The dilemma and potential threat was not lost on some contemporary American observers.[22] To have supported thorough denazification, as Jeffrey Herf has argued, would have been to risk losing support for Adenauer's party by a substantial number of voters more interested in reconstructing than remembering.[23]

As we have seen, the initial screening undertaken by Edward Hartshorne and the CIC in preparation for the partial reopening of the university—the reopening of the Medical Faculty—met with considerable resistance from professors, because their definition of what constituted a "Nazi" encompassed those who had come to Heidelberg in and after 1933 and whose appointments were due primarily to their party membership. As the other faculties prepared to resume instruction, they were screened by CIC agents and Military Government's "Special Branch" (denazification) officers. By the end of October, 46 instructors had lost their positions, with the Medical, Natural Sciences, and Philosophy Faculties hardest hit proportionally.[24] By early December, the Military Government had ordered the dismissal of 56 more instructors beyond those screened from the Medical and Theology Faculties that summer.[25] By the summer of 1946, 138 instructors and assistants (96 and 42 respectively) had been dismissed. This number amounted to just over half (51.1 percent) of the 270 members of the teaching staff listed at Heidelberg in the summer of 1944.[26]

Once extensive denazification got under way in the fall of 1945, professors rejected blanket removals based on party membership and advocated, in the words of the OSS officer Felix Gilbert, "investigation of individual cases by a commission of or including trusted Germans who know the people and the situation involved."[27] Gilbert also noted a clear divide between older and younger scholars in their views of denazification. Older scholars seemed prepared to "defend the established scholar who joined the Party in order to continue work and in any case insist upon his retention because of his proven educational and cultural value to future students, so long as investigation shows him to have been internally untouched by Nazism." On the whole (though Gilbert grants that Jaspers is an exception), the older scholars "show little sympathy for the younger instructors who entered academic life under the Nazis." Martin Dibelius, for instance, recommended that *all* young faculty members be suspended for the duration of denazification investigations, though they should be permitted to teach on a probationary basis in order to keep the university open. Conversely, younger scholars (Gilbert mentions only Alexander Mitscherlich) "feel not only that the established professors who yielded in the early years of the Nazi rule betrayed a responsibility commensurate with their position, but also that the older professors as a whole, anti-Nazi and Nazi alike, are of limited value for the future, since they have lost all contact with the temper of the students." Hence Mitscherlich, Gilbert noted, suggested that the age of the scholar should be "one of the primary criteria of denazification, with leniency varying in direct proportion to youth."[28]

Fritz Ernst gave Gilbert insights into his own views on denazification. For professors who had joined the party, Ernst proposed establishing a series of benchmark years to use in judging the extent of an individual's ideological commitment and assessing arguments for or against retention. A scholar who had joined the party before 1933, Ernst argued, was "no opportunist, but an enthusiast." Joining in the spring of 1933 might not be fair grounds for dismissal because anyone who joined then might have believed in the party's "ostensible legality" and because the party's "radicalism" was not yet fully apparent. Those who joined in 1935 could be dismissed because by that time the party's radicalism (exemplified by the "persecution of Jews and the Church") and the "abandonment of any pretense of legality" had become obvious. Yet even so one could have been induced to joint the party by foreign policy successes or "stronger pressures," such as those exerted by friends, family, or superiors. By the end of 1938, the evidence of "brutality"—here Ernst lists the annexation of Austria, the pogrom in November 1938, and the dissolution of Czechoslovakia—was clear. But party membership might be justified on the grounds of "greater [economic and political] stabilization" and growing pressures on people in important positions. Ernst also notes that by this time, party membership could be automatic for some civil servants. Finally, for the period after 1939, Ernst lists support for "Hitler's war" and "war methods" and for crimes committed in German-occupied countries and against Jews as a basis for dismissal, though continued support of the party could be justified by "stronger pressure [to join], no contact with the outside world, atrocities kept [a] military secret, [and the] psychology of standing together in [a] national emergency."[29]

In October 1945, Gustav Radbruch argued that Military Government officials had not yet grasped that there were "countless party members who were put under the most terrible pressures to join the party, but were never National Socialists and more often were the fiercest opponents of National Socialism." The main problem, he contended, was that "active Nazi" had been too broadly defined. The characteristics of a true "active Nazi" could be deduced not from "outer criteria" such as party membership, but only from an investigation of an individual's background. Such investigations could only be undertaken in cooperation with "trusted Germans."[30] A few months earlier, Radbruch and Walter Jellinek had attempted to draw a clear distinction between "active" and "passive" party members in the civil service in order to determine who should receive pensions. Active Nazis, they argued, were those who had misused their authority as civil servants and thus forfeited their right to receive a pension: "those who had participated [in or out of office] in riots, arson (the burning of synagogues!), plunder, [violent acts] against opponents or those of other races . . . but also those who refused to apply clear legal provisions because they were opposed—in reality or ostensibly—to National Socialist principles." Included in this category were those who acted as secret police informants and those who engaged in denunciations, as well as those who "as scholars designated so-called National Socialist body of thought as scientific truth without a critical test or against their better judgment." They did not, however, define what constituted a "passive Nazi." And, as we have seen, many more of their own colleagues could have qualified for the "active Nazi" category than either were prepared to admit. Walter Jellinek himself would certainly have qualified as a civil servant who had in 1933 and 1934 "designated so-called National Socialist body of thought as scientific truth without a critical test or against [his] better judgment."[31]

Karl Jaspers shared the belief that the Americans had cast the denazification net far too wide and, as we will see, resisted American-led investigatons of his colleagues. His best-known statement on the matter was made not regarding colleagues at Heidelberg, but about Martin Heidegger. In December 1945, Jaspers recommended to Freiburg University officials that Heidegger be barred from teaching "for several years." For Jaspers, what mattered was the individual's relationship to National Socialism. "In deciding how individual persons are to be treated," he wrote, "we must inevitably have an eye to the overall situation in which we find ourselves today. It is therefore essential that those who actively helped to put National Socialism in the driving seat be called to account. Heidegger is one of the few university professors who did just that." In evaluating Heidegger's engagement with National Socialism, Jaspers also concluded that Heidegger had become an anti-Semite.[32] Jaspers then offered a kind of schema for evaluating the engagement of intellectuals with National Socialism. He believed that Heidegger simply did not understand what he was getting into when he joined the party, but naiveté was no excuse. Without question, Heidegger, along with Carl Schmitt and Alfred Bäumler, had "blacken[ed] the reputation of German philosophy." Regarding Heidegger's supposed "disillusionment" with the Nazis, Jaspers added, a "change of heart brought about by a switch to the anti-Nazi camp has to be judged by the motives that underlie it." Jaspers then singled out three crucial dates that might be used as benchmarks in evaluating a supposed "change of heart": 1934, 1938, and 1941. "To my way of thinking," he concluded, "a change of heart that postdates 1941 is virtually meaningless—and indeed means very little unless it occurred decisively after the events of June 30, 1934 [the so-called night of the long knives, Hitler's murderous purge of the Sturmabteilung]." The year 1938 was no doubt a reference to the November pogrom. Jaspers, in short, could understand how an individual might have been swept up in the enthusiasm—however misguided—generated by the "Machtergriefung" and "Gleichschaltung." But Heidegger's anti-Semitic actions and statements, his activities as Rector, and his "mode of thinking, which seems to me to be fundamentally unfree, dictatorial, and uncommunicative" ought to have barred him from the lectern.[33]

Some professors saw denazification as a temporary impediment and simply an obstacle to be overcome. In a telling passage in his postwar diary, Karl Heinrich Bauer noted that a delegation of visiting American scholars informed him that their colleagues at home "denounced the ultra-radical removal of Nazis," a policy they attributed only to "the decisive power of public opinion." One of them promised to do what he could to influence this opinion and gain access for Bauer to "important American offices."[34] In a short memorandum on "the problem of rejected professors and Dozenten" dated November 2, 1945, Otto Regenbogen proposed that those who had been active "in a clearly criminal sense" should no longer be tolerated by the university. On the other hand, he hoped to help those who "had to be excluded on other grounds (early party membership, etc.) though without personal reproaches having been raised against them." Regenbogen ruminated over a plan to assist and protect those who had been dismissed. Physicians, for instance, should not be placed in "leading positions" in the clinics and hospitals, nor should natural scientists be given such positions in laboratories and research institutions. Scholars in the humanities could be "transferred" to work in the libraries, archives, museums, and similar institutions. Older or sick scholars should be granted emeritus status, and in other cases "German government offices" should intervene by granting pensions. In "less serious cases," those who had been temporarily suspended would be kept in mind for later reappointment.[35]

Karl Heinrich Bauer's protection of former Nazis, his decidedly "undemocratic" behavior as chairman of the Medical Faculty and Rector, and his career during the Third Reich would begin to plague him as early as the summer of 1945. In September, Alexander Mitscherlich informed Edward Hartshorne, who had just returned from one of his many trips around the American zone, that medical clinic employees had petitioned the Military Government for Bauer's removal as Rector. They accused Bauer of protecting and promoting former Nazis and excluding those with anti-Nazi credentials, and produced concrete evidence to back up their claims. Bauer considered the accusations an attempt by local communists to infiltrate and (re)politicize the university.[36] Although Mitscherlich compared Bauer to Paul Schmitthenner in his dictatorial manner in dealing with faculty committees, he recommended that given his "positive work" he be left in place. The conversation led Hartshorne—who undoubtedly had recent controversies in Bavaria in the back of his mind—to remark in his diary that "Bauer must evidently be carefully watched. God help us if his indiscretions ever get out of hand and we have to 'crack down' on him. If we ever have to close up a university for disciplinary reasons, I hope I am 3,000 miles away."[37]

Bauer—who recalled his attitude toward denazification as "we, the guiltless, operated according to the principle: we accuse none, but exonerate those where justifiable"—was indeed protecting former Nazis.[38] On June 8, 1945, Bauer, along with Ernst Engelking, Curt Oehme, Walther Schönfeld, and Alfred Seiffert, petitioned the CIC for Karl Schmidhuber's retention on the Medical Faculty, even though Schmidhuber had served as Dozentenbundführer from 1936 to 1945, had belonged to the Nazi Physicians' League, and had been an SS officer and an SD informant. Despite these credentials, Bauer was determined to retain him on the grounds that Schmidhuber "saw as his special task the protection of academic life from injurious interference by radical Nazi-elements and protecting the oppressed."[39] A month later, the same five men petitioned the Military Government for the retention of Johann Daniel Achelis. Admittedly, they wrote, he "belonged to those who played a role in National Socialism, above all in the first years." Yet they claimed he had never abused his authority while at Heidelberg, and indeed attempted to protect the faculty and the university. Achelis's role in securing Bauer's appointment at Heidelberg despite his colleague's marriage to a "one-quarter non-Aryan woman" was held to be proof that he was not an anti-Semite. Finally, Achelis was himself a fine scientist, and Bauer suggested that removing him would damage the quality of instruction in the faculty.[40]

The CIC and Edward Hartshorne would have none of this. After a meeting with the American on July 27, Bauer informed Curt Oehme that Achelis could not be retained, primarily because of his service in the Prussian Education Ministry. Although Bauer noted "altogether 1,800 professors had been fired" by the Ministry, he argued to Hartshorne that "they would have been fired anyway." To all this, an unmoved Hartshorne replied, "You have put forward much on behalf of Achelis. All of that, however, cannot budge the weight of 1,800 names."[41] Bauer also clashed with CIC agent Thomas Emmet over Schmidhuber's case, and on September 5, Emmet informed Bauer that retention of Achelis, Otto Dittmar, and Kurt Görttler was out of the question. Fritz Eichholtz and Hans Runge would be prohibited from lecturing, but would be allowed to retain the directorships of their clinics.[42]

Some of the rejected instructors had a right to petition the Military Government for reinstatement.[43] The petitions ignored or downplayed all involvement with National Socialism, often portraying the scholar in question as a victim of the Nazis who had been forced to join the SA or the party. In most cases, scholarly qualifications made retention on the various faculties necessary. For natural scientists, Karl Freudenberg believed, a clear line could be drawn between ideological engagement and scientific research. "The work of a physicist, chemist, zoologist, etc.," he wrote in January 1946, "differs from that of theologian, philosopher, historian, etc. insofar as it is not immediately connected with political meaning . . . A natural scientist, on the other side, did not necessarily fall into conflict with his own mental existence if he did the same . . . Most of the natural scientists are completely absorbed in their research work and do not occupy themselves with political reasoning. The decision [to join the party] was therefore taken more easily and in many cases with the intention of clearing away hindrances to research."[44] Freudenberg, then, hoped to retain Heinrich Vogt, who had joined the party in 1932 and played an active role (as Freudenberg was no doubt aware) in hounding Jewish scholars out of Heidelberg in 1933 and 1934. Despite his past, Freudenberg considered Vogt's scientific abilities too estimable to warrant his dismissal.[45]

Bauer was particularly intent on retaining not only Karl Schmidhuber and Johann Daniel Achelis, but also eight other instructors, including Hans Runge, the head of the women's clinic and the university's chief practitioner of forced sterilizations.[46] All eight had been members of the SA and the Nazi party and had been rejected unconditionally by the CIC in August. Bauer clearly envisioned submitting petitions on behalf of at least nine more men, including Viktor von Weizäcker, a renowned psychiatrist as well as a researcher in the T-4 ("euthanasia") program. That Bauer and others considered most professors' engagement with National Socialism to have been negligible is indicated by a list located in the Rector's files of names for which petitions would be submitted. Forty-four individuals are listed.[47]

On October 15, 1945, Gustav Radbruch and Walter Jellinek pleaded with Earl Crum, the American-appointed "University Officer" for Heidelberg, for the retention of Eugen Ulmer and Karl Engisch on the grounds that "both were enemies of National Socialism, both proved brave and active opponents." Engisch had belonged first to the Stahlhelm and then the SA and had joined the Nazi Party in 1937.[48] He was invited to Heidelberg by Wilhelm Groh, according to Jellinek and Radbruch, with the expectation that he would be "obedient." Engisch enjoyed a good reputation within certain party circles, they claimed, "on account of his kind and engaging manners." As for Ulmer, his rank as an SA-Truppführer was dismissed on the grounds that "he never applied for that rank nor actually acted as a Truppführer. But a refusal of this nomination was impossible and would have been regarded as high treason." Finally, Radbruch and Jellinek claimed that both men pressured Groh to halt student boycotts of the classes of their Jewish colleague Max Gutzwiller and intervened on behalf of the Jewish widow of a former faculty member who was threatened with deportation.[49] Neither Engisch nor Ulmer was dismissed by the Americans.

Less successful were Radbruch's efforts on behalf of Hermann Krause and Ernst Forsthoff. Radbruch was determined to keep both men on the Law Faculty, even though he acknowledged that they had been more than "nominal" party members. He argued that they had maintained their scholarly integrity and that Forsthoff had even become a "victim" of the Nazis because of his independent mind and religious convictions. Radbruch held Forsthoff to be an excellent scholar, a popular teacher, and not easily replaceable. The Senate concurred and supported the petition.[50] The Americans, however, demanded his dismissal. Forsthoff returned to his former chair at Heidelberg in 1950, having spent the intervening years as a successful freelance writer on legal and political subjects. Krause went on to teach law in Mannheim.

The Theology Faculty also attempted to retain compromised colleagues. Gustav Hoelscher petitioned Crum for the reinstatement of two junior faculty members who had been dismissed, Günther Moldänke and Heinrich Greeven. Hoelscher claimed both men were competent scholars, and had been forced against their wills to join the party. He claimed that "Moldänke was obliged to become a member of the party like all young officials."[51] As for Greeven, his "political attitude is quite clear and perspicacious. It is the straight line of an unfailing Christian conservatism. In the summer of 1933, not willing to enter the SA, he joined the so-called Stahlhelm, the counter-party opposed to the SA. But against his expectations, the Stahlhelm was incorporated by force and as a whole into the SA. So he became an SA man against his will."[52] But the CIC considered them both unacceptable. Regarding Moldänke, CIC Special Agent Thomas Emmet reported: "Subject joined the NSDAP in 1936 while teaching in a German Lutheran Seminary in Tartu, Estonia, where Nazism was outlawed and limited to subversive underground activities. During 1936 and 1937 he was a member of the Auslandsorganisation der NSDAP in Estonia. Joined the Marine-SA in 1934 and became a Rottenführer . . . In a letter dated July 19, 1939, Professor Odenwald (the Nazi theologian) reports to the Reichsminister für Wissenschaft [Bernhard Rust] that: 'After long hesitation, it can now be said without doubt that he [Moldänke] does not hold to the views of the so-called Confessional Church.'"[53]

Emmet's assessment of Greeven was even more unsparing: "Subject joined the Stahlhelm in 1932, which was incorporated into [the] SA in 1933. Became an SA Rottenführer. He received membership in the NSDAP automatically after 1937. In spite of being a clergyman of the Confessional Church and a Theologian, he did not withdraw from the SA or later from the NSDAP. He states that his only objection to National Socialism is that it turned against the Church. Otherwise, he is a strong believer in the National unity and 'Geistige Einheit' of the German race. He is anti-Semitic and militaristic. Was a front line Infantry Captain in this war." Daniel Penham concurred, adding "I do not think that Professor Greeven should be allowed to teach."[54] Apparently unmoved by the CIC's evidence, Earl Crum approved the reinstatement of both men to the Theology Faculty on the grounds that they were both qualified scholars and were needed as teachers and had not been more than "nominal members" of the Nazi party.[55]

The Heidelberg professor most intent on seeing his own faculty purged was Alfred Weber. As noted in the previous chapter, he would not accept what he considered to be compromised scholars and did more than most to bring back victims of the Nazi purges. He opposed Bauer and the rest of the Senate in his refusal to support Ernst Schuster's petition for reinstatement (Schuster had been dismissed by order of the Americans on January 16, 1946).[56] In Weber's view, Schuster's involvement with the regime was too extensive to justify his retention. Weber was similarly opposed to the reinstatement of Horst Jecht, also on the grounds that he had put his scholarship to use on behalf the Nazis' policies of territorial expansion.[57] But Weber's position on this issue was exceptional. By the end of 1945, Heidelberg's most influential professors had come to oppose American denazification policies outright and actively sought to reinstate compromised colleagues. It was in this increasingly tense atmosphere that Daniel Penham arrived at Heidelberg.

Evidence in support of some occupation officers' critique of the quality of local Military Government personnel—"largely untrained, often incompetent, and sometimes corrupt," as William Griffith put it—is provided by events at Heidelberg. The "University Officer" assigned full-time to Heidelberg in October 1945 was Earl Crum. Like Hartshorne and Penham, Crum was an academic—a professor of classical languages at Lehigh University in Pennsylvania—but there the similarities ended. In stark contrast to Hartshorne and Penham, he knew little about Germany, German academic culture, or the German language. What passed for his knowledge of the universities was a reflexive devotion to Humboldtian idealism.[58] He accepted the Heidelberg myth and was determined to take a hands-off approach to denazification. His views on the university's reopening simply parroted Karl Heinrich Bauer's. "By many of the Germans," he recalled in a 1949 article published in *The American-German Review,* "their oldest university, Heidelberg, is looked upon as a fortress of democratic liberal opinion ... As late as 1933, so far as I can ascertain, not a single full professor was a member of the Nazi party. Because of this fact, the hatred of the Nazi regime against Heidelberg was intensified.

Special Nazi agents removed most of the open-minded minded professors from their offices, replaced them by Nazis, and tried, against the intention of the staff of teachers, to make of it a 'Nazi university.'"[59] The responsibility for rebuilding the university was to belong to the faculty, and denazification was to be lenient.[60] There is no evidence in the records of the occupation, Crum's personal papers, Heidelberg University archives, or Baden state government archives that Crum devoted any substantial effort to investigating the past activities and present claims of any professors. Over and over, he took their side and opposed a thorough purge. Crum was enormously popular among the professors. Karl Jaspers admitted years later that he "helped us against the CIC [meaning Penham]—quietly, of course."[61] "Crum always represented American interests," Fritz Ernst recalled, "but it was our good fortune that he saw those interests best assured by giving the university entrusted to him the opportunity to demonstrate the value of its old spirit—in both old and new forms."[62] His departure occasioned a formal ceremony and fawning, sentimental tributes. Memoir accounts speak glowingly of his tenure there, and Crum conducted a friendly personal correspondence with Karl Heinrich Bauer into the 1960s.

Diametrically opposed to Crum was Daniel Penham. Penham was born Siegfried Oppenheim in Bad Hersfeld in 1914. He left Germany for France in 1933 and studied at the College de France and at the University of Besançon. While teaching in Besançon he became an outspoken critic of the Nazis and joined the French army and later the resistance. Following France's capitulation to the Germans in 1940, he relocated to the south of the country. Wanted by both German and French authorities, he obtained a visa to the United States in Marseilles. While he was en route, however, the Germans commandeered his ship and Penham was brought to Morocco and interned in the Ouedzem concentration camp. A sympathetic Moroccan official helped him secure release on the grounds of illness. In Rabat, Penham convinced officials at the U.S. Consul that his background and language skills would be an asset to the American military, and he was granted another visa. In the United States, Penham joined the Counter Intelligence Corps, which counted many émigrés among its ranks. Like many CIC agents, he was a scholar and was familiar with German intellectual and academic traditions. His virulent anti-Nazi sentiments were only intensified by what he witnessed when he returned to Germany in the Allied invasion of France in June 1944. Having fought in France, Belgium, and Germany, Penham participated in the liberation of the Nordhausen ("Dora") concentration camp, where the Nazis employed slave labor in building V-1 flying bombs and V-2 rockets.[63] His first encounter with postwar German academic culture took place not at Heidelberg, but at the University of Leipzig during the brief American occupation of that city in 1945. There Penham was in charge of the initial screening of the faculty and helped direct the forced evacuation of German scientists to the U.S. zone.[64]

Crucial to the course of his later investigations at Heidelberg was that Penham considered his experience in Leipzig a successful one. At Leipzig, he wrote in February 1946, "a committee of completely reliable professors was set up led by Rector [Bernhard] Schweitzer, and Professor [Theodor] Litt, men about whose political reliability there can be no question of doubt. These men made a sincere effort to be of assistance in every way they could."[65] Schweitzer's own account of the period supports Penham's assessment.[66] Professors at Leipzig were eager to conduct their own investigations of their colleagues and make recommendations as to who should be dismissed. They felt, like professors elsewhere, that to simply rely on information provided in the Fragebogen might result in the same kind of categorical purges conducted by the Nazis in 1933 and 1934. After lengthy negotiations, American officials agreed to permit a faculty-led investigation on the condition that they were consulted. Daniel Penham was placed in charge of overseeing the investigation. But at Leipzig, unlike Heidelberg, there was a greater willingness among the professors to conduct a thorough inquiry and to work closely with the Americans. The initial investigation was aimed, Schweitzer noted, "against professors or Dozenten who were installed in their positions by political offices without sufficient scientific qualifications or those who promoted the goals of the NSDAP by disavowing the idea of science in or outside of party offices and had therefore gained personal advantages or had allowed National Socialist teaching entry into their own research."[67] Schweitzer and his colleagues provided the Americans with "incriminating material" on charged professors and Dozenten and considered the investigation's scope to have met the demands of the strict denazification directives. Penham apparently concurred.[68] The first screening ended in June with sixteen instructors dismissed, the investigation concluding "without fundamental differences in opinions between the occupying power and the university." Schweitzer certainly did not recall Penham as a renegade agent or a lunatic. On the contrary, he recalled, "the university owes considerable thanks to the leader of the investigation, Dr. Penham, and to the head of the Military Government's religious and educational affairs division, Captain Wakefield, for their intelligent responsiveness."[69]

Most likely in connection with his involvement in the evacuation of Leipzig scientists to Weilburg (near Frankfurt), Penham arrived in Heidelberg in October and replaced fellow Special Agent Thomas Emmet. Penham's presence elicited considerable interest among some professors, given his German background and familiarity with academic culture. Penham then undertook an investigation of the situation at the university that went beyond that conducted by Hartshorne the previous summer. Not only did he have access to both documents captured by the Americans and the university's own files, but he also made a point of consulting the published works of the professors he was investigating. He was well aware that party membership alone, while important, was hardly a sufficient indicator of the extent to which a professor had supported National Socialism. In addition, he sought out the imprisoned former Nazi student leader Gustav Adolf Scheel, who supplied Penham with all kinds of information about Heidelberg professors.[70] The university's own files, Penham recalled, provided him with no shortage of informants and witnesses: "There were dozens of letters involving the mutual denunciation of professors, as well as many other items incriminating them. During my interrogation I presented this evidence to the person being questioned. I found the general reply, 'Ich bin gezwungen worden' ['but I was forced'], utterly unacceptable and unworthy of a scholar when referring to his own words. Either they believed their own words or [were motivated] by . . . ambition. This was further evidenced in letters addressed to the Dozentenbundführer requesting [that] a new [Nazi Party membership card] be issued in order that it appear that they had joined the party at an earlier date than they actually had."[71]

Penham became particularly interested in Willy Andreas's past. As we have seen, Andreas had been an outspoken supporter of the Nazi "Machtergreifung" in 1933 and 1934.[72] In the initial investigations of the faculty conducted by the CIC and Edward Hartshorne, Andreas was excluded from the first postwar election for Rector because of evidence that local party officials considered him reliable politically (see Chapter 4), though he was allowed to conduct lectures after the university reopened.

Penham, however, considered Andreas too compromised to continue teaching. On November 30, he sent a message to Andreas:

> We would like to ask you to bring to our office from your array of publications the following books and essays:
> "Bismarck's Speeches"
> "Rektoral Address, July 1933"
> "The German People of the Reformation," 1937
> "Strassburg and Its Turning Points from the Middle Ages to Modern Times"
> "Richelieu," 1922 and 1941 editions
> Other than these, we request the essay which you edited in cooperation with Wilhelm von Scholz: "The Great Germans from Arminius to Horst Wessel."[73]

The last title aroused considerable suspicion in Penham, not least because Andreas had failed to list it along with his other publications in his Fragebogen.[74] As Penham subsequently noted in his report on Heidelberg: "Professor Andreas, for instance, who taught modern history at Heidelberg University, mentioned all the publications he had written except 'The Great Germans from Arminius to Horst Wessel.' In other words, he had so little respect for historical truth that he compared the pimp and Nazi 'martyr' Horst Wessel with the Great German leaders of history."[75] Other factors also led Penham to demand Andreas's dismissal. One was the fact that he had not resigned as Rector when the Nazis took power. Another reason was that Penham had found Andreas's March 27, 1933, letter to Joseph Goebbels (see Chapter 1), in which the historian offered to help the nascent Propaganda Ministry counter foreign anti-German "propaganda."[76] On February 18, 1946, Karl Heinrich Bauer informed Andreas that the Military Government had demanded his dismissal.[77] Although Penham concluded that Andreas was not fit to teach, he believed he should be granted emeritus status, which Andreas received in 1949.

Penham also concluded that Bauer was unfit to be the Rector. Bauer's encounter with Penham was not the surgeon's first with a German-Jewish émigré officer. On July 19, Military Government Special

Branch officer Frederick Wallach appeared in Bauer's office with information regarding Otto Dittmar, the head of the university's orthopedics clinic. Wallach had been a student at Heidelberg in the 1920s and a member of "Bavaria," the prestigious Jewish student organization. He accused Dittmar—who belonged at that time to a right-wing student organization—of inciting an anti-Semitic brawl against the members of Bavaria at a local wine bar in 1924.[78] Dittmar later went on to become a Storm Trooper, a party member, a member of the Dozentenbund and the Nazi Physicians' League, and a full professor at Heidelberg and director of the orthopedics clinic.[79] Wallach, who was imprisoned in Dachau, later managed to emigrate to the United States. By 1945 he had returned to Germany as a first lieutenant in the U.S. Army. He became a denazification officer in Bavaria but was reassigned amidst rumors that he had threatened professors at Erlangen with the closing of the university there.[80] In July, he confronted Bauer personally about Dittmar's continued presence on the Medical Faculty. Bauer, who recalled the encounter as "most unpleasant," accused Wallach of attempting to secure Dittmar's position for his uncle, Sigmund Weil.[81]

Penham's own investigation of Bauer led him to conclude that he was unfit to serve as Rector. Penham read Bauer's 1926 book, *Rassenhygiene,* noting the passages that advocated a race war, sterilization, and other measures of "racial protection." But he had also found examples of Bauer's vociferous advocacy of forced sterilization, and accused him of maintaining contacts with high-level members of the Nazi Party. All of these charges were accurate, and Bauer either denied or downplayed them. His first line of defense was to assert repeatedly to Penham, "Look here, I have a clean Fragebogen." But Penham was uninterested in Bauer's questionnaire. What mattered to him were Bauer's words and deeds from the Weimar Republic to 1945, and Bauer did not consider these to have compromised his suitability to serve as Rector.[82] Regarding *Rassenhygiene,* Bauer argued that it rejected explicitly the ideas of "racial fanatics" and received negative reviews from known Nazis and positive reviews from Jews.[83] To the charge, for instance, that he had delivered a lecture advocating forced sterilization to a surgical congress in Berlin (which he had done), Bauer replied, "Sterilization was first, if I have been informed correctly, implemented in the United States. In Nazi Germany it was the law. My predecessor at Heidelberg, the well-known anti-Nazi Professor Kirchner, entrusted me with the lecture (and himself confided in me that he took me to be a true hereditary biologist and anti-Nazi) in order to bring the matter out of the realm of propaganda."[84] This was a risky endeavor, Bauer noted, because many in the audience were sympathetic to National Socialism. He considered any statements that appeared to advocate forced sterilization to be only "a bit of necessary camoflauge"—necessary "provided that one's main purpose was to achieve the rescue of those with operable hereditary disorders from sterilization."[85] Bauer was thus claiming to have promoted the Nazi sterilization law in order to protect people from the Nazi sterilization law.

On February 12, 1946, Penham confronted the Senate with his charges and thirteen days later submitted a lengthy report to his superior officers in the CIC on his investigations. In Penham's view, the university had been opened precipitously. "In this agent's opinion," he wrote, "a tremendous mistake was made in opening Heidelberg University at the time it was done. Hardly had the last echoes of gunfire died way in the distance when with a hurry and flurry completely unjustified by the situation at the time, the doors of the medical school were thrown open last September without consideration for the fact that Heidelberg University, as well as all of the German Universities had been, over a period of twelve years, Nazified to the core. It will require at least another six months of careful, methodical investigation before it can be said that elements of potential threat to the security of the American occupation have been removed."[86] Penham agreed that the initial screening relied too heavily on the Fragebogen, which he believed were easily falsified. What was needed were exactly the kind of individual investigations in cooperation with "reliable Germans" for which so many Germans had been calling for months. Penham's investigation at Leipzig was conducted in this manner, and he had attempted the same at Heidelberg, basing his inquiries on individual interviews, cross-examinations, university files, and—most important—the published works of the professors themselves. Yet just such investigations met with fierce resistance. "Evidence thus far has shown," he charged, "that the University officials are either incapable or unwilling to take the responsibility for denazifying the University even partly upon their own shoulders. This agent has been compelled to undertake this tremendous task against the combined efforts of virtually every member of the University faculty and administrative personnel who out of fear expend their entire efforts in covering up for one another."[87] Penham also produced considerable evidence that unscreened students were being enrolled in clear violation of Military Government regulations, a problem endemic at other universities in the American zone.

Penham described in detail what he considered a pro-Nazi environment inimical to the occupation's goals and the security of occupation forces. Students, he claimed, regularly expressed approval for nationalist and pro-Nazi statements, expressions that only Karl Jaspers appeared unwilling to tolerate:

> Shortly after the occasion of the well-known incident at Erlangen University in January, where Pastor [Martin] Niemöller was so poorly received in his attempt to discuss the question of war guilt, Professor K. H. Bauer of Heidelberg discussed the problem in one of his lectures on medicine. Rector Bauer stated as follows: "You all know what happened recently at Erlangen. We don't want any similar incidents here. We want discipline and order here." With an eloquent gesture he declaimed then, "After fifteen or twenty years, history will tell who really bears responsibility for this war." At this time again . . . the students applauding what they obviously interpreted as Nazi sentiments drowned out the speaker's voice. No effort was made on the part of the Rector to stop this demonstration . . . In a medical lecture, Professor [Conrad] Spang mentioned a specific disease affecting only Jews. He said, "Unfortunately, we cannot observe this disease here any more, as the Jews are"—At this point, the Professor was interrupted by raucous laughter and trampling of feet. The Professor's only answer was a weak gesture; no attempt was made to stop the uproar.[88]

In the face of this evidence, Penham recommended that the university be closed temporarily so that a complete screening could be undertaken. He envisioned such a screening being conducted by Americans and reliable Germans, as many professors had demanded. But Penham had in mind only those truly uncompromised: "They should not have a trace of sympathy for persons who were Nazis. The Rectorate of Heidelberg University under American occupation should be held by a man with an absolutely clear background who is willing to lead a crusade for democracy. If persons in these positions, whom we appoint, are not ardent democrats and anti-Nazis, it is difficult to see how anyone can be expected to be one."[89] Heidelberg University, however, remained open and no such screening took place.

Around the time Penham submitted his report to his superiors, Bauer pleaded for help from the Military Government in a long memorandum to Earl Crum. "Heidelberg University," he began, "finds itself in a severe crisis." The arrival of Daniel Penham, Bauer claimed, threatened to undo the Committee of Thirteen's efforts to reopen the university. Bauer's revealing assessment of Penham's investigation is worth quoting in full:

> Whereas until now, and also as at other universities, the screening was limited to activism within the party, party membership, and membership in its organizations, now a searching has set in with the non-Nazis and anti-Nazis as to whether they had had any suspicious connection with the Nazis . . . It is clear that when one has been forced to go through a swamp for twelve years, one gets dirty in the process once in some form. With the greatest alarm we saw that suddenly an immense demonstrative force was attributed to Nazi documents; whereas in the whole world the Nazi system is known as a system of lies, Nazi documents, all of a sudden, have become the source of pure truth when non-Nazis or anti-Nazis are concerned. We have witnessed and we continue to witness that a Nazi document of the year 1935 exceeds the importance of the statements of 10 or 20 anti-Nazis of the year 1945. Not only are the long-since accepted professors screened again and again, but this screening was done and is done, as the man in question [Penham] said himself, "with passion," yet not objectively. Unimportant trifles are exaggerated enormously, and many simple facts are perverted into the very contrary, without our own statements being believed, even when they are given by ten or more anti-Nazis.

Bauer concluded that Penham, though "highly intelligent," was "filled with an inner hatred toward the university and that this hatred is developing into the pathological." In Bauer's mind, the case was one of lawlessness versus justice.[90]

Bauer won not only Earl Crum's unqualified support, but also that of the Senate, which refused his offer to resign as Rector. Toward the end of February 1946, the Senate compiled for Earl Crum a detailed list of grievances about Penham's investigations.[91] Signed by Fritz Ernst, Karl Jaspers, Gustav Hoelscher, Gustav Radbruch, Ernst Engelking, Otto Regenbogen, and Herbert Seiffert, the report began by noting that before Penham's arrival, the Committee of Thirteen enjoyed a good working relationship with the CIC. When Penham arrived, the members of the Senate expected "the new representative of the CIC to carry on the screening in the old way." By this they certainly meant cooperatively. Penham quickly disabused them of any notion that he might serve as a rubber stamp. The Senate's first complaint against him was that "again and again he shouted at professors whom he interviewed, even at those who were unconditionally accepted. He ordered a member of the teaching staff to sing the 'Horst Wessel-Lied' [a Storm Trooper marching song]. When the professor did not know any more of the song, Mr. Penham himself sang the last two stanzas . . . Concerning the university professors he said more than once: 'They are all Nazis!'"[92] Although there were efforts to address the various individual accusations leveled in Penham's report, the emphasis was on his methods and supposed mental instability.

Bauer and his allies, as we have seen, had repeatedly called for close cooperation between "trusted Germans" and qualified American officials in screening the faculties. Such an approach to denazification, they claimed, would be fairer than relying on blanket dismissals based on the Fragebogen. Daniel Penham concurred and attempted to conduct just such a careful and differentiated investigation. Certainly, given his scholarly background and experience at Leipzig, Penham was a "qualified American official." Yet when he turned up evidence of the Heidelberg professorate's extensive complicity with National Socialism and demanded a more extensive inquiry into the university's immediate past, Bauer and other professors forgot their earlier advocacy of detailed individual investigations and claimed that Penham was motivated by "inner hatred toward the university" and that his recommendations were therefore baseless. Had Penham really been so motivated, of course, he would not (as he later recalled) have spent "night and day reviewing the writings of the faculty" but would simply have condemned them en masse without reference to the evidence.[93]

Particularly disappointing to Penham in this context was Karl Jaspers's refusal to cooperate with his investigation. When Penham brought copies of the publications and dossiers of Heidelberg professors to Jaspers, he simply refused to read them, telling Penham that "I just don't have time for that." Without considering the evidence before him, Jaspers attempted to convince an incredulous Penham that the majority of his colleagues were not "real Nazis" but "fellow travelers" (Mitläufer). Jaspers instead supported Bauer's continued tenure as Rector and signed the university Senate's condemnation of Penham's investigation.[94] Though Jaspers would later claim that Bauer used him in order to limit denazification and to secure the quick reopening of the university, Jaspers himself bears partial responsibility for the retention or return of former Nazis to prominent positions in the university and the thickening of an atmosphere hostile to any reckoning with the professorate's support for National Socialism.

How do we explain the discrepancy between Jaspers's well-known reputation as the philosopher who, as Anson Rabinbach has written, publicly "endorsed the Nuremberg trials and conceded that Germans had justly been forced to become a 'pariah people,' deprived of their state because of its crimes" and his steadfast refusal to confront the widespread complicity of his own Heidelberg colleagues?[95] Jaspers, like dozens of professors, opposed extensive purges and considered them indiscriminate and fueled by blind vengeance. Penham later concluded that a combination of fear, naiveté, and a desire to "be magnanimous [and] cultivate friendships no matter what had happened before" led Jaspers to protect former Nazis. Penham could understand this position, but never accept it, since he considered it his "duty" to "remove professors who had participated in the building of the Nazi regime."[96] Jaspers's attitude toward émigrés also offers an answer to this question. He considered both those like Daniel Penham and those like himself who remained in Germany to be "outcasts" of a sort. That is, he believed that both categories of Germans rejected the nation that turned to National Socialism and remained loyal to the civilized and humane society they knew to have survived twelve years of barbarism. In *The Question of German Guilt,* Jaspers admonished those who left Germany to avoid passing categorical judgments on those who remained behind: "At present, a bad example of dodging into mutual accusations is given in many discussions between emigrants and others who stayed here ... Each has its ordeal ... [but] there is no growth of life in mutual accusation." He may have believed, in short, that Penham was indulging in the kind of sweeping indictments that could only impede Germany's process of self-healing.[97]

The response of American officials to Penham's charges was also overwhelmingly negative. His superior officer, Loran Elliott, was his only defender. "Merely reading this report," he wrote to the Seventh Army's intelligence division, "is sufficient to make the blood of any American boil with anger, aroused by the stubborn defiance of the so-called intellectual elements of what was once a famous, but of what is now a notorious, Heidelberg University." Elliott subsequently ordered copies of the report sent to Military Government officers responsible for educational affairs. "Rektor Bauer," he recommended, should "be summoned for a hearing; . . . be told in definite and harsh terms that his attitude thus far has been one that practically justifies his hanging; that he be given one month in which to denazify and demilitarize the university" or face prosecution for obstructing the work of occupation authorities.[98] Earl Crum's own response indicates that he seemed to be only dimly aware of what was going on around him until Bauer sent him the long memorandum of February 19. In any case, he took the university's side. On February 27, Crum wrote to his commanding officer that "Mr. Penham appears to have developed a hostile attitude toward the University. [I believe that I have] gained the confidence of the members of the faculty by giving them all possible aid in meeting and solving the delicate problems of reconstruction, with [the] result that no demonstrations have occurred. [I am] not at all sure that [I] can avoid outbursts of some sort if CIC continues to be active in university affairs."[99]

To defend his recommendations to his superior officers in Berlin, Penham showed them a sample of dossiers containing incriminating information on professors from the university's files. But he found no interest there in the evidence he had amassed. Officials in Berlin took Jaspers's side, informing Penham that the esteemed philosopher was "wise enough to decide whether a professor is a nazi or not."[100] When Penham returned to Heidelberg, he discovered that the remaining dossiers had vanished. In early March, Military Government officials decided not to close Heidelberg. John Steiner, then head of the Military Government's education and religious affairs division section in Stuttgart, informed a *New York Herald Tribune* reporter that "we found [Penham's] evidence to be trivial and inconsequential . . . It seemed to us that it was a tempest in a teapot."[101] On March 22, Steiner submitted his own report on the situation at Heidelberg, concluding that the main problem was Penham's personality.[102] Noting that Penham later rescinded his recommendation that the university be closed but continued to maintain that Bauer be removed as Rector, Steiner believed that this course might be necessary given Bauer's past publications. Indeed, partly as a result of Penham's investigations, seventeen more instructors were dismissed in early 1946.[103] Penham's influence at Heidelberg had been curtailed, however. The CIC was forced to move its office out of the university, and Special Branch officers took over the screening process.[104] Crum, who had revealed himself to be the Military Government's University Officer in name only, requested redeployment.

Penham's accusations should be seen in the context of the growing body of evidence that universities in the American zone had not been thoroughly screened and that substantial pro-Nazi or former Nazi elements remained on the faculties and among the student bodies.[105] Once again, a series of scathing reports published in the American press, particularly in *The New Republic* and the *New York Times*, fanned these flames of suspicion.[106] Exactly two months after Penham submitted his report on Heidelberg, Karl Loewenstein reported that Munich University's Law Faculty was packed with former Nazis and that its chairman was protecting compromised professors, while the university had not yet eliminated a chair in "racial sciences."[107] Walter Dorn, an American political scientist involved in denazification, concurred in an analysis written for Lucius Clay that echoed Daniel Penham's assessment of Heidelberg: "In my non-authoritative opinion, Military Government has made a nearly irreversible mistake by reviving the old university of Munich and other universities. Instead of charging a group of politically reliable and energetic professors with the construction of a truly democratic university, Military Government has sought to reconstitute the *old* university of Munich, naturally without Nazis. What was the result? No chairs are being occupied as long as there is the slightest chance that one or another Nazi professor might still be exonerated . . . [but] professors and Dozenten are available."[108] Franz Neumann also concurred with Penham. Noting in the journal *Commentary* in 1946 that the examination of professors' publications had led to the discovery that "the majority of them had preached pro-Nazi, militarist, and anti-democratic doctrines," Neumann concluded that "the mistake of hastily opening all universities, instead of opening a few with teaching personnel of unimpeachably democratic views, has now to be paid for."[109] Edward Hartshorne was similarly dismayed when he surveyed the situation at Würzburg. "The sad fact," he wrote in his diary six days before his death, "is that Rector [Josef] Martin is about the only reliable anti-Nazi there, and that there is no such thing as an anti-Nazi leadership. Würzburg is at about the stage that Frankfurt, Marburg and Heidelberg were, on average, a year ago."[110] Hartshorne and other officials were not much more optimistic about the university at Erlangen.[111] Colonel Gordon Browning also found the situation at Würzburg intolerable: "Not only was the clinic Nazi, but every member of the library [staff], two thirds of the administrative staff, and two members of the division of liberal arts were shown to be Nazis. One was teaching 'Germanics,' which was the system of mysticism on which the 'superior race' theory partly rested."[112]

Marvin Boyle, the chief of the Military Government's Policy Enforcement Branch, summarized the situation in November 1946. Investigations revealed that, according to current German law, 1,035 out of a zonewide total of 2,477 faculty and staff could be considered Nazis, yet regional (Land) Military Government directors had only ordered the dismissal of 239 of the 1,035: "In this connection, attention is particularly invited to [a] report on the university of Heidelberg where, of a total of 313 staff and faculty members, 104 were listed as Nazis and of this number the director of Baden-Württemberg has not seen fit to remove even one; although [a] casual check indicates that in at least 17 cases the evidence is so obvious that there is no question concerning the need for immediate removal . . . Clearly the present policy in Württemberg-Baden is to 'leave the rats alone to insure that the house is not burned down.'"[113] Boyle admitted that if all 1,035 instructors were fired, some universities would have to close. The Military Government did not take this step, but ordered another wave of dismissals that affected most of the universities in the U.S. zone. Thirty-three instructors at Munich were fired, 33 at Frankfurt, and 30 at Erlangen. At Erlangen's institution, the Law Faculty virtually ceased to exist.[114]

At Heidelberg, Special Branch teams conducted a series of investigations, including one of Karl Heinrich Bauer, which produced a particularly detailed and damning report confirming all of Daniel Penham's accusations. Rudolf Urbach, chief of Special Branch, concluded that Bauer "did not seriously oppose National Socialism actively. His ambitions were partly thwarted due to his one-fourth Jewish wife, but subject has no reason to consider himself as politically persecuted or a victim of National Socialism. On account of his background, he is not recommended for the position of Rektor of the University."[115] At the end of the year, the Special Branch teams recommended that seventy-two instructors be dismissed owing "to past party membership," though they had been cleared for employment by the Military Government or by the Spruchkammer (local civilian denazification tribunal). The list included four members of the Committee of Thirteen: Bauer, Fritz Ernst, Wolfgang Gentner, and Ernst Engelking.[116] Yet most of those recommended for dismissal remained on the faculty rosters and in the classrooms. Bauer served out his term as Rector and remained one of the most influential figures at the university for the next two decades. By the end of 1946, the American-led policy of denazification was coming to an inglorious conclusion, the slack supposedly being taken up by the Spruchkammern. The situation at Heidelberg and other universities at this point was summarized in a gloomy June 1947 U.S. State Department intelligence report. Structurally, the universities had retreated to their old forms, determined to protect themselves from state interference as they presided over the creation of a "small elite of intellectuals." Regarding denazification, too much autonomy had been granted to faculty committees, which fought to protect compromised colleagues while refusing to recruit clearly non-Nazi professors from elsewhere in Germany or from abroad.[117]

In late 1945 and early 1946, the Military Government was under enormous pressure from a variety of sides. Public support in the United States for extensive arrests and dismissals was for a time high, and occupation authorities, acting on the most comprehensive denazification policy of any of the four occupying powers, ordered thousands of Germans dismissed from their jobs. Yet American officials were also responsible for maintaining a functioning civil order that was to be administered largely by Germans. Meanwhile, resentment toward denazification among the German public grew steadily. The situation at the universities reflected these dilemmas. Both American officials and German professors wanted the universities reopened as quickly as possible. On the German side, however, resistance to denazification at Heidelberg and other universities was extremely strong. Indeed, a 1948 State Department intelligence report noted that the greatest resistance to denazification came from Germany's cultural elite (including university professors).[118] Such an atmosphere was hardly conducive to the kind of thorough purges deemed necessary by the minority of vocal anti-Nazis working in the Military Government. Daniel Penham, like Karl Loewenstein, Moses Moskowitz,

Stefan Heym, Frederick Wallach, and others, believed that German society had been thoroughly nazified and that extensive denazification was necessary to achieving and maintaining the peace. At Heidelberg, Penham faced a number of formidable obstacles. Virtually all professors opposed extensive purges. They believed that the number of "genuine Nazis" was in fact very small and proved willing to defend and retain compromised colleagues. By the fall of 1945, a solid consensus among them had developed that ranged from principled opposition to large-scale dismissals to outright sabotage of Military Government policy.

More important, there can be no question that German-speaking Jewish émigré officers elicited particularly strong fears among their former countrymen. The CIC's reputation among many Germans as "an American Gestapo" may have been a factor in the overwhelmingly negative response to Penham, despite the fact that the professors' experience with Heidelberg's CIC detachment up to the fall of 1945 had been largely positive.[119] In the alarmed responses of many Germans one can detect the resonance of Joseph Goebbels's propaganda exhorting them to fight or face the "avenging Jew." In a telling 1951 letter to Willy Andreas, Paul Schmitthenner recalled that he was identified and arrested by "a Jewish American professor of Germanistik in the service of the CIC." In a camp reserved for members of the SS, he noted that "an American Jew" had assaulted him.[120] In this context, therefore, it is not surprising that the presence of a thirty-one-year-old German Jewish occupation officer thoroughly at home in German academic culture and determined to conduct a thorough investigation sparked a hostile reaction among Heidelberg's professorate.

The large numbers of instructors dismissed by the Americans in the fall of 1945 must not be allowed to obscure the fact that the atmosphere at Heidelberg was one of steadfast refusal to confront the university's past engagement with National Socialism. Further, the hypocrisy of the near-universal German demand that investigations of individuals be conducted by U.S. authorities and "qualified" Germans was revealed when most professors rejected such a course of action in practice. Within a short period of time most professors were able to regain positions in academia at Heidelberg or elsewhere. That they were able to do so is attributable to the pervasiveness of the Heidelberg myth and the evolution of the entire denazification program from one that aimed primarily at purging former Nazis from positions of influence and authority to one that aimed only to remove the "taint" of Nazism. Denazification became, as Franz Neumann put it in 1947, "simply an administrative procedure, no longer a problem of right and wrong."[121] This evolution was realized in the Spruchkammer process and is the subject of the following chapter.

CHAPTER SIX

Whitewashing the Ivory Tower

My struggle within [the Nazi Party] and ultimately my opposition cannot be judged in a purely political sense, but must—by my way of thinking—be connected with my research and thinking on folklore. This was and has remained in a certain sense unpolitical.
—Eugen Fehrle to the Heidelberg Spruchkammer, September 28, 1947

In March 1946, the United States turned the bulk of the responsibility for denazification over to the Germans in the form of local civilian tribunals known as Spruchkammer.[1] The tribunals whitewashed the Nazi pasts of thousands of Germans and facilitated the return of many compromised people to positions in the civil service, education, the media, business, and cultural life. Based on the long-inaccessible files of the tribunals in and around Heidelberg, this chapter examines the Spruchkammer process at the university. The purpose of this chapter is not to revisit the many shortcomings and failures of the process itself. My emphasis is on the ways in which the accused explained their relationships to National Socialism. Professors charged by the Spruchkammer constructed elaborate and remarkably similar narratives of defense and justification regarding their engagement with National Socialism. Above all, these narratives severed politics and ideology from scholarship and allowed compromised professors to present themselves as nominal party members and "purely objective" scholars and thus as not implicated in the regime's crimes. By respecting the autonomy of scholarship, acting as bulwarks against radical party elements, and by helping Jews and other persecuted individuals, they had, they said, become opponents of the regime, and they claimed they had "suffered" the consequences. The narratives thus bolstered the Heidelberg myth at the level of hundreds of individuals and contributed to an emerging political culture in West Germany that favored forgetting over remembering the past.

On March 5, 1946, Lucius Clay promulgated the "Law for the Liberation from National Socialism and Militarism." It was intended, in Clay's words, "to separate the nominal Nazi from the active Nazi so that the former could regain his place as a citizen and contribute properly to the economic revival of Germany."[2] The law decreed that hundreds of tribunals were to be constructed throughout the American zone, their judges and juries composed of German civilians with anti-Nazi or at least non-Nazi credentials. Every adult German was required to fill out yet another questionnaire—the Meldebogen. On the basis of the information provided, the tribunal would charge the individual in one of five categories: (1) major offenders (Hauptschuldiger); (2) activists, militarists, and profiteers (Belastet); (3) those with probational status (Minderbelastet, or "less incriminated"); (4) followers or fellow travelers (Mitläufer); and (5) those exonerated (Entlastet).[3] Penalties included incarceration, temporary suspension from or loss of employment, and a range of fines. American authorities were involved in that they provided information to the tribunals and could intervene and overturn tribunal decisions, but the job of oversight was undertaken primarily by local "Ministries for Political Liberation." The men placed in charge of the ministries and the tribunal judges and prosecutors were drawn from the major political parties, the Sozialdemokratische Partei Deutschlands, or SPD, and the Christlich Demokratische Union, or CDU.[4]

The most common category in which individuals were charged and classified was category four: Mitläufer, or fellow traveler. Of 950,126 cases tried in the American zone by 1950, over half (485,057) were so categorized.[5] In all of West Germany by the same date, 3,660,648 cases had been tried, and of those 1,005,874 resulted in Mitläufer verdicts. A total of 1,213,873 were exonerated, and 1,365,749 were amnestied or had their cases dismissed on other grounds. In addition, 150,425 were categorized as Minderbelastet, 23,060 as Belastetet, and 1,167 as Hauptschuldiger. Hence thousands of former Nazis now possessing clean legal bills of health began to return to positions in the public and private sectors. By the late 1940s and early 1950s, the German press was frequently reporting on former Nazis occupying high-level positions in the civil service, reflecting a concern—albeit a short-lived one—about the "renazification" of West German society.⁶ This situation also provided a propaganda windfall for the East German government, which considered West Germany to be a continuation of the Third Reich.⁷

The problems with the Spruchkammer process were legion. Finding enough genuine non- and anti-Nazi Germans to staff the "lay bureaucracy" proved impossible.⁸ A November 1946 Military Government intelligence unit (G-2) report listed several serious deficiencies on the German side: corrupt or incompetent German tribunal officers, inadequate sentences, a "lack of German interest and/or cooperation," political party interference ("especially by the KPD [Communist Party]"), and "fear of reprisals on the part of the Spruchkammer judges handing down a severe sentence and on the part of witnesses whose testimony would be detrimental to the accused."⁹ Conversely, the accused could often rely on neighbors, colleagues, pastors, or other acquaintances to provide positive affidavits (Gutachten, also known derisively as Persilscheine, after a popular brand of detergent) on their behalf.¹⁰ For the émigré scholar and former occupation officer Karl Loewenstein, the root of these problems was evident. "It seemed to me psychologically impossible," he wrote in *Social Research* in 1947, "for the Germans to condemn today what they had accepted as legal and utterly desirable only yesterday."¹¹ Further, the process revealed the tensions between memory and justice on the one side and democracy on the other: German officials were placed in charge of a program that was unpopular among the electorate to which it had to answer.

Given the vastness of the undertaking, the trials went on for nearly five years. The Military Government ended its supervisory role after two fitful years. To reduce the daunting caseload (one American reporter calculated in late October 1946 that at the current rate of evaluation the entire process would not be completed until 2018), Lucius Clay ordered a series of amnesties. German resistance and problems with the process itself were only part of the reason for the end of American involvement in 1948. Opposition from within the U.S. Congress was growing on the grounds that the program appeared inefficient and unworkable.¹² More important, denazification became the victim of a fundamental transformation in Europe's postwar political landscape. Four-power governance of Germany negotiated between the wartime Allies never materialized, and a string of foreign ministers' conferences from 1946 to 1948 failed to agree on the nature of a new German government and the terms of a peace treaty. The West had "changed enemies," as the late diplomat and historian Noel Annan put it.[13] Germans in the western occupation zones were seen by American and British officials as crucial allies in the emerging confrontation with the Soviet Union and securing this allegiance took precedence over denazification. The Soviets also curtailed denazification in their zone in August 1947. Changing enemies was to have profound implications for the postwar memory of National Socialism in both West and East Germany, because the crimes of the past and the extent of the support for the Nazis were to be forgotten in the face of present threats.

Existing records indicate that Heidelberg followed the general pattern of the rest of the American zone. That is, most charged by the Spruchkammer were convicted as Mitläufer or exonerated altogether. The cases of three of the university's most notorious Nazis never went to trial. Philipp Lenard, Ernst Krieck, and Carl Schneider—all charged in the Hauptschuldiger category—died before they could be tried. The other professors charged as Hauptschuldiger were Paul Schmitthenner, Karl Schmidhuber, Johann Duken, Ludwig Wesch, and Eugen Fehrle. Proceedings against Schmitthenner were suspended in 1951. Schmidhuber, Wesch, Duken, and Fehrle were all eventually convicted as Mitläufer. None except Schmidhuber returned to academia. Of the remaining thirty-seven full professors charged by the tribunals, twenty-four were convicted as Mitläufer, four were exonerated, six had the original charges against them dropped, and three died before they could be tried.[14] In short, not a single full professor was convicted in a category more serious than fellow traveler. Although the evidence is incomplete, most non-full professors charged by the tribunals were either convicted as Mitläufer or exonerated. The Spruchkammer did not, in the long run, have any substantial long-term impact on Heidelberg's or other universities' personnel structures.

I have selected for close examination nine cases—those of Eugen Fehrle, Fritz Ernst, Willy Andreas, Wolfgang Panzer, Ernst Forsthoff, Johann Duken, Hans Runge, Ernst Rodenwaldt, and Ludwig Wesch—representing the spectrum of disciplines, generations, extent of formal political engagement, and initial tribunal charges. The oldest,

Rodenwaldt, was born in 1878, the youngest (Wesch) in 1909. Rodenwaldt, Fehrle, and Wesch had belonged to the Nazi Party before 1933, while Duken, Runge, Panzer, and Forsthoff became members in or after 1933. Ernst and Andreas never joined the party. Fehrle was a folklorist, Ernst and Andreas historians, Panzer a geographer, Forsthoff a jurist, Wesch a mathematician and physicist, and Rodenwaldt, Duken, and Runge medical scientists. Fehrle was something of an academic outsider before 1933, and both he and Wesch owed their positions after that date primarily to their party membership. The others were established, well-known scholars (Duken, Runge, and Rodenwaldt) or clearly destined to become insiders (Forsthoff and Ernst) thanks to their own talents and the influence of their respective academic mentors. Fehrle's and Andreas's affiliations with Heidelberg extended back into the days of the Weimar Republic, and Rodenwaldt and Wesch studied there in the 1920s. Duken, Wesch, Rodenwaldt, Runge, and Panzer owed their full professorships at Heidelberg to the vacancies created by the purges, and Duken, Ernst, and Forsthoff were hired between 1937 and 1943. The sample also reflects a range of initial charges from Hauptschuldiger to Mitläufer. Finally, in five cases (Forsthoff, Ernst, Runge, Panzer, and Rodenwaldt), the professors were able to continue careers in the Federal Republic.

Eugen Fehrle was one of the very few instructors at Heidelberg who joined the Nazi Party before 1933. He became a party member in 1931, joined the SA two years later and the SS in 1940, and became an informant for the SD. As we have seen, he became one of the most prominent folklorists in the Third Reich by using his research to support Nazi claims to the superiority of the German "race." His rapid ascent up the academic hierarchy was also due to his party connections. Both the Gau personnel office and the Nazi students considered Fehrle one of the university's most important figures.[15]

In 1945, Fehrle fled advancing American troops but was soon arrested and then interned for two years in a Karlsruhe hospital. Both the Americans and the newly constituted Philosophy Faculty demanded his dismissal from the university. On January 5, 1948, the Heidelberg Spruchkammer charged him as Hauptschuldiger.[16] The initial case against Fehrle was unusually detailed and accurate. Most damning—beyond his various formal memberships—was his tenure as a university personnel adviser to the Baden Ministry of Culture from 1933 to 1935 (see Chapter 1). The tribunal considered him "responsible" for the firing of numerous professors, and did not regard him as simply a cog in a machine driven by forces beyond his control. His promotion from assistant to full professor and his numerous awards and memberships in scientific organizations in and outside Heidelberg (such as the Heidelberg Academy of Sciences and the German Academy in Munich) were attributed to his party connections. Further, the tribunal charged that he had put his research and teaching in German folklore to propagandistic purposes. "It is self-evident," the formal charges read, "that purely objective treatment of the field of German folklore as such does not entail activism in a political sense," but Fehrle had clearly attempted to justify National Socialism as an outgrowth of the German people's "historical and cultural development." Such propagandistic endeavors were particularly dangerous because Fehrle was a university professor, had direct influence over students, and had used his high-level position in the Culture Ministry and other offices to propagate his views.[17]

Fehrle had prepared for his own defense before he was charged. "My activities within the party," he argued in a thirty-two–page brief dated September 28, 1947, "my struggle within it, and ultimately my opposition cannot be judged in a purely political sense, but must—by my way of thinking—be connected with my research and thinking on folklore. This was and has remained in a certain sense unpolitical." This claim notwithstanding, the divisive political atmosphere of the Weimar Republic moved him in the direction of an academic field that could serve as a unifying force in German public life. His purpose was to back not just another political party's narrow agenda, but the entire German people through a movement of "national socialism" of the kind proposed by Friedrich Naumann. It was this idealistic impulse that drew him to the Nazi Party.[18]

Like many other German scholars in the 1920s, Fehrle was fascinated by the fascist regime in Italy, but after two visits there claimed to have been disappointed in what he regarded as Mussolini's "Machiavellian" theories of the state as "the end in itself." Hitler, however, considered the state a means to an end, "namely the maintenance and promotion of the people." Thus in 1935 Fehrle wrote in support of the new constitution, emphasizing the difference between the National Socialist conception and the "inner emptiness of the Wilhelmian state." But his hopes were soon dashed. The central problem was Fehrle's self-professed Catholicism. He claimed to have believed that religious sentiment was an integral part of the "Volkstum," an ideal not shared by party ideologues. Another issue was his professed devotion to the autonomy of scholarship. On this matter, Fehrle professed to have rejected the party's "racial" policies and anti-Jewish measures. Proof of this latter conviction was the assistance he provided to persecuted individuals. As for his tenure in the Culture Ministry during the height of the purges, he had only been carrying out orders. Finally, as one who remained committed to "objective scholarship," he worked as a moderate bulwark against the party's fanatics, such as Alfred Rosenberg, who worked to destroy German university traditions.[19]

Like other professors charged by the Spruchkammer, Fehrle produced a sheaf of affidavits from personal acquaintances, former students, and a diverse group of his former Heidelberg colleagues. Friedrich Panzer, for instance, defended Fehrle's academic appointment within the university as entirely in keeping with academic traditions in folklore and Germanistik and said it had had nothing to do with interference by the party.[20] In a similar vein, Martin Dibelius wrote that "Fehrle never struck me as a fanatical political theoretician; rather always as an objective-thinking scholarly worker."[21] Paul Schmitthenner claimed that Fehrle did everything in his power to alleviate the harshness of measures taken against the university in 1933 and after, and, most important, strove to protect the university from "radicalism and political irrationality."[22] Karl Meister, Willy Hellpach, and the Freiburg historian Gerhard Ritter all testified that Fehrle had tried to protect them from boycotts, house searches, pension cuts, and other forms of harassment. The tribunal also received an affidavit from Karl Jaspers. Although he stressed that he in no way was providing "an opinion about the overall behavior of an active National Socialist" and would not comment on "rumors" that came to him in the regime's early years, Jaspers did contend that Fehrle had taken steps to prevent or at least delay the deportation from Heidelberg of Jaspers's own wife and the elderly widow of Viktor Goldschmidt.[23]

On March 3, 1948, the Heidelberg tribunal held a hearing on Fehrle's case. Speaking on his own behalf, Fehrle repeated some of the basic arguments of his written statement. Otto Regenbogen was unconvinced and stated that Fehrle, Ernst Krieck, and Paul Schmitthenner had ruled the university as a "triumvirate," and that he believed that Fehrle was a National Socialist out of genuine conviction, the first on the Philosophy Faculty. Willy Andreas conceded that Fehrle probably helped to moderate the effect of the purges, recalling that he had confided to him that "a 200 percent Nazi" would have been installed in the Ministry if he had not served as an adviser to the Culture Ministry.[24]

The same day, the tribunal convicted Fehrle in category two (activist). Although the public prosecutor had recommended that he be categorized as Hauptschudiger, the tribunal concluded that mitigating factors warranted a milder sentence. It accepted, for instance, Fehrle's and his supporters' arguments that he had tried to thwart radical party influence at the university. It admitted that he indeed shared partial responsibility for the purges in 1933 and 1934, but his influence was "in no way solely determinative" and in some cases was used to mitigate some punitive measures taken against his colleagues. The tribunal also decided that although Fehrle did not espouse the most radical racial doctrines of Alfred Rosenberg, several of his publications had promoted Nazi ideology.[25]

The following month, Fehrle and his lawyers petitioned the appeals court in Karlsruhe to have the verdict changed to fellow traveler, and the public prosecutor responded with a demand that he be charged as a Hauptschuldiger, a move that was dismissed on a technicality. On October 2, the appeals court granted Fehrle's appeal on the grounds that "all the evidence indicates that the accused had been an opponent of the National Socialist rule of terror."[26] But Baden's Ministry for Political Liberation did not concur, noting in its rejection of the appeals court decision that it had not sufficiently appreciated the strongly condemnatory letters against Fehrle provided by the Philosophy Faculty and the Baden Ministry of Culture: "the accused was responsible for the dismissals of numerous scientifically important personalities from research and teaching, at least until 1935. As chairman he exercised tyrannical rule in the Philosophy Faculty along with Schmitthenner and Krieck, which all good elements of the faculty would consider unbearable. He was made a chair holder by the party, and not appointed by free scholarly agreement. As a teacher without exceptional importance, he abused his lectern to launch attacks against other scholarly sections of his faculty."[27] Fehrle appealed yet again, and on December 29 was convicted as a fellow traveler by the appeals court.[28] In July 1949, the verdict was reduced to Minderbelastete with no other justification than Fehrle's claims to have helped numerous foreign students during the war.²⁹ The Central Spruchkammer of North Baden finally resolved the case in January 1950 when it reversed the July 1949 verdict and categorized Fehrle as a Mitläufer.³⁰ Throughout this contorted process, Fehrle stuck to his basic defense: that he had been drawn early on to National Socialism out of idealistic and humanitarian considerations, had remained an "unpolitical" scholar, and had sought to mitigate the pernicious influence of the party on the university.

Fehrle was sixty-five years old in 1945. He never returned to academia after the conclusion of his Spruchkammer process, but was granted emeritus status at Heidelberg by Baden's Culture Ministry in October 1950. He died in 1957. As Peter Assion has noted, some of his works, cleansed of their racist contents, enjoyed a minor revival in the 1950s.³¹

In sharp contrast to Fehrle's case, that of the historian Fritz Ernst was dispensed with in a matter of months. In August 1946, the Heidelberg Spruchkammer charged Ernst as a Mitläufer and assessed him a fine of 500 Reichsmarks. An indignant Ernst considered the charges "characterized by exceptional pettiness" and appealed. The basis of his objection was that his membership in the SA was forced upon him and that he sought to leave it as soon as possible. He did give up his membership a year later "without the security of a position or income," and he resisted several requests at Heidelberg to join the NSDAP itself. Finally, he demanded exoneration on the grounds of his "active opposition" to National Socialism. "I have influenced students against National Socialism," he wrote, ". . . I suffered disadvantages from my well-known oppositional stance, which had an influence on students: public attacks by the Studentenführer, restrictions on my teaching through Wehrmacht duty . . . removal from the directorship of the regional studies institute and my replacement by Fehrle, removal of my assistants on the basis of political denunciations."³² In his defense, Ernst collected affidavits from several former students and Richard von Kienle, the Dozentenbundführer's "trusted man" in the Philosophy Faculty, who supported Ernst's claim that he had twice resisted requests that he join the Nazi Party.

Most striking was a sworn statement from the Tübingen historian Heinrich Dannenbauer. Dannenbauer reported that it was well known among colleagues and students that Ernst was highly critical of National Socialism. "From the beginning," he noted, "he had difficulties with the university party organizations" and was mistrusted by the Württemberg Culture Ministry in Stuttgart. Hence Dannenbauer advised Ernst to give in to pressure from the local Dozentenfüher, a Professor Matthaei, to join the SA. Since Ernst was already considered "politically untrustworthy" in local party circles and Matthaei's "invitation" in reality was a "demand," it would have been career suicide for Ernst not to join. Ernst, however, proved to be an unenthusiastic Storm Trooper and left the SA voluntarily in 1935.[33]

This was not Dannenbauer's assessment of Ernst at the time. In a May 7, 1934, letter to the Württemberg Culture Ministry, Dannenbauer praised not only Ernst's abilities as a scholar and his collegiality, but also his political reliability. The best witness in support of this judgment, Dannenbauer suggested, was the Dozentenfüher, Professor Matthaei. Matthaei, "after thorough consultations with old party members," named Ernst as "deputy leader" of the Philosophy Faculty's Dozentenschaft, because Ernst was "the most dedicated and reliable man among the young instructors that we could find for this assignment, despite the fact that he was one of the youngest." Dannenbauer himself could attest that Ernst had "the strongest interest in all questions regarding military policy" and that only poor health had prevented him from pursuing a career as an officer. Finally, during a brief assignment teaching at a German school in Buenos Aires in 1929 and 1930, he clashed with the school's directors and local German Foreign Office officials in his drive to maintain the "pure German character of the foreign schools." Ernst was, Dannenbauer claimed, subsequently drummed out of the school as a "crass nationalist."[34]

The tribunal, which included Emil Henk as one of the assessors, reviewed Ernst's case in September and concurred with his defense. Its final decision—"Entlastet," or exonerated—was in fact taken word for word from Ernst's own letter to the tribunal. It noted that he "formally" belonged in the Mitläufer category because of his two-year membership in the SA and his membership in the Dozentenbund after 1942. But he would not be charged as such because of his "active resistance" to National Socialism. The evidence for Ernst's "resistance" was that he willingly left the SA as a Privatdozent without regard for his own professional advancement, that he twice refused to join the NSDAP, and that he wielded unspecified "influence over students in an anti-National Socialist manner." The tribunal then concluded that such resistance had cost him in the form of "public attacks by the Studentenführer" and the endangering of his position at Heidelberg.³⁵ Forty years old when he was acquitted, Ernst continued to teach at Heidelberg, serving two consecutive terms as Rector from 1961 to 1963. In December 1963, he took his own life.

Ernst's colleague Willy Andreas, sixty-one years old in 1946, had never belonged to the NSDAP or any of its affiliated organizations. A conservative nationalist, he had been an outspoken supporter of the Nazi "national revolution" in 1933 and viewed National Socialism as "Germany's destiny" (see Chapter 1). He dutifully oversaw the first wave of dismissals in the wake of the Law for the Restoration of the German Civil Service. In the ideologically charged atmosphere of 1933 and 1934, Nazi students and his successor as Rector, Wilhelm Groh, considered him more of a relic of the past than a builder of the future National Socialist university. He left the post of Rector under a barrage of criticism from Groh and Nazi students, but continued to teach and publish. As we have seen, he was dismissed by order of the Americans in February 1946 because of his role as Rector in 1933, his publications, and the party's positive assessments of his political reliability.

In his Meldebogen, Andreas set the tone for his Spruchkammer defense. He had not belonged to the Nazi Party or any party organization. He had, between 1933 and 1937, been a "förderndes Mitglied" of the SS, meaning a contributor of regular "donations," though he claimed to have twice rejected requests from the local solicitor. Not only did Andreas's lack of party membership place him in the exonerated category, he further claimed that "in October 1933 I was denounced officially and publicly by the first Nazi Rector of the University and in the name of the government and party as an enemy of the state."³⁶ In September 1946, the public prosecutor recommended to the Heidelberg Spruchkammer that Andreas be convicted as a fellow traveler. Though he had not been a party member, he had nonetheless belonged to the German Academy in Munich since 1935, had been a contributor to the SS, and had remained co-editor of the biographical encyclopedia *Grosse Deutsche (The Great Germans)* at the time when it included an entry on the Nazi martyr Horst Wessel.³⁷ The public prosecutor also made reference to an October 1945 report by CIC Special Agent Thomas Emmet, which concluded that Andreas was a "strong anti-Nazi [during] 1933–1936" but "beginning [in] 1937 showed more cooperation with Nazis and found limited approval."[38]

Andreas rejected the charge of fellow traveler. Regarding his donations to the SS, he noted that this fact was known to the Americans in 1945, and not even Daniel Penham found the matter objectionable. Regarding his co-editorship of *The Great Germans* he claimed that he had nothing to do with the volume that included the entry on Horst Wessel (though he had remained a co-editor of the series). Regarding his political views, Andreas argued that they "proceeded—unbroken despite single concessions forced upon me—from my well-known advocacy for the Weimar Republic, for the Weimar constitution, and for Reichspresident [Friedrich] Ebert, from the honorary doctorate conferred upon [Jacob Gould] Schurman and [Gustav] Stresemann consistently until the military occupation of Heidelberg. Files will identify open and secret opposition during the dictatorship." Andreas also noted that he had become a member of the confessing church in November 1934 and maintained relationships with Jews before and during the war. He also recalled his defense of the university's autonomy and called attention to the attacks against him by Groh and Gustav Adolf Scheel. Regarding his offer to Joseph Goebbels in March 1933 to counter anti-German propaganda in the United States—the offer Andreas had initially told Daniel Penham he had not made—Andreas argued that it had been written in response to a request from the Propaganda Ministry to all university rectors, and Andreas felt it his duty to reply.[39]

Swayed by these arguments and the numerous positive statements from Friedrich Meinecke, Theodore Heuss, Gustav Radbruch, Martin Dibelius, Walter Jellinek, and others, the Heidelberg tribunal exonerated Andreas in March 1947. Neither in the public prosecutor's initial charge nor in the Spruchkammer's final decision was any reference made to Andreas's public pronouncements heralding the National Socialist revolution. Nor had there been any attempt to assess the extent of his responsibility for the first stage of the purges. None of his publications (other than *The Great Germans*) had been examined. Andreas, with the help of his supporters, had reconstructed his past to present himself as pro-republican, anti-Nazi, and a victim of Nazi persecution.[40]

Although exonerated by the tribunal, Andreas regained his former position in the Philosophy Faculty only in July 1949. During his period of suspension from the faculty, the Culture Minister for North Baden, Franz Schnabel, a professor of modern history at the Technical College in Karlsruhe, attempted to secure Andreas's vacant chair for himself. The Philosophy Faculty fought what it considered a blatant incursion into its autonomy by the state government, but it seemed cool to the idea of Andreas's return.[41] As Otto Regenbogen pointed out in a letter to the Spruchkammer, the faculty considered Andreas to have been not a convinced National Socialist but a conservative nationalist.[42] The problem may have been the antipathy of Andreas's longtime nemesis, Fritz Ernst, whom Andreas had denounced to American officials in 1945. In any case, Andreas retired as an emeritus professor in November 1949, just four months after he finally won reinstatement to the faculty.

The geographer Wolfgang Panzer, dismissed from Heidelberg by order of the Americans in November 1945, was charged by the Heidelberg Spruchkammer as Minderbelastet in January 1948. He had belonged to the NSDAP from 1934 to 1939, had served as a Referent in the Reich Ministry of Education, had been the co-founder of Heidelberg's Westforschung Institute, had been an army aide de camp in France, and later had served as a high-level official responsible for wartime cartography in the army's high command. In 1943, he was transferred to a newly created military geography group in Italy.[43] In his statement to the tribunal, Panzer claimed to have joined the party in 1934 while he was a visiting professor at Sun Yat-Sen University in Canton, China: "I had never before belonged to a party. I had not been forced to join the [Nazi] Party, but took this step—not an easy one for me as a scholar—in awareness of a duty that I could not elude . . . it appeared to me proper in order to improve the nation's living conditions and to guide it along a peaceful path to a better reputation among other nations (I had lived abroad nearly uninterrupted[ly] since 1929). At that time, nearly the entire small German community in Canton—about one hundred people in a city of one million inhabitants—belonged to the party. It was an avowal of German identity and not of a political orientation."[44] Panzer returned to Germany, however, to find local party officials petty and diffident, and regretted that "the ideals that we had in mind abroad and that had been loudly declared were felt so appallingly little" at home. Thus disillusioned, he felt himself to be only a nominal party member. In any case, he did not need to use his party membership as a "political tool" in his professional life, since "as a scholar, I kept political thought at a distance."[45]

Yet he served briefly in the Reich Ministry of Education during the period of the most extensive purges at the universities. While lecturing at the University of Berlin after his return from China in 1935, he was asked by representatives of the Ministry to advise it on the creation of a German university abroad (Auslandhochschule) and at the same time lend his support as an adviser in the Ministry's sections for geography, folklore, and geopolitics. He felt he had no choice but to accept, because his teaching position in Berlin was not secure. At the Ministry, he asserted that "I had the task of processing, commenting, and advising, but no authority to sign anything. I can affirm that in all opinions in my area of specialty I applied the strictest objectivity and endeavored to compensate and abrogate all existing antagonisms between certain tendencies in the schools, particularly where they threatened to become shifted onto a political track."[46] Further, he claimed that no dismissals took place during his brief service in the Ministry, and that even prominent non–party members received invitations to teach at universities. His own invitation to Heidelberg in early 1936 was the result of recommendations by the Philosophy Faculty and a decision of the Culture Ministry in Karlsruhe and not that of the Education Ministry in Berlin.[47]

Panzer claimed to have rejected all forms of Nazi race doctrines, saying his extensive travels among "foreign races" had imbued in him tolerance and respect for non-Western cultures, and claimed to have fostered and maintained contacts with numerous Jews in the United States and in Germany. Further, he said, his service in World War I had deepened his religious convictions and he had henceforth never abandoned his evangelical Christian faith. In short, he had a "strictly scholarly personality" and was a person of ideals and humanity. "Idealism alone" had brought him into the Nazi Party "because I believed in the possibility of the realization of ideals" that Hitler had later "abandoned so abysmally."[48] On March 10, 1948, the tribunal convicted Panzer as Mitläufer. It based its decision on the grounds that his scholarship had not been compromised by Nazi ideology (namely, that he had never advocated "imperialism"), that he had held Jewish scientists in high regard, had remained true to the evangelical church, and had received numerous positive affidavits from four Heidelberg colleagues, Fritz Ernst, Johannes Hoops, Karl Freudenberg, and Willy Hellpach.[49] Although he did not regain his former chair at Heidelberg, he remained a prominent presence among West German academic geographers and by the early 1950s was teaching again at the University of Mainz.

The Americans, as we have seen, ordered Ernst Forsthoff dismissed from his position in early 1946 despite strong support for his retention by the Law Faculty and the Senate. On November 25, 1946, the Heidelberg Spruchkammer charged him as an "activist, militarist, and profiteer." Forsthoff's various formal memberships—NSDAP since 1938, SA from 1933 to 1934, and the Dozentenbund from 1938 to 1945—placed him in the fellow traveler category. It was his publications, however, that led the tribunal to charge him as an activist. According to the public prosecutor: "he publicly contributed materially through his writings and through his employment of the personal esteem of the university instructor in political and cultural life to the strengthening and maintenance of the National Socialist rule of terror."[50] The references here were to Forsthoff's *Total State* and his odious edited collection, *German History in Documents since 1918*. Regarding the former, the prosecutor cited numerous passages and argued that Forsthoff had "almost page for page moved away from democratic principles, belittled them, and instead advocated the National Socialist conception of the state, meaning that of brutal power." In short, "the accused negated painstakingly achieved findings of constitutional law of nineteenth-century German legal instruction, stepped consciously in opposition to the democratic principles of the nations of the West, and propagated the National Socialist state conception in various sectors: the leadership principle, the leadership hierarchy, obedience and loyalty, military preparedness, the sanctity of orders, the justification of racial hatred."[51] As for *German History in Documents since 1918*, it could not have been a stronger propaganda tract had it been written by Joseph Goebbels himself. Its justification of Nazi laws, glorification of the army, and vilification of communists and Jews (one of the book's sections is titled "The Jews as Racially Foreign Bodies") was considered particularly pernicious, since the book was aimed at the broad reading public and not simply other jurists. The fact that the third edition appeared in 1943 cast considerable doubt in the prosecutor's mind on Forsthoff's claims that he had long been disillusioned with the party.[52]

On the content of his publications and his enthusiasm for National Socialism, Forsthoff commented:

> I counted among many Germans who greeted the seizure of power with great hopes, only after to be bitterly disappointed. Because I held that the bourgeois constitutional state in the form of the Weimar constitution was no longer viable after the inflation and world economic crisis (since 1929), I believed that National Socialism was at that time capable of giving the German people politically and socially a new form and order. In this sense I wrote in early 1933 my brochure, *The Total State*. With it was joined the further goal of opposing the total claims of the party and strengthening the positions of the relevantly experienced and moderate tenured civil service. That is what was meant by the title. It is the writing of an outsider, who felt himself as such and therefore not consciously an advocate of the party. The essay would be sharply rejected by the party and in the total state generally. After I was won over in 1934 to a critical and ultimately sharply negative position on National Socialism, I hindered a further edition of the essay, which I also in my later writings never cited because I recognized it as based on mistaken assumptions and also because my personal views had changed fundamentally. On the same justification was my *German History in Documents since 1918* created. It was at the time of the seizure of power about half finished and would be completed in 1934. A new edition appeared in 1943 at the inducement of the army high command.[53]

When he talked about party criticism of his work, Forsthoff was referring to Alfred Rosenberg's disapproval of *The Total State*. Disagreements among scholars and between scholars and party figures during the Third Reich could, as this example illustrates, be useful to those facing the Spruchkammer. The bulk of Forsthoff's defense is devoted to presenting himself as only a formal member of the party and later as not only a victim of Nazi persecution, but an active opponent of the regime. At the University of Frankfurt, the chairman of the Law Faculty "requested" that its members join the party or one of its affiliates. Forsthoff chose the SA but claimed to have withdrawn from it in the wake of the Röhm purge. In 1937, he joined the Nazi Party under compulsion from the Gauleiter. Forsthoff was at that time teaching in Königsberg, and was informed that he could not remain in the Prussian civil service without party membership. Since he was also chairman of the Law Faculty and thought it was in the faculty's best interests that he remain in that position, he acceded to the "request."[54]

Like other Spruchkammer defendants, Forsthoff proclaimed that he had protected persecuted colleagues at great professional and personal risk. "I was opposed from the beginning," he claimed, "to the terror measures of the regime, which began with the coordination and the persecution of dissenters." As chairman of the Law Faculty at Königberg he endeavored to keep party influence at bay. In his teaching, he rejected Nazi legal doctrine and strove to "convey an ethically founded conception of law" to his students. Regarding his writings (excluding *The Total State* and *German History in Documents*), he called attention to publications in the late 1930s and early 1940s that advocated limits on arbitrary state power and stressed that they had come under heavy fire from party ideologues.[55]

Forsthoff, like other professors, also claimed to have been guided in these antiparty measures by deeply rooted religious convictions (in his case, the evangelical church). In particular, he became an outspoken opponent of an SS proposal to turn the cathedral in Quedlinburg into an SS shrine. He also stated that he had advocated the rights of the church in the Nazi state and championed the independence of the church from state authority. Finally, Forsthoff noted that since August of 1942, he had joined a resistance circle that included conspirators in the assassination attempt against Hitler in July 1944. Although he was not identified among the conspirators, he argued that he had been "persecuted" by the party, particularly after accepting an invitation to teach at the University of Vienna in 1941. This "persecution" amounted to various kinds of petty harassment and was probably a result of Alfred Rosenberg's and Gauleiter Baldur von Schirach's dislike of Forsthoff's activism on behalf of the church and of some of his writings. Such protestations formed the basis of his request to the Spruchkammer that he be exonerated.[56] Like most of his colleagues, Forsthoff was able to produce a large number of positive affidavits in support of most of his claims.

He was finally charged as a fellow traveler. From 1946 to 1950, he enjoyed success as an independent writer on legal and political issues and served in the state government of Schleswig-Holstein. He was tried by the Kiel Spruchkammer in 1947 and exonerated in January 1948.[57] In the summer of 1950, Forsthoff was invited by the Heidelberg Law Faculty—at that time the chairman was Forsthoff's former colleague Eugen Ulmer—to hold lectures on public law. In the winter semester of 1950–51, he was reappointed to his former full professorship on the basis of Article 131 of the "Basic Law" (the West German constitution), which facilitated the reinstatement of former Nazi Party members into the civil service.[58] Having become one of the most influential conservative legal theorists in West Germany, he retired as an emeritus professor in 1967.

Johann Duken, along with Eugen Fehrle, was one of the few Heidelberg professors to be charged in the Hauptschuldiger category. Duken was head of the pediatrics clinic when the war ended. Among the first group of instructors rounded up by the CIC in early April 1945, he was interned for the next two years. Duken was also one of the few members of the Medical Faculty whom even Karl Heinrich Bauer considered unacceptable for reinstatement in 1945. At Heidelberg, Bauer wrote to the Baden Ministry of Culture in June 1945, it was well known that Duken had long been an "extreme National Socialist" who had advocated "euthanizing" sick children in his lectures and had become "one of the most important members of the SD."[59] Upon his release Duken moved his family to Sinsheim, near Heidelberg. On January 8, 1948, the Sinsheimer Spruchkammer charged him as a Hauptschuldiger.[60]

The tribunal's case against Duken was strong. He not only had belonged to the NSDAP, SA, Dozentenbund, and the Doctors League, but had joined the SS "on special assignment" in 1933 and had become a Oberstürmführer in 1939, had reported to the SD on the university, and had served in the SS's Racial Policy Office. Further, according to Duken himself, he had been charged in early 1933 by the government of Thüringia with the task of "partly reorganizing and partly creating anew the entire presecondary educational system" in that state. Following his transfer to the University of Giessen in October 1933, he was charged by local party officials with overseeing political education at that institution. Finally, the tribunal—again drawing from Duken's own autobiographical statements—recounted his participation in numerous Free Corps units following the end of World War I and his subsequent participation in the Kapp Putsch (a failed attempt by right-wing paramilitaries to overthrow the Weimar Republic in 1920) and in the campaign against the breakaway communist regime in Munich.[61]

In his own defense, Duken prepared a lengthy statement entitled "A Defense of Professor Dr. Johann Duken concerning His Membership in the NSDAP and Its Organizations." Duken served as a troop doctor at the front in World War I and was decorated for bravery. After the war, he continued the study of medicine under Jussuf Ibrahim at the University of Jena, specializing—like his mentor—in pediatrics. He also claimed to have established Germany's first children's tuberculosis clinic. He admitted to having belonged to certain unnamed "volunteer military organizations," the members of which were "rightist oriented," but stated that "not a single one of them sought to overthrow the state." He was, as his efforts on behalf of sick children from poor families demonstrated, committed to "socialism," but not socialist parties, since they were "materialistic" and "ridiculed religious convictions." He was drawn to "volunteer units" in Jena because he hoped to avoid civil war, and claimed to have used his position as a moderating influence from within. Like others, idealism drew him to the Nazi Party: "I must emphasize emphatically that my connection to the party and its organizations did not result from personal opportunism or because pressure had been brought to bear on me. I sought to exert influence and this resulted from my sense of responsibility and from my love of mankind." Duken's professed humanitarianism was also evidenced by his devotion to evangelical Christianity, which went unbroken during the Third Reich.[62]

In 1933 he had believed that a "true Volksgemeinschaft" would arise in Germany. The Enabling Law, being backed by "nearly the entire German people" and supported by President Hindenburg, did not raise serious doubts in his mind about the Nazi Party's intentions. Although the decision to join the party was not necessarily an easy one, he believed that not doing so would have jeopardized his professional ability to serve the sick. Regarding his membership in the SS, Duken claimed that Heinrich Himmler himself had approached him about serving as an "adviser" on unspecified matters pertaining to "tasks of national education." Without having agreed to join, Duken nonetheless received an SS membership card. He claimed never to have held a rank (though after the war, the CIC had identified him as a Hauptsturmführer). He said nothing about serving as an informant for the SD in Heidelberg.[63]

The tribunal held a hearing with witnesses at the end of January 1948. Several longtime acquaintances of Duken's from Jena and

Giessen, including the theologian Heinrich Bornkamm, attested to his social and religious consciousness and his resistance to joining the SS. The only two figures from Heidelberg University present were Johann Daniel Achelis and Curt Görttler, two of the Medical Faculty's most notorious Nazis. Both testified that their former colleague had in fact been mistrusted by the SD because of his unwavering religious convictions.[64] Shortly after the hearing, Dukan was exonerated. The tribunal accepted at face value every positive assessment of Duken and was persuaded that, despite considerable evidence to the contrary, he was an opponent of National Socialism. He was, the verdict concluded, "an idealist" motivated by a strong religious and social consciousness. When National Socialism came to power, he believed that the National Socialist demand for a "Volksgemeinschaft" could serve as "cover" for his Christian-dominated worldview, which impelled him to serve the general public. The result was that Duken actually made an enemy of the party, which responded to his stubborn humanitarianism with "hostility, severe slander, and disciplinary actions."[65]

The decision sparked a public outcry and an appeal by the public prosecutor that sent Duken's case back to the tribunal. Following the verdict, the *Rhein-Neckar Zeitung* weighed in with several editorials. One noted that after Duken's release from internment, he had moved to Sinsheim, where he was unknown, and hence "not one member of the Spruchkammer knew anything about the political activity of the former head of the children's clinic in Heidelberg. Inquiries to the Ministry and political committee of the university resulted in no exhaustive disclosure. At the hearing, representatives from both bodies had excused themselves. A request to the political committee in Giessen went unanswered. So a thick fog was spread over everything incriminating but much glaring sunshine on that which was exculpatory."[66] The article then cited a letter found in the university archives dated October 21, 1936, from the leader of the Dozentenbund in Giessen to Carl Schneider heaping praise on Duken's "work for the building of the National Socialist state." The university responded that it had indeed informed the tribunal of its rejection of Duken, and since the tribunal had access to Duken's university files, the Medical Faculty did not consider it necessary to send representatives to the hearing.[67] On February 17, the newspaper reported that the Culture Ministry in Baden claimed that it had sent the tribunal a detailed report on Duken and had never received any notice of a hearing.[68]

Around the same time, the Sinsheim tribunal received several letters expressing shock at the verdict. One, dated February 17 and signed only "several Heidelbergers," echoed a common criticism of the tribunals: "It is a mockery that such a man, a member of the SS, SD, etc., should be exonerated. Is there any justice? It is an error of justice and a miscarriage and one demands the public ask—*who is the public prosecutor?* . . . One hangs the little man, the bigshots are let loose, so it was earlier and so it is today. Abolish the Spruchkammer because it is becoming laughable."[69]

On April 5, the public prosecutor assigned to the Sinsheimer Spruchkammer appealed the verdict and again charged Duken as a Hauptschuldiger based on evidence that the tribunal had ignored, namely Duken's own autobiographical statements and affidavits from Heidelberg and Giessen universities identifying him as a fanatical National Socialist.[70] In November, another hearing was held in which witnesses produced conflicting testimony. One, a former assistant in the clinic, considered Duken a "convinced National Socialist," while another clinic assistant declared the exact opposite.[71] The tribunal overturned its January 29 decision, but convicted Duken only as a fellow traveler. It refused to revise its previous assessment of his activities in light of new evidence and testimony. A Christmas-time amnesty relieved him of any penalties.[72] However, he, unlike many other academics, would not find another teaching position. The Medical Faculty at Heidelberg certainly had no intention of reconsidering him for reinstatement.[73] By July 1954, however, the faculty had reversed its position and sought to secure emeritus status for him and hence a larger pension.[74] But Duken died in August of that year.

The Medical Faculty was determined to retain Hans Runge, the former head of the university's women's clinic. In their initial report on Heidelberg, however, the CIC had listed Runge as among those faculty members "reputed to have been ardent pro-Nazis" and who "should be excluded from any future reorganization of the University along democratic lines."[75] Subsequently, Runge had been "unconditionally rejected" by Edward Hartshorne and the CIC in August 1945 on account of his membership in the party, SA, Dozentenbund, and Doctors League; he was dismissed in October, though he was approved for reinstatement in January 1946. The Americans had incomplete information about his past—the CIC's August 14 assessment of the Medical Faculty noted that "in spite of his excellent character, conduct, and mentality, it would be incorrect to say that he had never been more than a nominal Nazi. His party files are unfortunately missing."[76] Runge, as noted in Chapter 1, was responsible for carrying out forced sterilizations at his clinic in the wake of the "Law for the Prevention of Genetically Diseased Offspring." His case went before the Spruchkammer in late 1946. Although his party memberships technically placed him in category two, the tribunal concluded that on the basis of "credible witnesses" who testified that Runge had not been an active National Socialist, classification in the Minderbelastet category seemed justifiable. Since Runge had declared himself to be a fellow traveler and the Military Government had cleared him for reinstatement to the Medical Faculty, the tribunal noted that he could not be charged in a category higher than Mitläufer.[77]

In a letter to the Spruchkammer, Runge noted that as a full professor at Greifswald, where "fundamental political struggles did not take place," he was not politically active, above all because he "could not as a civil servant belong to a party that fought against the government." Further, he claimed to be "completely unpolitical," a (non)position that comported with the demands his profession made on his time. Yet in 1933 he did join both the Nazi Party and the SA. "My entry into the party," he wrote, "ensued following the establishment of the Papen-Hitler government out of a sense that after the splitting up of many small parties a great party of unity would arise and that on the other hand the NSDAP would lose its radicalism if it were in a position of responsibility. Reichspresident Hindenburg appeared to me to offer protection here." In an unusually frank admission, he added that he was not pressured to join the party, nor did he do so for professional gain "since I was already a fully tenured professor." His membership in the SA resulted from a demand from the Rector that all faculty members join one formation or another (the SA, SS, or Stahlhelm). It was the Röhm purge of June 1934 that "opened his eyes for the first time to true developments." He thus used the opportunity of his invitation to teach at Heidelberg to leave the SA, though leaving the party itself "had already in this time become impossible." Memberships in the Nazi Teachers' League and Physicians' League were justified as required by his profession.[78]

Like his colleagues, Runge claimed to have helped politically and "racially" persecuted individuals, especially Jews: "During the entire [Third Reich], I cared for Jewish patients continuously and particularly well, and consulted and maintained contact with Jewish doctors." Also like many others, he claimed a fundamental devotion to Christianity; he was "the grandson, son, and brother of evangelical pastors" and himself likewise a member of an evangelical congregation. Overall, his principal devotion was to the practice of medicine guided by ethical and humanitarian considerations: "I am convinced that not a single provable accusation brought against me on the grounds of [party] activity or an offense against human and medical laws can be proved." Only his nominal party memberships account for his temporary dismissal by the Americans in 1945, and his otherwise spotless record accounts for his rapid reinstatement in January 1946.[79]

The tribunal concurred and a few months later convicted him as a fellow traveler, imposing a 2,000-mark fine but no temporary suspension from his profession. The Spruchkammer based its decision on Runge's own self-defense and the strong support of Runge by Rector Bauer and the Medical Faculty. The only reference to his involvement in forced sterilizations was a single cryptic comment at the close of the verdict: "the accused supported objectively a population policy for a healthy Germany." But it was his nominal party membership, his efforts on behalf of the politically and racially persecuted, and his clean bill of political health from the Americans that were the deciding factors in his case.[80] Runge continued his career as a prominent gynecologist at Heidelberg into the 1950s.

Alongside Carl Schneider, Ernst Rodenwaldt was Heidelberg's foremost specialist in "racial sciences." As noted in previous chapters, he was well established as an epidemiologist and expert in "racial hygiene" before 1933. After arriving at Heidelberg in 1935, he taught the courses on race formerly assigned to Schneider. His publications reveal that he maintained a steady interest in finding ways to "purify" and "protect" a given "race." Although he had abandoned the party, he enjoyed the regime's support for his research and became a prominent instructor in military medicine during the war. As late as July 1944 he boasted in a curriculum vita (possibly for the military) of his "expertise as an assessor in Nazi 'hereditary biology.'"[81]

Rodenwaldt was arrested by the Americans and interned in a British camp. American authorities demanded his dismissal from the university because he had been a party member before 1933, because of his military service, and because—in the CIC's words—he had "held courses . . . on Nazi racial theories." Karl Heinrich Bauer wanted to retain him, but, knowing of Rodenwaldt's past, took a wait-and-see approach pending the outcome of the CIC's investigation. Although the Americans unconditionally rejected him for reinstatement in August 1945, he had already been identified as an important scientist by the American agency responsible for evaluating German scientific advances during the Third Reich—the Military Government's Field Information Agency, Technical, or FIAT. FIAT agents had accompanied occupation forces into Germany, sweeping up scientists, research, blueprints, patents, equipment, and other materials. Like many other scientists, Rodenwaldt was invited by FIAT to prepare a report on hygiene, epidemiology, and preventive and industrial medicine for "a series of reviews of recent advances in German science."[82] He accepted, and the results were published in 1948.[83] Rodenwaldt's expertise in hygiene was also needed by the nascent government in Baden, which supported his petition for reinstatement to the Medical Faculty.[84]

In his Meldebogen, Rodenwaldt recorded that he had belonged to the NSDAP from July to November 1932, the Doctors League from 1935 to 1945, the Dozentenbund from 1936 to 1945, and several other related organizations. He also noted that he had been an adviser to the military on sanitation and tropical hygiene, director of the Tropical Medicine Institute of the army's medical academy, and had been promoted to physician-general in 1939. He categorized himself as a Mitläufer.[85] In October 1946, the Spruchkammer could not seem to decide how to charge him. His membership in the Dozentenbund and National Socialist Aviator Corps (Fliegerkorps) placed him by the letter of the law in the Mitläufer category. But his early party membership pointed to a more substantial charge, as did the fact that he had been head of the Tropical Medicine Institute at the military medical academy. The tribunal concluded that it would study the case without reference to the public prosecutor's charges and decide on a charge.[86]

On May 5, 1947, the Heidelberg Spruchkammer declared Rodenwaldt to be Minderbelastet, fined him 5,000 marks, and imposed a two-year probation that prohibited him from teaching, publishing, or occupying high-level positions of any kind. The tribunal did not assign much importance to his five-month membership in the party in 1932, or to the fact that he had taught courses in racial hygiene at Heidelberg, or to evidence provided by a faculty colleague that he had infused his lectures with Nazi ideology and maintained good standing in the university's leadership during Paul Schmitthenner's rectorship. It did, however, examine in some detail Rodenwaldt's publications and speeches on "racial hygiene" from 1934 to 1940, and concluded that they revealed an "unjustifiable collaboration with Nazism" by legitimizing and supporting the regime's policies.[87]

Rodenwaldt's lengthy narrative in his defense also addressed specific charges against him, particularly those related to his advocacy of "racial purification." He claimed to have been shocked to find upon his return from internment in April 1946 that the Americans had ordered his dismissal.[88] He had not, after all, "during the existence of the Third Reich" belonged to the NSDAP, SA, SS, or SD. As for his brief membership in the party in 1932:

> When during the year 1932 I was in Dutch service in the Dutch Indies I joined the NSDAP in June [sic]. I thought it well to take this step as, seen from abroad, the splitting into many parties seemed to me to be ruinous for Germany, as it hampered the building of a government—and because I supposed that a great a uniform party would be another step toward the desirable two-party system. In November of the same year I resigned from the party after a perusal of the literature sent to me from Germany, from which I gathered that the party [sought to govern Germany by] totalitarian, i.e., absolutist, methods, and after having heard from Germany through private channels that the party did not stick to a single point of its program. Another decisive factor for me was that the foundation of Ortgruppen [local groups] was planned for the Dutch Indies. In my opinion, the excellent harmony of the German colony in the "Deutscher Bund" [League of Germans] would have been destroyed, a development which I believed would have been a considerable drawback for Germans residing abroad.

His resignation from the party was rewarded with a denunciation and the denial to him of a chair in eugenics at Munich University (it went instead to a party hack, Lothar Tirala) and the directorship of the institute dealing with sailors' and tropical diseases at Hamburg University. After a brief tenure at Kiel University he accepted an invitation to teach at Heidelberg. But his troubles with the party did not end here, since he resisted ideological agitation by the Hygiene Institute's assistants. Because of my "exceedingly open and frank utterances," he courted trouble with the party. He also "refused to remove Jewish authors from my library, in spite of regulations to that effect." Further, in a very common defense, he claimed that he "never hesitated to take up relations with a Jewish scientist and to stick to such a relationship, in spite of the prohibition and repeated warnings."[89]

How did he account for his advocacy of racial hygiene? Rodenwaldt contextualized the field this way: "'Racial hygiene' . . . is the expression proposed by Alfred Plötz for Germany for the field of research, for which in American and English literature the term 'eugenics' (created by Francis Galton) is used. To deal with the branch of science called 'racial hygiene' in Germany has thus the same meaning as working in eugenics. It therefore does not mean that a German 'racial hygienist' must necessarily be a representative and propagator of National Socialist race theories. Almost every civilized country, also America and England, maintains eugenic associations." For Rodenwaldt, his research in this area was strictly "objective" and unpolluted by politics. When he delivered lectures on "racial hygiene" in 1937, he did so to protect "objective" science: "I took over these lectures with the consent of the faculty because I believed that an objective and scientific handling of the problems of hereditary biology could be thus guaranteed. This would not have been possible by entrusting such lectures to a younger National Socialist lecturer. In 1938 I took over the course on lectures on 'Volk und Rasse' [People and Race] as well, which so far had been under the direction of [Carl Schneider]. This course had originally been intended as a National Socialist training lecture, but I changed its tendency into a purely anthropological one as to the descent of mankind." As a defender of objective science, he also noted that—though he was never offered the position—he might have accepted a post in Baden's Office of Racial Policy "in order to prevent impossible measures in this field." Further evidence of his "objectivity" was that he "never failed to emphasize the internationalism of scientific research" because he "worked for almost thirteen years within the boundaries of a foreign people in the Dutch Indies."

Rodenwaldt thus portrayed himself as one who served above all the interests of "objective science." By "internationalizing" racial hygiene and eugenics, he removed the particular German stain and severed the connection between mainstream medical science—of which Rodenwaldt was a prominent representative—and the regime's racial policies and medical crimes. Nowhere does he address his advocacy in publications stretching from 1934 to 1940 of the regime's laws regarding "racial purification." His military service represented patriotism and a sense of duty—"one does not necessarily become a militarist if one has been called to service in wartime and wore the uniform of a higher rank." In any case, he "considered a war between the peoples of Europe as the greatest disaster, and . . . I thought it to be the task of science to remove all misunderstandings which might lead to a war."[90]

Rodenwaldt also had the support of some of his colleagues, most notably Willy Hellpach. The assessment of a special committee of the Medical Faculty created to consider the case was more ambiguous. "It is not known to us," its brief report to the Spruchkammer noted, "that Professor Rodenwaldt was himself active in National Socialist activities or else displayed a demonstrative National Socialist attitude, if he also did not keep himself distant from party circles and to a certain extent enjoyed their trust. He was not held as someone with which one had to be careful in conversation."[91] Rodenwaldt's colleague Friedrich Pietrusky, however, took the unusual step of denouncing his former colleague. "In university circles," Pietrusky stated, "Professor Rodenwaldt was pronounced a typical opportunist . . . His arrogance and his sense of self-worth made him a sustaining pillar of the university as represented by [Paul] Schmitthenner. His lectures were clearly oriented toward Nazism, of this there was no doubt in the Studentenschaft! . . . During the war Professor Rodenwalt spent three days a week in Berlin as the leading doctor for troops in Africa." He made no secret, Pietrusky charged, of his party affiliations and connections.[92] Pietrusky's negative assessment was an anomaly, however, and it is clear that the tribunal was swayed by the abundant positive statements made by his current colleagues.

Rodenwaldt's lawyer appealed his client's conviction as Minderbelastet, and in March 1948 the charge was lifted and Rodenwaldt was exonerated. An appeals court had also examined Rodenwaldt's writings from the late 1930s and 1940s and had concluded that he had indeed endorsed National Socialist race laws. But Rodenwaldt "had not made any more concessions than had other scholars" and was not "a convinced National Socialist."[93] Despite his age—he was sixty-nine when the charges against him were lifted—he continued his stellar career in the Federal Republic. In 1967, the West German army's Institute of War Medicine and Hygienics was named in his honor.

Finally, there is the case of Ludwig Wesch, one of the university's most prominent promoters of "Aryan physics." Wesch, thirty-six years old in 1945, had studied at Heidelberg, earned his doctorate in physics, and then joined the Natural Sciences Faculty, first as an assistant professor and then (in 1942) as a full professor. Without question, he owed his rapid advancement to the influence of his mentor, Philipp Lenard, and to his party memberships, which were perhaps more extensive than any other Heidelberg instructor. Wesch had joined the NSDAP as a student in 1929, the SA the same year, the SS in 1931 (and later the Reichssicherheitshauptamt, or Reich Main Security Office), and had belonged to the National Socialist Studentenbund from 1929 to 1931 and the Dozentenbund from 1936 to 1945. He was arrested in 1945, and while in American captivity, he willingly provided Samuel Goudsmit of the Alsos mission with an extensive report on his research at Heidelberg, which Goudsmit considered to be of subpar scientific value.[94]

Following two years of internment, he was charged as a Hauptschuldiger by the Heidelberg Spruchkammer in early 1947. After three hearings in the spring and summer of 1947, Wesch was convicted in the Minderbelastet category on July 8, 1947. His defense ranks among the most deceitful and tendentious of the Spruchkammer narratives examined in this chapter. The son of a family of modest means, he had to support himself at the university as a student worker: "As such, I concerned myself with social questions and it is understandable that I came into contact with the NSDAP. I joined, like numerous fellow students, confident in its social program of 1929. At that time racial or anti-Semitic views did not at all enter my field of view." His membership in the SS was due to his technical expertise: "Because of particular familiarity in the field of radio, I was approached in 1931/32 by the SS to serve as an instructor in radio broadcasting technologies." But his avowed "pro-Jewish" position embroiled him in disputes with fellow Nazi students and other party figures, and he henceforth attempted to devote himself exclusively to scientific research.[95]

Wesch's claim to have held party memberships in name only and to have conducted purely objective research was supported by numerous affidavits, including one from Philipp Lenard himself, who stated that Wesch had picked up the threads his own research on phosphors, cathode rays, and electrons and had distinguished himself as an scientist. There was no mention of politics or "Aryan physics"; only Wesch's alleged scientific and technical competence was noted.[96] A similar assessment was provided by another leading "Aryan physicist," Rudolf Tomaschek.[97] In one hearing, August Seybold admitted that while "everyone" knew that Wesch was "formally" a National Socialist, he was nonetheless an "upstanding fellow." He also claimed to have known nothing about Wesch's rapid promotion. Most important, Seybold suggested that Wesch did not mix politics and science. "I attended two of his lectures," he argued in a tribunal hearing on July 2, 1947; both "were not National Socialist lectures."[98] Seybold, himself sympathetic to "Aryan physics" (see Chapter 2), undoubtedly knew that Wesch had indeed mixed politics and science at Heidelberg, but his claims to the contrary before the tribunal contributed to Wesch's eventual exoneration.

As was the case with other ardent Nazis, the Natural Sciences Faculty was determined to exclude Wesch permanently from its ranks. In May 1947, the chairman, Ludwig Rüger, informed the Rector that Walter Bothe and Karl Freudenberg had insisted that Wesch be excluded from the faculty because he had been a fanatical Nazi. Although he had been a good student, they recalled, "his futher promotion resulted without the consultation of the faculty . . . Under normal circumstances, no faculty would have permitted his doctorate." Clearly, Wesch owed his later advancement to his party connections in general and to Philipp Lenard's sponsorship in particular.[99] During a hearing a year later, both men repeated these charges, adding that Wesch was politically very dangerous and that the rest of the faculty feared him.[100]

A month later, the Baden Ministry for Political Liberation overturned the decision, citing Wesch's extensive involvement with the party. In July 1949, the appeals court in Heidelberg finally convicted him as a fellow traveler on the grounds that his party memberships were nominal (the tribunal even accepted the argument that Wesch had been forced to join the SS and the Reich Main Security Office) and that he was a competent scientist. As such, he had not profited from his party connections. Reputable testimony to the contrary on all these points from Walther Bothe and Karl Freudenberg was ignored. Wesch was, like other colleagues facing the Spruchkammer, successful in recasting himself as a nonpolitical technician and scientist whose research adhered to the highest standards of "scientific objectivity," though his return to academia, like Eugen Fehrle's, was foreclosed not by the decision of the Spruchkammer but by the determination of his former colleagues to exclude him from the faculty.

The Spruchkammer at Heidelberg served as a "fellow traveler factory" for scholars as it did for other sectors of the West German public. As these cases reveal, what the tribunals knew about a given instructor and the determination of the public prosecutor varied considerably. Swayed by professors' constructions of their own pasts and numerous positive affidavits, the tribunals resisted convicting compromised professors in any category above that of "fellow traveler." This "Mitläuferfabrik," the passage of Article 131 of the Basic Law, the migration of scholars from eastern to western Germany, and a memory-clouding Cold War consciousness allowed the return of hundreds of former Nazis to academia in the late 1940s and throughout the 1950s. The decisive factor keeping some former Nazis out of postwar academia was not denazification or the Spruchkammer, but rather the determination of individual faculties to prevent the retention of those instructors deemed too compromised with National Socialism. At Heidelberg the number of instructors in this group was not large, and more often than not they represented fields outside the traditional German university, such as folklore or the kind of Volkswirtschaft represented by Ernst Schuster and Horst Jecht, or had owed their positions largely to party connections (Ludwig Wesch) rather than to scholarly achievements.

The narratives of defense and justification constructed by Heidelberg professors absolved them of any responsibility for supporting the regime and its policies. Joining the party was described as an act of idealism fueled by frustration over the Weimar Republic's political turmoil and the economic disaster of 1929. But the idealists claimed to have become quickly disillusioned when the party revealed its true self—brutal, criminal, and crassly anti-intellectual. Many added that the regime's policies and actions had transgressed religious convictions. Finally, a staple claim was that professors, party members or not, always protected the autonomy of scholarship from ideological and political interference. Professors claimed to have remained purely objective "technicians" and, given the party's alleged hostility to the universities, even resisters.

Presumed adherence to unpoliticized scholarly inquiry, therefore, was finally solidified into a form of resistance to National Socialism. This particular narrative had been a standard defense immediately after the war and appears in every Spruchkammer narrative examined in this study. It neatly removed the scientist from the taint of Nazism by portraying National Socialism as inherently and immutably hostile to "objective scholarship." Activities of the regime that required and received the support of professors—forced sterilization, "euthanasia," and other variants of "racial hygiene," weapons and high technology research, Ost- and Westforschung, historical justifications for territorial expansion, the construction of the "Aryan Jesus," Germanic folklore and "ancestral heritage," "Grossraumwirtschaft," and other endeavors—were not addressed. If one read only these postwar narratives, in other words, one would never know that the regime relied extensively upon the nation's best academic talent to support its policies of territorial and "racial" expansion.

A related defense—articulated most elaborately by Eugen Fehrle—was to claim that one was serving in some position of responsibility in the party hierarchy in order to protect academic culture from ideological fanatics who would no doubt do far more damage if they had the chance.[101] This was a common tactic employed by former Nazis from the Nuremberg trials through the 1960s. Alfred Rosenberg's lawyer at Nuremberg, for instance, argued that "the slipping of anti-Semitism into crime took place without his knowledge or will. The fact in itself that he preached anti-Semitism justifies his punishment as the murderer of Jews as little as one could hold Rousseau and Mirabeau responsible for the subsequent horrors of the French revolution."[102] The former SS officer and wartime German commissioner of Denmark Werner Best portrayed his own role as ruler of that nation in a similar fashion.[103] Hans Globke, the jurist who helped shape the Nueremberg race laws, also relied on this strategy in responding to the public outcry following Konrad Adenauer's appointment of him to several high-level government positions in the late 1940s and early 1950s.[104]

Respecting the autonomy of scholarship also precluded anti-Semitism. Professors claimed repeatedly to have proffered help to those in distress, especially Jews, presumably at considerable personal risk. This narrative supports Frank Stern's arguments regarding the pervasiveness of philo-Semitism in postwar West German society.[105] Hence professors claimed to have been opposed to Nazi race theories and anti-Semitism, maintained contacts with Jewish colleagues abroad, kept books by Jewish authors in their libraries, and cited (always admiringly) the research of Jewish scholars in their lectures and also to have "helped" individual Jews. In some cases (such as those of Paul Schmitthenner, Karl Engisch, and Eugen Fehrle) the last claim was true. A few had Jewish colleagues write affidavits on their behalf, and the tribunals were usually swayed favorably by such remonstrations. For professors, this defense was used to separate the individual from anti-Semitism and Nazi race policies and to portray the accused as an "objective" scientist who ignored arbitrary boundaries to research such as nationality or "race."

These defenses were bolstered through the support of former Nazi and non- or even anti-Nazi colleagues. Professors sought to protect each other almost immediately after the occupation of Heidelberg. They continued to do so through steadfast resistance to denazification and through a densely woven web of positive affidavits for colleagues facing the Spruchkammer. These statements not only described the accused as personally "respectable," but also claimed that they had always held to strictly objective standards in their research and teaching. Little, if anything, was said about party membership. Similarly, non-Nazi and anti-Nazi scholars supported former Nazi colleagues. They also did so primarily on the grounds that the accused had defended the autonomy of science and that they had intervened on behalf of a persecuted colleague or spouse of a colleague. Such justifications further reinforced the perception that scholarship was divorced from ideology.

Conversely, there were few cases at Heidelberg of professors denouncing each other. Friedrich Pietrusky's denunciation of Ernst Rodenwaldt was an anomaly, as was Alfred Weber's determination to hold both Ernst Schuster and Horst Jecht accountable for their support of the regime's policies of continental domination.[106] The rule was mutual protection, not condemnation. As Jerry Muller, Dirk van Laak, and Eberhard Demm have shown, in the 1950s former Nazis continued to support each other, form alliances, and exclude those whose pasts and views were different from their own, and steadfastly avoided discussing their past relationships to National Socialism.[107]

The narratives of defense and justification employed by Heidelberg professors were absorbed and diffused throughout West German academic and political culture in the 1950s and 1960s. The extent to which the Heidelberg myth and the defenses produced for the Spruchkammer had become the dominant features of accounts of the Nazi past in postwar German academic culture can be seen in festschrifts, in memoirs, and in other publications. In the 1950s and 1960s, festschrifts written for former Nazis contained few, if any, references to the Third Reich, let alone references to the Nazi past of the individual in question. A 1961 festschrift dedicated to Wolfgang Panzer, for instance, presented his past this way:

> In 1936 Panzer left Berlin and the numerous friends he had won there to accept a call to the chair for geography at Heidelberg. He was permitted to work here for only three undisturbed years as a successful academic teacher when war again called to arms this officer of the First World War as a major. After participating in the campaign in France he was transferred to the section for war cartography and land surveys, first to Berlin, then to Italy. So the geographer remained close to his trusted field, maps. The return to the deeply missed teaching profession in the confused postwar period resulted in severe hindrances. The Military Government ordered an automatic suspension from office on the grounds of his short-term and part-time activity as a Referent in the Ministry of Culture and membership in a section of the army high command, *even though these assignments had been of a purely technical kind*. Heidelberg did not wait for the dismissed Ordinarius, a person of integrity later completely successfully exonerated, and an appointment to the University of Saarbrücken, already confirmed by nomination, was crossed out because of an obscure French personnel policy. These were dark years for the man we are honoring today.[108]

The similarity to Panzer's own Spruchkammer narrative is striking. Indeed, there could hardly be a more concise summary of an apologetic reconstruction of a former Nazi academic's past. Ideology, it is said, played no part in Panzer's scholarship or his activities from 1933 to 1945. The perpetrator is presented as a reputable scholar "called" to a war in which he provides "purely technical" expertise, and who then becomes a victim after the war of an unjust purge. Another tactic was to repeat the common claim that a scholar's adherence to objectivity in his work had earned him the party's enmity. A collection of essays in honor of Hermann Güntert, for instance, noted that his assertion that the original homeland (Urheimat) of the Indo-Germanic peoples lay in Asia brought him into conflict with the Nazis, who then worked to derail his career. Güntert was himself no Nazi, his scholarship was above reproach, unpolluted by ideology, and hence he was rejected by the party.¹⁰⁹ By the time of Eugen Fehrle's death in 1957, his work had been "mainstreamed" and depoliticized within folklore studies and his own past whitewashed by fellow folklorists.¹¹⁰

More evidence that the Spruchkammer narratives resonated beyond the confines of the tribunals is found in memoirs written in the 1950s and 1960s by Heidelberg professors. A particularly interesting case is that of Fritz Ernst. In 1959, Ernst prepared a short manuscript for the Institute of Contemporary History in London, unpublished until 1996, and titled "A Look Back at Those Twelve Years of the Third Reich."¹¹¹ Here he expanded upon his Spruchkammer narrative and portrayed himself as an opponent of National Socialism who had suffered attacks by the Tübingen Studentenschaft, resisted joining the party on several occasions, and supervised the dissertation of "a half Jewess," but who was nonetheless protected by a few clear-sighted and humane party members (such as Dozentenführer Karl Schmidhuber) at Tübingen and Heidelberg.

Ernst drew on this reconstruction of his own past for a series of popular public lectures he delivered at Heidelberg in 1961 and 1962, later published as *Die Deutschen und Ihre Jüngsten Geschichte* (translated into English as *The Germans and Their Modern History*).¹¹² Regarding his experience as a student at Tübingen at the outset of the Third Reich he wrote: "Why did a large number of students in Tübingen also join the SA at that time? For one thing, the public pressure that was being exerted on all classes and age groups may also have had its effect on some, even on the younger ones. On the whole, however, it was more the result of a desire not to stand idly by in the general turmoil. 'We march!' These words had a magical meaning... In Tübingen, where only a handful of Jews could be found, anti-Semitism scarcely existed, at least not at the University. For that reason, many who became victims of propaganda were all the more ready to believe what was said about the alleged domination of the Jews in Berlin."¹¹³ At this point, of course, Ernst was under no obligation to admit that he himself had been a member of the SA. But regarding SA and party members, he argued that "there were various kinds of SA units. Those who in the beginning behaved outrageously were usually not the young members but the old core of the SA who had long before won their spurs in street fights in Berlin." Some had even distinguished themselves during the pogrom of November 1938: "To the credit of the leaders of the local party in Heidelberg it must be said, however, that the sections of the city north of the Neckar escaped [the] destruction."[114] Ernst omitted the fact that there were no synagogues or Jewish communities in this part of Heidelberg to destroy.

This benign take on Nazi Party members was carried over to his experience at Heidelberg university. His account is worth quoting at length:

> Here, as in all fields of endeavor, there were those who were members of the National Socialist party and those who were not. But that was not indicative of the real borderline of political viewpoints and human decency . . . We who did not join the National Socialist party or, rather, who explicitly refused to join, would not have been in a position to continue lecturing if we had not continuously been protected by members of the National Socialist party . . . both by the professors and by the students. Here again, just as much is being wrongly oversimplified today as was oversimplified by the Americans during the denazification trials after 1945 . . . Among the professors as well as among the students there were fanatical "fighters for the Führer," but they practically formed an island to which the other university members sought no access. Among the professors these radicals formed a small group. Not even the leader of the National Socialist Dozentenbund [Karl Schmidhuber], who did much to protect those whose opinions were different from his own, belonged to this group. At most German universities the professors who were the most prominent National Socialists had first been appointed in 1933; only a few of the older professors joined the radical camp. In the middle, between us and the radicals, was a heterogeneous group of which the majority were irreproachable in their lectures as well as in their research.[115]

Drawing on a common Spruchkammer narrative, Ernst claimed that it was idealism—short-lived as it was—that led many to the arms of the party. Such people only wanted the best for Germany. If they found cause to criticize the regime, they kept silent during the war "because they considered that to be their duty as Germans."[116] Given this conception of the relationship between National Socialism and the universities, Ernst's judgment of denazification was particularly harsh. The Americans, he argued, "operated with conceptions that by no means corresponded with the actual nature of the dictatorship they were trying to destroy."[117] Echoing a widely held view, he also maintianed that the Spruchkammer were a failure, because "far too many people were punished . . . The men who were the first to be brought before these tribunals were, for the most part, sorely needed at their administrative posts and in their businesses because they were trusted and considered to have political judgment . . . Even at the universities the National Socialists had introduced the 'leadership principle' and thus had destroyed academic self-government. The result was that after 1935 a predominant number of the rectors and deans at German institutions of higher education owed their positions to National Socialism. In spite of this, every new appointment was fought over in most of the faculties, and in general, respectable standards were maintained. This speaks well for many of the men in charge of university affairs at the various ministries."[118]

Here, Ernst not only blended elements of his own narrative written for the tribunal and later for the Institute for Contemporary History but also offered something of a variation on the Heidelberg myth. The party, he claimed, tried to pack the faculties with its own men, but failed to do so not only because most professors did not want National Socialists on their faculties, but also because responsible Ministry officials remained true to traditional standards of scholarly appointment-making. This claim was not totally at odds with what occurred at Heidelberg and elsewhere in the period of the Gleichschaltung. The men in charge of university affairs at the various ministries"—men like Eugen Fehrle, Johann Daniel Achelis, Wolfgang Panzer, and many others—hardly "protected" the university by overseeing the purges of hundreds of scholars. Yet it was not false to claim that such officials considered scholarly qualification an important factor in filling vacant positions. The point that was deliberately obfuscated in the postwar years was that hundreds of professors were both National Socialists and competent scholars.

Ernst's account of the Nazi past at the universities must also be placed in the context of the Cold War reorientation of past enemies and the importance of "stories of German suffering" inflicted above all by the Soviet army upon German civilians. In addition, the misery of expellees from Eastern Europe was very real, but conservatives like Ernst chose to recall this suffering at the expense of what caused the expulsions in the first place: Hitler's war in Europe and the colossal destruction visited upon Eastern Europe and the Soviet Union by the German army. Ernst was, in other words, "changing enemies" in the sense that he downplayed National Socialism and the crimes committed in its name and turned the spotlight on the true enemy: the Soviet Union and communism. In 1943, Ernst blamed Hitler's megalomania for squandering the "greatest war machine of the time." His disappointment at the military loss and resulting establishment of Bolshevism in Germany was still felt in the early 1960s. The ire of former Nazis and conservative nationalists like Ernst was directed eastward and away from their own complicity in bringing about the postwar division of their country.

Another memoirist was Ernst Rodenwaldt. His 470-page memoir is largely devoted to technical descriptions of his career as a specialist in tropical hygiene interspersed with sentimental recollections of many years spent living in exotic locales.[119] It contains few references to politics. Rodenwaldt, according to his memoir, was a proud nationalist who favored the authoritarian rule of the Kaiser over a democratic republic. As was the case in his Spruchkammer defense, he does not discuss Nazi race theory as it informed his own work in the 1930s and 1940s. During the war, he was simply a technician, called to serve his country's army, which had been "threatened by epidemics in the wide expanses of Europe."[120] At the war's end, he notes that his dismissal from the university was ordered by the Americans—despite the fact that he "was not a member of the NSDAP"—because of his "general's rank." Rodenwaldt, not surprisingly, makes no mention of his brief party membership in 1932. He then heaps scorn upon the entire denazification process—"a monstrous little changeling" that had "given rise to the devil of hatred from the violated body of the Goddess of Justice." Even though the process, he said, had robbed him of the better part of two productive years, he refused to become embittered, because he was able to continue working as a scientist, even while temporarily suspended from his teaching position.[121]

The professor of Romance languages Walter Mönch provides yet another example. As we have seen, Mönch had participated in the network of "German scientific institutes" in German-occupied or Allied nations during the war. As a result of these activities and his Nazi Party membership, the Heidelberg Spruchkammer charged him as Minderbelatet and then as Mitläufer in June 1947. Like many of his colleagues, Mönch maintained that his activities abroad had no connection to the party or its cultural imperialism and that his own scholarship was untainted by politics.[122] In 1981, his memoirs were published. With diffidence and pathos, Mönch recalled his past and denazification:

> I was dismissed from the university and no longer permitted to enter the seminar buildings. The primary reason: as a guest professor abroad dur-

ing the Third Reich, I had disseminated National Socialist propaganda and consequently contributed to the regime's atrocities. I finally came out of the appeals process as a "Mitläufer"—a terrible appellation, which applied not at all to my personality and independence ... Such is life. Absolutely nothing new. But the affair hardly distressed me at all. I knew enough about the ways of the world. Through my intensive study of Voltaire and the world-wise, experienced, and clear-sighted Prussian king I was sufficiently informed about the moral inaccessibility of man and the crooked course of history.[123]

It would be too easy to conclude that these examples simply reflect the unwillingness of the German elite to examine with any honesty the extent of its complicity with National Socialism. They reveal the ways in which this elite had individually and collectively come to terms with its past. It should be added that such an aversion should not be confused with an aversion to examining National Socialism itself as a political and historical phenomenon. Indeed, scholars and journalists from across the political spectrum produced a large amount of literature in the immediate postwar period on the roots and causes of the Third Reich and politicians spoke out frequently on the subject.[124] When it came to accounting for their own roles in the catastrophe, however, they were intent on separating themselves from the regime they had supported.

How professors assessed their work privately, however, is another matter. Defeat and occupation had apparently not changed Edgar Glässer's mind regarding his own research. "My *Einführung in die rassenkundliche Sprachforschung* [see Chapter 2] incriminates me—grotesquely," he wrote his fellow philologist Werner Krauss in March 1946, "because in it I have only put forward the same views in a Herder-esque sense, perhaps like Georges Lakhovsky [. . .], which interpreted the heterogeneity of humanity—like other things—as something necessary and thus in a way permissible ... But where in any connection the word race, particularity, or the syllable bio- appears, one suspects something."[125] The disruption in Glässer's career was only temporary since he took a position in Mainz the same year, though published little thereafter. Conversely, while the philosopher Alfred Bäumler remained defensive in public about his past ("the 'philosopher' and pedagogue of N[ational] S[ocialism] was Krieck and not I," he wrote in the course of his Spruchkammer trial), in private he lamented his intellectual collaboration with the Nazis.[126]

Most public reflections, in any case, avoided close examination of the role of intellectuals and academic culture in supporting National Socialism. We have already seen how Karl Jaspers's critique of academic culture—despite its claim that "science as such could only be ruined by scientists"—fell short of addressing the widespread complicity of many of his colleagues at Heidelberg and elsewhere. The historian Friedrich Meinecke, in his 1946 book *The German Catastrophe,* did not identify intellectuals and university professors as implicated in the emergence of National Socialism. Similarly, the philosopher Theodore Litt noted in 1955 that "the representatives of so-called 'culture' ought to have been the first to show up the emptiness of the National-Socialist ideology." Although university professors "by no means passed into the National-Socialist camp with banners flying," he wrote, "even when the Party had come into power, those who subscribed to it heart and soul formed only a minority within the whole. But those were also only a small minority who, in obedience to tradition and to the spiritual mission of the university[,] felt it their duty to offer resistance to the rise of the Party when it menaced the essence of scientific research and education, and to refuse to follow the Party at its zenith, when it attacked the spirit of the educational institutions by brutal interventions." That professors did not "show up the emptiness of National-Socialist ideology" was thus due not only to a deep-seated sense of obligation to the state in whatever form, but also because Nazi Party ideologues "were able to attach themselves to moods and opinions which had long been traditional." Although unusually critical, Litt nonetheless concluded that German university professors had been misguided idealists swindled by cynical propagandists.[127]

A far more exculpatory example, as noted in the Introduction to this study, was Gerhard Ritter's influential 1945 essay, "Der Deutsche Professor im 'Dritten Reich.'"[128] In Ritter's view the universities were under siege from the party but the extent of its control was always uneven. Anti-Nazis such as himself could retreat within the arcana of their disciplines, avoid persecution, and thus maintain personal integrity and the integrity of their institutions. Ritter, like Ernst, defended the numerous advisers to the Nazi culture ministers on the grounds that they had tried to defend the gates of the German university against the hordes of anti-intellectual party Visigoths, despite the fact that they had dutifully overseen the firing of hundreds of scholars.[129]

This justification, as we have seen, echoed to the reading public Ritter's private defense of one such adviser—Eugen Fehrle—for the Spruchkammer.

Such sentiments were not limited to conservative nationalists like Ritter. In 1946 Hannah Arendt wrote that "it is true that some outstanding scholars went out of their way and did more to aid the Nazis than the majority of German professors, who fell into line simply for the sake of their jobs."[130] She dismissed what she believed to be the fleeting dalliance of her former teacher Martin Heidegger with the Nazi Party as an isolated instance of sheer idiocy. To Max Weinreich's claim in *Hitler's Professors,* also published in 1946, that "there was participation of German scholarship in every single phase" of the Holocaust, she concluded that one should not take "Nazi professors" and "Nazi science" too seriously.[131] Yet, as Weinreich understood, the "German spirit" in scholarship was taken seriously enough at that time to lead hundreds of professors to back the regime and its genocidal war of expansion in word and deed. But by the time *Hitler's Professors* appeared the Heidelberg myth was already an imposing edifice and far too strong to breach.

"Denazification"—from the first actions of the Counter Intelligence Corps in April 1945 through the Spruchkammer process—was not a "failure" in the sense that National Socialism returned to the universities. It must also be noted that the postwar purges sidelined those former Nazis who might otherwise have had a significant impact on the creation of the West German government.[132] Dismissals, internment, retirements, and temporary suspensions from teaching mandated by the Spruchkammer indeed led to a steep, if temporary, drop in the number of instructors at Heidelberg. In 1944 and 1945, there were 196 full professors, assistant professors, and Dozenten. In 1946–47, that number had fallen to 78. By 1947–48, however, the figure had risen to 105, and by 1952–53 to 186.[133] The end of denazification and the Spruchkammer, the passage of Article 131, and migration from the Soviet occupation zone largely fueled this sharp increase.

The entire denazification process—from the earliest suspensions through the Spruchkammer trials—quickly came to be regarded by most West Germans as an infamy. At best it was considered a reflection of American naiveté, at worst a violation of justice (Ernst Rodenwaldt's "monstrous little changeling"). Yet in the end many professors made effective use of the process that so many of them considered illegitimate. Heidelberg professors facing the Spruchkammer, for instance, rarely failed to mention the exonerated status of a colleague writing an affidavit on their behalf. A variation on this defense was to deflect uncomfortable questions about one's past by referring to the decision of the Spruchkammer. Hence the Heidelberg theologian Karl Georg Kuhn, responding in the late 1960s to Rolf Seeliger's questions regarding his membership in the Nazi Party and lengthy anti-Semitic publication record, noted that he had indeed published one regrettable article on the "Jewish question" in 1939 but that he had also been completely exonerated by Spruchkammer in the American and French occupation zones.[134] This and other examples lend credence to Franz Neumann's assertion that the denazification process had devolved from judging right and wrong to a state-sanctioned "administrative procedure."

Without question, former National Socialists returned to Heidelberg and other institutions en masse. Of sixty-three instructors (full professors, assistant professors, and Dozenten) ordered dismissed by the Americans between April 1945 and March 1946, fifty returned to academic teaching positions in German universities (twenty-five of them to Heidelberg) and technical colleges from the late 1940s to the mid-1950s. This figure, of course, does not include former Nazis who had come to Heidelberg from other institutions, or those who had not been dismissed by the Americans but who had pro-Nazi pasts (such as Karl Heinrich Bauer or Fritz Ernst).[135] In the 1950s many scholars with substantially compromised backgrounds would remain at Heidelberg. Virtually absent from the postwar rosters of all German universities were those who had lost their positions from 1932 to 1937. It is to the implications for Heidelberg of this modified restoration that I turn in the next chapter.

CHAPTER SEVEN

A Culture of Forgetting

> If one thinks back on the events of 1933, one would think it would be unnecessary to waste a word about them, because those of today's adult generation *aere perennius* must have been branded by those events and, from the accounts they passed down, so too the adolescent youth. My experiences of the years 1952–1954, however, have shown me that this is surely not the case: all of the base acts of National Socialism were either forgotten or were supposed to be ignored. Those who participated in these acts or at least quietly looked on believed that they atoned for them through the sufferings that they themselves experienced—albeit as a result of a regime that they had accepted.
> —Gerta von Ubisch, unpublished memoirs, ca. 1955

A long period of silence about the past in West Germany followed the brief "Nuremberg interregnum." After 1947, American and British officials were interested primarily in ensuring the reconstruction of Germany as an ally in the emerging Cold War, and by the mid-1950s they had succeeded. West Germany's postwar political leadership, dominated by the figure of Konrad Adenauer, was instrumental in engineering this realignment, which came at the expense of facing the crimes of National Socialism. The West German public seemed willing not only to forget the past but to forgive former Nazis as resistance to denazification and widespread support for the provisions of Article 131 of the Basic Law indicate. As noted in previous chapters, university professors also resisted denazification and campaigned to have compromised colleagues retained or reinstated to former positions. Many did not avoid analyzing the Third Reich as a political phenomenon, but as the case of Heidelberg illustrates, a willingness to address academic culture's compromised past was virtually nowhere in evidence. Most closed ranks around the exculpating Heidelberg myth. It would not be until the 1960s that cracks in the myth's façade would appear.

In this chapter I survey important developments at Heidelberg in the 1950s.[1] In 1945, as we have seen, the structure of the university was largely restored to its pre-1933 form and would remain unaltered until the 1960s. The immediate postwar years witnessed a surge in antifascist, pro-democratic sentiment that included a degree of willingness to talk about the past, but this situation was changing by the late 1940s and early 1950s. Denazification and the decisions of the postwar faculties prevented the return of a few of the most extreme former Nazis, yet many other compromised professors began to return to academia. Conversely, there were few individuals willing to examine closely the relationship between the ivory tower and National Socialism, and those who attempted such examinations were ostracized or had their careers sabotaged. Although the Nazi-era emphasis on "racial" and military sciences would disappear from the research agendas and curricula of the post-1945 university, the scholarship of former Nazis would undergo a series of transformations and revisions with significant consequences for academic culture in Germany.

The 1950s were years of expansion for the university.[2] As noted, the number of instructors increased steadily after 1946. In the 1946–47 academic year, there were 78 full and assistant professors and Dozenten, 9 honorary professors, and 50 graduate student lecturers. There were 3,996 students registered in the same period, 1,209 of them women. The university hosted fifty institutes and thirteen clinics. These numbers increased steadily throughout the following decade. By the 1957–58 academic year, there were 238 instructors (full and assistant professors and Dozenten), 35 honorary professors, and 136 graduate student lecturers. There were 6,353 students attending Heidelberg (1,905 of them women). By 1960, 8 percent of the university's students were non-Germans, a fact that restored Heidelberg's prewar reputation as a magnet for foreign students. The number of institutes and clinics had grown to fifty-nine and fourteen, respectively.[3] Several interdisciplinary institutes and those dealing with the practical problems of modern industrial societies proliferated in the 1950s and early 1960s. The Institute for Political Science drew its directors from the Philosophy and Law faculties, and the Working Group for Modern Social History (1957) and the South Asian Institute (1963) were both heavily interdisciplinary. The Philosophy Faculty created seminars in international comparative social statistics and Eastern European history, while the Law Faculty sponsored a variety of new institutes devoted to criminology and finance, and to tax, economic, and social law. The Medical and Natural Sciences faculties also expanded considerably.⁴

In the postwar decade Heidelberg's academic culture experienced a process of revival, albeit along different channels. Shortly after the end of the war, numerous small discussion groups and salon circles devoted to discussing contemporary social and political developments reformed themselves, most notably around Corinna Sombart (the widow of the economist Werner Sombart), Marie Baum, Marianne Weber, and Alfred Weber.⁵ These groups were dominated by a generation that came to political maturity in Wilhelmine Germany. Although thoroughly anti-Nazi, most remained after 1945 German nationalists—they could not they accept the Oder-Neisse line any more than they could accept Germany's territorial losses after 1918. Politically, they sought a unified, neutral Germany governed by a social democratic government infused with Christian principles as an alternative to American-dominated capitalism and Soviet-dominated communism (also called "Free Socialism").⁶ It should be noted, however, that Heidelberg's anti-Nazis were not all of one mind—Alfred Weber and Karl Jaspers, for instance, differed notably over conceptions of national identity and its implications for Germany's political future.⁷

In addition to the revived salon circles, a political discussion group created by Alfred Weber and the publisher Lambert Schneider, the Heidelberg Action Group for Democracy and Free Socialism, included the durable core of the university's liberals, such as Dolf Sternberger and Hans von Eckardt. The group held debates before large audiences on contemporary political issues such as the postwar settlement, Germany's future position in Europe, and even Nazi crimes.⁸ The group also created a remarkable but short-lived journal published in Heidelberg from 1945 to 1949, *Die Wandlung (Metamorphosis)*. With regular contributions from Weber, Karl Jaspers, and other prominent anti-Nazis (and a few, like Viktor von Weizsäcker and Fritz Ernst, whom most at the time considered anti-Nazis), the journal included essays on freedom, state power, tolerance, "the renewal of law," university reform, and German guilt; published poetry and essays by Montesquieu, Franz Kafka, Bertolt Brecht, and T. S. Eliot; and reprinted documents on current diplomatic developments and Nazi medical crimes. *Die Wandlung* served as a kind of expression of liberation from dictatorship as well as a refresher course in democratic civil society.⁹

One of the most influential attempts in Germany to reckon with the catastrophe of National Socialism, Karl Jaspers's *The Question of German Guilt (Die Schuldfrage),* was first published in 1946.¹⁰ Jaspers had been speaking publicly in Heidelberg on this subject for nearly two years, often to audiences that were less than receptive to his message. *Die Schuldfrage* was one of the very few attempts by an academic of high stature to grapple with personal and national responsibility in Germany for National Socialism. Its appearance also made its author one of West Germany's leading and most controversial political commentators.¹¹ But antifascist voices calling for a renewal of German civil society along democratic lines and demanding forthright discussions of the past were relatively few, and the leading lights behind *Die Wandlung* were mostly old and would soon depart from the scene. Alfred Weber was seventy-seven in 1945 (he died in 1958). In 1948, Karl Jaspers accepted an invitation to teach at the University of Basel. Although at the time he denied that dissatisfaction with developments in postwar Germany drove him to Switzerland, he later noted with apparent bitterness that a great opportunity to renew the German university in 1945 had been squandered and that he himself had been used by Karl Heinrich Bauer and others more interested in his reputation than his ideas.¹² A year after Jaspers's departure, finally, Gustav Radbruch died, and yet another liberal voice was removed from Heidelberg's postwar academic culture.

Throughout most of the 1950s, conversely, former Nazis or those with pro-Nazi pasts dominated the university. In the winter semester of 1951–52, for instance, the Medical Faculty's rosters included Karl Heinrich Bauer, Viktor von Weizsäcker, Fritz Eicholtz, Ernst Rodenwaldt, Hans Runge, two of Carl Schneider's former assistants, Karl Friedrich Wendt and Joachim Rauch, and Hans Klein, a former assistant at an SS sanatorium (Hohenlychen). In 1957, the Philosophy Faculty included Reinhard Herbig, Johannes Kühn, Erich Maschke, Werner Conze, and Helmut Meinhold—all substantially compromised with National Socialism. The same year, Karl Georg Kuhn—a leading member of Walter Frank's Reich Institute for the History of the New Germany's Research Department for the Jewish Question and of the Institute for the Study and Eradication of Jewish Influence in German Church Life and also the author of numerous anti-Semitic publications—served as the chairman of the Theology Faculty.¹³

How could someone like Kuhn, a member of the Nazi Party from

1932 to 1945 and of the SA from 1933 to 1945—and whose efforts at "dejudaizing" Christianity were well known in the postwar era—secure a position at Heidelberg? We have seen how professors, most notably Karl Heinreich Bauer, protected their own colleagues. But what about those who had not taught at Heidelberg during the Third Reich? Kuhn's case is instructive. In general, of course, one can point to the same broader developments in West Germany that affected academic culture: the onset of the Cold War, the end of denazification, and the passing of Article 131 of the Basic Law. Like many other scholars, Kuhn received a clean legal bill of health from both the Württemberg Spruchkammer and a special Tübingen University tribunal in 1948 on the grounds that his party memberships were nominal, his scholarship "objective," and his activities in the Reich Institute for the History of the New Germany aimed at limiting the influence of ideological fanatics. The Institute for the Study and Eradication of Jewish Influence in German Church Life was not mentioned.[14] Further, the chairman of Heidelberg's Theology Faculty considered Kuhn a "pioneer of modern, critically sharply focused religious history methodology" and one of Germany's foremost experts on Judaism. Aware of his brief suspension from teaching "on political grounds," the faculty concluded that there were no longer any grounds to delve into the matter, since it had been "settled in a formal sense."[15]

The results of this modified restoration were not just unwillingness to discuss National Socialism. Gone was the solidarity of the immediate postwar months, when professors with diverse experiences in the Third Reich, such as Karl Jaspers, Karl Heinrich Bauer, and Alexander Mitscherlich, cooperated in getting the university reopened. After a brief visit to Heidelberg in the summer of 1950, Karl Jaspers reported to Hannah Arendt that "I feel *no* guilt for leaving this Germany and for *not* yearning to go back.—A small detail: I'm a member of the Heidelberg academy. They happened to have a meeting while I was there. They *forgot* to invite me. A clear sign of how little I mean to those people."[16] Another result was the emergence of academic circles comprised of former Nazis or pro-Nazis.[17] As noted in the previous chapter, Ernst Forsthoff returned to Heidelberg's Law Faculty in 1951. He became the leading transmitter of Carl Schmitt's ideas to West German academic culture (an unrepentant Schmitt had gone into largely self-imposed exile, having been barred from academia for refusing to undergo a denazification process). These ideas enjoyed a healthy postwar life and Schmitt's influence on several generations of scholars, intellectuals, and high-ranking civil servants is difficult to overstate. By the late 1940s, former students like Forsthoff and younger admirers of Schmitt had formed an organization, Academia Moralis, and several informal circles that served not only to keep Schmitt's ideas alive but also to provide a kind of support network for former Nazis. Forsthoff himself drew young admirers of Schmitt to a series of summertime courses—the Ebrach seminars—beginning in 1957.[18]

Also notable in this context is the Heidelberger Juristenkreis (Heidelberger Jurists Circle) that formed around the legal scholar Eduard Wahl in 1949. Wahl, who joined the Law Faculty in 1941, had belonged to the SA, Nazi Party, and the Dozentenbund, and had served as co-editor of the pro-Nazi legal journal *Zeitschrift für Völkerrecht*.[19] Completely exonerated by the Spruchkammer in 1947, Wahl migrated to the Christian Democrats and became a deputy in the West German Bundestag. He had also served as a prominent member of the legal defense team for the chemical giant I. G. Farben at Nuremberg. The Juristenkreis was one of several influential private lobbies in Germany working to overturn or at least ameliorate war crimes verdicts reached in the highly contentious U.S. Army war crimes trials.[20] Its membership included a variety of regional and national political figures, legal scholars, judges, and church officials. The Juristenkreis exploited fears of an extreme right-wing threat to the young West German democracy to pressure both American (and French) officials and Chancellor Adenauer to put an end to the entire war crimes process. Wahl's and the Juristenkreis's basic position was that most actions considered "war crimes" could not really be considered such, because of the viciousness of the war in the East and because the entire process violated the provisions of West Germany's constitution. Their efforts and those of like-minded pressure groups was a reflection of the widespread resistance among the West German elite to denazification and a legal reckoning with Nazi crimes.[21]

In the late 1940s, further implications of a shift in the university's political balance became evident. Rumors of incomplete denazification and a reactionary atmosphere at German universities in the American occupation zone appeared in the American press in late 1945 and contributed to Lucius Clay's decision to launch a round of investigations and dismissals the following spring. On December 16, 1947, the *New York Times* published yet another stinging critique of American university policy and the enduring "reactionary atmosphere" at German universities, this time singling out Heidelberg.[22] The author was Delbert Clark, who later published a sensationalist account of his travels in occupied Germany.[23] "An attempt to create a liberal atmosphere at Heidelberg university has failed," Clark began in his *Times* exposé, "the ancient seat of learning is rapidly coming again under the control of the old reactionary elements." With the passing of denazification, he claimed, American officials relaxed their supervision of the university with the result that "the feeble liberals were set on their feet like dolls and left to stand alone":

> Now what is described as an old-line reactionary administration is running the university again and the democratic-minded professors who returned after the defeat of the Nazis say that they are subjected to constant pressure in a variety of ingenious ways of making them uncomfortable in their positions. One, a world-famous scholar, has told friends that he will soon give up and retire. Recently one professor, who had been rejected two years ago as a Nazi, was finally readmitted, and announced it as his main purpose to get all his old friends back on the faculty as soon as possible . . . A famous Swiss medical professor was invited to deliver a series of lectures for a stated fee. He accepted, but ran into so many obstacles that he left without completing his course. Classrooms would be mysteriously unavailable. Transportation could not be had. Many other vexatious things happened that finally convinced him that he was not wanted . . . When the trial of Nazi doctors at Nuernberg [*sic*] brought to light certain evidence of experimentation on human beings, one member of the medical faculty, profoundly shocked, published a book commenting on the documents. He was immediately vigorously attacked by a large number of the medical faculty as "unpatriotic."[24]

The unnamed "world-famous scholar," Clark admitted in a private letter to Alfred Weber, was Karl Jaspers.[25] The similarly unnamed "member of the medical faculty" was the young psychologist Alexander Mitscherlich. The "Swiss medical professor" was Edgar Salin (an economist and not a medical scientist), who had been fired from Heidelberg in the 1930s. Clark claimed to Weber that his sources, instructors and a few students, had requested anonymity for the sake of their own security.

The article caused a considerable stir within the university. On January 13, 1948, Rector Wolfgang Kunkel called a general assembly of the teaching body. Although some of the substantive charges leveled in Clark's article were discussed, with Kunkel even recommending a faculty-by-faculty review of "the problem of the reinstatement of the politically charged (Mitläufer)," the Rector in fact believed that Clark's charges had no basis in reality. Whether any "faculty-by-faculty" review ever took place is unclear.[26] In a long letter to the Culture Ministry in Stuttgart, however, Kunkel rejected every claim in the article. Relying on the Heidelberg myth, he argued that there had never been a "reactionary atmosphere" at Heidelberg to begin with: "It should be noted here that until 1933, Heidelberg University had had a well-known, particularly liberal atmosphere. At no other German university in the time of the Weimar constitution had a liberalism of scholarly work and political opinion flourished so . . . Because of this liberal and democratic attitude, the university had been particularly deeply struck by National Socialism . . . In general, the representatives of the good old Heidelberg tradition restored in office in 1945 such as Professors Jaspers, Alfred Weber, Regenbogen, Radbruch, Ranke, Jellinek, Grisebach, Hoepke . . . as before authoritatively engaged in the university's leadership."[27] In a letter to the *New York Times* dated February 20 (and published April 19), Karl Heinrich Bauer also dismissed Clark's accusations out of hand, adding that "there is not a single person connected with the university who could be accused of harboring reactionary tendencies."[28] Even Alfred Weber rejected the accusations. "As someone who was removed at an early date on political grounds and then reinstated," he wrote to Clark (here distorting his own past, given that he had not been "removed," but had resigned on his own initiative), "I am in a position to ascertain that [the charge of a reactionary atmosphere] is from start to finish baseless. Full unanimity in the general political orientation dominates the university. Since the opening of the university and all its acts henceforth, this orientation rested upon solemnly expressed denunciations in the sharpest manner of the previous regime and rests on the basis of intellectual immersion and inner revision."[29] There was no genuine interest within the university, in short, in investigating Clark's claims. Like Daniel Penham before him, Clark was branded a liar and his accusations were dismissed as groundless.

Those among the university's own ranks who inquired into the relationship between academic culture and National Socialism, conversely, found themselves ostracized. The most notorious incident involved Alexander Mitscherlich. Despite his relatively young age (he was thirty-eight in 1946), Mitscherlich and a young medical student, Fred Mielke, had been selected to represent the German Medical Commission at the military tribunal in the Nuremberg medical trial.[30] Not only was Mitscherlich not uncompromised with National Socialism, but apparently (and tellingly) no one else from the medical community wanted the job. The trial, which got under way in December 1946, involved twenty-three physicians and scientists charged with "murders, tortures, and other atrocities committed in the name of medical science."[31] Fifteen of the accused were found guilty, and seven of them received the death sentence; eight were acquitted. A year later, Mitscherlich and Mielke published an account of the trial that included documentation and a damning indictment of the entire German medical profession.[32] Mitscherlich's accusations stood the Heidelberg myth on its head: "Science and government alike have proliferated to a degree too vast to be [comprehended]. During the war years especially, their interests were so closely interwoven that often the individual was no longer able to check the effects of his work. What had been the fruit of scientific research but yesterday, suddenly turned into a weapon of war, an adjunct in the killing of men, founded on *Weltanschauung* . . . As for the doctor, he could become a licensed murderer, a publicly appointed torturer, only in the merging of two trends—at the point where his aggressive quest for truth coincided with the ideology of dictatorship." Regarding the relationship between the accused physicians and the German medical profession as a whole, Mitscherlich and Mielke concluded that "even had [the defendants] been individually of greater importance than they were, this corporal's guard could never have effected so vast a tide of suffering . . . We leave it to historians with a broader approach to delve into the characters and biographies of the individuals who here stand accused, to assign them to their rightful places in the total picture, composed of traditional elements and new. Such a presentation far transcends the scope of this trial."[33]

A backlash against Mitscherlich ensued. "My medical colleagues at that time," he recalled in his memoirs, "not only defamed me as a traitor to the Fatherland, but defamed and impaired me professionally."[34] Several physicians he had named in the book sued him, attempts were made to block the publication of the book (which was largely ignored in Germany when it was published), and Mitscherlich was ostracized by the medical profession.35 At Heidelberg, Karl Heinrich Bauer seemed determined to hound him from the faculty, in part because of his antipathy to Mitscherlich's field, modern psychology.36 Mitscherlich did, however, have the support of what was left of Heidelberg's anti-Nazis. Karl Jaspers considered his book to be of "great value," while Gustav Radbruch called it "a publication of the greatest importance and thoughtfulness" and Alfred Weber described it as a "courageous and patriotic act."37 Yet they were in the minority, their influence at Heidelberg on the wane and nonexistent in the German medical community.

As we have seen, Weber was the single Heidelberg professor determined to make no concessions to former Nazis in reconstructing the university after 1945. Further, he did more than any other instructor to facilitate the return of instructors dismissed in the 1930s. Despite his sharp rejection of Delbert Clark's accusations in the *New York Times*, he seemed to come to broadly the same conclusions two years later. In a 1949 article in *Die Wandlung*, he asked rhetorically, "Have we Germans failed since 1945?" and expressed considerable doubts about the capacity of West Germany's intellectual elite to reform itself and contribute to the building of a healthy democracy.38 But Weber's postwar influence at Heidelberg was short lived. His antifascism fell victim to the Cold War. Interest in his "Kultursoziologie" was short-lived in postwar Germany and by the early 1950s academic sociology would become dominated by former Nazis whose work was heavily empirically oriented.39 In the early and mid-1950s, as Weber's biographer, Eberhard Demm, has revealed, men like the historian Johannes Kühn and the sociologist Helmut Meinhold did not "forgive or forget" Weber's uncompromising stand on denazification. Although they could do little to the eminent Weber himself, they could—and did—turn on his students. Kühn seemed particularly determined to strike back at Weber in this manner. He sabotaged the academic careers of three of Weber's students, Herbert von Borch, who subsequently went on to become a well-known journalist and correspondent for the prestigious *Süddeutsche Zeitung*, and Heinz Markmann. Meinhold similarly prevented Gräfin Leonore Lichnowsky from receiving her degree.40

By the mid-1950s, the Philosophy Faculty had become a stronghold of former Nazis or pro-Nazis. One particularly notorious example was Helmut Meinhold, who joined the faculty in 1952. During the war, he had served as an assistant in the Institut für deutsche Ostarbeit (roughly, The Institute for German Labor in the East) in Cracow, where he formulated plans for the "depopulation" and resettlement of Poland.[41] By 1957 he had become the chairman of the faculty. In the late 1940s and well into the 1950s, there were several important additions to the faculty from the Soviet occupation zone (after 1949 the German Democratic Republic).[42] One was Johannes Kühn, who had been an early convert to National Socialism. Victor Klemperer, who had been on friendly terms with Kühn until the latter began to ignore him after 1935, was so disgusted with his former colleague's conversion to National Socialism that he was moved to record one of the more memorable passages in his diary: "If one day the situation were reversed and the fate of the vanquished lay in my hands, then I would let all the ordinary folk go and even some of the leaders . . . But I would have all the intellectuals strung up, and the professors three feet higher than the rest."[43] Kühn began to infuse his scholarship with racial concepts as early as 1936 and later became an outspoken proponent of the war.[44]

Two other scholars from the Soviet zone were Werner Conze and Erich Maschke. Conze was arguably the most influential historian in the Federal Republic. Not only did he revitalize the study of history at Heidelberg, but he—along with Theodor Schieder—revolutionized the historical profession in West Germany as a co-founder of modern social history. Conze had studied briefly with the sociologist Hans Freyer in Leipzig and later with Günther Ipsen and Hans Rothfels in Königsberg. He was trained in the tradition of "Volksgeschichte," which had its roots in the nineteenth century and emerged as a new field of historical research in the 1920s and 1930s. Volksgeschichte concerned itself with the histories of ethnically defined groups of people and drew on a variety of methodologies traditionally common to sociology, political economy, ethnography, and anthropology. Not surprisingly, Völksgeschichte lent itself almost seamlessly to the National Socialist conception of "racial science" and the regime's expansionist aims, particularly with regard to Eastern Europe and the Soviet Union. Conze and Schieder themselves had devoted considerable attention to the problem of Nazi settlement policies, including the matter of "depopulating" Poland of its Jewish population in order to make room for German settlers. Their involvement went beyond the writing of academic monographs and involved formal policy recommendations, in some cases delivered to the Ministry of the Interior.[45] Conze's colleague at Heidelberg, finally, was his longtime acquaintance Erich Maschke. Maschke, a former Storm Trooper and eventually Dozentenbundführer at Leipzig University, was another product of Königsberg and himself a prominent "Ostforscher," whose regional studies of Eastern Europe were pervaded by racist formulations.[46]

The modified restorations of the postwar decade included the revision of scholarly works written during the Third Reich.[47] These revisions appeared in several separate but related forms. One involved simply removing now-unacceptable passages from books and issuing the result as a revised edition. A second involved modifying conceptions that had previously supported the "German spirit" in scholarship, amounting to a kind of denazification of scholarship itself. The case of the philosopher Hans-Georg Gadamer's shifting interpretation of the eighteenth-century philosopher Gottfried von Herder is instructive. In 1940, Gadamer (originally addressing an audience of French prisoners of war) celebrated Herder's rejection of idea-centered French Enlightenment thought in favor of a conception of a society and its state as grounded in the blood of the "Volk." In a revised version of this lecture published in 1967, however, Gadamer removed all references to "Völkisch" ideology; and what had been celebrated in the 1940 version—German uniqueness and superiority—was either eliminated or recast in the revised text as unfortunate episodes of despotism that over the centuries had cost Germany dearly.[48] Eugen Fehrle engineered a similar modification in the early 1950s. Although no longer in academia, Fehrle was able to publish two widely read monographs in 1952 and 1955, which replaced hierarchical race-based conceptions of a "Volk" with a hazy notion of a "mystical soul."[49] From the 1950s through the early 1970s, as Frank-Rutger Hausmann has shown, Walter Mönch republished his wartime German Scientific Institute lectures on German and French art and music. In the context of Nazi Germany's wartime cultural imperialism, in which Mönch played an active role in Belgium (see Chapter 3), his lectures were aimed at promoting, as the pro-Nazi *Brüssler Zeitung* wrote in 1942, the "deep unity" of French and German culture "in the sense of a higher European order." In the postwar decades, the lectures could also be seen as promoting Franco-German reconciliation, albeit in the sense of a new Western European order forged by former enemies and based on economic cooperation and a mutual defense alliance.[50]

Another variation on this theme is found in the origins of social history in West Germany. In and immediately after 1945, interest among many historians in traditional, state-centered, and "top-down" approaches to historical problems surged briefly. Conze and his allies had long considered this approach highly unsatisfactory. Hence they sought to modify "Volksgeschichte" to examine the structural social problems of modern societies, initially with the aim of understanding the disaster of National Socialism. The result was the founding of the Working Group for Modern Social History at Heidelberg in 1957.[51] Conze, Schieder, and Otto Brunner subsequently trained what is today the leading stratum of the German historical profession. Conze removed the ethnic-racist "Völkisch" focus from his approach to studying modern society. In its place he put an emphasis on societal "structures." Although Conze, Schieder, Otto Brunner, and others approached the study of history "from below," rather than from the perspective of high politics, they concurred with conservative historians such as Gerhard Ritter that modernization as a European phenomenon was responsible for National Socialism, and not the peculiarities of Germany's own development.

Finally, some postwar scholarship also reflected what Jerry Muller has referred to as the "deradicalization" of radical conservative scholars and intellectuals. Ernst Forsthoff, as Muller suggested, was typical of several German radical conservatives (Hans Freyer, Arnold Gehlen, Hans Zehrer, and others) who had supported National Socialism but claimed to have become "disillusioned" with it during the course of the Third Reich. In the late 1930s and early 1940s Forsthoff began to reformulate his views of the "total state" (see Chapter 3). As a result of this disillusionment, the discrediting of National Socialism, and the defeat and occupation of Germany, he further modified his views regarding the state. In the 1950s, Peter Caldwell has pointed out, Forsthoff revived criticisms that he had leveled at the Weimar state in modified form. In the post–World War II period, he never really resigned himself to West German democracy, although he did not reject it outright, as he had the Weimar Republic. In the 1950s, he held that a strengthening of the state's administrative apparatus (staffed by "experts") was the only way to protect society not only from multiple and conflicting interests, but also from the ravages of modern technology. He did not so much "embrace" parliamentary democracy—which he believed was imposed on Western Germany by the victors—as resign himself to its existence. None of this is to say that Forsthoff or other former radical conservatives were willing to discuss the regime's crimes or express any regret for their earlier publications or engagement with the party. But their political views clearly had changed, if largely in the sense of becoming latter-day versions of the Weimar era's "republicans of the head."[52]

Heidelberg's confrontations with its Nazi past have come, as they have elsewhere in Germany, slowly and unevenly. The pages of the university's official magazine, *Ruperto Carola,* published in this period are eerily silent on the fate of the university during the Third Reich, as if dictatorship, war, and genocide had left no trace on the "living spirit" of the institution. Within its walls, however, the "German spirit" could and did make its continued presence felt. Substantial cracks in the Heidelberg myth began to appear in the 1960s. The establishment of the Central Office for the Investigation of National Socialist Crimes in Ludwigsburg in 1958, the trial of Adolf Eichmann in 1961, and the trials of Auschwitz commanders and camp guards in the mid-1960s heightened awareness in the Federal Republic of Nazi crimes and unpunished Nazi criminals.[53] University students in particular became increasingly unwilling to accept their parents' and elders' silence and complacency regarding the past. Banners paraded around West German universities in the late 1960s reading "unter den Talaren Muff von 1000 Jahren" (under these robes—the mustiness of a thousand years) not only called attention to the professoriate's conservatism and resistance to change, but also made clear reference to Hitler's promised "Thousand Year Reich." A few left-leaning writers and students in West Germany documented their professors' "Brown pasts."[54] At Heidelberg in 1968, a group of students occupied the offices of Karl Heinrich Bauer, organized a "teach-in" on the subject of Germany's medical profession and Nazi crimes, and demanded that Bauer account for his pro-Nazi past. Bauer, who enjoyed the full support of his colleagues, responded with a press release that repeated the self-serving justifications put to American authorities in 1946. The medical student leading the teach-in, Ernst Scheurlen, was expelled from the university.[55]

In 1986, Heidelberg celebrated its six hundredth anniversary, and the university community did not find it an auspicious occasion to delve too deeply into its darkest period. A series of commemorative books and articles honoring the university were published around this time, the centerpiece of which was a three-volume survey of the institution's entire history. Although several contributions were devoted to National Socialism, these and other works based their overall assessment of the university on the Heidelberg myth.[56] Only an "unofficial" edited volume, provocatively titled *Also a History of Heidelberg University*, took a more critical position and attempted to puncture the legend of a passive and victimized university.[57] It would not be until 1993 that the names of all of the Nazis' true victims among Heidelberg's professorate would be identified on a wall inside the university's oldest building.

That the universities would not confront their pasts and punished those who called for greater awareness of the relationship between academic culture and National Socialism should not be surprising. By the 1957–58 academic year, the average age of a full professor at Heidelberg was fifty-nine years. With the rare exception of the returned émigré scholar (such as Karl Löwith), in other words, the vast majority had entered academic culture shortly before the Third Reich and thus experienced some of their most formative and productive years as scholars in the 1930s and 1940s. The many who had supported National Socialism had their pasts legally whitewashed by the Spruchkammer and Article 131 and had the support of their colleagues. Most were averse, like former Nazis then serving in other branches of the civil service, to discussing their own pasts. "I don't have anything to report to you," Ernst Forsthoff wrote in response to Rolf Seeliger's questions about his past in the late 1960s: "only those of a weak nature hold the mistaken belief that through belated interpretations and clarifications one may make something better, or moderate it or even undo something. I hold myself to Ernst Jünger's aphorism (from *Blätter und Steine*): 'he who interprets himself stoops beneath his own level.'"[58]

Students of Forsthoff and others were disinclined to probe their mentors' memories of those years—at least not until well into the 1960s. And even in the 1960s some were not only protective but unprepared or unwilling to recognize the often close connection between politics, ideology, and academic culture in the Third Reich. In 1969, Forsthoff's students defended him publicly as "a sincere, uncompromised witness to the time of the Nazi regime."[59] But there was also the matter of what Wulf Kansteiner referred to as "the contract entered into in academia on an everyday basis," meaning that "in exchange for guidance, training, and long-term patronage, students agree to a certain degree of exploitation and long-term professional loyalty." Hans-Ulrich Wehler described the implications of this "contract" for the memory of National Socialism in academic culture:

> I came as a student to Cologne because of [Theodor] Schieder. Over the decades Schieder struck us as intellectually superior, extraordinarily versatile, theoretically astute, and eminently liberal-minded in his dealings with younger colleagues. There is nothing to regret about those years in Cologne. But Schieder was consistently silent about one thing. It was impossible to elicit even a single word from him about his years in Königsberg between 1934 and 1944. That gave cause to vague assumptions that, however, we could not put in concrete terms, let alone develop into a justified suspicion. Also, in the end, we did not feel that clarification was a pressing concern because of the predominant overall perception of his personality.[60]

The Nazi pasts of Schieder, Werner Conze, and others long held by academic and nonacademic observers alike to have been anti-Nazis would not undergo close critical examination until the 1990s.

Breaks and continuities with the past characterized the revival of Heidelberg's academic culture in the 1950s. For a few years after 1945, Heidelberg's famed salon culture of the Weimar era revived briefly. Antifascist voices calling for a renewal of political and academic culture along democratic lines as well as awareness of the crimes of National Socialism reached the apogee of their collective influence from 1945 to 1949. Yet resistance to these voices remained strong throughout the occupation years and only increased following the end of denazification and the departure or deaths of the pillars of Heidelberg's liberal culture. Although National Socialism was (largely) discredited and compromised, many professors had gone to considerable lengths to separate themselves and their work from any connection to Nazi ideology. But the past remained woven into the fabric of teaching and research throughout the Federal Republic's first decade and beyond.

Conclusion: Complicities and Silences

> Only those of a weak nature hold the mistaken belief that through belated interpretations and clarifications one may make something better, or moderate it or even undo something. I hold myself to Ernst Jünger's aphorism (from *Blätter und Steine*): "he who interprets himself stoops beneath his own level."
> —Ernst Forsthoff, to Rolf Seeliger, *Braune Universität,* ca. 1964

How did Heidelberg university professors respond to National Socialism? What impact did National Socialism have on research and teaching, and what role did professors play in the Nazi seizure and consolidation of power, in the construction of the "racial state" in Germany, and in Hitler's racist war of expansion? Finally, how did professors recall National Socialism after 1945, and what impact did the Heidelberg myth have on the emerging political culture of West Germany? Most scholarship that has addressed these questions has presented Heidelberg and other universities solely as victims of Nazi persecution. A still widely held consensus maintains that Heidelberg in particular was a bastion of tolerance, liberalism, and support for the Republic among its professors. In this version of the past, a rabidly anti-intellectual Nazi Party descended on the universities in 1933, hoping to form them into strongholds of "National Socialist" scholarship by purging Jews and "Marxists" and appointing pseudo-scholars to newly vacant professorships. In this crusade, the party had the support of the Nazi students, who had been among the earliest and most radical of converts to National Socialism. Still distrustful of the "Mandarin" elite that before 1933 had largely scorned it, the party also created or planned to create scholarly "institutes" to transcend the work of the traditional universities.

This account of events also contends that the vast majority of professors wanted nothing to do with the regime, its ideology, or its policies. They simply wished to be left alone to continue their scholarly pursuits largely as before. Admittedly, a few prominent scholars did support the regime at first, although more often than not out of misplaced idealism or nationalism. In any case, they soon became disillusioned with the reality of National Socialism. Although many others ultimately joined the party or an affiliated organization, most did so to protect their careers and their freedom to pursue research as they saw fit.

True, to a certain extent the university was indeed a victim of the Nazis. Above all, Jewish and liberal scholars and students were harassed, dismissed, and expelled. The loss of prominent Jewish academics and the reduced contact between German and foreign scholars hindered the progress of research in various fields. The university also lost some of its traditional autonomy of self-governance. The party impeded, although did not eliminate, the freedom to teach and learn, not least because the regime had stamped out freedom of expression throughout Germany. The party also attempted, albeit unsuccessfully, to control and reshape the professorate through a variety of channels, and enlisted professors in the service of the secret police to inform on their colleagues and students. In the awarding of some appointments, finally, political reliability was more highly prized than scholarly potential or accomplishment.

Evidence from Heidelberg's experience from 1933 to 1945 forces us to revise this complacent and comforting assessment. In the Weimar Republic, Heidelberg's professors indeed represented a wide spectrum of ideological engagement. About one-third were active with political parties, the majority belonging to the conservative DNVP or (in few cases the DVP), although a considerable number joined the liberal DDP. Only a very few joined the Nazi or socialist parties. The strongholds of pro-Republic sentiment and toleration were the Law Faculty and the Institute for Social and Political Sciences (Insosta), while the Medical and Natural Sciences faculties were the most conservative. Yet by the late 1920s, some former liberals had abandoned their previous support for the Republic, and a few outspoken democrats departed from Heidelberg. The university's leadership proved unwilling and unable to oppose the increasingly militant Nazi student organization. It would not be too great an exaggeration to state that the purges of German universities began at Heidelberg in 1932 when the Jewish pacifist and socialist Emil J. Gumbel was prohibited from teaching by the Baden state government with the overwhelming support of the teaching body.

Those who have claimed that Heidelberg was a bastion of tolerance and pro-Republic sentiment have been unable to explain not only why the professorate did not protest the Nazi seizure and consolidation of power but also why a considerable number of professors from all faculties and representing all age groups and levels on the university's hierarchy welcomed the regime and justified its policies while remaining silent as dozens of their colleagues were dismissed. Professors embraced the "National Revolution" because it promised the cultural, political, economic, and "racial" revival of Germany. It represented to many, as the historian Willy Andreas put it in 1933, "Germany's destiny." What concerned the few scholars who spoke up about the matter was the state's encroachment upon the institution's traditional autonomy and not the injustice of the anti-Semitic purge.

Despite unprecedented state incursion into their affairs, the faculties retained considerable influence over the selection of new members. The backgrounds and qualifications of those invited to replace dismissed scholars varied considerably from faculty to faculty. Party membership was not always the sole or even determining factor in the selection of replacements. Under the leadership of Carl Schneider, the Medical Faculty ensured that open positions were filled with qualified medical scientists and reliable National Socialists. Philipp Lenard wielded similarly decisive influence over the reconstruction of the Physics Institute and made Heidelberg one of the two centers in Germany of "Aryan physics." Alfred Weber's famed Insosta ceased to exist, its remnants being merged by the Culture Ministry with the Technical College in Mannheim. The new Faculty for Social and Political Sciences drew most of its members from this institution—principally economists and empirically oriented sociologists. By contrast, the Theology Faculty did not lose a single member in the purges.

From a very early point, Heidelberg's professors oriented their scholarship and teaching to the regime's objectives of creating a "racially pure" Germany and to its planned war of territorial expansion. The period from 1936 to 1939 represented a turning point in this regard for the university, as it did for all of Germany. In this period the regime accelerated the persecution of Jews and began to prepare for war. Like the "Gleichschaltung," interest in "racial" sciences and territorial expansion was driven from above and surged from within the university itself. Hence the regime ordered all remaining Jewish students dismissed and all Jewish scholars (including those "Aryans" married to Jews) expelled. The regime defined the "German spirit" in scholarship in opposition to the positivist "Jewish spirit," claiming that only "Aryan" scientists were capable of understanding the world. But from within Heidelberg itself, scholars embraced the "German spirit," became increasingly interested in race as a subject of study, and adopted race as a determining factor in the process of their scientific research. Some, of course, had been working in this direction for years. The most extreme manifestation of this development emerged from the Physics Institute, renamed after Philipp Lenard in late 1935. But the phenomenon can be noted across the faculties. Although unlike several other universities, Heidelberg did not see the creation of a special institute for the study of "racial sciences," the most influential figures in the Medical Faculty developed considerable interest in "racial hygiene," sterilization, and ultimately the systematic murder of the mentally ill and handicapped. Finally, the growing interest among professors in military and "racial sciences" was reflected in the creation of new courses in all faculties that addressed these topics. With good reason, then, Paul Schmitthenner could boast in November 1938: "we are no longer the university of the liberal age."

Another element of the "German spirit" was the contention—once again, held by many academics and nonacademic Nazi Party members alike—that research and teaching at the nation's universities was splintering into specializations without regard for an overarching whole and a fundamental connection to the German people it was supposed to serve. Between 1936 and 1939, then, a number of special institutes and seminars that focused on Germany's military preparedness, the Reich's western borders, and interdisciplinary research and teaching that sought to form such a bond between the university, scholarship, and the "Volksgemeinschaft" were created, all on the initiative of Heidelberg professors themselves. Each received varying degrees of state sanction and financial support.

The trends in research and teaching that emerged in the years 1936 to 1939 continued into the war. Far from neglecting research and teaching, the regime supported universities and scientific institutes. Scholars from all disciplines contributed their prestige and skills to the war effort by issuing publications and giving lectures, by helping plan for the exploitation and resettlement of conquered territories, and by participating in the mistreatment and murder of innocent human beings in the name of "purifying" the "Volksgemeinschaft." Several interdisciplinary institutes for the study of the economic integration of territories under German occupation or control were established during the war. The most direct link between Heidelberg University and the regime's crimes was found in the Medical Faculty, as was often the case at other universities. Carl Schneider became a leading researcher of the "euthanasia" program and forged his Heidelberg clinic into one of the program's major research and training centers. In stark contrast to these developments, resistance to the regime—organized or individual—by professors or students was rare.

What led so many scholars to support a murderous regime? In his classic study of Germany's "Mandarin elite," Fritz Ringer suggested that a pervasive (at least among the social scientists and historians that he examined) sense of decline in status combined with deeply rooted nationalism and cultural pessimism made the professors easy prey for the party in 1933, the point at which Ringer ended his study.[1] Outright opportunism was clearly another factor. In the late nineteenth century, German universities had witnessed rapid expansion in both numbers of students and in the number of those seeking to become academics. Yet the full professors, the elite of the elite who occupied the pinnacle of a rigid hierarchy, remained unreceptive to expanding their ranks or allowing junior colleagues any say in the management of university affairs. Budgetary constraints on state education ministries also proved to be a considerable impediment to creating new positions for the growing number of lower-level instructors without secure teaching positions. The significance of this development for the post-1933 period was, of course, that after the purges hundreds of positions were now open. Further, younger scholars were often put under pressure by party figures and colleagues to join at least the SA or another party-affiliated organization. Yet it is clear that party membership or lack of it was never the sole determining factor in academic advancement. Membership in the party could enhance a scholar's prospects, but it was possible to pursue a successful career without it. In short, the line between ideological engagement and opportunism was blurry, and the two were mutually reinforcing rather than distinct, as many academics wanted the world to believe after 1945.

Anti-Semitism and the widespread racist consciousness that pervaded scholarly fields from medicine to the study of ancient history was also another factor that made it easy for professors to accept or embrace the Nazi regime.[2] The kind of biological anti-Semitism prevalent within the Nazi Party was rarely found at the universities before 1933, but became increasingly common after that date and especially in the regime's final peacetime years. The anti-Semitism pervasive among Heidelberg's professors was summarized succinctly by the botanist Gerta von Ubisch, herself a victim of the purges: "In their heart of hearts, many Germans were anti-Semites and each one had one more or less large circle of Jews which he knew well and which he accepted as exceptions, while he rejected the Jews *in principle*." This strain was of a subtler and historically more common variety than that pronounced by Hitler and the Nazi Party, but it was nonetheless pernicious in that it contributed to the lack of any protest at the summary dismissals of thousands of the nation's finest scholars.

If many professors believed that National Socialism was good politics and good for Germany, however, many also believed *at the time* that its ideology comported with good scholarship. Postwar claims to the contrary, the boundaries between politics, ideology, and science during the Third Reich were porous. Drawing on developments in their fields that predated 1933, Heidelberg professors from all faculties made tangible contributions to the regime's policies of "racial purification" and territorial expansion in the name of the Führer, the "Volksgemeinschaft," and the "German spirit" in scholarship. The extent to which this antipositivist conception of science was adopted at other universities in the 1930s and 1940s and the role this rejection played in the postwar reemergence of positivism and Humboldtian idealism is a subject that requires much more investigation. At Heidelberg, the "German spirit" penetrated to the core of research and teaching, which is not to say that it was embraced uniformly by the professorate. A variety of intellectual currents flowed into and out of National Socialist Germany, and individual scholars disagreed with each other about their significance and applicability. The obfuscation of this element of "normalcy" in Germany's academic culture in the Third Reich was yet another casualty of the Heidelberg myth, which saddled a few fanatics such as Ernst Krieck, Eugen Fehrle, and Paul Schmitthenner with the blame for imposing the "German spirit" on the universities.

The practical problems faced by the American occupation authorities and the determination of a small group of professors account for Heidelberg's rapid reopening following the collapse of the Third Reich. This group consisted of well-known anti-Nazis, such as Karl Jaspers and Alfred Weber, as well as compromised individuals. Overall, they sought to restore the university's pre-1933 traditions and were determined to limit the influence of students in university affairs. They were almost without exception uninterested in structural reform, believing that National Socialism had "betrayed" Western scholarship and perverted the great liberal university traditions established in the early nineteenth century by Alexander von Humboldt and Friedrich Schleiermacher and had opened the gates of the ivory tower to hordes of anti-intellectual Visigoths.

Here lay the basis of the Heidelberg myth, which absolved all but a very few professors of complicity with National Socialism. Elements of it could be found in foreign and émigré assessments of Germany's nazified universities written in the 1930s. It was developed fully by Heidelberg professors in and after 1945 and has provided the basis for not only much of the consequent self-understanding of the West German professorate, but also most subsequent scholarly accounts. Before 1933, according to the myth, Heidelberg represented a stronghold of pro-Republic liberal tolerance. The National Socialists, determined to make an "example" out of "liberal" Heidelberg, did away with the university's autonomy and crushed academic freedoms, along the way ridding the university of the professors who had supported Germany's experiment with parliamentary democracy. The myth's earliest propagators rarely make reference to the fact that the Jews were the regime's principal targets, thus lending another element of distortion to an already warped portrait. The regime subsequently installed ideological fanatics with subpar scholarly qualifications to ensure Heidelberg's "nazification." The vast majority, however, kept their distance from the Nazis. If they had joined the party or could be shown to have made compromising statements, such instances could be excused because, as Karl Heinrich Bauer put it in 1946, "when one is forced to go through a swamp for twelve years, one gets dirty once in some form in the process." Such sentiments were held widely. "Nobody who remained in Germany," a report of the newly reconstituted Senate proclaimed in February 1946, "without being sent to a concentration camp, can be clean." Given the dark portrait of the university presented above, the myth obscured and attempted to excuse the willing complicity of the professorate with National Socialism.

The Heidelberg myth provided the main defense against U.S. denazification policies—initially the most extensive in all of occupied Germany—and was in turn reinforced by the professors' overwhelmingly negative response to several waves of dismissals. Under the leadership of a knowledgeable and perceptive officer, Edward Y. Hartshorne, all faculties would be screened thoroughly before being permitted to resume instruction. Yet like millions of Germans, most professors considered denazification to be unjust and the result of the occupiers' ignorance of the reality of life under the Nazis. They insisted that only a few had compromised themselves in any meaningful way with the Nazis and that most should remain in their positions despite formal party memberships. They argued that the number of "genuine Nazis" on the faculties had been few, that they had been imposed on the university by the regime, and that they were not scholars of merit.

This version of events connected scholarly accomplishment and political engagement and bolstered the myth that those who were productive, competent scholars were not Nazis. Hence the presence of a few men like Paul Schmitthenner, Eugen Fehrle, and Ernst Krieck ultimately proved highly convenient for many other compromised scholars who used their examples as the standard by which to gauge an individual's engagement—or lack of it—with National Socialism. A common defense in the postwar years, then, was to claim that since one had never embraced National Socialist ideology "as did Krieck" or "as did Alfred Rosenberg," one could not possibly be considered tainted by National Socialism. Although the historian Ulrich Herbert has memorably located the caricature of such "ideal Nazis" in fictionalized film and television productions, the case of postwar academic culture at Heidelberg indicates that such a figure also existed in the imaginations of professors and continues to obscure an understanding of the complexities of the years between 1933 and 1945.

Despite the fact that no organized effort was made at Heidelberg or anywhere else to secure the return of dismissed Jewish scholars (with the exception of those living in Heidelberg itself), Karl Heinrich Bauer and others insisted that qualified personnel who were not party members were simply not available. The resistance of the faculties to denazification—particularly that of the Medical Faculty under Bauer's dictatorial chairmanship—drove Edward Hartshorne to despair for the future of the universities and a democratic Germany.

The American policy of denazification reached its apogee in late 1945 and early 1946. Despite strong resistance, the purges hit the university particularly hard, even though the sharp reduction in the number of instructors was temporary. Although the Medical and Theology faculties resumed instruction in late 1945 and the entire university reopened early in 1946, widespread rumors that denazification at American zone universities was incomplete led the military governor, Lucius Clay, to order a close investigation of the situation and if necessary authorize a new round of purges. In this atmosphere, a German Jewish émigré officer of the Counter Intelligence Corps, Daniel Penham, arrived in Heidelberg and undertook just such a close investigation. Himself a scholar familiar with German academic culture and intellectual traditions, Penham was determined to extirpate all vestiges of National Socialist ideology from the university. After an initial inquiry that involved reading the publications of the professors themselves, Penham concluded that Heidelberg had been "Nazified to the core" and had reopened too quickly. He went so far as to propose that the university should be closed temporarily so that an extensive screening of the faculties and student body could be undertaken. Penham's activities fueled even greater resistance among the professors, many of whom no doubt felt considerable fear and loathing in the presence of a young uniformed German Jew. His investigations led professors to retrench even further behind the Heidelberg myth and to predict that his investigations would lead to the destruction of the university.

Penham, long regarded by contemporary German observers and later by historians as a mentally deranged and renegade agent of the CIC, was in fact representative of a vocal but minority strain among American occupation officials. Historians have often assessed the American denazification policy as an abysmal failure in that it favored the restoration of conservative elites, many of them compromised with National Socialism, at the expense of justice and social reform, while many West Germans considered it to have reflected hopeless naiveté on the part of the Americans.[3] But the voices of those like Penham present us with a more complex picture. Penham himself, in some ways like Edward Hartshorne, was hardly without experience or qualifications to assess the academic elite's engagement with National Socialism. Like other officers (many of them also émigrés), Penham believed that Germany's future as a peaceful and democratic state and not least the dictates of justice would best be served by a forthright reckoning with the past, even at the expense of administrative convenience. His investigation sabotaged and opposed by the entire professorate and his recommendations ignored by his superiors, Penham was reassigned. Ironically, a Military Government investigation of the faculties in the spring and summer of 1946 confirmed Penham's accusations. But with the often overwhelming burdens placed on American occupation officials and the emergence of the Cold War and its attendant emphasis on the quick resuscitation of the West German economy, little action was taken, and compromised professors like Karl Heinrich Bauer kept their positions.

The duel between Daniel Penham and Karl Heinrich Bauer described in Chapter 5 illustrates better than any other single incident the clashing interpretations of nazification that have dominated debate both among contemporaries and, in roughly similar form, among historians since 1946. Penham believed a close and detailed investigation of individual faculty members was necessary to determine the extent of the institution's "nazification." Such an investigation would take a variety of factors into account—the scholar's political track record, the courses he taught, and his scholarly work published both before and during the Third Reich. Penham's opponents, led by Bauer, rejected "blanket" denazification policies and demanded that each scholar's record be taken into account by American investigators and by the Spruchkammer. Yet the professors nonetheless bitterly resisted just such an investigation when it was proposed and pursued by Daniel Penham. Bauer and other professors instead succeeded in narrowing the meaning of nazification. This fundamental divide in the interpretation of the meaning of "nazification" persists in large part to the present, as historians continue to disagree over the extent of the professorate's engagement with National Socialism. Our understanding of the consensus behind Hitler and the Nazis in academic culture, however, will remain incomplete until historians undertake the kind of detailed and differentiated investigations advocated by Daniel Penham in early 1946.

The Heidelberg myth was solidified and further diffused in German political culture in the wake of the Spruchkammer, a legal whitewash that facilitated the return of thousands of former Nazis to positions of influence in German public life. The long-inaccessible records of these local civilian tribunals around Heidelberg reveal that professors constructed remarkably similar narratives regarding their relationships to National Socialism and supported each other in a densely woven web of mutual affidavits. The narratives severed politics and ideology from scholarship and allowed compromised professors to present themselves not only as nominal party members but as scholars who never deviated from the dictates of "objective" scholarship. They represented professors as men who respected the autonomy of research and teaching and became opponents of the regime because the Nazis clearly hoped to destroy "legitimate" scholarly methods of investigation. Further, nearly every professor standing before the tribunal claimed to have assisted Jews in one way or another or at least to have made positive references to Jewish scholarship in his lectures. These narratives were thereafter repeated in roughly similar forms in numerous festschrifts and memoirs, and later in many scholarly accounts, and formed an important element of the emerging culture of forgetting that marked the formative years of the Federal Republic.

What impact did National Socialism have on the quality of research and other scholarly endeavors at Heidelberg? Generalizations are difficult, and more research needs to be done on this important question. Certainly, as Alan Beyerchen concluded, the Aryan physicists failed not only as political infighters among the unforgiving bureaucratic jungles of the Third Reich but also as pioneers of "Aryan science."[4] The intense interest, however, among agents of the U.S. Field Information Agency Technical (FIAT) in research conducted in the medical and physical sciences during the Third Reich reveals that in many areas advances were made. As noted in Chapter 7, the defeat and occupation of Germany also led professors either to ignore or to revise some of their previous work. Such revisions have been little studied by historians but must be considered part of the "denazification" of academic culture after 1945. In a variation on this important theme, scholars such as Werner Conze and Ernst Forsthoff drew upon their academic collaborations with National Socialism—now modified to accommodate postwar democratic sensibilities—to forge a bold new direction in social history (in Conze's case) or in the reorienting and revival of conservative German cultural, legal, and political criticism.

I have suggested that the "nazification" of Heidelberg worked like an enormous pincer movement, with one arm of the pincer representing the party and its decrees and the other representing acceptance and implementation from below. Further, the case of Heidelberg reveals that "nazification" should be seen as a process that unfolded in the course of the regime's attempts to build a "racially pure" society and its concomitant war of territorial expansion. Scholars, having embraced National Socialism to varying degrees, did so out of a variety of personal and professional motives, including a clear desire to reconceptualize the nature of scholarly inquiry itself and a related desire to alter the purpose and structure of the university. They didn't "betray" academic culture but sought to reshape it. Hence, in their view, "freedom of research" was not seriously impeded at Heidelberg because the concept itself had been redefined.

Denazification involved more than a set of policies laid down by the occupiers. It also entailed a form of "coming to terms with the past" among the professors. By defining what constituted unacceptable engagement with the Nazis narrowly—namely, adherence to the most extreme manifestations of "Nazi scholarship," active engagement with the SS or the SD, and also engagement in a discipline that had been traditionally marginalized by academic culture (such as folklore or pedagogy)—professors relied on the construction of a past that absolved most of them of virtually any blame for the catastrophe of National Socialism. This maneuver exonerated dozens of scholars who had, party membership or not, put their talents in the service of the regime.

By the 1950s, this culture of forgetting at Heidelberg was entrenched as it was throughout West Germany. As the Spruchkammer process came to an inglorious conclusion and the Bundestag passed a sweeping amnesty law in 1951, hundreds of former Nazis returned to academia. As Karl Jaspers noted to Hannah Arendt in 1950, the years 1945 and 1946—years when figures like Jaspers and Alfred Weber had called for a democratic civil society alongside a reckoning with the past (if not necessarily extensive denazification)—had been forgotten. In place of the culture of forgetting there emerged what Dirk van Laak has memorably labeled "the security of silence."[5] Attempts to break the silence, such as those of the mid- and late 1960s or those of the late 1990s—have been met within much of German academic culture with skepticism, arrogant dismissal, or outright hostility. The Heidelberg myth remains a formidable, though not unbreachable, edifice.

APPENDIX A

The Structure of the German University

All German universities were (and continue to be) state institutions. Until 1934, their respective state (Land) ministries of education were responsible for budgetary matters and for approving or rejecting professorial appointments recommended by individual university faculties. By the early twentieth century, the universities were comprised of five or six faculties: theology, law, medicine, philosophy, the natural sciences, and the newer faculties (often quasi-independent institutes) of the social sciences. Each faculty was comprised of seminars, institutes, or clinics devoted to particular specialties. Hence, the History Seminar was located within the Philosophy Faculty, the Physics Institute within the Natural Sciences Faculty, and so forth. The entire institution was represented by a Rektor (or Rector, the equivalent of an English Vice-Chancellor or an American President), and a Great and Small Senate. The Great Senate consisted of the entire teaching body (except for the unsalaried lecturers, the Privatdozenten) and elected the Rector annually from among the full professors (Ordinarien). The Small Senate was elected by and consisted of the full professors and had the most influence over the institution's day-to-day affairs.

There were two broad groups of professors: Ordinarien and Nichtordinarien. Ordinarien were full, tenured professors who had the largest role in governing the university and recommending appointments and in general influencing the direction of research and teaching. They alone could be elected as Dekane (faculty chairmen) and rectors. Nichtordinarien were junior-level professors, (or ausserordentliche Professoren, or Extraordinarien) whose role in the governance of the university was limited but who could eventually be promoted to full professors. Privatdozenten, who carried only the *venia legendi* (the right to teach conferred by the university and the state), received only lecture fees and had no say in the institution's governance. By 1932, there were 2,061 full professors, 1,577 junior-level professors, and 1,753 Privatdozenten at Germany's twenty-two universities.

Those aspiring to a career as an academic had to seek out a professor willing to serve as an adviser, complete the requirements for a doctorate, and then write a dissertation. A candidate would then often serve as an assistant to a professor while preparing a completely new scholarly work, the Habilitationsschrift, which would finally establish the scholar's credentials within his discipline. The new instructor would then wait for a call from a state Ministry of Education to fill a vacant chair at a university. The entire process, from Habilitationsschrift to the attainment of full-professor status, could take thirty to forty years.[1]

APPENDIX B

Dissertations Supervised by Paul Schmitthenner, 1932–1941

1932

"The U-Boat War against England and the German Daily Press from 1.8.14 to 1.2.17" (O. Stadler)

1934

"State and Nation in the Thought of Carl von Clausewitz" (A. Brügmann)
"The Army of Baden, 1866–1870/1" (H. Riese)

1935

"On Farmers, the Bourgeoisie, and the Workers in the Army" (H. Gauer)
"The Evolution of Youth Journals and Their Formation in the Social Democratic, Communist, and National Socialist Youth Movements" (F. Sellmeyer)
"The Development and Change of the Use of Airships in Sea Warfare" (H. Beelitz)
"Count Wilhelm von Schaumberg-Lippe and His Army: The Roots of Universal Conscription in Germany" (E. Hübinger)
"Military Considerations in Germany after the War of 1918–1921: An Investigation of the Weimar Constitution, Political Party Programs, and the Large Party Presses" (K. Rau)
"The Historical Development of German Pacificism since 1900: A Contribution to the Collapse of Germany in the World War" (G. Starker)

1936

"Sport, Politics, and the Press: Sport as a Means of Political Struggle and Party-Political Propaganda in the Time of the Weimar System, 1919–1933" (E. Bayer)

"Military Policy of the German Reich under Reich Chancellor Fuerst Buelow" (E. Rausch)

1937

"The Anti-German Climate of Opinion in the United States of America during the World War and 1933/34" (A. Dittmann)
"Military Considerations in the History of German Physical Education" (O. Neumann)
"The Freemasons and the Assassination in Sarajevo" (H. Zinnecke)

1938

"The Burgenland in the Light of Czech Plans for Sovereignty" (E. Falk)
"The Military-Political Development of Germany's Soldiers Reflected in Farmer's and Soldier's Songs" (G. Klein)

1939

"The Military Education of Youth in the Prewar Period, 1871–1914" (R. Fechter)
"Foreign Policy as Racial and Spatial Problems Seen from Bismarck's Eastern Policy" (H. Grathwohl)
"Enmity toward the Reich of Political Catholicism in Alsace-Lorraine, 1870–1918," (H. Gerke)
"Friedrich Naumann's Political Desires from a Military-Political Viewpoint" (O. Gramm)
"The Army Contingent of the Cloister at Salem" (H. Schmiedel)
"Baden's Military Condition, 1750–1806" (O. Wollweber)
"The Three Corners of Germany, Switzerland, and France as Contested Territory [Volksraum]" (E. Gäng)

1940

"The Catholic Press and Parliament Policy in Hesse as Mirrored in Mainz Journals" (W. Schmiedmüller)
"The Work of the German Military Organizations and the Military Situation of Germany before the World War" (E. Schwinn)

1941

"The Military-Political Importance of Ireland and the Irish Question" (B. Herr)

Listed with No Dates

"The Struggle for the Ruhr in 1923 and Its Importance for the Nation. A Military-Political Study" (L. Noack)
"Political Catholicism and World War" (F. W. Albrecht)

Listed as Works in Progress

"Women's Service Duty in the World War, 1914/1918" (U. Geiseler)
"The Black Forest as a Strategic Barrier in History" (H. Krebs)
"Friedrich Wilhelm Ruestow" (H. Hofferberth)
"The Baden-Baden Army Contingent in the Reich Army" (M. Wasmer)
"Military Enthusiasm and Military Action of the German Student Body in the War of 1870/1" (H. Mayer)
"Military Thought and the Idea of a Greater Germany in the Youth Movement of 1918–1933" (H. Kullmer)
"The Development and Military Significance of the English Mandate in Palestine" (M. Struve)
"The Military-Political Significance of Poenitz" (H. Seidenadel)[1]

Archival Sources

Germany

BA: BUNDESARCHIV, BERLIN
    R21 (Reichserziehungsministerium)

GLAK: GENERALLANDESARCHIV KARLSRUHE
    Dienerakte
    Ministerium des Kultus und Unterrichts
    Nachlass Willy Andreas
    Nachlass Willy Hellpach
    Nachlass Ernst Krieck
    Spruchkammerakte

STADTARCHIV HEIDELBERG

UAH: UNIVERSITÄTSARCHIV HEIDELBERG
    Fakultätsakte
    Nachlass Karl Heinrich Bauer
    Nachlass Karl Freudenberg
    Personalakte
    Rektoratsamt
    Senatprotokolle

UBH: UNIVERSITÄTSBIBLIOTHEK HEIDELBERG
    Nachlass Martin Dibelius
    Nachlass Gustav Radbruch
    Nachlass Gerta von Ubisch

United States

AMERICAN INSTITUTE OF PHYSICS, COLLEGE PARK, MARYLAND
Papers of Samuel Goudsmit

GEORGE C. MARSHALL RESEARCH LIBRARY, LEXINGTON, VIRGINIA
Smith-Crum Papers

HOOVER INSTITUTION, STANFORD UNIVERSITY
West European Collections

NARA: UNITED STATES NATIONAL ARCHIVES AND RECORDS ADMINISTRATION, COLLEGE PARK, MARYLAND
Record Group 260 (Records of the Office of Military Government United States)
Record Group 226 (Records of the OSS)
Record Group 242 (Berlin Document Center)

TRUMAN STATE UNIVERSITY, KIRKSVILLE, MISSOURI
Papers of Harry Hamilton Laughlin

UNIVERSITY OF CHICAGO SPECIAL COLLECTIONS
Papers of Emil J. Gumbel

Notes

Introduction

1. There are multiple ways to use the term "myth." I use it here as a coherent narrative strategy employed by a particular group that blends elements of truth and falsehood to legitimize that group's claims to knowledge and power. On the difficulties of defining myth, see Elizabeth Baeten, *The Magic Mirror: Myth's Abiding Power* (Albany: State University of New York Press, 1996).
2. See Michael Kater, "The Burden of the Past: Problems of a Modern Historiography of Physicians and Medicine in Nazi Germany," *German Studies Review,* 10, no. 1 (February 1987), 31–56; Rüdiger Hohls and Konrad Jarausch, eds., *Versäumte Fragen: deutsche Historiker im Schatten des Nationalsozialismus* (Stuttgart: Deutsche Verlagsanstalt, 2000); James R. Dow and Hannjost Lixfeld, "Epilogue: Overcoming the Past of National Socialist Folklore," in James R. Dow and Hannjost Lixfeld, eds., *The Nazification of an Academic Discipline: Folklore in the Third Reich* (Bloomington: Indiana University Press, 1994), pp. 264–296; and Carsten Klingemann, "Reichssoziologie und Nachkriegssoziologie: Zur Kontinuität einer Wissenschaft in zwei politischen Systemen," in Renate Knigge-Tesche, ed., *Berater der braunen Macht. Wissenschaft und Wissenschaftler im NS-Staat* (Frankfurt am Main: Anabas Verlag, 1999), pp. 70–93.
3. Gerhard Ritter, "Der Professor im 'Dritten Reich,'" *Die Gegenwart,* December 24, 1945, pp. 23–26, and in English translation as "The Professor in the Third Reich," *Review of Politics,* 8, no. 2 (April 1946), 242–254. Also see Hannah Arendt, "The Image of Hell," *Commentary,* 2 (September 1946), 291–295.
4. In addition to Ritter, see Fritz Ernst, "Die Wiederöffnung der Universität

Heidelberg, 1945–1946. Aus Anlass des 70. Geburtstag von Karl Heinrich Bauer am 26. September 1960," *Heidelberger Jahrbücher,* 4 (1960), 1–28; Wolfgang Kunkel, "Der Professor im Dritten Reich," in Helmut Kuhn et al., *Die Deutsche Universität im Dritten Reich* (Munich: R. Piper & Co. Verlag, 1966), pp. 103–133; and the essays in Hans Herzfeld et al., *Universitätstag 1966. Nationalsozialismus und die deutsche Universität* (Berlin: Walter de Gruyter, 1966). Also see Ernst Nolte, "Behavioral Patterns of University Professors in the Third Reich," in Ernst Nolte, *Marxism, Fascism, Cold War* (Assen: Van Gorcum, 1982), pp. 106–120, and Jeremy Noakes, "The Ivory Tower under Siege: German Universities in the Third Reich," *The Journal of European Studies,* 23 (1993), 371–407.

5. Max Weinreich, *Hitler's Professors: The Part of Scholarship in Germany's Crimes against the Jewish People* (New York: Yiddish Scientific Institute–YIVO, 1946). Yale University Press republished it in 1999.

6. Ibid., p. 6.

7. Rolf Seeliger, *Braune Universität. Dokumentation mit Stellungnahmen. Dokumentenreihe,* 6 vols. (Munich: Verlag Rolf Seeliger, 1964), and Hans Peter Bleuel, *Deutschlands Bekenner. Professoren zwischen Kaiserreich und Diktatur* (Bern: Scherz Verlag, 1967).

8. See Margit Szöllösi-Janze, "National Socialism and the Sciences: Reflections, Conclusions, and Historical Perspectives," in Margit Szöllösi-Janze, ed., *Science in the Third Reich* (Oxford: Berg, 2001), pp. 1–35, and the excellent contributions to Knigge-Tesche, ed., *Berater der braunen Macht.*

9. See Hohls and Jarausch, *Versäumte Fragen.* In his fine study of intellectuals and tyranny, Mark Lilla concludes that "in the Walpurgisnacht of 1933, scores of Germany's leading professors and writers engaged themselves foolishly and ignorantly in politics ... Most concluded that their forays into politics had been errors and returned quickly to their studies and laboratories." Mark Lilla, *The Reckless Mind: Intellectuals in Politics* (New York: New York Review Books, 2001), pp. 205–206.

10. On Heidelberg, see Christian Jansen, *Professoren und Politik: Politisches Denken und Handeln der Heidelberger Hochschullehrer, 1914–1935* (Göttingen: Vandenhoeck & Ruprecht, 1992); Eike Wolgast, "Die Universität Heidelberg in der Zeit des Nationalsozialismus," *Zeitschrift für die Geschichte des Oberrheins,* 135 (1987), 359–406; Wilhelm Doerr, ed., *Semper Apertus: Sechshundert Jahre Ruprecht-Karls-Universität Heidelberg, 1386–1986* (Berlin: Springer, 1985), vol. 3; Birgit Vezina, *"Die Gleichschaltung" der Universität Heidelberg im Zuge der nationalsozialistischen Machtergreifung* (Heidelberg: C. Winter, 1982); Dorothee Mussgnug, *Die vertriebenen Heidelberger Dozenten: zur Geschichte der Ruprecht-Karls-Universität nach 1933* (Heidelberg: C. Winter, 1988); and Karin Buselmeier, Dietrich Harth, and Christian Jansen, eds., *Auch eine Geschichte der Universität Heidelberg* (Mannheim: Edition Quadrat, 1985).

11. Karl-Dietrich Bracher, *Turning Points in Modern Times: Essays on German*

and European History (Cambridge: Harvard University Press, 1995), p. 152.

12. See Ian Kershaw, *The Nazi Dictatorship: Problems and Perspectives of Interpretation* (New York: Oxford University Press, 2000), and his *Hitler, 1889–1936: Hubris* (New York: W. W. Norton, 1998), p. 539.

13. The literal English translation of the German word "Wissenschaft" is "science," but in the context of German academic culture, "Wissenschaft" encompasses all scholarly endeavors. I have translated the term as "scholarly" or "scholarship" and use it to denote the hard sciences, the humanities, and the social sciences.

14. A good introduction to this subject is Steven Shapin, "History of Science and Its Sociological Reconstructions," *History of Science,* 20, no. 49 (1982), 157–211. Important works addressing the sociology of scientific knowledge are Ludwik Fleck's writings, collected in R. S. Cohen and Thomas Schnelle, eds., *Cognition and Fact: Materials on Ludwik Fleck* (Dordrecht: D. Reidel, 1986); Karl Popper, *The Logic of Scientific Discovery* (London: Hutchinson, 1959); Robert Merton, *The Sociology of Science: Theoretical and Empirical Investigations* (Chicago: University of Chicago Press, 1973); Thomas Kuhn, *The Structure of Scientific Revolutions* (Chicago: University of Chicago Press, 1962); Bruno Latour, *Laboratory Life: The Social Construction of Scientific Facts* (Beverly Hills: Sage Publications, 1979); Jean-François Lyotard, *The Postmodern Condition: A Report on Knowledge* (Minneapolis: University of Minnesota Press, 1984); Steven Shapin and Simon Schaffer, *Leviathan and the Air-Pump: Hobbes, Boyle, and the Experimental Life* (Princeton: Princeton University Press, 1985); Mario Biagioli, *Galileo, Courtier: The Practice of Science in the Culture of Absolutism* (Chicago: University of Chicago Press, 1993); and Christopher Norris, *Against Relativism: Philosophy of Science, Deconstruction, and Critical Theory* (Oxford: Blackwell, 1997). Also see Alan Sokal and Jean Bricmont, *Fashionable Nonsense: Postmodern Intellectuals' Abuse of Science* (New York: Picador, 1998). On "national styles" of science, see Jonathan Harwood, *Styles of Scientific Thought: The German Genetics Community, 1900–1933* (Chicago: University of Chicago Press, 1993), esp. pp. 1–17.

15. Alan Beyerchen, "What We Now Know about Nazism and Science," in Margaret C. Jacob, ed., *The Politics of Western Science, 1640–1990* (Atlantic Highlands, N.J.: Humanities Press, 1994), pp. 129–155; Mario Biagioli, "Science, Modernity, and the 'Final Solution,'" in Saul Friedländer, ed., *Probing the Limits of Representation: Nazism and the "Final Solution"* (Cambridge: Harvard University Press, 1992), pp. 185–205; and Herbert Mehrtens, "The Social System of Mathematics and National Socialism: A Survey," in Monika Renneberg and Mark Walker, eds., *Science, Technology, and National Socialism* (Cambridge: Cambridge University Press, 1994), pp. 291–311.

16. See Fritz Ringer, *The Decline of the German Mandarins: The German Academic Community, 1890–1933* (Cambridge: Harvard University Press, 1969); George Mosse, *The Crisis of German Ideology: The Intellectual Origins of the Third Reich* (New York: Grosset & Dunlap, 1964); Kurt Sontheimer, *Antidemokratisches Denken in der Weimarer Republik: die politischen Ideen des Deutschen Nationalismus zwischen 1918 und 1933* (Munich: Nyphenburger Verlagshandlung, 1969); Jeffrey Herf, *Reactionary Modernism: Technology, Culture, and Politics in Weimar and the Third Reich* (Cambridge: Cambridge University Press, 1984); Notker Hammerstein, *Antisemitismus und deutsche Universitäten* (Frankfurt am Main: Campus Verlag, 1995); and Harwood, *Styles of Scientific Thought*.

17. I have used Leszek Kolakowski's definition of positivism as "a certain philosophical attitude concerning human knowledge; strictly speaking, it does not prejudge questions about how men arrive at knowledge—neither the psychological nor the historical foundations of knowledge." Positivism thus encompasses (1) "the rule of phenomenalism," whereby "we are entitled to record only that which is actually manifested in experience"; (2) "the rule of nominalism," which assumes that "every abstract science is a method of ordering, a quantitative recording of experiences, and has no independent cognitive function in the sense that, via its abstractions, it opens access to empirically inaccessible domains of reality"; (3) a rejection of assigning "cognitive value to value judgments and normative statements"; and (4) "the unity of the scientific method," whereby "the methods for acquiring valid knowledge, and the main stages in elaborating experience through theoretical reflection, are essentially the same in all spheres of experience." Positivism, in short, demands that the acquisition of knowledge be "entirely free of metaphysical assumptions," that is, "value-free." Leszek Kolakowski, *The Alienation of Reason: A History of Positivist Thought* (Garden City: Doubleday, 1968), pp. 1–10.

18. See, for instance, Joachim Lerchenmueller, *Die Geschichtswissenschaft in den Planungen der Sicherheitsdienstes der SS. Der SD-Historiker Hermann Löffler und seine Denkschrift "Entwicklung und Aufgaben der Geschichtswissenschaft in Deutschland"* (Bonn: Verlag J. H. W. Dietz Nachf., 2001), and the Sicherheitsdienst report on academic Germanists reprinted in Gerd Simon, *Germanistik in den Planspielen des Sicherheitsdienstes der SS,* vol. 1 (Tübingen: GIFT Verlag, 1998).

19. Charlotte Koehn-Behrens, ed., *Was ist Rasse? Gespräche mit den grössten deutschen Forschern der Gegenwart* (Munich: F. Eher, 1934).

20. Ringer, *Decline of the German Mandarins,* pp. 200–252, 305–434. Also see Robert Proctor, *Value-Free Science? Purity and Power in Modern Knowledge* (Cambridge: Harvard University Press, 1991), pp. 65–154, and Sylvia Paletschek, "The Invention of Humboldt and the Impact of National Socialism: The German University Idea in the First Half of the Twentieth Century," in Szöllösi-Janze, ed., *Science in the Third Reich,* pp. 37–58.

21. Gustav Radbruch, *Der Innere Weg. Aufriss meines Lebens* (Stuttgart: K. F. Koehler, 1951), pp. 88–89.
22. Marianne Weber, "Akademische Geselligkeit, 1924–1944," manuscript, Universitätsbibliothek Heidelberg (hereafter cited as UBH), Nachlass Gustav Radbruch, Heid. Hs. 3716, and published as "Academic Conviviality," *Minerva,* 15, no. 2, (1977), 214–246.
23. On the history of Insosta, see Klaus Brintzinger, Carsten Klingemann, and Reinhard Blomert, *Intellektuelle im Aufbruch: Karl Mannheim, Alfred Weber, Norbert Elias und die Heidelberger Sozialwissenschaften der Zwischenkriegszeit* (Munich: Hanser, 1999), and Klaus Brintzinger, *Die Nationalökonomie an den Universitäten Freiburg, Heidelberg und Tübingen 1918–1945: eine institutionenhistorische, vergleichende Studie der wirtschaftswissenschaftlichen Fakultäten und Abteilungen südwestdeutscher Universitäten* (Frankfurt am Main: Lang, 1996).
24. Karl Mannheim, "Heidelberg Letters," in David Kettler and Colin Loader, eds., *Karl Mannheim: Sociology as Political Education* (New Brunswick, N.J.: Transaction, 2001), p. 90.
25. Volker Berghahn, *America and the Intellectual Cold Wars in Europe: Shepard Stone between Philanthropy, Academy, and Diplomacy* (Princeton: Princeton University Press, 2001).
26. On Schurman, see Detlev Junker, "Jacob Gould Schurman, die Universität Heidelberg und die deutsch-amerikanische Beziehungen," in Doerr, ed., *Semper Apertus,* vol. 3, pp. 328–358.
27. Paul Oskar Kristeller and Margaret L. King, "Iter Kristellerianum: The European Journey (1905–1939), *Renaissance Quarterly,* 47 (1994), 915. I am grateful to my colleague Margaret King for suggesting this source.
28. Jansen, *Professoren und Politik,* pp. 394–406.
29. Most of the information about Heidelberg during the Weimar Republic has been drawn from ibid.; Helene Tompert, "Lebensformen und Denkweisen der akademischen Welt Heidelbergs im Wilhelmischen Zeitalter," *Historische Studien,* 411 (1969); and Reinhard Riese, *Die Hochschule auf dem Wege zum wissenschaftlichen Grossbetrieb: die Universität Heidelberg und das badische Hochschulwesen, 1860–1914* (Stuttgart: Ernst Klett Verlag, 1977). Important memoir accounts include Walter Pauly, ed., *Aus meinem Leben: Erinnerungen von Gerhard Anschütz* (Frankfurt: Klostermann, 1992); Karl Freudenberg, "Lebenserinnerungen," *Heidelberger Jahrbücher,* 1988, pp. 151–187; Weber, "Akademische Geselligkeit, 1924–1944"; Radbruch, *Der innere Weg;* Willy Hellpach, *Hellpach-Memoiren, 1925–1945* (Cologne: In Kommission bei Böhlau, 1987); Marie Baum, *Rückblick auf mein Leben* (Heidelberg: F. H. Kerle Verlag, 1950); Philipp Lenard, "Erinnerungen eines Naturwissenschaftlers, der Kaiserreich, Judenherrschaft und Hitler erlebt hat," unpublished manuscript, Institut für Fränkisch-Pfälzische Geschichte und Landeskunde, Heidelberg University; Helmut Joachim Fischer, *Erinnerungen,* vol. 1, *Von der Wissenschaft zum*

Sicherheitsdienst (Ingolstadt: Quellenstudien der Zeitgeschichtlichen Forschungsstelle Ingolstadt, 1984–85); Ludwig Curtius, *Deutsche und Antike Welt. Lebenserinnerungen* (Stuttgart: Deutsche Verlags-Anstalt, 1950); Hermann Glockner, *Heidelberger Bilderbuch. Erinnerungen* (Bonn: H. Bouvier, 1969); Gustav Hoelscher, "Gelehrter in Politischer Zeit," *Ruperto Carola*, 58/59 (December 1976/June 1977), 53–59; Karl Jaspers, "Philosophical Autobiography," in Paul Arthur Schilpp, ed., *The Philosophy of Karl Jaspers* (La Salle, Ill.: Open Court, 1957), pp. 3–94; Hans Speier, *The Truth in Hell and Other Essays on Politics and Culture, 1935–1987* (New York: Oxford University Press, 1989); Gerta von Ubisch, unpublished memoirs, ca. 1955, UBH, Nachlass Gerta von Ubisch, Heid. Hs. 4029; Emil J. Gumbel, "The Professor from Heidelberg," in William Allen Neilson, ed., *We Escaped: Twelve Personal Narratives of the Flight to America* (New York: MacMillan, 1941); chap. 2; Günther Dehn, *Die alte Zeit die vorigen Jahre. Lebenserrinerungen* (Munich: Chr. Kaiser Verlag, 1962); Golo Mann, *Reminiscences and Reflections: A Youth in Germany* (New York: Norton, 1990); Norbert Elias, *Reflections on a Life* (Cambridge: Polity Press, 1994); Dolf Sternberger, "Erinnerungen an die Zwanziger Zahre in Heidelberg," in *Die Geschichte der Universität Heidelberg. Vorträge im Wintersemester 1985/86* (Heidelberg: HVA, 1986), pp. 176–185; Nahum Goldmann, *The Autobiography of Nahum Goldmann: Sixty Years of Jewish Life* (New York: Holt, Rinehart & Winston, 1969); Carl Zuckmayer, *A Part of Myself* (New York: Harcourt Brace Jovanovich, 1970); and Ernst Toller, *Ein Jugend in Deutschland* (Amsterdam: Querido Verlag N.V., 1936).

30. See Alice Gallin, *Midwives to Nazism: University Professors in Weimar Germany, 1925–1933* (Macon: Mercer University Press, 1986).
31. The best accounts of the Gumbel affair are in Christian Jansen, *Emil Julius Gumbel. Porträt eines Zivilisten* (Heidelberg: Verlag das Wunderhorn, 1991), and Arthur David Brenner, *Emil J. Gumbel: Weimar German Pacifist and Professor* (Boston: Humanities Press, 2001).
32. "'Heldenverehrung' in Heidelberg," *Deutsche Republik*, July 2, 1932, p. 1271.
33. Edgar Julius Jung, "Niebelungen von Weimar?" *Deutsche Rundschau*, 231 (1932), 158.
34. See, for instance, Willy Hellpach, *Politische Prognose für Deutschland* (Berlin: S. Fischer, 1928); Karl Jaspers, *Die geistige Situation der Zeit* (Berlin: Walter de Gruyter, 1931); Ernst Robert Curtius, *Deutscher Geist in Gefahr* (Stuttgart: Deutsche Verlags-Anstalt, 1932); and Martin Dibelius, "Die Zersetzung des Bürgertums," 1932, reprinted in Friedrich Wilhelm Graf, ed., "Martin Dibelius über die Zerstörung der Bürgerlichkeit. Ein Vortrag im Heidelberger Marianne-Weber-Kreis 1932," in *Zeitschrift für die neuere Theologiegeschichte*, 4 (1997), 114–153.
35. See, for example, Willy Hellpach's "Das Bündnis des Faschismus mit dem

Geist," *Reich und Länder,* 1 (January 1933), 10–18, and his "Das faschistische Italien und der europaeische Geist," *Minerva-Zeitschrift,* 9, nos. 1/2 (January/February 1933), 1–7. On Hellpach's political transformation, see Christian Jansen, "Antiliberalismus und Antiparlamentarismus in der bürgerlich-demokratischen Elite der Weimarer Republik. Willy Hellpachs Publizistik der Jahre 1925–1933," *Zeitschrift für Geschichtswissenschaft,* 49, no. 9 (2001), 773–795. Also see Dirk Käsler and Thomas Steiner, "Academic Discussion or Political Guidance? Social-scientific Analyses of Fascism and National Socialism in Germany before 1933," in Dirk Käsler and Stephen P. Turner, eds., *Sociology Responds to Fascism* (London: Routledge, 1992), pp. 88–126.

1. Embracing National Socialism

1. Karl Dietrich Bracher, Wolfgang Sauer, and Gerhard Schulz, *Die nationalsozialistische Machtergreifung: Studien zur Errichtung des totalitären Herrschaftssystems in Deutschland, 1933/34* (Cologne: Westdeutscher Verlag, 1960).
2. On the Gleichschaltung at the universities, see Edward Y. Hartshorne, Jr., *The German Universities and National Socialism* (London: George Allen & Unwin, 1937); Karl-Dietrich Bracher, "Die Gleichschaltung der deutschen Universität," in Hans Herzfeld et al., *Universitätstag 1966. Nationalsozialismus und die deutsche Universität* (Berlin: Walter de Gruyter, 1966), pp. 126–142; Bruno Reimann, "Die 'Selbst-Gleichschaltung' der Universitäten 1933," in Jörg Tröger, ed., *Hochschule und Wissenschaft im Dritten Reich* (Frankfurt: Campus Verlag, 1986), pp. 38–52; Helmut Heiber, *Universität unterm Hakenkreuz. Die Kapitulation der Hohen Schulen. Das Jahr 1933 und seine Themen* (Munich: K. G. Saur, 1991); and Karl Löwith, *My Life in Germany before and after 1933: A Report* (Urbana: University of Illinois Press, 1986), pp. 70–84. On the Gleichschaltung at Heidelberg, see Emil J. Gumbel, *Auf der Suche nach Wahrheit* (Berlin: Dietz Verlag, 1991), pp. 207–217; Birgit Vezina, *Die 'Gleichschaltung' der Universität Heidelberg im Zuge der nationalsozialistischen Machtergreifung* (Heidelberg: C. Winter, 1982); Dorothee Mussgnug, *Die vertriebenen Heidelberg Dozenten: zur Geschichte der Ruprecht-Karls-Universität nach 1933* (Heidelberg: C. Winter, 1988); and Dorothee Mussgnug, "Die Universität Heidelberg zu Beginn der nationalsozialistischen Herrschaft," in Wilhelm Doerr, ed., *Semper Apertus: Sechshundert Jahre Ruprecht-Karls-Universitat Heidelberg, 1386–1986* (Berlin: Springer Verlag, 1985), pp. 464–503; Christian Jansen, *Professoren und Politik: Politisches Denken und Handeln der Heidelberger Hochschullehrer, 1914–1935* (Göttingen: Vandenhoeck & Ruprecht, 1992), pp. 276–297; Christian Peters and Arno Weckbecker, eds., *Die "Gleichschaltung" der Universität Heidelberg* (Heidelberg: Zeitsprung-Verlag GdbR, 1983); Arno Weckbecker, *Die Judenverfolgung in*

Heidelberg, 1933–1945 (Heidelberg: Müller, Juristischer Verlag, 1985); pp. 142–187; and Joachim-Felix Leonhard, ed., *Bücherverbrennung. Zensur, Verbot, Vernichtung unter dem Nationalsozialismus in Heidelberg* (Heidelberg: Heidelberger Verlagsanstalt und Druckerei GmbH, 1983).

3. On the Reich Education Ministry and the Dozentenbund, see Reece Conn Kelly, "National Socialism and German University Teachers: The NSDAP's Efforts to Create a National Socialist Professoriate and Scholarship" (Ph.D. diss., University of Washington, 1973). On Rust, see Ulf Pederson, *Bernhard Rust: ein nationalsozialistischer Bildungspolitiker vor dem Hintergrund seiner Zeit* (Braunschweig: Forschungsstelle für Schulgeschichte und Schulentwicklung, 1994).

4. Jansen, *Professoren und Politik,* pp. 394–397. "Report of Preliminary Interrogation," 7th Army Internment Camp, Ludwigsburg, October 5, 1945, "Klageschrift," April 11, 1947, and OMGUS NSDAP Records Check, July 7, 1947, in Spruchkammerakte Karl Schmidhuber, Generallandesarchiv Karlsruhe (hereafter cited as GLAK), 465a/59/54/603–39449.

5. They were: Karl Schmidhuber, Walter Thoms, Carl Schneider, Theodor Odenwald, Ernst Krieck, Ludwig Wesch, Eugen Kruppke, Heinrich Vogt, Udo Wegner, Johannes Duken, Georg Mollier, Alex Ritzert, Otto Dittmar, Eugen Fehrle, and Paul Schmitthenner. Memorandum for the Officer in Charge, 307th Counter Intelligence Corps Detachment, April 9, 1945, April 13, 1945, and August 14, 1945, reprinted in Jürgen Hess, Hartmut Lehmann, and Volker Sellin, eds., *Heidelberg 1945* (Stuttgart: Franz Steiner Verlag, 1996), pp. 393–401, 402–404, and 405–417, respectively.

6. Minister of Culture to the rectors of Heidelberg, Freiburg, and the Technical College in Karlsruhe, January 16, 1933, GLAK, 235/29820.

7. "Die Verfassungen der badischen Universitäten und der Techn. Hochschule in Karlsruhe," August 21, 1933, and October 7, 1933, GLAK, 235/29820. Also see Hermann Weisert, *Die Verfassung der Universität Heidelberg. Überblick, 1386–1952* (Heidelberg: Carl Winter Universitätsverlag, 1974), pp. 125–131. On the "Rector as Führer," see Helmut Seier, "Der Rektor als Führer. Zur Hochschulpolitik des Reichserziehungsministeriums, 1934–1945," *Vierteljahrhefte für Zeitgeschichte,* 12 (1964), 105–146.

8. Kelly, "National Socialism and German University Teachers," p. 63, and Vezina, *Die "Gleichschaltung" der Universität Heidelberg,* pp. 59–61.

9. *Heidelberg Neueste Nachrichten,* July 1, 1933; "Rektor Willy Andreas a.D.," *Volksgemeinschaft,* October 6, 1933; and *Der Heidelberger Student,* winter semester, 1 (1933–34). On Heidegger's speech, see Victor Farias, *Heidegger and Nazism* (Philadelphia: Temple University Press, 1989), pp. 137–140; Gerd Tellenbach, *Aus errinnerter Zeitgeschichte* (Freiburg im Breisgau: Verlag der Wagnerschen Universitätsbuchhandlung, 1981), pp. 40–42; and Karl Jaspers, "Philosophical Autobiography," in Paul Arthur Schilpp, ed., *The Philosophy of Karl Jaspers* (La Salle, Ill.: Open Court, 1957), p. 75.

10. On Groh's background, see Heiber, *Universitäten unterem Hakenkreuz,* part 2, p. 292. On his election as Rector, see Vezina, *Die "Gleichschaltung" der Universität Heidelberg,* pp. 67–68.
11. A copy of Groh's memorandum is in GLAK, Nachlass Willy Andreas, no. 760.
12. Karl Jaspers to Spruchkammer Heidelberg, October 11, 1946, Spruchkammerakte Johann Daniel Achelis, GLAK, 465a/59/48/3725.
13. Wilhelm Groh, circular, October 1, 1933, GLAK, 235/29820.
14. Wilhelm Groh, "Aus der Praxis einer Universitätsverfassung," *Deutsches Recht,* 5 (1935), and Groh circular, October 1, 1933, GLAK, 235/29820. Also see Vezina, *Die "Gleichschaltung" der Universität Heidelberg,* pp. 68–69, and Mussgnug, "Die Universität zu Beginn der Nationalsozialistischen Herrschaft," pp. 482–489.
15. Seier, "Der Rektor als Führer," pp. 140–141.
16. On German university students in Nazi Germany, see Geoffrey Giles, *Students and National Socialism in Germany* (Princeton: Princeton University Press, 1985); Michael Grüttner, *Studenten im Dritten Reich* (Paderborn: Ferdinand Schöningh, 1995); and Norbert Giovanni, *Zwischen Republik und Faschismus: Heidelberger Studentinnen und Studenten, 1918–1945* (Weinheim: Deutsche Studien Verlag, 1990). On the "political soldier," see Goetz von Chelius, "Der politische Soldat," *Heidelberger Studentenführer,* winter semester (1933–34), 11–12. Also see Richard Oeschle to Eugen Fehrle, April 14, 1933, GLAK, 235/1884, and Gustav Adolf Scheel, "Kamaraden!" *Heidelberg Studentenführer,* winter semester (1933–34), 7–8.
17. Quoted in Heiber, *Universitäten unterem Hakenkreuz,* part 2, pp. 282–283. Also see Birgit Arnold, "'Deutscher Student, es ist nicht nötig, dass Du lebst, wohl aber, dass Du Deine Pflicht gegenüber Deinem Volk erfüllst.' Gustav Adolf Scheel, Reichsstudenführer und Gauleiter von Salzburg," in Michael Kissener and Joachim Scholtyseck, eds., *Die Führer der Provinz: NS-Biographien aus Baden und Württemberg* (Constance: Universitätsverlag Konstanz, 1997), pp. 567–594. On Scheel's role in the purges, see Mussgnug, *Die vertriebenen Heidelberger Dozenten,* pp. 21, 41, 46, 60, 97.
18. Eugen Fehrle to the rectors of Heidelberg, Freiburg, Karlsruhe (Technical College), and Kuratorium of the Mannheim Trade School, August 18, 1933, GLAK, 235/30040. Also see Eike Wolgast, "Die Universität Heidelberg in der Zeit des Nationalsozialismus," *Zeitschrift für die Geschichte des Oberrheins,* 135 (1987), 359–406, esp. 381–382. On the results of the search of the house of the art historian August Grisebach, see SA Oberführer W. Ziegler to Eugen Fehrle, April 14, 1933, GLAK, 235/1884.
19. Heidelberger Studentenschaft, "Wochenplan vom 14. bis 21. Jan. 34," GLAK, 235/30040. On these developments, see Giovanni, *Zwischen Republik und Faschismus,* pp. 192–220, and Weckbecker, *Die Judenverfolgung in Heidelberg,* pp. 167–184. On the book burning in Heidelberg, see Clemens Zimmermann, "Die Bücherverbrennung am 17. Mai

1933 in Heidelberg, Studenten und Politik am Ende der Weimar Republik," in Leonhard, ed., *Bücherverbrennung*, pp. 55–84.

20. See Otto Wacker to the Rector and Senate of Heidelberg University, April 6, 1933, Universitätsarchiv Heidelberg (hereafter cited as UAH), B-3026/4a. The text of the April 7 law and the "First Ordinance on the Implementation of the Law for the Restoration of the Professional Civil Service" of April 11 are reprinted in Klaus Hentschel, ed., *Physics and National Socialism: An Anthology of Primary Sources* (Basel: Birkhäuser Verlag, 1996), pp. 21–26. A person of "Aryan descent" was defined four days later as "anyone descended from non-Aryan, and in particular Jewish, parents or grandparents . . . [it being] sufficient that one parent or one grandparent be non-Aryan." On the law's origins, see Saul Friedländer, *Nazi Germany and the Jews*, vol. 1: *The Years of Persecution* (New York: HarperCollins, 1997), pp. 9–60. A related policy was to strip Jewish and "politically unwanted" Heidelberg graduates of their degrees. Between 1933 and 1942, 124 former students had their diplomas rescinded; 41 of these were restored in the late 1940s and early 1950s. See Werner Moritz, "Die Aberkennung des Doktortitels an der Universität Heidelberg während der NS-Zeit," in Armin Kohnle and Frank Engehausen, eds., *Zwischen Wissenschaft und Politik. Studien zur deutschen Universitätsgeschichte* (Stuttgart: Franz Steiner Verlag, 2001), pp. 540–562.

21. See Hartshorne, *The German Universities and National Socialism*; Claus-Dieter Krohn, *Intellectuals in Exile: Refugee Scholars and the New School for Social Research* (Amherst: University of Massachusetts Press, 1993), pp. 11–19; and Mussgnug, *Die vertriebenen Heidelberger Dozenten*, pp. 111, 113. There were 201 active instructors at Heidelberg in the winter semester of 1932–33. Of the 58 active professors fired, 27 were dismissed in 1933, 23 in 1935, and 8 in 1937.

22. Mussgnug, *Die vertriebenen Heidelberger Dozenten*, pp. 139–186.

23. Ibid., pp. 155–156.

24. Hans-Georg Gadamer, "Interview: The German University and German Politics: The Case of Heidegger," in Dieter Misgeld and Graeme Nicholson, eds., *Hans-Georg Gadamer on Education, Poetry, and History: Applied Hermeneutics* (Albany: State University of New York Press, 1992), p. 9.

25. Löwith, *My Life in Germany*, p. 82.

26. See, for instance, the April 20, 1933, letter from the Frankfurt university historian Ernst Kantorowicz to the Ministry of Culture, reprinted in *Dokumente zur Geschichte der Frankfurter Juden, 1933–1945* (Frankfurt: Verlag Waldemar Kramer, 1963), pp. 99–100.

27. Klaus Kempter, *Die Jellineks, 1820–1955: eine Familienbiographische Studie zum deutschjüdischen Bildungsbürgertum* (Düsseldorf: Droste, 1998), p. 485. Also see Weckbecker, *Die Judenverfolgung in Heidelberg*, p. 162, and Victor Klemperer, *I Will Bear Witness: A Diary of the Nazi Years, 1933–1941* (New York: Random House, 1998).

28. Löwith, *My Life in Germany*, p. 79.
29. Quoted in ibid., p. 81.
30. UAH, B-3026/4a. Siebeck also sent a copy to the chairman of the Medical Faculty at Freiburg and "confidentially" to the chairman of the German University Association in Bonn. I found no response in the university's or the Ministry's archives. On anti-Semitism among the professorate after 1933, see Saul Friedlander, "The Demise of the German Mandarins: The German University and the Jews, 1933–1939," in Christian Jansen, ed., *Von der Aufgabe der Freiheit: politische Verantwortung und bürgerliche Gesellschaft im 19. und 20. Jahrhundert* (Berlin: Akademie Verlag, 1995), pp. 69–82, and Löwith, *My Life in Germany*, pp. 70–84.
31. Fritz Stern, *Einstein's German World* (Princeton: Princeton University Press, 1999), esp. pp. 31–34 and 272–288, and Notker Hammerstein, *Antisemitismus und deutsche Universitäten* (Frankfurt am Main: Campus Verlag, 1995).
32. Gerta von Ubisch, unpublished memoirs, ca. 1955, Universitätsbibliothek Heidelberg, Nachlass Gerta von Ubisch, Heid. Hs. 4029. Emphasis in the original. Portions were published in the journal *Mädchenbildung und Frauenschaffen* in 1956 and 1957, but all references to the anti-Semitism of her former colleagues at Heidelberg found in the original document were omitted. See *Mädchenbildung und Frauenschaffen,* 10–11 (October-November 1956), and 1 (January 1957), 413–422, 598–507, and 35–45, respectively. On von Ubisch's career, see Meike Sophia Baader, "'Wissenschaft als Beruf' in den Naturwissenschaften. Gerta von Ubisch (1882–1965)—die erste habilitierte und dennoch weithin unbekannte Frau an der Universität Heidelberg," in Hubert Treiber and Karol Sauerland, eds., *Heidelberg im Schnittpunkt intellektueller Kreise: zur Topographie der geistigen Geselligkeit eines Weltdorfes, 1850–1950* (Opladen: Westdeutscher Verlag, 1995), pp. 445–460. Karl Löwith echoed these sentiments in *My Life in Germany,* pp. 77–84.
33. Willy Andreas to Otto Wacker, September 19, 1933, UAH, B-1015/3.
34. Quoted in Vezina, *Die "Gleichschaltung" der Universität Heidelberg,* pp. 35–36.
35. *Vorlesungsverzeichnis,* Universität Heidelberg, winter semester, 1935–36.
36. Karl Freudenberg to Chairman of the Natural Sciences–Mathematics Faculty, May 23, 1946, UAH, Rep. 14/65.
37. Marianne Weber, "Academic Conviviality," *Minerva,* 15, no. 2 (1977), 230.
38. Alfred Weber, "Parteifahnen auf dem Rathaus," *Heidelberger Tageblatt,* March 7, 1933, and Eberhard Demm, "Zivilcourage im Jahre 1933. Alfred Weber und die Fahnenaktionen der NSDAP," *Heidelberger Jahrbücher,* 21 (1982), 69–80.
39. Demm, "Zivilcourage im Jahre 1933," p. 77. See also Hubert Schrade (writing for Ernst Krieck) to the Ministry of Culture and Education, July

21, 1938, and the Ministry's own dispatch to the REM, July 28, 1938, both in GLAK, 466/20780.
40. Gustav Radbruch, *Der innere Weg. Aufriss meines Lebens* (Stuttgart: K. F. Koehler Verlag, 1951), p. 185. Victor Klemperer took a similar path after his own dismissal from the Technical College in Dresden, immersing himself in a study of eighteenth-century French political philosophy. See his *I Will Bear Witness,* vol. 1.
41. Karl Jaspers, "Lebensbeschreibung," n.d., but probably 1945 or 1946, GLAK, 235/2133.
42. Quoted in Eberhard Demm, *Von der Weimarer Republik zur Bundesrepublik. Der politische Weg Alfred Webers, 1920–1958* (Düsseldorf: Droste, 1999), p. 237.
43. Weber, "Academic Conviviality," pp. 230–232.
44. Quoted in Jeremy Noakes, "The Ivory Tower under Siege: German Universities in the Third Reich," *Journal of European Studies,* 23 (1993), p. 380.
45. These examples are from Reimann, "Die 'Selbst-Gleichschaltung' der Universitäten im 1933," pp. 45–46. Also see the commentaries included in *Bekenntnis der Professoren an den deutschen Universitäten und Hochschulen zu Adolf Hitler und dem nationalsozialistischen Staat überreicht vom Nationalsozialistischen Lehrerbund* (Dresden: W. Limpert, 1933).
46. See, for example, "Aufruf des Bundes für deutsche Volkskunde e.V.," *Niederdeutsche Zeitschrift für Volkskunde,* 11 (1933), 255–256. By the summer of 1933, about 20 percent of Germany's university instructors had joined the Nazi Party. See Michael Grüttner, "Wissenschaft," in Wolfgang Benz, Hermann Graml, and Hermann Weiss, eds., *Enzyklopädie des Nationalsozialismus* (Stuttgart: Klett-Cotta, 1997), p. 147.
47. Hans Himmel to Ministry of Education, September 27, 1935, UAH, B-3027/2.
48. Andreas Duhm, *Die Kampf um die deutsche Kirche: eine Kirchengeschichte des Jahres 1933/1934* (Gotha: L. Klotz, 1934), p. 71.
49. Christian Jansen was the first scholar to systematically explore the response of Heidelberg's professors to National Socialism. See his *Professoren und Politik,* pp. 276–294.
50. *Der Heidelberger Tageblatt,* May 15, 1933. Paul Schmitthenner expressed similar sentiments in *Reden zur Feier der Nationalen Erhebung am Tage der Deutschen Arbeit* (Heidelberg: Carl Winters Universitätsbuchhandlung, 1933). Andreas and Schmitthenner, as Karen Schönwälder has pointed out, were hardly unusual among German historians, many of whom made similar statements around this time. See her "'Lehrmeisterin der Völker und der Jugend.' Historiker als politische Kommentatoren, 1933 bis 1945," in Peter Schöttler, ed., *Geschichtsschreibung als Legitimationswissenschaft, 1918–1945* (Frankfurt am Main: Suhrkamp, 1997), pp. 128–165.
51. Willy Andreas, "Hindenburg zum Gedächtnis," *Velhagen & Klasings Monatshefte,* 49, no. 1 (September 1934).
52. Walter Jellinek, "Le droit public de l'Allemagne," *Annuiare de L'Institut In-*

ternational de Droit Public, 1934 and 1935, 43–77 and 350–363, respectively.
53. Otto Erdmannsdörfer, *Reden zur Feier der Nationalen Erhebung in der Aula der Universität Heidelberg am Tage der Deutschen Arbeit*, (Heidelberg: Carl Winters Universitätsbuchhandlung, 1933), pp. 15–19.
54. Heinz Hildebrandt, *Rechtsfindung im neuen deutschen Staate* (Berlin: Walter de Gruyter, 1935), p. 15.
55. Quoted in Jansen, *Professoren und Politik*, p. 277.
56. Willy Andreas to Joseph Goebbels, March 27, 1933, UAH, B-1015/4a. Philipp Gassert, *Amerika im Dritten Reich. Ideologie, Propaganda und Volksmeinung, 1933–1945* (Stuttgart: Franz Steiner Verlag, 1997), pp. 136–147.
57. Arnold Bergsträsser, "The Economic Policy of the German Government," *International Affairs* (London), 13, no. 1 (January 1934), 26–46. Also see his *Nation und Wirtschaft* (Hamburg: Hanseatischen Verlagsanstalt, 1933).
58. Martin Dibelius to Eugen Fehrle, May 4, 1934, "Bericht über die Teilnahme an der Englandreise deutscher Professoren," June 29, 1933, Dibelius to the Evangelical Oberkirchenrat, Karlsruhe, September 30, 1933, and his report on the Ecumenical Seminar at the University of Genf, August 29, 1935, all in GLAK, 235/1884.
59. Walter Jellinek, "Le droit public de l'Allemagne en 1933," *Annuaire de L'Institut International de Droit Public*, 1934, 52–53.
60. Jellinek, "Le droit public de l'Allemagne en 1934," *Annuaire de L'Institue de Droit Public*, 1935, 363–363, and "Verfassungsneubau," *Reich und Länder*, 7, no. 5 (May 1933), 129–136.
61. Reinhard Höhn, *Die Wandlung im staatsrechtlichen Denken* (Hamburg: Hanseatische Verlagsanstalt, 1934), esp. pp. 42–46.
62. Hildebrandt, *Rechtsfindung*, p. 15.
63. Radbruch, *Der Innere Weg*, p. 134, and Georg Dahm and Friedrich Schaffstein, *Liberales oder autoritäres Strafrecht?* (Hamburg: Hanseatische Verlagsanstalt, 1933).
64. Ingo Müller, *Hitler's Justice: The Courts of the Third Reich* (Cambridge: Harvard University Press, 1991), pp. 68–81.
65. Carl Brinkmann, "Theoretische Bermerkungen zum nationalsozialistischen Wirtschaftsprogramm," *Schmollers Jahrbuch*, 58, no. 1 (1934), 1–4.
66. Bergsträsser, "The Economic Policy of the German Government," pp. 31–32.
67. Hermann Güntert, *Der Ursprung der Germanen* (Heidelberg: Carl Winters Universitätsbuchhandlung, 1934), pp. 7, 182–183.
68. Kurt von Raumer, "Das Reich der Deutschen: Erbe und Aufgabe," *Wort und Tat*, 4 (1934), 115–126. Also see his "Revolutionen als Volksbewegung," *Volksspiegel*, 1935, pp. 24–36.
69. Jellinek, "Verfassungneubau," p. 136, and von Raumer, "Revolutionen als Volksbewegung," p. 36. Also see Dibelius's reports cited above in n. 58; Duhm, *Die Kampf um die deutsche Kirche*, pp. 213–228; Otto Mann,

"Jüdische Methoden," *Nationalsozialistische Monatshefte,* 6 (1935), 473–474; and Hermann Güntert, "Das germanische Erbe in der deutschen Seele," *Zeitschrift für Deutschkunde,* 48 (1934), 459–460. For other examples, see Jansen, *Professoren und Politik,* pp. 289–294, and Friedländer, "The Demise of the German Mandarins, pp. 69–82.

70. On race consciousness and racism in European history, see George Mosse, *Toward the Final Solution: A History of European Rascism* (Madison: University of Wisconsin Press, 1985). For an example of pre-1933 racist concepts applied to history at Heidelberg, see Ernst Wahle, "Die rassenkundliche Auswertung vorgeschichtlicher Forschungsergebnisse," in Walter Scheidt and Ernst Wahle, eds., *Rassenkunde. Allgemeine Rassenkunde als Einführung in das Studium der Menschenrassen* (Munich: J. F. Lehmanns Verlag, 1925), pp. 548–570.

71. Quoted in Walter Pauly, ed., *Aus meinem Leben: Erinnerungen von Gerhard Anschütz* (Frankfurt: Klostermann, 1992), pp. 328–329.

72. Hans von Eckardt to Willy Andreas, March 24, 1933, UAH Personalakte (hereafter cited as PA), 3614 (von Eckardt).

73. Lutz Hachmeister, *Der Gegnerforscher: die Karriere des SS-Führers Franz Alfred Six* (Munich: C. H. Beck, 1998), pp. 53–56.

74. Eugen Täubler, "Heidelberger Gespräch. (25. März 1933)," in Geza Alföldy, ed., *Eugen Täubler. Ausgewählte Schriften zur Alten Geschichte* (Stuttgart: Franz Steiner Verlag Wiesbaden GmbH, 1987), pp. 312–325.

75. Hans Gerth, affidavit, May 26, 1943, Emil J. Gumbel Papers, University of Chicago Library, Box 3, Folder 7.

76. Jansen, *Professoren und Politik,* pp. 394–397, and Jansen, "Antiliberalismus und Antiparlamentarismus in der bürgerlich-demokratischen Elite der Weimarer Republik. Willy Hellpachs Publizistik der Jahre 1925–1933," *Zeitschrift für Geschichtswissenschaft,* 49, no. 9 (2000), 789–795.

77. Franz Neumann, *Behemoth: The Structure and Practice of National Socialism, 1933–1944* (New York: Octagon Books, 1972), pp. 38–39.

78. Ian Kershaw, *Hitler, 1889–1936: Hubris* (New York: W. W. Norton, 1999), pp. 529–591.

79. Robert Gellately, *Backing Hitler: Consent and Coercion in Nazi Germany* (Oxford: Oxford University Press, 2001).

80. See Sylvia Paletschek, "The Invention of Humboldt and the Impact of National Socialism: The German University Idea in the First Half of the Twentieth Century," in Margit Szölleosi-Janze, ed., *Science in the Third Reich* (Oxford: Berg, 2001), pp. 37–58.

81. Ernst Krieck, "Die Erneurung der deutschen Universität," in Ernst Krieck and Friedrich Klausing, eds., *Die deutsche Hochschule* (Marburg: N. G. Elwertsche Verlagsbuchhandlung, G. Braun, 1933), pp. 1–5, and Ernst Krieck, *Wissenschaft, Weltanschauung, und Hochschulereform* (Leipzig: Urmanen Verlag, 1934).

82. See Helmut Seier, "Universität und Hochschulpolitik im nationalsozialistischen Staat," in Klaus Malettke, ed., *Der Nationalsozialismus an der*

Macht. Aspekte nationalsozialistischer Politik und Herrschaft (Göttingen: Vandenhoeck & Ruprecht, 1984), pp. 143–165; Ernst Nolte, "Behavioral Patterns of University Professors in the Third Reich," in Ernst Nolte, *Marxism, Fascism, Cold War* (Assen: Van Gorcum, 1982), pp. 106–120; Geoffrey Giles, "Die Idee der politischen Universität: Hochschulreform nach der Machtergreifung," in Manfred Heinemann, ed., *Erziehung und Schulung im Dritten Reich* (Stuttgart: Klett-Cotta, 1980), pp. 50–60; and Jeremy Noakes, "The Ivory Tower under Siege," pp. 371–407, esp. pp. 378–384. On Krieck, see Gerhard Müller, *Ernst Krieck und die nationalsozialistische Wissenschaftsreform. Motive und Tendenzen einer Wissenschaftslehre und Hochschulreform im Dritten Reich* (Weinheim: Beltz Verlag, 1978), and Helmut Wojtun, *Die politische Pädagogik von Ernst Krieck und ihre Würdigung durch die westdeutsche Pädagogik* (Frankfurt am Main: P. Lang, 2000).

83. On Heidegger, National Socialism, and the universities, see Bernd Martin, ed., *Martin Heidegger und das "Dritte Reich": ein Kompendium* (Darmstadt: Wissenschaftliche Buchgesellschaft, 1989), and Gadamer, "Interview: The German University and German Politics," in Misgeld and Nicholson, eds., *Hans-Georg Gadamer on Education, Poetry, and History*, pp. 3–14.

84. Martin Heidegger, "The Self-Assertion of the German University," in Günther Neske and Emil Kettering, eds., *Martin Heidegger and National Socialism: Questions and Answers* (New York: Paragon House, 1990), pp. 5–13.

85. Rüdiger Safranski, *Martin Heidegger: Between Good and Evil* (Cambridge: Harvard University Press, 1998), pp. 248–253.

86. Karl Jaspers to Martin Heidegger, August 23, 1933, reprinted in Richard Wisser and Leonard Ehrlich, eds., *Karl Jaspers: Philosopher among Philosophers* (Würzburg: Königshaussen & Neumann, 1993), pp. 332–333.

87. Ibid.

88. Karl Jaspers, "How Can the Universities be Rejuvinated? Some Theses," ca. July-August, 1933, reprinted in ibid., pp. 312–331, and Jaspers to Heidegger, August 23, 1933, in ibid., pp. 332–333.

89. For defenses of Jaspers, see Hans Saner, "Jaspers's 'Theses' on the Question of University Rejuvination (1933): A Critical Comparison with Heidegger's 'Rectorial [sic] Address,'" in ibid., pp. 139–152, and Leonard Ehrlich, "Heidegger's Philosophy of Being from the Perspective of His Rectorate," in Alan M. Olson, ed., *Heidegger and Jaspers* (Philadelphia: Temple University Press, 1994), pp. 29–48, esp. pp. 33–35.

90. Grüttner, "Das Scheitern der Vordenker: Deutsche Hochschullehrer und der Nationalsozialismus," in Michael Grüttner, Rüdiger Hachtmann, and Heinz-Gerhard Haupt, eds., *Geschichte und Emanzipation. Festschrift für Reinhard Rürup* (Frankfurt: Campus Verlag, 1999), pp. 458–481.

91. Johannes Stein, "Universität und Volk" and Paul Schmitthenner, "Die politische Universität," both in *Der Heidelberger Student*, May 18, 1933. Similar is Nicolai von Bubnoff, "Universität und Nation," ibid.

92. Andreas, *Der Heidelberger Tageblatt*, May 15, 1933; Gerd Tellenbach, "Kämpfende Wissenschaft. Von den Erlebnissen des Heidelberger Universitätsjubiläums," *Der Führer*, July 5, 1936; Hermann Glockner, "Gedanken über den Einbau einer deutschen Körperschaft in unsere Universitäten," *Volk im Werden*, 1, no. 2 (1933) 8–10.

93. Otto Regenbogen, "Das Altertum und die politische Erziehung," *Neue Jahrbücher für Wissenschaft und Jugendbildung*, 10 (1934), 211–225. Wilhelm Waldkirch, *Die Zeitungspolitische Aufgabe* (Ludwigshafen: Verlag Julius Waldkirch, 1935), 3 vols. Similar statements are found in Hubert Schrade, *Schicksal und Notwendigkeit der Kunst* (Leipzig: Armanen-Verlag, 1936); Philipp Lenard, "Die Naturwissenschaft im neuen Staat," *Heidelberger Tageblatt*, May 24, 1933; and Hans-Hermann Adler, "Das Gesicht der deutschen Universität," *Hochschule und Ausland*, 13, no. 11 (1935), 48–55.

94. Adler, "Das Gesicht der deutschen Universität."

95. Ibid., pp. 51–54.

96. Carl Brinkmann, "Gibt es eine politische Universität?" *Der Heidelberger Student*, May 18, 1933.

97. On academic thologians and theology faculties in the Third Reich, see Robert P. Ericksen, *Theologians under Hitler: Gerhard Kittel, Paul Althaus, and Emmanuel Hirsch* (New Haven: Yale University Press, 1985); Leonore Siegele-Wenschkewitz and Carsten Nicolaisen, eds., *Theologische Fakultäten im Nationalsozialismus* (Göttingen: Vandenhoeck und Ruprecht, 1993); and Kurt Meier, *Die Theologischen Fakultäten im Dritten Reich* (Berlin: De Gruyter, 1996). On Heidelberg, see Karl-Heinz Fix, *Universitätstheologie und Politik: die Heidelberger Theologische Fakultät in der Weimarer Republik* (Heidelberg: C. Winter Heidelberg, 1994), and Leonore Siegele-Wenschkewitz, "Die Theologische Fakultät im Dritten Reich. 'Bollwerk gegen Basel,'" in Doerr, ed., *Semper Apertus*, vol. 3, pp. 504–543. The rosters were taken from *Vorlesungsverzeichnisse*, Universität Heidelberg, summer 1933 and winter semesters 1944-45.

98. On the "German Christians," see Doris L. Bergen, *Twisted Cross: The German Christian Movement in the Third Reich* (Chapel Hill: University of North Carolina Press, 1996).

99. *Vorlesungsverzeichnis*, Universität Heidelberg, 1944–45.

100. See Duhm, *Die Kampf um die deutsche Kirche*.

101. See Fix, *Universitätstheologie und Politik*, pp. 126–130.

102. Theology Faculty to the Senate Commission, Heidelberg University, October 31, 1945, UAH PA, 4380 (Jelke). Also see Fix, *Universitätstheologie und Politik*, pp. 138–144, and Siegele-Wenschkewitz, "Die Theologische Fakultät."

103. A summary of his career can be found in "Spruch," n.d., but probably 1948, Spruchkammerakte Theodor Odenwald, GLAK, 465a/59/5/5740. On the institute, see Susannah Heschel, "Making Nazism a Christian Movement: The Development of a Christian Theology of Antisemitism dur-

ing the Third Reich," in Betty Rogers Rubenstein and Michael Berenbaum, eds., *What Kind of God? Essays in Honor of Richard L. Rubenstein* (Lanham, Md.: University Press of America, 1995), pp. 159–199; Susannah Heschel, "When Jesus Was an Aryan: The Protestant Church and Antisemitic Propaganda," in Susannah Heschel and Robert Ericksen, *Betrayal: German Churches and the Holocaust* (Minneapolis: Fortress Press, 1999), pp. 68–89; and Max Weinreich, *Hitler's Professors: The Part of Scholarship in Germany's Crimes against the Jewish People* (New Haven: Yale University Press), pp. 62–67.

104. Fix, *Universitätstheologie und Politik,* pp. 185–198, and Weber, "Academic Conviviality," pp. 245–246.
105. Richard Oeschle to Eugen Fehrle, April 14, 1933, GLAK, 235/1884.
106. Karl Schmidhuber to Paul Schmitthenner, May 12, 1939, GLAK, 235/1884.
107. Dibelius to Wilhelm Groh, October 6, 1933, GLAK, 235/1884, and Langmann to REM (?), April 29, 1937, UAH PA, 3545 (Dibelius).
108. On the Theology Faculty at Bonn, see Paul Kahle, *Bonn University in Pre-Nazi and Nazi Times, 1923–1939* (privately printed, 1945), pp. 12–14. On Hoelscher, see Gustav Hoelscher, "Gelehrter in Politischer Zeit," *Ruperto Carola,* 58–59 (December 1976–June 1977), 53–59, and Siegele-Wenschkewitz, "Die Theologische Fakultät." On Jelke's attitude toward Hoelscher, see Karl Wichmann, affidavit, October 26, 1945, UAH PA, 248 (Jelke). On the boycott of Hoelscher's lectures, see Hoelscher to Wilhelm Groh, May 25, 1935, UAH PA, 4248 (Hoelscher). Also see Martin Dibelius to Military Government, Heidelberg, July 21, 1945, UAH, B-1520.
109. Vezina, *Die 'Gleichschaltung' der Universität Heidelberg,* pp. 132–145.
110. Ibid., pp. 143–145. On Hubert Schrade, see Karl-Ludwig Hofmann and Christmut Präger, "'Volk, Rasse, Staat und deutscher Geist.' Zum Universitätsjubiläum 1936 und zur Kunstgeschichte in Heidelberg im *Dritten Reich,*" in Karin Buselmeier, Dietrich Harth, and Christian Jansen, eds., *Auch eine Geschichte der Universität Heidelberg* (Mannheim: Edition Quadrat, 1985), pp. 337–345.
111. On historians in the Third Reich, see Hartmut Lehmann and James Van Horn Melton, eds., *Paths of Continuity: Central European Historiography from the 1930s to the 1950s* (Cambridge: Cambridge University Press, 1994); Karen Schönwälder, *Historiker und Politik. Geschichtswissenschaft im Nationalsozialismus* (Frankfurt: Campus Verlag, 1992); Ursula Wolf, *Litteris et patriae: das Janusgesicht der Historie* (Stuttgart: Steiner Verlag, 1996); Heinz Wolf, *Deutsch-jüdische Emigrationshistoriker in den USA und der Nationalsozialismus* (Bern: P. Lang, 1988); Beat Näf, *Von Perikles zu Hitler? Die athenische Demokratie und die deutsche Althistorie bis 1945* (Bern: P. Lang, 1986); Schöttler, ed., *Geschichtsschreibung als Legitimationswissenschaft;* Winfried Schulze, Gerd Helm, and Thomas Ott, *Deutsche Historiker im Nationalsozialismus. Beobachtungen und Überlegungen zu einer Debatte* (Frankfurt am Main: Fischer Taschenbuch Verlag, 1999); and Joachim Lerchenmueller, *Die Geschichtswissenschaft in den Planungen*

des Sicherheitsdienstes der SS. Der SD-Historiker Hermann Löffler und seine Denkschrift "Entwicklung und Aufgaben der Geschichtswissenschaft in Deutschland" (Bonn: Verlag J. H. W. Dietz Nachf., 2001).

112. For the creation of the Military Sciences Seminar, see GLAK, 235/29988, and Ulrike Lennartz, "Ein badischer 'Preusse.' Paul Schmitthenner, Badischer Staatsminister," in Kissener and Scholtyseck, eds., *Die Führer der Provinz*, pp. 623–653.

113. Vezina, *Die "Gleichschaltung" der Heidelberg Universität*, pp. 133–136. On Franz, see Wolfgang Behringer, "Bauern-Franz und Rassen-Günther. Die politische Geschichte des Agrarhistorikers Günther Franz (1902–1992)," in Schulze and Oexle, eds., *Deutsche Historiker im Nationalsozialismus*, pp. 114–141.

114. On Fehrle, see Peter Assion, "Eugen Fehrle and the 'Mythos of Our Folk,'" in James Dow and Hannjost Lixfeld, eds., *The Nazification of an Academic Discipline: Folklore in the Third Reich* (Bloomingon: Indiana University Press, 1994), pp. 112–134. For Fehrle's own account of his place in the tradition of folklore research at Heidelberg, see Eugen Fehrle, "Die deutsche Volkskunde in Heidelberg," *Festausgabe der Volksgemeinschaft*, June 30, 1936.

115. "Spruch," March 3, 1948, Spruchkammerakte Eugen Fehrle, GLAK, 465a/59/1/17838-33573.

116. Assion, "Eugen Fehrle and the 'Mythos of Our Folk,'" pp. 116–129.

117. Groh to Ministry of Culture, October 26, 1935, and Berlin Document Center, File Hans Hermann Adler, United States National Archives and Records Administration, Record Group 242. On the Institut für Zeitungswissenschaft, see Albrecht Ackermann, "Das Institut für Zeitungswesen (Zeitungswissenschaft) an der Universität Heidelberg, 1927–1945," in Rüdiger vom Bruch and Otto B. Roegele, eds., *Von der Zeitungskunde zur Publizistik. Biographisch-institutionelle Stationen der deutschen Zeitungswissenschaft in der ersten Hälfte des 20. Jahrhunderts* (Frankfurt am Main: Haag & Herchen, 1986), pp. 143–180, and Hachmeister, *Der Gegnerforscher*, pp. 52–76.

118. Alfred Weber, "Neue Universität," *Rheinische Neuzeitung*, May 5, 1946.

119. See Reinhard Bollmus, *Handelshochschule und Nationalsozialismus: das Ende d. Handelshochsch. Mannheim u. d. Vorgeschichte d. Errichtung e. Staats- und Wirtschaftswiss. Fak. an d. Univ. Heidelberg, 1933–34* (Meisenheim: Hain, 1973).

120. Carsten Klingemann, "Social-Scientific Experts—No Ideologues: Sociology and Social Research in the Third Reich," in Stephen P. Turner and Dirk Käsler, eds., *Sociology Responds to Fascism* (London; New York: Routledge, 1992), pp. 127–154, and Hans Derks, "Social Sciences in Germany, 1933–1945," *German History*, 17, no. 2 (1999), 177–219.

121. These samples were taken from *Vorlesungsverzeichnis*, Universität Heidelberg, winter semesters 1935–36 and 1936–37.

122. On the fate of Insosta, see Klaus-Rainer Brintzinger, *Die Nationalökonomie*

an den Universitäten Freiburg, Heidelberg und Tübingen, 1918–1945: eine institutionenhistorische, vergleichende Studie der wirtschaftswissenschaftlichen Fakultäten und Abteilungen südwestdeutscher Universitäten (Frankfurt am Main: Lang, 1996), pp. 184–199; Carsten Klingemann, "Das 'Institut für Sozial- und Staatswissenschaften' an der Universität Heidelberg zum Ende der Weimarer Republik und während des Nationalsozialismus," in *Jahrbuch für Soziologiegeschichte,* 1990, pp. 79–120; and Reinhard Blomert, *Heidelberger Sozial- und Staatswissenschaften: das Institut für Sozial- und Staatswissenschaften zwischen 1918 und 1945* (Marburg: Metropolis-Verlag, 1997).

123. On Bergsträsser and Brinkmann, see Klingemann, "'Das 'Institut für Sozial- und Staatswissenschaften,'" pp. 88–94.
124. Walter Thoms, Lebenslauf, n.d., but probably 1932 or 1933, UAH PA, 6079 (Thoms). Also see the biographical notes in UAH PA, 6080 (Thoms).
125. Walter Thoms, *Wirtschaft und Betrieb. Vorträge und Beiträge zur Neuordnung der deutschen Volks- und Betriebswirtschaft* (Leipzig: Verlag August Lutzeyer, 1943).
126. UAH PA, 5818 and 5819 (Schuster).
127. On Panzer, see Michael Fahlbusch, *Wissenschaft im Dienst der nationalsozialistischen Politik? die "Volksdeutschen Forschungsgemeinschaften" von 1931–1945* (Baden-Baden: Nomos, 1999), p. 359, and Spruchkammerakte Wolfgang Panzer, GLAK, 465a/59/2/11822–25869. On his place among Nazi geographers and his activities in the early years of the regime, see Eugen Wirth, *Einhundert Jahre Geographie in Erlangen* (Erlangen: Junge & Sohn, 1995), p. 16.
128. Figures cited in Müller, *Hitler's Justice,* p. 69.
129. On law faculties and legal scholars in the Third Reich, see ibid. and Michael Stolleis, *The Law under the Swastika: Studies in Legal History in Nazi Germany* (Chicago: University of Chicago Press, 1998).
130. Endemann joined the NSDAP in 1932, Jellinek was in the DVP, and von Rauchhaupt was in the DVP and the Stahlhelm. Groh, Dahm, Hildebrandt, and von Rauchhaupt would join the NSDAP after 1933. Mitteis would become a member of the Dozentenbund. Information from Jansen, *Professoren und Politik,* p. 394.
131. On continuities in legal thought between the Weimar Republic and the Third Reich, see Oliver Lepsius, *Die gegensatzaufhebende Begriffsbildung: Methodenentwicklungen in der Weimarer Republik und ihr Verhältnis zur Ideologisierung der Rechtswissenschaft im Nationalsozialismus* (Munich: C. H. Beck, 1994). For contemporary examples, see Heinz Hildebrandt, *Reichsfindung,* esp. "Vorwort" and pp. 27–37, and Carl Bilfinger, "Das Reichsstatthaltergesetz," *Archiv des öffentlichen Rechts,* 24 (1934), 131–165.
132. On the creation of these laws, culminating in the Nuremberg race laws of 1935, see Friedländer, *Nazi Germany and the Jews,* pp. 145–173.
133. On medical science in Nazi Germany see Alexander Mitscherlich and Fred

Mielke, *The Death Doctors* (London: Elek Books, 1962); Robert Jay Lifton, *The Nazi Doctors: Medical Killing and the Psychology of Genocide* (New York: Basic Books, 1986); Michael Kater, *Doctors under Hitler* (Chapel Hill: University of North Carolina Press, 1999); and Robert Proctor, *Racial Hygiene: Medicine under the Nazis* (Cambridge: Harvard University Press, 1988). On Heidelberg's Medical Faculty, see Sophinette Backer, Petra Becker-von Rose, and Bernd Laufs, "Einblicke in die Medizin während des Nationalsozialismus—Beispiele aus der Heidelberger Zeit," in Buselmeier et al., eds., *Auch eine Geschichte*, pp. 315–335, and Bernd Laufs, "Vom Umgang der Medizin mit ihrer Geschichte," in Gerritt Hohendorf and Achim Magull-Seltenreich, eds., *Von der Heilkunde zur Massentötung. Medizin im Nationalsozialismus* (Heidelberg: Wunderhorn, 1990), pp. 233–253.

134. Viktor von Weizäcker to the chairman of the Medical Faculty, December 28, 1949, UAH PA, 1161 (Schneider).

135. On Schneider, see Christine Teller, "Carl Schneider. Zur Biographie eines deutschen Wissenschaftlers," *Geschichte und Gesellschaft*, 16, no. 4 (1990), 464–478, and Petra Becker-von Rose, "Carl Schneider—wissenschaftlicher Schrittmacher der Euthenasieaktion und Universitätspsychiater in Heidelberg, 1933–1945," in Hohendorf and Magull-Seltenreich, eds., *Von der Heilkunde zur Massentötung*, pp. 90–112. Also see Becker-von Rose et al., "Einblicke in die Medizin," pp. 324–331.

136. See Paul Weindling, *Health, Race, and German Politics between National Unification and Nazism, 1870–1945* (Cambridge: Cambridge University Press, 1989); Gisela Bock, *Zwangssterilisation im Nationalsozialismus: Studien zur Rassenpolitik und Frauenpolitik* (Opladen: Westdeutscher Verlag, 1986); and Michael Burleigh, *Death and Deliverance: "Euthanasia" in Germany c. 1900–1945* (Cambridge: Cambridge University Press, 1994).

137. Henry Friedlander, *The Origins of Nazi Genocide: From Euthanasia to the Final Solution* (Chapel Hill: University of North Carolina Press, 1995), pp. 28, 30.

138. Carl Schneider, *Behandlung und Verhütung der Geisteskrankeheiten. Allgemeine Erfahrungen Grundsätze, Technik, Biologie* (Berlin: Verlag von Julius Springer, 1939), esp. pp. 91–147.

139. Kater, *Hitler's Doctors*, p. 236, and *Vorlesungsverzeichnis*, Heidelberg University, summer semester, 1935.

140. See Runge's telling comments in "Berichte aus gynäkologischen Gesellschaften. Nordwestdeutsche Gesellschaft für Gynäkologie, Sitzung vom 28.IV.1934," *Zentralblatt für Gynäkologie*, 58, no. 37 (1934), 2212. Also see Becker-von Rose et al., "Einblicke in die Medizin während des Nationalsozialismus," p. 320, and Laufs, "Vom Umgang der Medizin mit ihrer Geschichte." One such dissertation was Elisabeth Hofmann's "Körperliches Befinden und Einstellung von Frauen, die nach dem Erbgesundheitsgesetz sterilisiert wurden" (doctoral thesis, Heidelberg University,

1937). Hofmann began her study with a quote from *Mein Kampf*: "who are physically and intellectually not healthy and worthy, must not be allowed to perpetuate their affliction in the body of their children! The state must see to it that only those who are healthy may be allowed to sire children." Also see Dora Neeff, "Die bisherigen Erfahrungen über Eingriff und Verlauf der sterilisierenden Operation bei der Frau: nach 285 Tubensterilisierenden, die in Ausführung des Gesetzes zur Verhütung erbkranken Nachwuchses vorgenommen sind" (doctoral thesis, Heidelberg University, 1936).

141. Figure cited in Hofmann, "Körperliches Befinden und Einstellung von Frauen," p. 3.
142. Spruchkammerakte Hans Runge and Otto Dittmar, GLAK, 465a/59/6/8663–1885 and 465a/59/7/354, respectively, and Vezina, *Die "Gleichschaltung" der Heidelberg Universität*, p. 159.
143. UAH PA, 3607 (Duken), and Spruchkammerakte Johann Duken, GLAK, 465a/61/13/503. Also see Vezina, *Die "Gleichschaltung" der Heidelberg Universität*, pp. 156–162.
144. Dr. Eckert (Oberbürgermeister of Worms) to Ernst Engelking, October 12, 1946, and Sigmund Weil, "Separatvotum über Professor Achelis," November 4, 1946, both in Spruchkammerakte Johann Daniel Achelis, GLAK, 465a/59/48/3725. Also see Jerry Muller, *The Other God That Failed: Hans Freyer and the Deradicalization of German Conservatism* (Princeton: Princeton University Press, 1987), pp. 221, 229–230, 236, and Helmut Heiber, *Universität unterm Hakenkreuz. Der Professor im Dritten Reich* (Munich: K. G. Saur, 1991), p. 392.
145. Annegret Ehmann, "From Colonial Racism to Nazi Population Policy: The Role of the So-called Mischlinge," in Michael Berenbaum and Abraham Peck, eds., *The Holocaust and History: The Known, the Unknown, the Disputed, and the Reexamined* (Bloomington: Indiana University Press, 1998), pp. 115–133.
146. Carl Schneider to Rector, May 28, 1936, UAH PA, 5490 (Rodenwaldt).
147. Dozentenschaft der Universität Heidelberg to Rector, June 22, 1936, UAH PA, 5490 (Rodenwaldt).
148. Studentenschaft der Universität Heidelberg to Rector, June 17, 1936, UAH PA, 5490 (Rodenwaldt).
149. On Rodenwaldt, see Kater, *Doctors under Hitler*, pp. 2–3, and Becker-von Rose et al., "Einblicke in die Medizin."
150. Alan Beyerchen, *Scientists under Hitler: Politics and the Physics Community in the Third Reich* (New Haven: Yale University Press, 1977).
151. Ibid., p. 100.
152. Ibid., pp. 123–188.
153. Mark Walker, *Nazi Science: Myth, Truth, and the German Atomic Bomb* (New York: Plenum Press, 1995). On the Kaiser Wilhelm Institute, see Kristie Macrakis, *Surviving the Swastika: Scientific Research in Nazi Ger-

many (New York: Oxford University Press, 1993). The Göttingen physicist Georg Joos, for instance, was hounded out of the university and became the director of Zeiss-Werke. Kelly, "National Socialism and German University Teachers," p. 305.

154. "Spruch," September 23, 1948, Spruchkammerakte Heinrich Vogt, GLAK, 465a/59/1/8863–8615, and Arthur Rosenhal to Wilhelm Groh, June 2, 1935, UAH PA, 5515 (Rosenthal). Also see the essays collected in Winfried Scharlau, ed., *Mathematische Institute in Deutschland, 1800–1945* (Braunschweig: F. Vieweg, 1990). Also informative is Helmut Joachim Fischer's *Erinnerungen*, 2 vols. (Ingolstadt: Quellenstudien der Zeitgeschichtlichen Forschungsstelle Ingolstadt, 1984–1985).

155. Statement by Otto Erdmannsdörfer, November 5, 1945, in Spruchkammerakte Udo Wegner, GLAK, 465a/59/4/10896.

156. "Klageschrift," November 28, 1947, in GLAK, 465a/59/4/10896. See Freudenberg's assessment quoted in Vezina, *Die "Gleichschaltung" der Heidelberg Universität*, p. 156.

2. The "German Spirit" in Scholarship

1. Meinhold Lurz, "Öffentliches Gedächtnis in den Jahren 1945 und 1946," in Jürgen Hess, Hartmut Lehmann, and Volker Sellin, eds., *Heidelberg 1945* (Stuttgart: Franz Steiner Verlag, 1996), pp. 231–254.

2. See Meinhold Lurz, "Die 550-Jahr-Feier der Universität Heidelberg als nationalsozialistische Selbstdarstellung von Reich und Universität," *Ruperto Carola*, 28, no. 57 (1976), 35–41; Karl-Ludwig Hofmann and Christmut W. Präger, "'Volk, Rasse, Staat und deutscher Geist.' Zum Universitätsjubiläum 1936 und zur Kunstgeschichte in Heidelberg im 'Dritten Reich,'" in Karin Buselmeier, Dietrich Harth, and Christian Jansen, eds., *Auch eine Geschichte der Universität Heidelberg* (Mannheim: Edition Quadrat, 1985), pp. 337–345; and Philipp Gassert, *Amerika im Dritten Reich: Ideologie, Propaganda und Volksmeinung, 1933–1945* (Stuttgart: Franz Steiner Verlag, 1997), pp. 194–198.

3. Saul Friedländer, *Nazi Germany and the Jews*, vol. 1: *The Years of Persecution, 1933–1939* (New York: HarperCollins, 1997), pp. 177–333.

4. The speeches at the event were published in August Becker, ed., *Naturforschung im Aufbruch. Reden und Vorträge zur Einweihungsfeier des Philipp-Lenard-Instituts der Universität Heidelberg am 13. und 14. Dezember 1935* (Munich: J. S. Lehmanns Verlag, 1936).

5. The best description of the "canon" of Aryan physics is found in Alan Beyerchen, *Scientists under Hitler: Politics and the Physics Community in the Third Reich* (New Haven: Yale University Press, 1977), pp. 123–140. See also Philipp Lenard, "Vergangenheit und Zukunft deutscher Forschung," Lothar Tirala, "Nordische Rasse und Naturwissenschaft," Wolfgang Schultz, "Nordische Physik und nordisches Ermessen," and Rudolf Tomas-

chek, "Die Entwicklung der Äthervorstellung," all in Becker, ed., *Naturforschung im Aufbruch,* pp. 18–25, 27–38, 70–74, and 39–50, respectively.
6. Ernst Krieck, "Der Wandel der Wissenschaftsidee und des Wissenschaftssytems im Bereich der nationalsozialistischen Weltanschauung," in Becker, ed., *Naturforschung im Aufbruch,* pp. 51–53.
7. August Seybold, "Die Gemeinschaftsarbeit physikalischer und biologischer Forschung—eine Aufgabe der deutschen Wissenschaft!" in Becker, ed., *Naturforschung im Aufbruch,* p. 55.
8. Johannes Stein, "Arzt und Naturwissenschaft," in Becker, ed., *Naturforschung im Aufbruch,* p. 54.
9. Hans Rukop, "Physikalische Probleme in der Wissenschaft und in der Industrie," Becker, ed., *Naturforschung im Aufbruch,* pp. 61–69.
10. Beyerchen, *Scientists under Hitler.* Also see the relevant documents in Klaus Hentschel, ed., *Physics and National Socialism: An Anthology of Primary Sources* (Basel: Birkhäuser Verlag, 1996).
11. Beyerchen, *Scientists under Hitler,* pp. 126–140. Also see Friedländer's comments on the "Aryan physicists" in his *Nazi Germany and the Jews,* pp. 193–194.
12. Beyerchen, *Scientists under Hitler,* p. 169.
13. Regierungsassessor Dr. Müller to Wilhelm Groh, December 24, 1935, Universitätsarchiv Heidelberg (hereafter cited as UAH), B-1812/7.
14. Wilhelm Groh to Adolf Schmid, January 8, 1936, UAH, B-1812/16; Karl Seiler to Ernst Krieck, February 16, 1936, and "Bericht des Vorläufigen Arbeitsausschusses an den Rektor über die grundsätzlichen Fragen der 550 Jahrfeier," June 1, 1935, both in UAH, B-1812/7.
15. Representatives of the universities of Oxford, Cambridge, and London to state secretary of the Reich Chancellery, May 18, 1933, copy in Generallandesarchiv Karlsruhe (hereafter cited as GLAK), 235/5007.
16. "Nazi-Socialism and International Science," *Nature,* December 14, 1935, pp. 927–928.
17. "Philipp-Lenard-Institut at Heidelberg: Ceremonial Dedication" and "Nationalism and International Science," *Nature,* January 18, 1936, pp. 93–94 and 100, respectively.
18. "Heidelberg, Spinoza, and Academic Freedom," *Nature,* February 22, 1936, pp. 303–304.
19. Hentschel, ed., *Physics and National Socialism,* p. 118.
20. August Becker to Wilhelm Groh, January 31, 1936, UAH, B-1812/16.
21. Quoted in Gerhard Müller, *Ernst Krieck und die nationalsozislistische Wissenschaftsreform: Motive und Tendenzen einer Wissenschaftslehre und Hochschulreform im Dritten Reich* (Weinheim: Beltz, 1978), p. 126.
22. August Seybold to Wilhelm Groh, February 4, 1936, UAH, B-1812/16.
23. Müller, *Ernst Krieck,* p. 500.
24. Herbert Dunelm to the London *Times,* February 4, 1936. The most important correspondence related to this affair, as well as articles from *Nature,*

The Cambridge Review, and *The Universities Review* were collected and published in 1936 as *Heidelberg and the Universities of America* (New York: Viking, 1936). Also see Robert A. Brady, . . . *The Spirit and Structure of German Fascism* (New York: Viking, 1937); S. D. Stirk, *German Universities—through English Eyes* (London: V. Gollancz, 1946); and the commentary in the Paris-based émigré newspaper *Das neue Tagebuch* ("Wer geht nach Heidelberg?"), February 15, 1936.

25. See the responses in the *Times* published February 5, 7, 8, 10, 11, 13, 20, 24, 26, 28, and 29, 1936.
26. Charles Grant Robertson to the *Times,* February 16, 1936. On the decision of King's College to decline its invitation, see *The Cambridge Review,* February 14, 1936 (letter dated February 8), p. 259.
27. Harold Stannard to the *Times,* Feburary 18, 1936. Emphasis added.
28. Goebbels's address is reprinted in *Heidelberger Neueste Nachrichten,* June 29, 1936. Also see Joseph Goebbels, diary entries for June 28 and June 29, 1936, in Elke Fröhlich, ed., *Die Tagebücher von Joseph Goebbels Sämtliche Fragmente,* part 1, vol. 2 (Munich: K. G. Saur, 1987), p. 635. Hitler's telegram is reprinted in *Volksgemeinschaft,* June 29, 1936.
29. "550 Jahre Universität Heidelberg," copy located in the Institut für Fränkisch-Pfälzische Geschichte und Landeskunde, Heidelberg University.
30. Groh quoted in "Empfang der Reichsregierung im Königssaal," *Heidelberger Tageblatt,* June 29, 1936.
31. Ibid.
32. Ernst Krieck to the Deutsche Kongress-Zentrale, no date (1937), UAH, B-1812/40.
33. Thomas Mann, "The Living Spirit," in Thomas Mann, *Die Forderung des Tages. Abhandlungen und kleine Aufsätze über Literatur und Kunst* (Frankfurt am Main: S. Fischer Verlag, 1986), pp. 309–316.
34. Although virtually no public debate on the scale of the one in Great Britain took place in the United States, students and some professors at Columbia University pressured that institution's president without success to refuse the invitation. Events at Columbia can be followed in the *New York Times,* March 2, 4–5, 7, 10, 28, 31, 1936. The *Times*'s editorial page pronounced the death of academic freedom in Germany on April 12, 1936.
35. Helmut Heiber, *Die Universität unterm Hakenkreuz. Die Kapitulation der Hohen Schulen. Das Jahr 1933 und seine Themen* (Munich: K. G. Saur, 1991), part 2, pp. 294–300.
36. Robert Proctor, "Nazi Medicine and the Politics of Knowledge," in Sandra G. Harding, ed., *The "Racial" Economy of Science* (Bloomington: Indiana University Press, 1993), pp. 344–358.
37. Wilhelm Classen, "Das Ausland und die nationalsozialistische Wissenschaft," *Volk im Werden,* 5, no. 3 (March 1937), 113–121.
38. *Das nationalsozialistische Deutschland und die Wissenschaft, Heidelberger Reden von Reichsminister Rust und Professor Ernst Krieck* (Hamburg:

Reichsinstitut für Geschichte des neuen Deutschlands, 1936) and in English translation as *National Socialist Germany and the Pursuit of Learning* (Hamburg: Reichinstitut für Geschichte des neuen Deutschlands, 1936). The honorary professor of medicine, Heinrich Kunstmann, made a similar argument in a graduation speech on November 23, 1936. See Kunstmann, "Rede zur feier der Immatrikulation gehalten in der Aula der Neuen Universität Heidelberg 23. November 1936 (Heidelberg: Carl Winter's Universitätsbuchhandlung, 1937).

39. Rust, "National Socialist Germany and the Pursuit of Learning," in *National Socialist Germany and the Pursuit of Learning*, pp. 8–9, 4–5.
40. Robert Proctor, *Value-Free Science? Purity and Power in Modern Knowledge* (Cambridge: Harvard University Press, 1991), pp. 85–98 and 171–173.
41. Bernhard Rust, "Bildung eines Reichsforschungsrats," *Deutsche Wissenschaft, Erziehung und Volksbildung*, 3, no. 7 (1937), 151–152. Also see Carl Krauch, "Jugend an die Front. Die Nachwuchsfrage in Wissenschaft und Technik" (1937), reprinted in Hentschel, ed., *Physics and National Socialism*, pp. 161–167.
42. See Rust's pointed warning quoted in the *New York Times*, October 8, 1936.
43. Müller, *Ernst Krieck*, p. 125.
44. Ernst Krieck, "The Objectivity of Science: A Crucial Problem," *National Socialist Germany and the Pursuit of Learning*, pp. 17, 20, 21.
45. *Festausgabe der Volksgemeinschaft*, June 30, 1936. Also see Hans Hermann Adler's summary, "Das Gesicht der deutschen Universität," *Hochschule und Ausland*, 13, no. 11 (1935), 48–55.
46. H. Hagenbuch, "Älteste und jüngste Universität," *Festausgabe der Volksgemeinschaft*, June 30, 1936.
47. Eugen Fehrle, "Die deutsche Volkskunde in Heidelberg," *Festausgabe der Volksgemeinschaft*, June 30, 1936. On Fehrle's debt to Dietrich's ideas, see Peter Assion, "Eugen Fehrle and the 'Mythos of our Folk,'" in James R. Dow and Hannjost Lixfeld, eds., *The Nazification of an Academic Discipline: Folklore in the Third Reich* (Bloomington: Indiana University Press, 1994), pp. 113–114.
48. Hermann Güntert, "Aufgaben und Bedeutung der Sprachwissenschaft," *Festausgabe der Volksgemeinschaft*, June 30, 1936.
49. Eduard Bötticher, "Staats- und wirtschaftswissenschaftliche Fakultät," *Festausgabe der Volksgemeinschaft*, June 30, 1936.
50. Paul Schmitthenner, "Die Universität als Stätte wehrpolitische Erziehung," *Festausgabe der Volksgemeinschaft*, June 30, 1936.
51. Ludwig Wesch, "Das Philipp-Lenard-Institut eine Stätte deutscher Forschung," *Festausgabe der Volksgemeinschaft*, June 30, 1936.
52. See "Wesch Report," 1945, American Institute of Physics, Samuel Goudsmit Papers, Series IV, Subseries A (ALSOS Mission), Box 27, Folder 27.

53. "Professor Stein über 'Volkstum und Arzt,'" *Heidelberger Tageblatt,* July 1, 1936.
54. Carl Schneider, "Der deutsche Arzt," *Festausgabe der Volksgemeinschaft,* June 30, 1936. Also see Johann Daniel Achelis, "Über den medizinischen Unterricht," *Festausgabe der Volksgemeinschaft,* June 30, 1936.
55. "Die neuen Ehrendoktoren der Universität," *Volksgemeinschaft,* July 1, 1936.
56. A copy of Groh's circular requesting nominations, dated September 21, 1935, can be found in UAH, Theol.Fak 169.
57. Karl Engisch to Wilhelm Groh, January 29, 1936, UAH, B-1523/5.
58. "Die neuen Ehrendoktoren der Universität," *Volksgemeinschaft,* July 1, 1936. The relevant files in Heidelberg University's archives contain no recommendations from the Theology Faculty.
59. Karl Freudenberg to Heinrich Vogt, January 27, 1936, and Otto Ermannsdörfer to Heinrich Vogt, October 29, 1936, both in UAH, B-1523/5.
60. Hermann Güntert to Wilhelm Groh, October 29, 1935, and January 31, 1936, UAH, B-1523/5.
61. Eduard Bötticher to Wilhelm Groh, January 17, 1936, UAH, B-1523/5. The recommendations were made by Brinkmann.
62. Ibid.
63. Ibid.
64. Ernst Rodenwaldt to Carl Schneider, December 11, 1935, UAH, B-1523/5.
65. Carl Schneider to Harry Laughlin, May 16, 1936, and Harry Laughlin to Carl Schneider, May 28, 1936, and Universitätsbibliothek Heidelberg to Eugenics Record Office, Cold Springs Harbor, June 15, 1936, all in the Papers of Harry Hamilton Laughlin, Truman State University, Kirksville, Mo., Box E, 1–3.
66. Stefan Kühl, *The Nazi Connection: Eugenics, American Racism, and German National Socialism* (New York: Oxford University Press, 1994), pp. 77–95.
67. Acting director of the Anatomical Institute to Carl Schneider, December 2, 1935, UAH, B-1523/5.
68. Paul Schmitthenner to Baden state minister, Culture Minister, and NSDAP Gauleitung, February 1, 1936, GLAK, 235/29988.
69. "Universität Heidelberg Zusammenstellung der Universitätsinstitute und ihrer Aversen für 1941," n.d., but likely 1941 or 1942, GLAK, 235/29988.
70. Paul Schmitthenner to Culture Minister, January 24, 1936, GLAK, 235/29988.
71. The subjects are taken from the respective *Vorlesungsverzeichnisse,* Universität Heidelberg.
72. On "Westforschung" see Burkhard Dietz, "Die interdisziplinäre 'Westforschung' der Weimar Republik und NS-Zeit als Gegenstand der Wissenschafts- und Zeitgeschichte. Überlegung zu Forschungsstand und Forschungsperspektiven," *Geschichte im Westen,* 14, no. 2 (1999), 189–

209; Peter Schöttler, "Von der rheinischen Landesgeschichte zur nazistischen Volksgeschichte," in Winfried Schulze and Otto Gerhard Oexle, eds., *Deutsche Historiker im Nationalsozialismus* (Frankfurt: Fischer Taschenbuch Verlag, 1999), pp. 89–113; and Michael Fahlbusch, *Wissenschaft im Dienst der Nationalsozialistischen Politik? die "Volksdeutschen Forschungsgemeinschaften" von 1931–1945* (Baden-Baden: Nomos, 1999), pp. 350–440. On "Ostforschung," see Michael Burleigh, *Germany Turns Eastward: A Study of Ostforschung in the Third Reich* (Cambridge: Cambridge University Press, 1988), and Martin Burkert, *Die Ostwissenschaften im Dritten Reich. Teil I, Zwischen Verbot und Duldung: die schwierige Gratwanderung der Ostwissenschaften zwischen 1933 und 1939* (Wiesbaden: Harrassowitz in Kommission, 2000).

73. See Irmline Veit-Brause, "The Place of Local and Regional History in German and French Historiography: Some General Reflections," *Australian Journal of French Studies,* 16, part 5 (1979), 447–477.

74. See, for instance, Ernst Anrich, *Die Geschichte der deutschen Westgrenze* (Leipzig: Verlag von Quelle & Meyer, 1939), esp. pp. 116–121. Also see Schöttler, "Die historische 'Westforschung'," pp. 233–234, and Fahlbusch, *Wissenschaft im Dienst,* p. 380.

75. "Denkschrift über die Notwendigkeit der Errichtung eines Instituts für fränkisch-pfälzisch Landes- und Volksforschung an der Universität Heidelberg," June 1937, GLAK, 235/29965.

76. Fritz Ernst, "Institut für Fränkisch-Pfälzische Landes- und Volksforschung," *Volksgemeinschaft* (Heidelberg), July 5, 1939.

77. Wolfgang Panzer, "Der Aufbau des deutschen Lebansraumes," *Zeitschrift für Erdkunde,* 4, no. 6 (March 15, 1936), 241–247.

78. Spruch, September 9, 1946, Spruchkammerakte Fritz Ernst, GLAK, 465a/59/5/4876.

79. Richard Kienle (to Spruchkammer Heidelberg), August 4, 1946, and Meldebogen (Fritz Ernst), April 27, 1946, both in Spruchkammerakte Fritz Ernst, GLAK, 465a/59/5/4876. Also see Ernst's own account in Diethard Aschoff, *Fritz Ernst. Im Schatten des Diktators. Rückblick eines Heidelberger Historikers auf die NS-Zeit* (Heidelberg: Manutius Verlag, 1996).

80. Richard Scherberger to Gauleitung Baden, January 15, 1941, UAH Personalakte (hereafter cited as PA) 3690 (Ernst).

81. Aschoff, *Fritz Ernst. Im Schatten des Diktators,* pp. 5–37.

82. Two widely cited statements on this issue are Wolfgang Kunkel's "Der Professor im Dritten Reich," in Helmut Kuhn et al., *Die Deutsche Universität im Dritten Reich* (Munich: R. Piper, 1966), pp. 103–133, and Gerhard Ritter's "Der deutsche Professor im 'Dritten Reich,'" *Die Gegenwart,* December 24, 1945, pp. 23–26.

83. See Reece Conn Kelly, "National Socialism and German University Teachers: The NSDAP's Efforts to Create a National Socialist Professoriate and Scholarship" (Ph.D. diss., University of Washington, 1973), pp. 374–376.

84. Scherberger to Gauleitung Baden, January 15, 1941, UAH PA 3690 (Ernst).
85. See his "Zum Verhältnis von politischer und völkischer Einheit der Deutschen im Mittelalter," in Heinrich Dannenbauer and Fritz Ernst, eds., *Das Reich. Idee und Gestalt* (Stuttgart: J. G. Cotta'sche Buchhandlung Nachfolger, 1940), pp. 203–216, and his *England und Indien. Zur Geschichte ihrer Beziehungen* (Stuttgart: W. Kohlhammer Verlag, 1935–36).
86. See Fritz Ernst to the Ministry of Culture, January 6, 1939, GLAK, 235/29965, and *Volksgemeinschaft* (Heidelberg), December 29, 1938.
87. See Carsten Klingemann, *Soziologie im Dritten Reich* (Baden-Baden: Nomos Verlagsgesellschaft, 1996), and Klaus Brintzinger, *Die Nationalökonomie an den Universitäten Freiburg, Heidelberg und Tübingen: eine institutionenhistorische, vergleichende Studie der wirtschaftswissenschaftlichen Fakultäten und Abteilungen südwestdeutscher Universitäten* (Frankfurt: Lang, 1996), pp. 184–230, 238–242.
88. See, for instance, Ernst Schuster, "Saarpfalz," and Carl Brinkmann, "Baden," both in Konrad Meyer and Klaus Thiede, eds., *Die ländische Arbeitsverfassung im Westen und Süden des Reiches. Beiträge zur Landfluchtfrage* (Heidelberg: Kurt Vowinckel Verlag, 1941), pp. 232–245 and 246–254, respectively, and Carl Brinkmann, "Gesundung der bäuerlichen Verhältnisse und Siedlerreserve in Nordbaden," *Raumforschung und Raumordnung*, 4 (1940).
89. Carsten Klingemann, "Reichssoziologie und Nachkriegssoziologie: Zur Kontinuität einer Wissenschaft in zwei politischen Systemen," in Renate Knigge-Tesche, ed., *Berater der braunen Macht: Wissenschaft und Wissenschaftler im NS-Staat* (Frankfurt: Anabas Verlag, 1999), pp. 70–93.
90. Carsten Klingemann, "Sociology and Social Research in the Third Reich," in Stephen Turner and Dirk Käsler, eds., *Sociology Responds to Fascism* (London: Routledge, 1992), pp. 127–129, 149–150.
91. Ibid., pp. 128–129.
92. On Sombart, see Jeffrey Herf, *Reactionary Modernism: Technology, Culture, and Politics in Weimar and the Third Reich* (Cambridge: Cambridge University Press, 1984), pp. 130–151.
93. Thoms, "Nationalsozialistische Wirtschaftsdenken," originally published in *Zeitschrift für Organisation*, 12 (1939), and reprinted in Thoms, *Wirtschaft und Betrieb. Vorträge und Beiträge zur Neuordnung der Deutschen Volks- und Betriebswirtschaft* (Leipzig: Verlag August Lutzeyer, 1943), pp. 40–45.
94. Thoms, "Der betriebliche Arbeitseinsatz im europäischen Grossraum," in *Wirtschaft und Betrieb*, pp. 61–82.
95. Ernst Krieck to the Minister of Culture, September 29, 1936, GLAK, 235/3826.
96. Ernst Krieck, "Über die Errichtung eines volks- und kulturpolitischen Instituts an der Universität Heidelberg," September 1936, GLAK, 235/3826.

97. For a list of such institutes, see Robert Proctor, *Racial Hygiene: Medicine under the Nazis* (Cambridge: Harvard University Press, 1988), pp. 327–329.
98. A revealing window onto Schneider's outlook is provided by an article intended to accompany the official program to the 1937 traveling exhibit of confiscated modern art deemed "degenerate" by the regime. Although not included in the program, Schneider's essay was published as "Degenerate Art and Lunatic Art" ("Entartete Kunst und Irrenkunst") in the *Archiv für Psychiatrie und Nervenkrankenheiten*, 110 (1939), 135–164.
99. Henry Friedlander, *The Origins of Nazi Genocide: From Euthanasia to the Final Solution* (Chapel Hill: University of North Carolina Press, 1995).
100. "Wie Bewahrt der Deutsche die Reinheit seines Blutes in Ländern mit farbiger Bevölkerung," *Der Auslandsdeutsche*, 19 (1936), 623; "Die nicht gemeinsamen Rasseelemente der Balischen Kasten" and "Die Rückwirkung der Rassenmischung in den Kolonialländern auf Europa," both in *Archiv für Rassen- und Gesellschaftsbiologie (einschliesslich Rassen- und Gesellschaftshygiene)*, 32 (1938); and "Rassenhygiene und Kolonialpolitik. Nationalsozialistische Rassenerkenntnis als Grundlage für die koloniale Betätigung des neuen Europas," *Deutscher Kolonialdienst*, 4, no. 7 (1939), 180–185; and "Rassenbiologische Probleme in Kolonialländern," *Verhandlungen der Deutschen Gesellschaft für Rassenforschung*, 10 (1940), 1–17.
101. Rodenwaldt, "Rassenhygiene und Kolonialpolitik," pp. 180, 184–185.
102. See Benno Müller-Hill, *Murderous Science: Elimination by Scientific Selection of Jews, Gypsies, and Others in Germany, 1933–1945* (Plainview, N.Y.: Cold Spring Harbor Laboratory Press, 1998), pp. 99–100, and Friedlander, *The Origins of Nazi Genocide*, pp. 128, 155.
103. Wilhelm Rimpau, "Viktor von Weizäcker im Nationalsozialismus," in Gerritt Hohendorf and Achim Magull-Seltenreich, eds., *Von der Heilkunde zur Massentötung. Medizin im Nationalsozialismus* (Heidelberg: Wunderhorn, 1990), pp. 113–130.
104. Undated questionnaire, UAH PA 5599 (Schachermeyr).
105. Fritz Schachermeyr, "Zur Rasse und Kultur im Minoischen Kreta," *Wörter und Sachen*, n.s., 2 (1939), 97–157.
106. See Fritz Schachermeyr, "Die nordische Führerpersönlichkeit im Altertum," in Hermann Gieselbuch, ed., *Humanistische Bildung im nationalsozialistische Staat* (Leipzig: Verlag und Druck von B. G. Teubner, 1933), pp. 36–43, and his *Indogermanen und Orient. Ihre kulturelle und machtpolitische Auseinandersetzung im Altertum* (Stuttgart: W. Kohlhammer, 1944).
107. *Der Nomos Chinas und das Evangelium. Eine Untersuchung über die Bedeutung von Rasse und Volkstum für die missionarische Verkündigung in China* (Leipzig: J. C. Hinrichs Buchhandlung, 1936).
108. Ibid., pp. 4, 8.
109. On the language arts see Ruth Römer, *Sprachwissenschaft und Rassen-*

ideologie in Deutschland (Munich: Wilhelm Fink Verlag, 1985), esp. chap. 9.
110. Hermann Güntert, "Zum heutigen Stand der Sprachforschung," *Wörter und Sachen*, 12 (1929), p. 389.
111. Hermann Güntert, "Neue Zeit—neues Ziel," *Wörter und Sachen*, n.s., 1 (1938), pp. 6–7.
112. Hermann Güntert, *Geschichte der germanischen Völkerschaften* (Leipzig: Bibliographisches Institut, 1943), pp. 7–8.
113. Ahnenerbe Memorandum, 1944, reprinted in Hannjost Lixfeld, *Folklore and Fascism: The Reich Institute for German Volkskunde* (Bloomington: Indiana University Press, 1994), pp. 194–200.
114. Richard von Kienle, *Germanische Gemeinschaftsformen* (Stuttgart: W. Kohlhammer Verlag, 1939), p. 3.
115. See Frank-Rutger Hausmann, *"Vom Strudel der Ereignisse Verschlungen." Deutsche Romanistik im "Dritten Reich"* (Frankfurt: Vittorio Klostermann, 2000), and his *"Deutsche Geisteswissenschaft" im Zweiten Weltkrieg. Die "Aktion Ritterbusch," (1940–1945)* (Dresden: Dresden University Press, 1998). On philology see Peter Sturm, *Literaturwissenschaft im Dritten Reich. Germanistische Wissenschaftsformation und politisches System* (Vienna: Verlag Edition Präsens, 1995).
116. On Mönch, see Hausmann, *"Vom Strudel der Ereignisse verschlungen"*, pp. 334–337, 554–567, and 643–646.
117. Biographical information from Spruchkammerakte Walter Mönch, GLAK, 465a/59/38/2847.
118. *Frankreichs Literatur im XVI. Jahrhundert. Eine Nationalpolitische Geistesgeschichte der Französischen Renaissance* (Berlin: Walter de Gruyter, 1938).
119. Ibid., pp. 193–194.
120. Ibid., p. 207.
121. "Das heutige Deutschland im Spiegel französischer Bücher. Bemerkungen zu einem Deutschlandbuch von Chateaubriant," *Geist der Zeit*, 16, no. 4 (1938), 258–263.
122. Ibid., pp. 261, 262.
123. "Rasse und Stil bei Alphonse de Lamartine," *Zeitschrift für französische Sprache und Literatur*, 62, no. 4 (1938), 158.
124. Edgar Glässer, *Einführung in die rassenkundlich Sprachforschung: Kritische-historische Untersuchungen* (Heidelberg: C. Winters Universitätsbuchhandlung), p. 87.
125. Ibid., p. 86.
126. Dienerakte Wilhelm Groh, GLAK, 235/2031.
127. On Krieck as Rector, see Eike Wolgast, "Die Universität Heidelberg in der Zeit des Nationalsozialismus," *Zeitschrift für die Geschichte des Oberrheins*, 135 (1987), 392–394, and Heiber, *Universität unterm Hakenkreuz*, part 1, pp. 464–474.

128. Paul Schmitthenner, "Politik und Kriegführung als wehrpolitisches Problem. Eine grundsätzliche Erwiderung," *Historische Zeitschrift,* 159 (1939), 550.
129. Paul Schmitthenner, "Rede des Rektors der Universität Heidelberg Staatsministers Prof. Dr. Schmitthenner zur 552. Jahresfeier der Universität Heidelberg," *Heidelberger Universitätsreden,* n.s., no. 5 (Heidelberg: Carl Winter's Verlag, 1939), p. 6.
130. Ulrike Lennartz, "Ein badischer 'Preusse.' Paul Schmitthenner, Badischer Staatsminister," in Michael Kissener and Joachim Scholtyseck, eds., *Die Führer der Provinz: NS-Biographien aus Baden und Württemberg* (Constance: Universitätsverlag Konstanz, 1997) pp. 623–653.
131. Dorothee Mussgnug, *Die vertriebenen Heidelberger Dozenten: zur Geschichte der Ruprecht-Karls-Universität nach 1933* (Heidelberg: C. Winter, 1988), pp. 95–111.
132. Wilhelm Groh to Ministry of Culture, January 13, 1937, GLAK, 235/2133.
133. Aktenvermerk, Minister of Culture and Education, March 18, 1937, GLAK, 235/2133.
134. Ernst Krieck to Baden Ministry of Culture, May 3, 1937, GLAK, 235/2133.
135. Minister of Culture to Baden state minister, May 14, 1937, GLAK, 235/2133.
136. Reich Education Ministry to the Reichstatthalter in Baden, June 16, 1937, and Baden state chancellor's office to Ministry of Culture, June 22, 1937, both in GLAK, 235/2133.
137. Karl Jaspers to Reich Education Minister and Minister of Culture in Karlsruhe, July 14, 1937, UAH PA, 4369 (Jaspers).
138. Ernst Krieck to Minister of Culture, July 14, 1937, GLAK, 235/2133.
139. Minister of Culture to Reich Ministry of Education, July 23, 1937, GLAK, 235/2133, and Minister of Culture to Finance and Economics Minister, Karlsruhe, August 24, 1937, GLAK, 466/9647.
140. Karl Jaspers, "Lebensbeschreibung," n.d., but probably 1945 or 1946, GLAK, 235/2133. Reprinted in Renato de Rosa, ed., *Briefwechsel, 1945–1948 / Karl Jaspers, K. H. Bauer* (Berlin: Springer Verlag, 1983), pp. 1–7.
141. Jaspers, "Philosophical Autobiography," in Paul Arthur Schilpp, ed., *The Philosophy of Karl Jaspers* (La Salle, Ill: Open Court, 1957), p. 62.
142. Ibid., p. 63.
143. Ibid.
144. Victor Klemperer, *I Will Bear Witness: A Diary of the Nazi Years, 1933–1941* (New York: Modern Library, 1999).
145. On the pogrom, see Marion Kaplan, *Between Dignity and Despair: Jewish Life in Nazi Germany* (New York: Oxford University Press, 1998), pp. 119–144. On the pogrom in Heidelberg, see Frank Moraw, "Das November-Pogrom 1938 und die lokale Politik in Heidelberg," in Norbert Giovanni et al., eds., *Jüdisches Leben in Heidelberg: Studien zu einer unterbrochenen Geschichte* (Heidelberg: Wunderhorn, 1992), pp. 121–141, and

Arno Weckbecker, *Die Judenverfolgung in Heidelberg, 1933–1945* (Heidelberg: Juristischer Verlag, 1985), pp. 188–196.
146. See Karl Heinrich Bauer to Johannes Hoops, June 18, 1945, GLAK, 235/29831.
147. Kaplan, *Between Dignity and Despair*, p. 123.
148. Hugo Ott, "Der Freiburger Kreis," in Rudolf Lill and Michael Kissener, eds., *20. Juli 1944 in Baden und Württemberg* (Constance: Universitäts Verlag Konstanz, 1994).
149. Quoted in Friedländer, *Nazi Germany and the Jews*, p. 293.
150. Friedländer, "The Demise of the German Mandarins," and Lennartz, "Ein badischer 'Preusse,'" pp. 642–645.
151. Schmitthenner, "Rede des Rektors der Universität Heidelberg." Also see his "Bewegung und Universität," *Heidelberger Hochschulführer*, summer semester, 1939, pp. 42–46.

3. The National Socialist University at War

1. "Rede zur Feier der Immatrikulation," January 30, 1940, *Kriegsvorträge der Universität Heidelberg*, vol. 2 (Heidelberg: Carl Winter's Universitätsbuchhandlung, 1940), p. 23.
2. On professors and the war, see Klaus Schwabe, "Deutsche Hochschullehrer und Hitler's Krieg (1936–1940)," in Martin Broszat and Klaus Schwabe, eds., *Die deutschen Eliten und der Weg in den Zweiten Weltkrieg* (Munich: Beck, 1989), pp. 291–333, and Hans Peter Herrmann, "German Professors and the Two World Wars," in Reinhold Grimm and Jost Hermand, eds., *1914/1939: German Reflections of the Two World Wars* (Madison: University of Wisconsin Press, 1992), pp. 154–173. Also see Michael Burleigh, *Germany Turns Eastward: A Study of Ostforschung in the Third Reich* (Cambridge: Cambridge University Press, 1988), Frank-Rutger Hausmann, *"Deutsche Geisteswissenschaft" im Zweiten Weltkrieg. Die "Aktion Ritterbusch" (1940–1945)* (Dresden: Dresden University Press, 1998), and Michael Fahlbusch, *Wissenschaft im Dienst der nationalsozialistischen Politik? die "Volksdeutschen Forschungsgemeinschaften" von 1931–1945* (Baden-Baden: Nomos, 1999).
3. Karl Freudenberg, memorandum, November 5, 1945, Universitätsarchiv Heidelberg (herefter cited as UAH), B-1590/1.
4. Figures cited in Michael Fahlbusch, "Für Volk, Führer und Reich! Volkstumsforschung und Volkstumspolitik, 1931–1945," paper delivered at the University of Constance, May 2000.
5. Ute Deichmann, *Biologists under Hitler* (Cambridge: Harvard University Press, 1996), p. 130.
6. Kristie Macrakis, *Surviving the Swastika: Scientific Research in Nazi Germany* (New York: Oxford University Press, 1993), pp. 131–161, figure cited on p. 157.

7. Leslie E. Simon, *German Research in World War II: An Analysis of the Conduct of Research* (New York: John Wiley & Sons, 1947).
8. Twelve such institutes were established between 1940 and 1943. The tradition of aggressive cultural foreign policy predated the Nazis. See Kurt Düwell, *Deutschlands auswärtige Kulturpolitik: Grundlinien und Dokumente, 1918–1932* (Cologne: Böhlau, 1976), and Volkhard Leitenberger, *Akademischer Austausch und auswärtiger Kulturpolitik: Der Deutsche Akademischer Austauschdienst (DAAD) 1923–1945* (Göttingen: Musterschmidt, 1976).
9. On Forsthoff, see Jerry Muller, *The Other God That Failed: Hans Freyer and the Deradicalization of German Conservatism* (Princeton: Princeton University Press, 1987), pp. 392–395, and Ulrich Storost, *Staat und Verfassung bei Ernst Forsthoff* (Frankfurt am Main: Lang, 1979).
10. Ernst Forsthoff, *Der Totale Staat* (Hamburg: Hanseatische Verlagsanstalt, 1933). The ideas in this work were foreshadowed in Forsthoffer's contribution, under the pseudonym Friedrich Grüter, to a collection of essays by young conservative scholars edited by Albrecht Günther, *Was wir vom Nationalsozialismus erwarten* (Heilbronn: E. Salzer, 1932).
11. Military Government of Germany Fragebogen, Ernst Forsthoff, May 11, 1945, UAH Personalakte (hereafter cited as PA), 3789 (Forsthoff).
12. *Deutsche Geschichte in Dokumenten seit 1918* (Leipzig: Alfred Kröner Verlag, 1935, and Stuttgart: A. Kröner, 1938 and 1943). See Forsthoff's suggestive comments in the foreword to the final edition.
13. Ernst Forsthoff, "Lebenslauf," June 27, 1949, UAH PA, 3787 (Forsthoff).
14. Fragebogen, Ernst Forsthoff, May 11, 1945, UAH PA, 3789 (Forsthoff).
15. Much of the information presented here on Bauer is taken from an extensive American Military Government investigation of him conducted in the spring and summer of 1946; the report of that investigation is in the United States National Archives and Records Administration (hereafter cited as NARA), RG 260, Office of Military Government Württemberg-Baden (hereafter cited as OMGWB), Records of the Education & Civil-Religious Affairs Division, Box 917A, File: "Denazification of Heidelberg University 1945–1947 (Col. Irvin)"; and cited hereafter as Bauer Report. For secondary accounts see Barbara Zimmermann, "Karl Heinrich Bauer," in Bernd Ottnad, ed., *Badische Biograhien. Neue Folge* (Stuttgart: W. Kohlhammer, 1982), vol. 3, pp. 23–24, and Eike Wolgast, "Karl Heinrich Bauer—der erste Heidelberger Nachkriegsrektor. Weltbild und Handeln, 1945–1946," in Jürgen Hess, Hartmut Lehmann, and Volker Sellin, eds., *Heidelberg 1945* (Stuttgart: Franz Steiner Verlag, 1997), pp. 107–129. These uncritical accounts should be read alongside Bernd Laufs, "Vom Umgang der Medizin mit ihrer Geschichte," in Gerritt Hohendorf and Achim Magull-Seltenreich, eds., *Von der Heilkunde zur Massentötung. Medizin im Nationalsozialismus* (Heidelberg: Wunderhorn, 1990), pp. 233–257.
16. Karl Heinrich Bauer, "Lebenslauf," in Renato de Rosa, ed., *Briefwechsel,*

1945–1968 / Karl Jaspers, K. H. Bauer (Berlin: Springer Verlag, 1983), p. 13.
17. Karl Heinrich Bauer, *Rassenhygiene* (Leipzig: Quelle & Meyer, 1926). On the context of "racial hygiene" in Europe, see George Mosse, *Toward the Final Solution: A History of European Racism* (Madison: University of Wisconsin Press, 1978), pp. 77–93.
18. Bauer, *Rassenhygiene,* pp. 204, 207. Bauer's advocacy of a race war is on p. 168.
19. See Karl Heinrich Bauer, "Technik und Methodik der Sterilisation beim Manne," in "Berichte aus wissenschaftlichen Gesellschaften. 59. Tagung der Deutschen Gesellschaft für Chirurgie in Berlin, 24.-27. April 1935," *Zentralblatt für Gynäkologie,* 59 (1935), 1465–1466, and Bauer Report.
20. Karl Heinrich Bauer, "Die Bedeutung des Gesetzes zur Verhütung erbkranken Nachwuchses für die Chirurgie," *Der Chirurg,* 4 no. 9 (May 1, 1934); Karl Heinrich Bauer, "Berichte aus wissenschaftlichen Gesellschaften. Tagung der Deutschen Gesellschaft für Chirurgie in Berlin 4.-7. April 1934," *Zentralblatt für Gynäkologie,* 58, no. 28 (1934), 1660–1662; and Karl Heinrich Bauer and Felix von Mikulicz-Radecki, *Die Praxis der Sterilisierungsoperationen* (Leipzig: J. A. Barth, 1936).
21. Interrogation Report, Johann Daniel Achelis, May 11, 1946, Bauer Report.
22. Rector of Göttingen to Bernhard Rust, January 1, 1941, UAH PA, 3204 (Bauer).
23. Karl Heinrich Bauer to Kurator of the University and Technical College of Breslau, February 12, 1942, UAH PA, 3204 (Bauer).
24. Bauer Report.
25. See the report of Bauer's trip to Bulgaria in 1941, December 17, 1941, UAH PA, 3204 (Bauer).
26. *Lehrbuch der Chirurgie* (Berlin: Springer, 1941).
27. Bernhard Rust to Paul Schmitthenner, December 31, 1942, copy in Bauer Report.
28. Interrogation Report, Johann Daniel Achelis, corroborated by an affidavit by Waldemar Kutscher, May 7, 1946, both in Bauer Report.
29. Ibid.
30. Ernst Krieck, "Der Wille zum Reich," May 5, 1940, *Kriegsvorträge der Universität Heidelberg,* vol. 3 (Heidelberg: Carl Winter's Universitätsbuchhandlung, 1940), p. 5. Also see Karl Bilfinger, "Englische Völkerrechtspolitik," November 21, 1939, *Kriegsvorträge der Universität Heidelberg,* vol. 1 (Berlin: Verlag Junker und Dünnhaupt, 1940).
31. Schmitthenner, "Rede zur Feier der Immatrikulation."
32. Ernst Schuster, "Der Wehrgeist In der Volkswirtschaft," January 30, 1940, *Kriegsvorträge der Universität Heidelberg,* vol. 2, pp. 3–15.
33. Herbert Krüger, "Vertrauen als seelische Grundlage der Volksgemeinschaft," June 5, 1940, *Kriegsvorträge der Universität Heidelberg,* vol. 2, pp. 3–20.

34. Gerhard Dulckeit, "Das Recht In Geschichte und Gegenwart," November 22, 1940, *Kriegsvorträge der Universität Heidelberg*, vol. 2, pp. 3–16.
35. Ibid., p. 7.
36. Ibid., p. 13.
37. Ibid., p. 15.
38. August Becker, "Naturerkenntnis und Wehrkraft," June 2, 1940, *Kriegsvorträge der Universität Heidelberg*, vol. 4 (Heidelberg: Carl Winter's Universitätsbuchhandlung, 1940), and Jeffrey Herf, *Reactionary Modernism: Technology, Culture, and Politics in Weimar and the Third Reich* (Cambridge: Cambridge University Press, 1984), pp. 1–17.
39. Becker, "Naturerkenntnis und Wehrkraft," p. 15.
40. Joseph Goebbels, *Der geistige Arbeiter im Schicksalkampf des Reiches. Rede vor der Heidelberger Universität am 9. Juli 1943* (Munich: Zentralverwaltung der NSDAP, 1944), pp. 21, 22.
41. Culture Ministry Aktenvermerk, Semesterfrontkursen, October 9, 1939, Generallandesarchiv Karlsruhe (hereafter cited as GLAK), 235/4868.
42. Oberkommando der Wehrmacht to Baden State Chancellery, October 11, 1939, GLAK, 235/4868.
43. Karl Bilfinger to Paul Schmitthenner, September 8, 1939, GLAK, 235/4868.
44. Hubert Schrade to Paul Schmitthenner, October 7, 1939, GLAK, 235/4868.
45. Paul Böckmann to Paul Schmitthenner, October 9, 1939, GLAK, 235/4868.
46. Quoted in Eike Wolgast, "Die Universität Heidelberg in der Zeit des Nationalsozialismus," *Zeitschrift für die Geschichte des Oberrheins*, 135 (1987), p. 399.
47. Walter Thoms to Paul Schmitthenner, September 5, 1939, GLAK, 235/4868.
48. Hans Runge to Reich Education Ministry, September 6, 1939, GLAK, 235/4868.
49. Fritz Eichholtz to Paul Schmitthenner, October 6, 1939, GLAK, 235/4868.
50. August Becker to Paul Schmitthenner, October 6, 1939, GLAK, 235/4868.
51. Karl Freudenberg to Paul Schmitthenner, October 6, 1939, GLAK, 235/4868.
52. Julius Wilser to Paul Schmitthenner, October 6, 1939, GLAK, 235/4868.
53. *Vorlesungsverzeichnisse*, Universität Heidelberg, 1940–1944, and Wolgast, "Die Universität Heidelberg," pp. 398–399.
54. *Vorlesungsverzeichnis*, Universität Heidelberg, winter semester, 1943–44.
55. Thoms to Schmitthenner, September 5, 1939, GLAK, 235/4868.
56. *Vorlesungsverzeichnisse*, Universität Heidelberg, 1940–1944, and Wolgast, "Die Universität Heidelberg," pp. 398–399.
57. Ibid., p. 401.
58. Rutger-Hausmann, *"Aktion Ritterbusch,"* pp. 24, 34.
59. Martin Debelius, *Britisches Christentum und Britische Weltmacht* (Berlin: Junker und Dünnhaupt, 1940); Carl Brinkmann, *Der wirtschaftliche Liberalismus als System der britischen Weltanschauung* (Berlin: Junker und

Dünnhaupt, 1940) and *Der Englische Wirtschaftsimperialismus* (Berlin: Junker und Dünnhaupt, 1940); Carl Bilfinger, *Der Völkerbund als Instrument britischer Machtpolitik* (Berlin: Junker und Dünnhaupt, 1940), *Die Stimsondoktrin* (Essen: Essener Verlagsanstalt, 1943), and *Das wahre Gesicht des Kellogpaktes* (Essen: Essener Verlagsanstalt, 1942); and Eugen Fehrle, *Deutsches Volkstum im Elsass* (Berlin: Junker und Dünnhaupt, 1941).

60. Brinkmann, *Der Englische Wirtschaftsimperialismus*, esp. pp. 54–58.
61. Dibelius, *Britisches Christentum und Britische Weltmacht*, pp. 43, 45, 65, 66.
62. Fehrle, *Deutsches Volkstum im Elsass*, quotes on pp. 9, 54–55.
63. Frank-Rutger Hausmann, *"Vom Strudel der Ereignisse Verschlungen." Deutsche Romanistik im "Dritten Reich"* (Frankfurt: Vittorio Klostermann, 2000), esp. pp. 393–616.
64. "Tätigkeitsbericht für das S.S. 1941," August 25, 1941, and "Bericht über das Studienjahr 1941/42 an der Universität Lüttich," June 10, 1942, both in UAH PA, 5044 (Mönch).
65. "Fruchtbarer geistiger Austausch. Lütticher Studenten hören deutsche Gast-Professoren," *Brüsseler Zeitung*, March 5, 1942.
66. Mönch, "Bericht über das Studienjahr."
67. Ibid. Also see Mönch's *Voltaire und Friedrich der Grosse. Das Drama einer Denkwürdigen Freundschaft* (Stuttgart: W. Kohlhammer Verlag, 1943).
68. Spruchkammerakte Walter Mönch, GLAK, 465a/59/38/2847.
69. Volker Losemann, "The Nazi Concept of Rome," in Catherine Edwards, ed., *Roman Presences: Receptions of Rome In European Culture, 1789–1945* (Cambridge: Cambridge University Press, 1999), pp. 221–235, and Diemuth Königs, *Joseph Vogt: ein Althistoriker in der Weimarer Republik und im Dritten Reich* (Basel: Helbing & Lichtenhahn, 1995).
70. Joseph Vogt, ed., *Rom und Karthago. Ein Gemeinschaftswerk* (Leipzig: Köhler & Amelang, 1943).
71. Reinhard Herbig, "Das archaeologische Bild des Puniertums," in ibid., pp. 176–177.
72. Quoted in Mark Mazower, *Dark Continent: Europe's Twentieth Century* (New York: Vintage Books, 1998), p. 146.
73. Fritz Ernst, *England und Indien. Zur Geschichte ihrer Beziehungen* (Stuttgart: W. Kohlhammer Verlag, 1935–36), esp. pp. 38–40.
74. See Fritz Ernst to the Reich Education Ministry, February 1, 1938, and May 10, 1939, both in UAH PA, 3689 (Ernst).
75. Fritz Ernst, "Zum Verhältnis von politischer und völkischer Einheit der Deutschen im Mittelalter," in Heinrich Dannenbauer and Fritz Ernst, eds., *Das Reich. Idee und Gestalt* (Stuttgart: J. G. Cotta'sche Buchhandlung Nachfolger, 1940), pp. 203–216. Also see Ernst's *Lothringen; aus der geschichte eines grenzlandes* (Leipzig: Köhler & Amelang, 1941), which

Ernst "dedicated respectfully to the victorious army leaders on the recovery of Lothringia."
76. Friedrich Panzer, ed., *Deutsches Schicksal im Elsass. Vorträge Heidelberger Professoren* (Heidelberg: Carl Winter's Universitätsbuchhandlung, 1941). Also see Kurt von Raumer, *Der Rhein im deutschen Schicksal. Reden und Aufsätze zur Westfrage* (Berlin: Verlag von Georg Stilke, 1936), and his *Der politische Sinn der Landesgeschichte* (Kaiserslautern: Pfalz. Gesellschaft zur Förderung der Wissenschaften, 1938), and Ernst Wahle's *Vorzeit am Oberrhein* (Heidelberg: C. Winter, 1937) and *Frühgeschichte als Landesgeschichte* (Stuttgart: W. Kohlhammer, 1943).
77. Walther Köhler, "Humanismus und Reformation im Elsass," in Panzer, ed., *Deutsches Schicksal im Elsass,* p. 69.
78. Paul Böckmann, "Deutsches Schicksal in der elsässischen Literaturentwicklung der Neuzeit," in Panzer, ed., *Deutsches Schicksal im Elsass,* pp. 85, 86, 115.
79. Alan Milward, *War, Economy, and Society, 1939–1945* (Berkeley: University of California Press, 1977), pp. 132–165.
80. Klaus Brintzinger, *Die Nationalökonomie an den Universitäten Freiburg, Heidelberg und Tübingen 1918–1945: eine institutionenhistorische, vergleichende Studie der wirtschaftswissenschaftlichen Fakultäten und Abteilungen südwestdeutscher Universitäten* (Frankfurt am Main: Lang, 1996), pp. 233–237.
81. Walter Thoms to Reich Education Ministry, October 23, 1941, UAH, B-6693/1.
82. UAH, B-6949/2.
83. "Arbeitsbericht für das Jahr 1941/1942," Bundesarchiv Berlin (hereafter cited as BA), R21/10320, Folder 1.
84. "Ansprache des Staatssekretärs Dr. Landfried anlässlich der Überreichung der Urkunde und Sanatorenkette als Ehrensenator der Ruprecht-Carls-Universität zu Heidelberg," June 14, 1941, *Kriegsvorträge der Universität Heidelberg,* vol. 9 (Heidelberg: Carl Winter's Universitätsbuchhandlung, 1941), p. 23.
85. "Sitzung des Kuratoriums des Institute für Grossraumwirtschaft am 2.1.42," UAH, B-6693/1.
86. *Völkischer Beobachter,* January 8, 1942. Also see "Institut für Grossraumwirtschaft an der Universität Heidelberg," *Raumforschung und Raumordnung,* 1 (1942).
87. "Arbeitsbericht für das Jahr 1941/1942," BA, R21/10320, Folder 1.
88. "Protokoll des Seminars für Grossraumwirtschaft im Sommersemester 1944," July 26, 1944, BA, R21/10320, Folder 1.
89. UAH, B-6949/2.
90. "Forschungsprogramm des Institut für Grossraumwirtschaft," BA, R4901/10230.

91. Walter Waffenschmidt to Karl Heinrich Bauer, March 19, 1946, UAH, B-6693/1.
92. "Bericht über die Arbeitstagung des Instituts für Grossraumwirtschaft in Heidelberg vom 7. bis 12. Dezember 1942," February 26, 1943, UAH, B-6693/1. See also "Probleme des Grossraums Europa. Arbeitstagung des Instituts für Grossraumwirtschaft," *Volksgemeinschaft* (Heidelberg), December 19, 1942.
93. "Arbeitsbericht für das Jahr 1942/1943," BA, R21/10320, Folder 1.
94. Konstantin Bobtschev, *Die Eurpäische Grossraumwirtschaft und Bulgarien* (Heidelberg: Kurt Vowinckel Verlag, 1944).
95. Ibid., pp. 15, 29.
96. Walter Thoms to Paul Schmitthenner, July 17, 1944, UAH PA, 6079 (Thoms).
97. "Protokoll über die Kuratoriumssitzung des Instituts für Grossraumwirtschaft an der Universität Heidelberg," January 11, 1945, GLAK, 235/29959.
98. Institut für Volkswirtschaftslehre und Statistik an der Universität Heidelberg, "Betr. Forschungsaufgaben im Institut...," September 9, 1944, UAH PA, 5819 (Schuster).
99. "Bericht über das Dolmetscher-Insitut. (Stand vom 9.2.1940)," UAH, B6695/5.
100. SS Hauptsturmführer Focke to Anton Burkard, August 9, 1944, and Burkard's response on August 12, UAH, B-6695/5,6.
101. See Simon, *German Research in World War II,* p. 75, and Helmuth Trischler, *Luft- und Raumfahrtforschung in Deutschland, 1900–1970* (Frankfurt: Campus Verlag, 1992), pp. 273–275.
102. Beyerchen, *Scientists under Hitler,* pp. 167–198.
103. See Karl Heinrich Bauer to Military Government, January 28, 1946, UAH, B-6949/2.
104. Spruchkammerakte Ludwig Wesch, GLAK, 465a/50/2/23762.
105. Henry Friedlander, *The Origins of Nazi Genocide: From Euthanasia to the Final Solution* (Chapel Hill: University of North Carolina Press, 1995), chap. 6, and Götz Aly, ed., *Cleansing the Fatherland: Nazi Medicine and Racial Hygiene* (Baltimore: Johns Hopkins University Press, 1994).
106. See Peter Chroust, "Selected Letters of Doctor Friedrich Mennecke," in, Aly, ed., *Cleansing the Fatherland,* pp. 238–295.
107. See Ernst Klee, *Was sie taten—was sie wurden: Ärzte, Juristen und andere Beteiligte am Kranken-oder Judenmord* (Frankfurt: Fischer Taschenbuch Verlag, 1986), pp. 178–183, and Benno Müller-Hill, *Murderous Science: Elimination by Scientific Selection of Jews, Gypsies, and Others in Germany, 1933–1945* (Plainview, N.Y.: Cold Spring Harbor Laboratory Press, 1998), pp. 3–6, and especially Müller-Hill's simultaneously unrevealing and revealing interview with Hans-Joachim Rauch, pp. 177–183.
108. Carl Schneider to Reich Association of Mental Hospitals in Berlin, Janu-

ary 21, 1943, reprinted in Aly, "Pure and Tainted Progress," in Aly, ed., *Cleansing the Fatherland,* pp. 213–214.
109. Quoted in ibid., p. 217.
110. Quoted in ibid., p. 210.
111. The literature on this subject is enormous. See Michael Geyer and John Boyer, eds., *Resistance against the Third Reich, 1933–1990* (Chicago: University of Chicago Press, 1994).
112. Friedrich Wilhelm Graf, ed., "Martin Dibelius über die Zerstörung der Bürgerlichkeit. Ein Vortrag im Heidelberger Marianne-Weber-Kreis 1932," *Zeitschrift für neuere Theologiegeschichte,* 4 (1997), 114–153.
113. On Weber's contact with Henk, see Field Intelligence Study 31 (October 15, 1945), reprinted in Jürgen Heideking and Christoph Mauch, eds., *American Intelligence and the German Resistance to Hitler: A Documentary History* (Boulder, Colo.: Westview Press, 1996), p. 420. Also see Eberhard Demm, *Von der Weimarer Republik zur Bundesrepublik. Der politische Weg Alfred Webers, 1920–1958* (Düsseldorf: Droste Verlag, 1999), pp. 239–241. Henk also supplied Karl Jaspers with a steady stream of information during these years, and Haubach paid a call on the Jaspers shortly after the attempted assassination of Hitler in 1944. See Karl Jaspers to Karl Heinrich Bauer, August 23, 1945, in de Rosa, ed., *Briefwechsel, 1945–1968,* p. 75.
114. Diary of Edward Yarnall Hartshorne, Jr., May 16, 1945, published in James F. Tent, ed., *Academic Proconsul: Harvard Sociologist Edward Y. Hartshorne and the Reopening of German Universities, 1945–1946. His Personal Account* (Trier: Wissenschafter Verlag Trier, 1998), p. 53. Cited hereafter as Hartshorne diary, with the appropriate date.
115. Marianne Weber, "Academic Conviviality," *Minerva,* 15 no. 2 (1977), 214–246.
116. On this point, see Eric Johnson, *Nazi Terror: The Gestapo, Jews, and Ordinary Germans* (New York: Basic Books, 1999).
117. Weber, "Academic Conviviality," p. 232.
118. Hartshorne diary, May 16, 1945.
119. Weber, "Academic Conviviality," p. 233.
120. Ibid, pp. 235–236.
121. See Ian Kershaw, *The Nazi Dictatorship: Problems and Perspectives of Interpretation* (London: Edward Arnold, 1993), pp. 158–162.
122. Leo Strauss, *Persecution and the Art of Writing* (Glencoe, Ill.: Glencoe Press, 1952), p. 24.
123. Ibid.
124. But see J. M. Ritchie's study, *German Literature under National Socialism* (London: C. Helm, 1983), and Jerry Muller's excellent discussion of this issue in *The Other God That Failed,* pp. 290–305.
125. Fritz Ernst, "Lothringen und Bergund," *Die Welt als Geschichte,* 9 (1943), 1–12.

126. Müller-Hill, *Murderous Science,* pp. 74, 180.
127. "Arbeitstagung im Institut für Grossraumwirtschaft," *Volksgemeinschaft,* January 15, 1945.
128. "Protokoll über die Kuratoriumsitzung des Instituts für Grossraumwirtschaft an der Universität Heidelberg am 11. Januar 1945," GLAK, 235/29959.
129. Bauer Report.
130. UAH PA, 5709 (Schmitthenner).
131. Karl Jaspers, "Philosophical Autobiography," in Paul Arthur Schilpp, ed., *The Philosophy of Karl Jaspers* (La Salle, Ill.: Open Court, 1957), p. 62.
132. Paul Schmitthenner to Sicherheitsdienst des Reichsführers SS, Berlin, UAH PA, 4369 (Jaspers); Karl Jaspers, affidavit, April 20, 1948, Spruchkammerakte Paul Schmitthenner, GLAK, 465a/Ztr. Spr. K./B./Sv./1629; and Karl Jaspers, affidavit, February 28, 1948, Spruchkammerakte Eugen Fehrle, GLAK, 465a/59/1/17838-33573. On Krieck's attitude toward aiding the Jaspers, see Karl Jaspers to Ilse Krieck, January 9, 1946, GLAK, Nachlass Ernst Krieck, Number 8 (1).

4. Constructing the Myth

1. On the concept of *Stunde Null,* see Geoffrey Giles, ed., *Stunde Null: The End and the Beginning Fifty Years Ago* (Washington, D.C.: German Historical Institute, 1997).
2. My choice of the term "partial and modified restorations" has been influenced by Jeffrey Herf's conceptualization of "multiple restorations" in twentieth-century German political culture. See his "Multiple Restorations: German Political Traditions and the Interpretation of Nazism, 1945–1946," *Central European History,* 26, no. 1 (1993), 21–55.
3. On the initial months of the occupation and the reopening of the university, see Uta Gerhardt, "Die Amerikanischen Militäroffiziere und der Konflikt um die Wiederöffnung der Universität Heidelberg, 1945–1946," James F. Tent, "Edward Yarnall Hartshorne and the Reopening of the Ruprecht-Karls-Universität in Heidelberg, 1945: His Personal Account," Volker Sellin, "Die Universität Heidelberg im Jahre 1945," and Christian Jansen, "Mehr pragmatische denn liberal. Politische Initiativen und Argumentationsmuster von Walter Jellinek, Gustav Radbruch und Willy Hellpach im Kontext der Wiederöffnung der Universität Heidelberg," all in Jürgen Hess, Hartmut Lehmann, and Volker Sellin, eds., *Heidelberg 1945* (Stuttgart: Franz Steiner Verlag, 1996), pp. 30–54, 55–74, 91–106, 107–129, and 173–196, respectively. Also see Renato de Rosa, "Der Neubeginn der Universität 1945. Karl Heinrich Bauer und Karl Jaspers," in Wilhelm Doerr, ed., *Semper Apertus: Sechshundert Jahre Ruprecht-Karls-Universität Heidelberg, 1386–1986* (Berlin: Springer Verlag, 1985), vol. 3, pp. 544–568; Geoffrey Giles, "Reeducation at Heidelberg University, *Paedagogica His-*

torica, 33 (1997), 201–219; James Mumper, "The Reopening of Heidelberg University, 1945–1946: Major Earl L. Crum and the Ambiguities of American Postwar Policy," in F. X. J. Homer and Larry Wilcox, eds., *Germany and Europe in the Era of the Two World Wars: Essays in Honor of Oron James Hale* (Charlottesville: University Press of Virginia, 1986), pp. 211–248; and Fritz Ernst, "Die Wiederöffnung der Universität Heidelberg, 1945–1946. Aus Anlass des 70. Geburtstag von Karl Heinrich Bauer am 26. September 1960," *Heidelberger Jahrbücher,* 4 (1960), 1–28. Most of these accounts are overwhelmingly celebratory and uncritical and should be read with Frank Pfetsch, "Neugründung der Universität nach 1945?" in Karin Buselmeier, Dietrich Harth, and Christian Jansen, eds., *Auch eine Geschichte der Universität Heidelberg* (Mannheim: Edition Quadrat, 1985), pp. 365–380.

4. Ernst, "Die Wiederöffnung der Universität Heidelberg," p. 2.
5. A total of seven universities fell within the American zone: Heidelberg, Marburg, Giessen, Frankfurt, Würzburg, Erlangen, and Munich. Bonn, Cologne, Münster, Göttingen, Hamburg, Kiel, and the Medical Academy at Düsseldorf fell under British control. Freiburg and Tübingen lay in the French zone. The Soviet zone included Rostock, Greifswald, Jena, Leipzig, and Halle. The University of Berlin was put under the control (temporarily) of the four occupying powers. Königsberg and Breslau were dissolved as German universities.
6. Memorandum for the Officer in Charge, April 9 and 13, 1945, both reprinted in Hess et al., eds., *Heidelberg 1945,* pp. 393–401 and 402–404, respectively.
7. See "Liste der zur Zeit Abwesenden," n.d., but probably summer 1945, Universitätsarchiv Heidelberg (hereafter cited as UAH), B-3029/18.
8. Paul Schmitthenner to Willy Andreas, May 30, 1951, Generallandesarchiv Karlsruhe (hereafter cited as GLAK), Nachlass Willy Andreas, no. 764.
9. Samuel A. Goudsmit, *Alsos* (New York: Henry Schuman, 1947), pp. 84–86.
10. See Karl Jaspers to Karl Heinrich Bauer, August 23, 1964, in Renato de Rosa, ed., *Briefwechsel, 1945–1968 / Karl Jaspers, K. H. Baur* (Berlin: Springer Verlag, 1983), pp. 75–76. Also see Karl Jaspers, "Erfahrung des Augestossenseins. Karl Jaspers über seinen Weggang aus Deutschland," *Der Spiegel,* 41 (1967), 42.
11. This informal committee's membership varied slightly in number, though its name stuck. This list is from Karl Heinrich Bauer to Ministry of Education, Stuttgart, August 7, 1946, United States National Archives and Records Administration (hereafter cited as NARA), RG 260, Office of the Military Government Württemberg-Baden (hereafter cited as OMGWB), Records of Education and Civil-Religious Affairs Division, Box 916, File: "Higher Institutions of Learning."
12. Weekly Military Government Report, August 5, 1945, NARA, RG 226, Records of the OSS, Research and Analysis Branch Divisions Intelligence Re-

ports ("XL" Series), 1941–1946, Entry 19, Box 209, Folder XL 14168–XL 14174.
13. See Leonard Krieger, "The Inter-regnum in Germany: March-August 1945," *Political Science Quarterly,* 64, no. 4 (1949), 481–532. On local political initiatives in the immediate postwar period, see Lutz Niethammer, ed., *Arbeiterinitiative 1945: antifaschistische Ausschüsse und Reorganisation der Arbeiterbewegung in Deutschland* (Wuppertal: Hammer, 1976), and Rebecca Boehling, *A Question of Priorities: Democratic Reforms and Economic Recovery in Postwar Germany: Frankfurt, Munich, and Stuttgart under U.S. Occupation, 1945–1949* (Providence, R.I.: Berghahn Books, 1996).
14. "OSS Report 'Action Groups in Post-Collapse Germany,','" May 29, 1945, NARA, RG 84, Foreign Service Posts, U.S. Political Adviser—Berlin, Top Secret General Correspondence, 1945–1949, Box 1, File: "TS.800—Anti-Nazis (Germany)."
15. Quoted in OSS Field Intelligence Study 41, "The Liberal Universities of Baden II. Heidelberg," November 13, 1945 (hereafter cited as OSS report), copy in the Hoover Institution, Stanford University, West European Collections. The author of the report was the historian Felix Gilbert, who was assisted by Leonard Krieger. I am grateful to Barry Katz and Helen Solanum for helping me track down a copy of this valuable document. Also see Felix Gilbert, *A European Past: Memoirs, 1905–1945* (New York: W. W. Norton, 1988), pp. 204–210.
16. Ibid., p. 208.
17. "Statute of the University of Heidelberg, June 22, 1945, NARA, RG 260, OMGWB, Records of the Education and Civil-Religious Affairs Division, Box 912, File: "Heidelberg University—General." Also see the diary of Edward Hartshorne, July 1 and 15, 1945, reprinted in James Tent, ed., *Academic Proconsul: Harvard Sociologist Edward Y. Hartshorne and the Reopening of German Universities, 1945–1946. His Personal Account* (Trier: WVT Wissenschaftlicher Verlag Trier, 1998), and hereafter referred to as Hartshorne diary with the appropriate date. Also see Hermann Weisert, *Die Verfassung der Universität Heidelberg: Überblick, 1386–1952* (Heidelberg: Winter, 1974), pp. 138–146.
18. OSS report.
19. Alexander Mitscherlich, *Ein Leben für die Psychoanalyse: Anmerkungen zu meiner Zeit* (Frankfurt: Suhrkamp, 1980), p. 133.
20. UAH, Rep. 10/5. Hereafter cited as Bauer diary with the appropriate date.
21. Memorandum, November 5, 1945, UAH, B-1590/1.
22. Beginning in the early 1970s, the West German Constitutional Court reversed some of these reforms on the grounds that they threatened academic freedom. See David Currie, *The Constitution of the Federal Republic of Germany* (Chicago: University of Chicago Press, 1994), pp. 233–237.
23. Alfred Weber, "Die neue Universität und der studentische Nachwuchs.

Christentum und Antike als Grundlagen unserer Bildung," *Rhein-Neckar Zeitung,* June 15, 1946.
24. Eberhard Demm, *Von der Weimarer Republik zur Bundesrepublik. Der politische Weg Alfred Webers, 1920–1958* (Düsseldorf: Droste Verlag, 1999), pp. 333–339. Also see the recollections of Heinz Markmann, "Das InSoSta nach dem Zweiten Weltkrieg," in Reinhard Blomert, ed., *Heidelberger Sozial- und Staatswissenschaften: das Institut für Sozial- und Staatswissenschaften zwischen 1918 und 1958* (Marburg: Metropolis-Verlag, 1997), pp. 83–96; and Karl Heinrich Bauer to Military Government, December 12, 1945, NARA, RG 260, OMGWB, Records of the Education and Civil-Religious Affairs Division, Box 916, File: "Higher Institutions of Learning (Reports in German)."
25. Demm, *Von der Weimarer Republik zur Bundesrepublik,* pp. 333–334. Sitzung des Dreizehner-Ausschusses am 16.7.45 and 27.7.45, UAH, Rep. 10/2. On these debates, see Jansen, "Mehr Pragmatisch denn Liberal," pp. 178–179.
26. Memorandum for the Officer in Charge, April 9, 1945, reprinted in Hess et al., eds., *Heidelberg 1945,* pp. 393–401.
27. Karl Jaspers, "Heidelberger Erinnerungen," *Heidelberger Jahrbücher,* 5 (1960), 10.
28. Personalfragebogen für Hochschulbeamten, Karl Heinrich Bauer, July 9, 1945, UAH, Rep. 10/60. Also see Bauer, "Besinnung und Leistung," *Südkurier,* October 9, 1945.
29. Bauer to Jaspers, June 6, 1945, UAH, Rep. 10/2.
30. Bauer diary, August 24, 1945.
31. Karl Heinrich Bauer to Military Government, October 10, 1945, GLAK, OMGWB 17/138–1/14.
32. William Bauer to Major Earl Crum, February 4, 1946, and Christof Reiner to Lieutenant Colonel Leon Irvin, August 5, 1946, both in GLAK, OMGWB 17/138–1/10.
33. Shepard Stone, "Report on the Mood in Germany," *New York Times,* January 26, 1947, p. 8.
34. See the report by a joint commission of American, British, and Swedish academics, "The University Student in Germany," 1949, *The U.S. Occupation of Germany: Educational Reform, 1945–1949* (California, Md.: Congressional Information Service, 1991), 3A-150.
35. Karl Jaspers to Hannah Arendt, October 28, 1945, reprinted in Lotte Köhler and Hans Saner, eds., *Hannah Arendt / Karl Jaspers Correspondence, 1926–1969* (New York: Harcourt Brace Jovanovich, 1992), p. 22.
36. See James F. Tent, *Mission on the Rhine: Reeducation and Denazification in American-Occupied Germany* (Chicago: University of Chicago Press, 1982), esp. pp. 13–73; Manfred Heinemann, ed., *Hochschuloffiziere und Wiederaufbau des Hochschulwesens in Westdeutschland, 1945–1952,* part 2: *Die US-Zone* (Hildesheim: Lax, 1990); Uta Gerhardt, "The Medical

Meaning of Reeducation for Germany: Contemporary Interpretation of Cultural and Institutional Change," *Paedagogica Historica,* 33 (1997), 135–155; Jutta-B. Lange-Quassowski, *Neuordnung oder Restauration? Das Demokratiekonzept der amerikanischen Besatzungsmacht und die politische Sozialisation der Westdeutschen: Wirtschaftsordnung—Schulstruktur—politische Bildung* (Opladen: Leske und Budrich, 1979); and Charles Biebel, "American Efforts for Educational Reform in Occupied Germany, 1945–1955—a Reassessment," *History of Education Quarterly,* 22 (Fall 1982), 277–287.

37. See, for instance, I. L. Kandel, *The Making of Nazis* (New York: Bureau of Publications, Teachers College, Columbia University, 1935); Robert K. Merton, "Science and the Social Order" (1938), reprinted in Robert K. Merton, ed., *The Sociology of Science: Theoretical and Empirical Investigations* (Chicago: University of Chicago Press, 1973); Aurel Kolnai, *The War against the West* (New York: Viking, 1938); J. D. Bernal, *The Social Function of Science* (New York: MacMillan, 1939); Joseph Needham, "The Nazi Attack on International Science" (1940), reprinted in Yehuda Elkana et al., eds., *History, Philosophy, and Sociology of Science* (New York: Arno Press, 1975), pp. 154–198; George Kneller, *The Educational Philosophy of National Socialism* (New Haven: Yale University Press, 1941); and Abraham Wolf, *Higher Education in Nazi Germany or Education for World Conquest* (London: Methuen, 1944).

38. Frieda Wunderlich, "Education in Nazi Germany," *Social Research,* 4, no. 2 (1937), 356, 357, 358.

39. See, for instance, Henry P. Leverich, "Survey of Recent Events in the Field of Education in Germany," March 8, 1936, NARA, RG 59, Confidential U.S. State Department Central Files, Germany, Internal Affairs 1930–1941 (Frederick, Md.: University Publications of America, 1984), Reel 25.

40. William E. Dodd, "German Impressions," August 11, 1937, Franklin D. Roosevelt Library Digital Archives, Hyde Park, N.Y., Germany: William E. Dodd: 1936–1938 (i300).

41. "Nazi Education—V. Higher Education under the Nazis," February 18, 1943, NARA, RG 226, Records of the OSS, Research and Analysis Branch ("Regular" Series), 1941–1945, Roll #214, Report #31388, NARA Microfilm Publication M1499.

42. Memorandum for the Officer in Charge, April 9, 1945, reprinted in Hess et al., eds., *Heidelberg 1945,* pp. 393–401.

43. Quoted in Frank Stern, *The Whitewashing of the Yellow Badge: Antisemitism and Philosemitism in Postwar Germany* (New York: Pergamon Press, 1992), p. 163.

44. Tent, *Mission on the Rhine,* pp. 13–39.

45. Protocol of the Proceedings of the Berlin (Potsdam) Conference, August 1, 1945, reprinted in *Documents on Germany, 1944–1985* (Washington, D.C.: United States Department of State Publication 9446, 1985), pp. 54–

65, and "General U.S. Principles for Reeducation," Draft by the Committee on German Re-education, May 28 and 29, 1945, revised and approved by the State-War-Navy Coordinating Committee, May 16, 1945, *U.S. Occupation of Germany: Educational Reform, 1945–1949*, 3A-122.
46. By December 1944 SHAEF's Psychological Warfare Division had compiled a "white list" for Heidelberg, which included Radbruch, Regenbogen, Jaspers, Gustav Hoelscher, Eugen Täubler, Alfred Weber, Marianne Weber, Gerhard Anschütz, Franz Brecht, and Hans von Eckardt; "PWD 'White List' of Persons in Germany Believed to be Anti-Nazi or Non-Nazi," December 5, 1944, NARA, RG 226, Records of the OSS, Research and Analysis Branch Divisions, Intelligence Reports ("XL" Series), 1941–1946, Entry 19, Box 292, Folder XL 20084.
47. Uta Gerhardt, "American Sociology and German Re-education after World War II," in Giles, ed., *Stunde Null,* pp. 39–58, and Manfred Heinemann, "Emigranten, Remigranten und ihr Beitrag zur Erneuerung von Schul- und Hochschulverfassungen nach 1945," in Claus-Dieter Crohn and Martin Schumacher, eds., *Exil und Neuordnung. Beiträge zur verfassungspolitischen Entwicklung in Deutschland nach 1945* (Düsseldorf: Droste Verlag, 2000), pp. 377–400. Also see Vice President Henry Wallace's comments in Herschel V. Johnson to the Secretary of State, August 6, 1943, NARA, RG 226, Records of the OSS, Research and Analysis Branch ("Regular" Series), 1941–1945, Roll #336, Report #45559, NARA Microfilm Publication M1499.
48. Werner Richter, *Re-educating Germany* (Chicago: University of Chicago Press, 1945), p. 213.
49. Memorandum to the Director of Strategic Services from the Foreign Nationalities Branch, Number B-304, January 18, 1945, *U.S. Occupation of Germany: Educational Reform, 1945–1949,* 1A-3.
50. Franz Neumann, "Re-educating the Germans: The Dilemma of Reconstruction," *Commentary,* 3, no. 6 (1947), 517.
51. Ibid., pp. 519–520, 525.
52. Quoted in Giles, "Reeducation at Heidelberg University," p. 203.
53. Memordandum for the Officer in Charge, April 9, 1945, in Hess et al., eds., *Heidelberg 1945,* p. 398.
54. Ibid.
55. Giles, "Reeducation at Heidelberg University," pp. 201–219.
56. Hartshorne diary, July 1, 1945, and Tent, *Mission on the Rhine,* pp. 58–59.
57. Tent, ed., *Academic Proconsul,* pp. v–ix.
58. Hartshorne diary, July 1, 1945.
59. Edward Hartshorne, "Reopening German Universities," *Military Government Weekly Information Bulletin* (OMGUS), 43 (May 27, 1946), 5–9.
60. Hartshorne diary, September 11, 1945.
61. Ibid., July 15, 1945.
62. Ibid., September 20, 1945.

63. "Our Responsibility for German Universities," *Social Forum*, 105, no. 1 (January 1946), 396–402. As an active-duty officer Hartshorne was prevented by censorship regulations from signing his own name to the article.
64. Ibid., p. 402.
65. Hartshorne diary, July 10, 1945.
66. Muccio to Murphy, July 10, 1945, *The U.S. Occupation of Germany: Educational Reform, 1945–1949*, 1-B-18.
67. Hartshorne diary, July 15, 1945.
68. Ibid., July 12, 1945.
69. See Ziemke, *The U.S. Army in the Occupation of Germany*, pp. 380–390. The published memoirs of former occupation officers are generally critical—see Saul Padover, *Experiment in Germany: The Story of an American Intelligence Officer* (New York: Duell, Sloan, and Pearce, 1946), and Marshall Knappen, *And Call It Peace* (Chicago: University of Chicago Press, 1947). More favorable is Noel Annan, *Changing Enemies: The Defeat and Regeneration of Germany* (New York: W. W. Norton, 1995), pp. 202–212, and the contributions to Michael Ermarth, ed., *America and the Shaping of German Society, 1945–1955* (Providence, R.I.: Berg, 1993), part 3. The best scholarly studies are Clemens Vollnhalls, ed., *Entnazifizierung. Politische Säuberung und Rehabilitierung in den vier Besatzungszonen, 1945–1949* (Munich: Deutsche Taschenbuch Verlag, 1991); Lutz Niethammer, *Entnazifizierung in Bayern. Säuberung und Rehabilitierung unter amerikanischer Besatzung* (Frankfurt: S. Fischer, 1972); and Hans Woller, *Gesellschaft und Politik in der amerikanischen Besatzungszone: die Region Ansbach und Fürth* (Munich: Oldenbourg, 1986).
70. JCS 1067, *Documents on Germany, 1944–1985*, p. 19.
71. Ziemke, *The U.S. Army in the Occupation of Germany*, pp. 380, 383.
72. See Frank Horvay, "Military Government and Denazification in Ansbach, 1945–1946," in Ermarth, ed., *America and the Shaping of German Society*, pp. 166–174.
73. *Weekly Military Government Report*, August 5, 1945.
74. Quoted in Hartshorne, "Reopening German Universities," p. 8.
75. Hartshorne diary, July 20, 1945.
76. Karl Freudenberg to Johannes Hoops, June 10, 1945, UAH, B-3029/18, and Hartshorne diary, July 20, 1945.
77. Johannes Hoops to Military Government (Powhida), July 24, 1945, UAH, B-3029/18.
78. Karl Freudenberg to Rector, May 25, 1945, UAH, B-3029/18.
79. Otto Regenbogen to Rector, September 16, 1945, UAH, B-3029/18.
80. Otto Regenbogen to the president of the State District Government in Mannheim, October 1, 1945, GLAK, 235/29831.
81. Martin Dibelius to Military Government Heidelberg, July 23, 1945, and Gustav Hoelscher to Military Government Heidelberg, September 18, 1945, both in UAH, B-1540.

82. Vorbereitungs-Ausschuss der Theologischen Fakultät, July 21, 1945, UAH, B-1540.
83. See Memorandum for the Officer in Charge, August 14, 1945, in Hess et al., eds., *Heidelberg 1945*, pp. 405–417.
84. "Plan for Reopening the Medical Faculty of Heidelberg," July 4, 1945, UAH, B-1560/3.
85. "Report on the Present Situation of the Faculty of Medicine of the University of Heidelberg," November 1, 1945, GLAK, OMGWB 12/87–1/11.
86. Bauer diary, August 23, 1945.
87. Hartshorne diary, August 16 and September 12, 1945.
88. But other influential figures also propagated the myth. See Karl Freudenberg's comments appended to his Fragebogen, June 23, 1945, UAH, Rep. 14/592.
89. Karl Heinrich Bauer to Colonel Charles Winning, June 25, 1945, copy in GLAK, Nachlass Willy Andreas, no. 763.
90. Karl Heinrich Bauer to Earl Crum, October 9, 1945, Smith-Crum Papers (hereafter cited as Smith-Crum papers), George C. Marshall Research Library, Lexington, Va.
91. Hartshorne diary, July 24, 1945.
92. Ibid., August 8, 1945.
93. Ibid., August 7 and 10, 1945.
94. Ibid., September 12, 1945, Willy Andreas to Edward Hartshorne, September 14, 1945, GLAK, Nachlass Willy Andreas, no. 764, and Clifton Lisle to Karl Heinrich Bauer, September 15, 1945, UAH PA, 3123 (Andreas).
95. Hartshorne diary, July 24, 1945, and Hartshorne to Elsa Fay Hartshorne, July 24, 1945, in Tent, ed., *Academic Proconsul,* pp. 168–169.
96. Hartshorne diary, August 20, 1945.
97. Ibid., July 24, 1945.
98. This total is based on the faculty roster (excluding honorary and retired professors) for the winter semester of 1944–45, *Vorlesgungsverzeichnis,* Universität Heidelberg, winter semester 1944–45.
99. Memoradum for the Officer in Charge, August 14, 1945, reprinted in Hess et al., eds., *Heidelberg 1945,* pp. 405–417.
100. Hartshorne diary, August 16, 1945.
101. Protokoll der Senatssitzung vom 17. August, 1945, UAH, B-3029/18.
102. Brintzinger, *Die Nationalökonomie,* p. 245–246, and Demm, *Von der Weimarer Republik zur Bundesrepublik,* pp. 326–327.
103. Hans von Eckardt, "Es ist an der Zeit," *Die Neue Zeit,* October 25, 1945. For Radbruch's response, see Gustav Radbruch to Karl Heinrich Bauer, October 26, 1945, UAH, Rep. 10/79.
104. A transcript of the speech is in NARA, RG 260, Records of the Education and Civil-Religious Affairs Division, Box 914, File: "Heidelberg University—Staff."
105. Edward Hartshorne arranged for it to be translated and published as "The

Rededication of German Scholarship" in the journal *The American Scholar,* 15, no. 2 (1946), 180–188.
106. Ibid., p. 187.
107. Ibid., p. 183.
108. Ibid., pp. 187–188.
109. Hartshorne diary, August 15, 1945, and OSS report.
110. Karl Jaspers to Hannah Arendt, September 18, 1946, reprinted in Köhler and Saner, eds., *Hannah Arendt / Karl Jaspers Correspondence,* p. 58.
111. Jaspers, "The Rededication of German Scholarship," pp. 183, 184.
112. Karl Jaspers, "Die Wissenschaft im Hitlerstaat" (January 1946), in Karl Jaspers, ed., *Die Antwort an Sigrid Undset. Vermehrt um Beiträge über die Wissenschaft und die Universität* (Constance: Südverlag, 1947), pp. 12–17.
113. Hartshorne, "Reopening German Universities," p. 7.
114. Bauer to Military Government, August 26, 1945, Smith-Crum papers.
115. Tent, *Academic Proconsul,* pp. 291–292.
116. Hans Mayer, "Als der Krieg zu Ende war. Wir haben uns zu rasch mit der Vergangenheit eingerichtet," *Die Zeit,* February 1, 1985, and Claus-Dieter Crohn, *Intellectuals in Exile: Refugee Scholars and the New School for Social Research* (Amherst: University of Massachusetts Press, 1993), pp. 199–203.
117. Emil J. Gumbel to Max Seydewitz, May 38, 1947, Emil Gumbel Papers, University of Chicago Library, Box 2, Folder 7.
118. Dorothee Mussgnug, *Die vertriebenen Heidelberger Dozenten: zur Geschichte der Ruprecht-Karls-Universität nach 1933* (Heidelberg: C. Winter, 1988), pp. 198–283.
119. Ibid., pp. 265–267. On Olschki's dismissal from the University of California, see Arthur Evans, "Leonardo Olschki, 1885–1961," *Romance Philology,* 31, no. 1 (August 1977), 42–43.
120. Spruchkammerakte Walter Paatz, GLAK, 465a/59/3/11835–6589.
121. Quoted in Mussgnung, *Die vertriebenen Heidelberger Dozenten,* p. 215.
122. Florian Jung, "Die Mathematische Institut der Universität Heidelberg im Dritten Reich" (unpublished manuscript, Heidelberg, 1999), pp. 80–84.
123. Quoted in Mussgnug, *Die vertriebenen Heidelberger Dozenten,* pp. 275–276.
124. This account has been drawn from von Ubisch's unpublished memoirs, "Lebenserinnerungen," ca. 1955, Universitäts Bibliothek Heidelberg, Nachlass Gerta von Ubisch, Heid HS 4029; Mussgnug, *Die Vertriebenen Heidelberger Dozenten;* and Ute Deichmann, *Biologists under Hitler* (Cambridge: Harvard University Press, 1996), pp. 52–58.
125. Quoted in Deichmann, *Biologists under Hitler,* p. 57.
126. Von Ubish, "Lebenserinnerungen."
127. Demm, *Von der Weimarer Republik zur Bundesrepublik,* pp. 331–333, and Mussgnug, *Die vertriebenen Heidelberger Dozenten,* pp. 212–213.

Tent, ed., *American Proconsul: Edward Y. Hartshorne and the Reopening of German Universities, 1945–1946. His Personal Account* (Trier: WVT Wissenschaftlicher Verlag Trier, 1998) (hereafter cited as Hartshorne diary with the appropriate date).

38. Quoted in *Bubenreuther Zeitung,* 44 (1967), 32–56.
39. Karl Heinrich Bauer et al. to the Counter Intelligence Corps, June 8, 1945, UAH, Rep. 10/103. On Schmidhuber's past, see Spruchkammerakte Karl Schmidhuber, GLAK, 465a/59/54/603–39449. For CIC assessments of him, see Memorandum for the Officer in Charge, April 9 and August 14, 1945, reprinted in Hess et al., eds., *Heidelberg 1945,* pp. 397 and 413, respectively.
40. Karl Heinrich Bauer et al., to Military Government Heidelberg, July 13, 1945, UAH, Rep. 10/61.
41. Bauer to Oehme, July 27, 1945, UAH, Rep. 10/61.
42. Bauer diary, August 18 and September 5, 1945.
43. Bauer to the president of the State Government of North Baden, Culture Ministry, October 16, 1945, GLAK, 235/29831.
44. Karl Freudenberg, "General Remarks concerning Petitions for Members of the Natural Sciences Faculty," January 1, 1946, UAH, Rep. 14/592.
45. Freudenberg to the president of the Landesbezirks Mannhaim, September 26, 1945, UAH, B-1590/1.
46. Karl Heinrich Bauer to Military Government Heidelberg, August 31, 1945, UAH, B-3029/18.
47. Karl Heinrich Bauer, undated notes (likely October-November 1945), UAH, B-3029/18.
48. Karl Engisch, Meldebogen, April 25, 1946, in Spruchkammerakte Karl Engisch, GLAK, 465a/59/5/4312.
49. Walter Jellinek and Gustav Radbruch to Earl Crum, October 15, 1945, UAH, B-1550/2.
50. Gustav Radbruch, petition on behalf of Ernst Forsthoff, n.d. (March 1946), UAH Personalakte 3790 (Forsthoff). The petition included a statement in support of Forsthoff signed by 122 students.
51. Gustav Hoelscher to Military Government Heidelberg, October 15, 1945, UAH, B-1540.
52. Gustav Hoelscher to Military Government Heidelberg, September 18, 1945, UAH, B-1540.
53. CIC Statement, October 31, 1945, NARA, RG 260, Office of Military Government Württemberg-Baden (hereafter cited as OMGWB), Records of Education and Civil-Religious Affairs Division, File: "Settled Petitions of Professors and Lecturers—Heidelberg University."
54. Emmet and Penham quoted in CIC Statement, October 31, 1945, NARA, RG 260, OMGWB, Records of Education and Civil-Religious Affairs Division, File: "Settled Petitions of Professors and Lecturers—Heidelberg University."

22. See, for instance, David L. Robinson, Jr., to Charles Fahy, January 3, 1946, United States National Archives and Records Administration (hereafter cited as NARA), RG 260, Records of the Executive Office, Office of the Adjutant General, General Correspondence and Other Records ("Decimal File"), 1945–1949, Box 16, File: "Denazification Policy."
23. Herf, *Divided Memory*, pp. 226.
24. President of the Land Government Baden, Culture and Education Section, to Rector, Heidelberg University, October 25, 1945, Universitätsarchiv Heidelberg (hereafter cited as UAH), B-3029/18.
25. Earl Crum to president of the Education Ministry, Land Government of Baden, December 7, 1945, copy in Generallandesarchiv Karlsruhe (hereafter cited as GLAK), 235/2245.
26. Office of Military Government, Land Württemberg-Baden, Annual Report, August 19, 1946, NARA, RG 260, Records of the Education and Civil-Religious Affairs Division, Box 916, File: "Higher Institutions of Learning (Reports in English)." The report lists a total of 192 instructors. The university's faculty rosters for the summer semester of 1944 list 270 instructors and assistants (excluding "inactive" professors and instructors in the Dolmetscher Institut); *Vorlesungsverzeichnis,* Universität Heidelberg, summer semester, 1944, pp. 12–27.
27. OSS Field Intelligence Study 41, "The Liberal Universities of Baden II. Heidelberg," November 13, 1945 (hereafter cited as OSS report"), copy in the Hoover Institution, Stanford University, West European Collections. Also see Gustav Radbruch, untitled memorandum, October 25, 1945, UAH, Rep. 10/14.
28. OSS report.
29. Ibid.
30. Gustav Radbruch, untitled memorandum, October 25, 1945, UAH Rep. 10/14.
31. Gustav Radbruch and Walter Jellinek, "Die Ruhegeldfrage bei der Entlassung ehemaliger PG.," August 13, 1945, UAH, B-3029/18.
32. The full text of Jaspers's letter is reprinted in Hugo Ott, *Martin Heidegger: A Political Life* (New York: Basic Books, 1993), pp. 336–341.
33. Ott, *Martin Heidegger: A Political Life,* pp. 309–350.
34. UAH, Rep. 10/5, August 28, 1945. Hereafter cited as Bauer diary with the appropriate date.
35. Otto Regenbogen, "Probleme der rejected Professoren und Dozenten," November 2, 1945, UAH, H-IV, 335/1.
36. See Betriebsrat der klin. Univ. Anstalten to Max Bock, October 1, 1945, and Bauer's interpretation in a December 17, 1945, letter to Earl Crum, both in UAH, Rep. 10/21. Also see "Universität Heidelberg und Heidelberger Gewerkschaften. Tatsachenbericht," reprinted in Jaspers, *Erneuerung der Universität,* pp. 455–459.
37. Diary of Edward Hartshorne, September 12, 1945, reprinted in James F.

9. Earl Ziemke, *The U.S. Army in the Occupation of Germany, 1944–1946* (Washington, D.C.: Center of Military History, United States Army, 1975), pp. 383–390. Also see Marshall Knappen, *And Call It Peace* (Chicago: University of Chicago Press, 1947), pp. 121–137. The text of Law Number 8 is reprinted in Clemens Vollnhalls, *Entnazifizierung. Politische Säuberung und Rehabilitierung in den vier Besatzungszonen, 1945–1949* (Munich: Deutsche Taschenbuch Verlag, 1991), pp. 100–101.
10. Statistics cited in Vollnhalls, *Entnazifizierung*, p. 159.
11. James Tent, *Mission on the Rhine: Reeducation and Denazification in American-Occupied Germany* (Chicago: University of Chicago Press, 1982), pp. 74–109.
12. William E. Griffith, "Denazification in the United States Zone of Germany," *The Annals of the American Academy of Political and Social Science,* 267 (January 1950), 68–76. For other critical assessments by former occupation officers, see Knappen, *And Call It Peace;* Joseph Napoli, "Denazification from an American's Viewpoint," *The Annals of the American Academy of Political and Social Science,* 264 (July 1949), 115–123; and John Herz, "The Fiasco of Denazification in Germany," *Political Science Quarterly,* 63, no. 4 (December 1948), 569–594. Also see the commentary by Alvin Johnson, editor of the émigré journal *Social Research* (but not an occupation officer), "Denazification," *Social Research,* 14, no. 1 (March 1947), 59–61.
13. Napoli, "Denazification from an American's Viewpoint," p. 118.
14. Ibid., p. 121.
15. Karl Loewenstein, "Comment on 'Denazification,'" *Social Research,* 14, no. 3 (September 1947), 365, 366.
16. Moses Moskowitz, "The Germans and the Jews: Postwar Report. The Enigma of German Irresponsibility," *Commentary,* 2 (July 1946), p. 7. Also see Frank Stern, *The Whitewashing of the Yellow Badge: Antisemitism and Philosemitism in Postwar Germany* (Oxford: Pergamon Press, 1992), pp. 92–95.
17. Stefan Heym, "Die Probleme einer Besatzungsmacht," February 1946, reprinted in Stefan Heym, *Wege und Umwege. Streitbare Schriften aus fünf Jahrzehnten* (Munich: Goldmann, 1998), pp. 232–239.
18. Lucius D. Clay, *Decision in Germany* (Garden City, N.Y.: Doubleday, 1950), p. 88. Also see his comments in "Proconsul of a People, by Another People, for Both Peoples," in Robert Wolfe, ed., *Americans as Proconsuls: United States Military Government in Germany and Japan, 1944–1952* (Carbondale: Southern Illinois University Press, 1984), p. 105.
19. Anna J. Merritt and Richard L. Merritt, eds., *Public Opinion in Occupied Germany: The OMGUS Surveys, 1945–1949* (Urbana: University of Illinois Press, 1970), pp. 30–39.
20. Herf, *Divided Memory,* pp. 227–239.
21. Ibid., pp. 221–226.

5. The Limits of Denazification

1. See Jeffrey Herf, *Divided Memory: The Nazi Past in the Two Germanys* (Cambridge: Harvard University Press, 1997), pp. 201–209.
2. On the "Penham affair" at Heidelberg, see Fritz Ernst, "Die Wiederöffnung der Universität Heidelberg, 1945–1946. Aus Anlass des 70. Geburtstag von Karl Heinrich Bauer am 26. September 1960," *Heidelberger Jahrbücher,* 4 (1960), 1–28; Renato de Rosa, "Politische Akzente im Leben eines Philosophen. Karl Jaspers in Heidelberg, 1901–1946," in Karl Jaspers, *Erneuerung der Universität. Reden und Schriften, 1945/1946* (Heidelberg: Lambert Schneider Taschenbücher, 1986); and James Mumper, "The Reopening of Heidelberg University, 1945–1946: Major Earl L. Crum and the Ambiguities of American Postwar Policy," in F. X. J. Homer and Larry Wilcox, eds., *Germany and Europe in the Era of the Two World Wars: Essays in Honor of Oron James Hale* (Charlottesville: University Press of Virginia, 1986), pp. 211–248. More balanced and insightful are Cornelia Girndt and Abraham Lauve, "Eine Mauer des Schweigens und der Diskretion," *Communale,* October 16, 1986; Uta Gerhardt, "Der Konflikt um die Wiederöffnung der Universität Heidelberg, 1945–1946," in Jürgen Hess, Hartmut Lehmann, and Volker Sellin, eds., *Heidelberg 1945* (Stuttgart: Franz Steiner Verlag, 1996), pp. 30–54; and Anson Rabinbach, "The German as Pariah: Karl Jaspers's *The Question of German Guilt*," in Anson Rabinbach, *In the Shadow of Catastrophe: German Intellectuals between Apocalypse and Enlightenment* (Berkeley: University of California Press, 1997), pp. 129–165.
3. Fritz Ernst quoted in Diethard Aschoff, *Fritz Ernst. Im Schatten des Diktators. Rückblick eines Heidelberger Historikers auf die NS-Zeit* (Heidelberg: Manutius Verlag, 1996), p. 68. Ernst repeated this assessment in milder language in his essay "Die Wiederöffnung der Universität Heidelberg," pp. 18–19.
4. See Karl Heinrich Bauer to Karl Jaspers, January 11, 1968, in Renato de Rosa, ed., *Briefwechsel, 1945–1968 / Karl Jaspers. K. H. Bauer* (Berlin: Springer 1983), pp. 83–85. Penham returned to the United States and taught French literature and Romance philology for many years at Columbia University.
5. A student during those years told me Penham was "crazy" and claimed that her opinion was shared by numerous fellow students.
6. Mumper, "The Reopening of Heidelberg University," p. 234; De Rosa, "Politische Akzente," pp. 402–403; and Dorothee Mussgnug, *Die vertriebenen Heidelberger Dozenten: zur Geschichte der Ruprecht-Karls-Universität nach 1933* (Heidelberg: C. Winter, 1988), p. 193.
7. Geoffrey Giles, "Reeducation at Heidelberg University, *Paedagogica Historica,* 33 (1997), p. 214.
8. On the "Aachen affair," see Klaus-Dietmar Henke, *Die amerikanische Besetzung Deutschlands* (Munich: Oldenbourg, 1995), pp. 252–311.

55. Earl Crum to director of Office of Military Government, n.d. (November 1945), NARA, RG 260, OMGWB, Records of Education and Civil-Religious Affairs Division, File: "Settled Petitions of Professors and Lecturers—Heidelberg University."
56. Alfred Weber to Gustav Radbruch, October 1, 1945, UAH Personalakte, 5819 (Schuster).
57. Alfred Weber, "Gutachten an die Militärregierung," n.d. (likely late 1945 or early 1946), Spruchkammerakte Horst Jecht, GLAK, 465a/59/1/11154.
58. Mumper, "The Reopening of Heidelberg University," p. 215.
59. Earl Crum, "Heidelberg University Reopens," *The American-German Review,* 16 (December 1949), 11–16.
60. Ibid., p. 11.
61. Karl Jaspers, "Erfahrungen des Augestossenseins. Karl Jaspers über seinen Weggang aus Deutschland," *Der Spiegel,* 41 (1967), 46.
62. Ernst, "Die Wiederöffnung der Universität Heidelberg," p. 12.
63. I am grateful to Michael Penham, son of the late Daniel Penham, for providing me with this biographical information and other unpublished materials.
64. See "Report on the Situation of Certain Leipzig University Professors at Present Staying in Weilburg," October 3, 1945, NARA, RG 260, OMGWB, Records of the Education and Civil-Religious Affairs Division, Box 917A, untitled file. Also see Hans-Uwe Feige, "Vor dem Abzug: Brain Drain," *Deutschland-Archiv,* 12 (1991), 1302–1313.
65. Memorandum for the Officer in Charge, February 23, 1946, George C. Marshall Research Library, Lexington, Va., Smith-Crum Papers (hereafter cited as Smith-Crum papers). The report is cited hereafter as "Penham report."
66. See Bernhard Schweitzer, "Bericht über die Vorgänge an der Universität Leipzig vom 16. Mai 1945 bis zum 21. Januar 1946," reprinted in Helga Welsh, "Entnazifizierung und Wiederöffnung der Universität Leipzig 1945–1946. Ein Bericht des damaligen Rektors Professor Bernhard Schweitzer," *Vierteljahrhefte für Zeitgeschichte,* 33, no. 2 (1985), 339–372. On denazification at Leipzig university, also see Hans-Uwe Feige, "Zur Entnazifizierung des Lehrkörpers an der Universität Leipzig," *Zeitschrift für Geschichtswissenschaft,* 42, no. 9 (1994), 795–808.
67. Schweitzer, "Bericht," p. 758.
68. Ibid.
69. Ibid.
70. Penham report.
71. Daniel Penham to Abraham Lauve and Cornelia Girndt, August 28, 1986, unpublished correspondence in the possession of Michael Penham.
72. Any doubts that Andreas did not abandon his initial enthusiasm for "National Socialism as Germany's destiny" are dispelled by an article titled "Geschichte und Gegenwart," which called on historians to draw upon the lessons of the past in the "necessary" "struggle for a new European form of

life [Lebensform]," published in the *Mitteldeutsche Nationalzeitung* (Halle/Saale), March 12, 1943, in *Münchner Neueste Nachrichten,* December 25, 1942, in *Metzer Zeitung,* March 3, 1943, in *Deutsche Polarzeitung,* March 18, 1943, in *Deutsche Zeitung in Norwegen,* March 24, 1943, and in at least one other newspaper.

73. Daniel Penham to Willy Andreas, November 30, 1945, GLAK, Nachlass Willy Andreas, no. 760.
74. Fragebogen, Willy Andreas, May 11, 1945.
75. Penham report.
76. Andreas's daughter Ursula met with Penham several times on behalf of her father. Her detailed notes of their conversations shed a good deal of light on Penham's attitude toward the professorate. They are located in GLAK, Nachlass Willy Andreas, no. 760a.
77. Karl Heinrich Bauer to Willy Andreas, February 18, 1946, GLAK, Nachlass Willy Andreas, no. 760.
78. Friedrich Wallach to Karl Heinrich Bauer, August 20, 1945, UAH, B-3029/18.
79. Information from Spruchkammerakte Otto Dittmar, GLAK, 465a/59/7/354.
80. See Edwin Costrell, "An American University Officer in Occupied Germany: A Personal Account Thirty-Six Years Later," in Manfred Heinemann, ed., *Hochschuloffiziere und Wiederaufbau des Hochschulwesens in Westdeutschland, 1945–1952,* part 2: *Die US-Zone* (Hildesheim: Lax, 1990), pp. 23–33.
81. Bauer diary, July 19, 1945.
82. Handwritten notes by Daniel Penham, n.d., in the possession of Michael Penham.
83. Karl Heinrich Bauer, "Betr.: K. H. Bauer, Rassenhygiene, ihre biologischen Grundlagen," n.d. (January or February 1946), UAH, Rep. 10/6.
84. Bauer to Fritz Ernst and the university Senate, February 21, 1946, Smith-Crum papers.
85. Bauer to Ernst and the universtiy Senate, February 12, 1946. Bauer is referring to pro-Nazi statements he made in "Berichte aus wissenschaftliche Gesellschaften. Tagung der Deutschen Gesellschaft für Chirurgie in Berlin 4.-7. April 1934," *Zentralblatt für Gynäkologie,* 28 (1934), 1660–1662. Also see Chapter 3 above.
86. Penham report.
87. Ibid.
88. Ibid.
89. Ibid.
90. Bauer to Crum, February 19, 1946, Smith-Crum papers.
91. "Report of the Senate of Heidelberg University [to Earl Crum]," n.d. (February 1946), Smith-Crum Papers.
92. Ibid. A not uncommon practice among émigré occupation officers was to

force Germans to sing the "Horst Wessel-Lied," which many of these officers themselves knew all too well. I am grateful to the historian and former occupation officer Edward Peterson for sharing with me some of his recollections on this point.
93. Penham to Lauve and Girndt.
94. Penham, handwritten notes.
95. Rabinach, "The German as Pariah," p. 131.
96. Penham, handwritten notes.
97. Karl Jaspers, *The Question of Guilt* (New York: The Dial Press, 1947), pp. 105–106.
98. Loran Elliott to G-2, Seventh Army Headquarters, February 25, 1946, Smith-Crum papers.
99. Earl Crum to Commanding Officer, Office of Military Government, Württemberg-Baden, February 27, 1946, Smith-Crum papers.
100. Penham, handwritten notes.
101. John Elliott, "U.S. C.I.C. Man Causes Furore at Heidelberg," *New York Herald Tribune,* March 17, 1946.
102. John Steiner to Chief, I A and C Division, Office of Military Government United States (OMGUS), March 22, 1946, Smith-Crum papers.
103. "Verzeichnis der seit Oktober 1945 auf Anordnung der amerikanischen Militärregierung entlassenen Professoren, Beamten und Angestellten (Erl. Des Landesdirektors f. Kultus und Unterricht von. 21.2.1946 Nr. A I 229)," GLAK, 235/29831. Also see Sydney Gruson, "U.S. Army Purges Heidelberg Staff," *New York Times,* March 28, 1946.
104. Gruson, "U.S. Army Purges Heidelberg Staff."
105. See Tent, *Mission on the Rhine,* pp. 74–109, and Stern, *The Whitewashing of the Yellow Badge,* pp. 158–185.
106. Irving Wolfson, "The AMG Mess in Germany," *The New Republic,* March 4, 1946, pp. 310–313, and the *New York Times,* March 13, April 22, 23, and 26, 1946.
107. Karl Loewenstein, "Report on the Law School of Munich University and Related Matters," April 23, 1946, in *The U.S. Occupation of Germany: Educational Reform, 1945–1949* (California, Md: Congressional Information Service, 1991), 3A-147.
108. Walter Dorn, "Denkschrift," May 22, 1946, reprinted in Lutz Niethammer, ed., *Walter L. Dorn. Inspektionsreisen in der US-Zone. Notizen, Denkschriften und Errinnerungen aus dem Nachlass* (Stuttgart: Deutsche Verlags-Anstalt, 1973), p. 87. Subsequently, Clay ordered new investigations and, in September 1946, the removal of "important German officials." See Tent, *Mission on the Rhine,* p. 95.
109. Franz Neumann, "Re-educating the Germans: The Dilemma of Reconstruction," *Commentary,* 3, no. 6 (1946), 520.
110. Hartshorne diary, August 22, 1946. On Würzburg also see Gordon Browning to Marvin Boyle, August 31, 1946, NARA, Record Group 260,

OMGUS, Records of the Executive Office, Office of the Adjutant General, Box 19, File: "Denazification of Institutions of Higher Learning in the U.S. Zone."

111. Hartshorne diary, August 11, 1946, and the report of James Wilkinson, U.S. consul general in Munich, February 7, 1947, in *The U.S. Occupation of Germany: Educational Reform, 1945–1949,* 1A-158.
112. Browning to Boyle, August 31, 1946.
113. Marvin Boyle, "Report of Policy Enforcement Branch," November 19, 1946, NARA, RG 260, OMGUS, Records of the Executive Office, Office of the Adjutant General, Box 19, File: "Denazification of Institutions of Higher Learning in the U.S. Zone."
114. Tent, *Mission on the Rhine,* pp. 97–98. For a contemporary summary of the investigations, see "Der Fortschritt der Umerziehung in Deutschland" (Office of Intelligence Research Report No. 4237), June 3, 1947, reprinted in Alfons Söllner, ed., *Zur Archäologie der Demokratie in Deutschland,* vol. 2: *Analysen von politischen Emigranten im amerikanischen Aussenministerium, 1946–1949* (Frankfurt: Fischer Taschenbuch Verlag, 1986), pp. 177–216.
115. Rudolf Urbach to Military Government Headquarters, Württemberg-Baden, June 19, 1946, NARA, RG 260, OMGWB, Records of the Education and Civil-Religious Affairs Division, Box 917A, File: "Denazification of Heidelberg University, 1945–1947 (Col. Irvin)."
116. Milton Potter to Chief, Policy Enforcement Branch, OMGUS, November 15, 1946, NARA, RG 260, OMGWB, Records of the Education and Civil-Religious Affairs Division, Box 912, File: "University of Heidelberg—Policy Enforcement."
117. "Der Fortschritt der Umerziehung in Deutschland," pp. 182–187.
118. "Der gegenwärtige Stand der Entnazifizierung in Westdeutschland und Berlin" (Office of Intelligence Research, Report No. 4626, April 15, 1948), reprinted in Söllner, ed., *Zur Archäologie der Demokratie in Deutschland,* pp. 217–249, esp. p. 243.
119. On the CIC as an "American Gestapo," see Paul Rohrbach to Lucius Clay, May 4, 1946, NARA, RG 260, OMGUB, Records of Headquarters, General Records, 1945–1949, Box 1, File: "Letters Correspondence 1946"; and Stone, "Report on the Mood of Germany." Also see Woller, *Gesellschaft und Politik in der amerikanischen Besatzungszone;* Sayer and Botting, *America's Secret Army,* pp. 281–283, 295; and Ingrid Krüger-Bulcke, ed., *James K. Pollock. Besatzung und Staatsaufbau nach 1945. Occupation Diary and Private Correspondence, 1945–1948* (Munich: Oldenbourg, 1994), p. 269.
120. Paul Schmitthenner to Willy Andreas, May 30, 1951, GLAK, Nachlass Willy Andreas, no. 764. On anti-Semitism in occupied Germany, see Stern, *The Whitewashing of the Yellow Badge.*
121. Neumann, "Re-educating the Germans," p. 524.

6. Whitewashing the Ivory Tower

1. On the Spruchkammer, see Clemens Vollnhals, *Entnazifizierung. Politische Säuberung und Rehabilitierung in den vier Besatzungszonen, 1945–1949* (Munich: Deutsche Taschenbuch Verlag, 1991), pp. 259–338; Lutz Niethammer, *Die Mitläuferfabrik: die Entnazifizierung am Beispiel Bayerns* (Berlin: Dietz, 1982); and Hans Woller, *Gesellschaft und Politik in der amerikanischen Besatzungszone: die Region Ansbach und Fürth* (Munich: Oldenbourg, 1986).
2. Lucius Clay to Commanding General, USFET, December 26, 1946, United States National Archives and Records Administration (hereafter cited as NARA), RG 260, Office of Military Government United States (hereafter cited as OMGUS), Records of the Executive Office, Office of the Adjutant General, General Correspondence and Other Records, 1945–1949, Box 16, File: "Denazification Policy."
3. The most important portions of the law are reprinted in Vollnhals, *Entnazifizierung,* pp. 262–272.
4. Ibid., p. 276.
5. Ibid., p. 333.
6. See the reports reprinted in ibid., pp. 321–330. On fears of "renazification," see Norbert Frei, "'Vergangenheitsbewältigung' or 'Renazification'? The American Perspective on Gemany's Confrontation with the Nazi Past in the Early Years of the Adenauer Era," in Michael Ermarth, ed., *America and the Shaping of German Society, 1945–1955* (Providence: Berg, 1993), pp. 47–59. Also see Curt Garner, "Public Service Personnel in West Germany in the 1950s: Controversial Policy Decisions and Their Effects on Social Composition, Gender Structure, and the Role of Former Nazis," in Robert Moeller, ed., *West Germany under Construction: Politics, Society, and Culture in the Adenauer Era* (Ann Arbor: University of Michigan Press, 1997), pp. 135–195.
7. See, for instance, Nationale Front des Demokratischen Deutschland, *Brown Book: War and Nazi Criminals in West Germany* (Dresden: Verlag Zeit im Bild, 1965).
8. See Joseph Napoli, "Denazification from an American's Viewpoint," *The Annals of the American Academy of Political and Social Science,* 264 (July 1949), 115–123.
9. W. A. Burress to Chief of Staff, USFET G-2, November 21, 1946, NARA, RG 260, OMGUS, Records of the Executive Office, Office of the Adjutant General, General Correspondence and Other Records, 1945–1949, Box 16, File: "Denazification Policy."
10. See Woller, *Gesellschaft und Politik,* p. 132, and Niethammer, *Entnazifizierung in Bayern,* pp. 613–617.
11. Karl Loewenstein, "Comment on 'Denazification,'" *Social Research,* 14, no. 1 (March 1947), 366.

12. William E. Griffith, "Denazification in the United States Zone of Germany," *The Annals of the American Academy of Political and Social Science*, 267 (January 1950), 68–76.
13. Noel Annan, *Changing Enemies: The Defeat and Regeneration of Germany* (New York: W. W. Norton, 1996).
14. Volker Sellin, "Die Universität Heidelberg im Jahre 1945," in Jürgen Hess, Hartmut Lehmann, and Volker Sellin, eds., *Heidelberg 1945* (Stuttgart: Franz Steiner Verlag, 1996), pp. 98–105.
15. Klageschrift, January 5, 1948, Spruchkammerakte Fehrle, Generallandesarchiv Karlsruhe (hereafter cited as GLAK), 465a/50/1/17838–33573, and Richard Scherberger to Gauleitung Baden, January 15, 1941, Universitätsarchiv Heidelberg (hereafter cited as UAH) Personalakte (hereafter cited as PA), 3690 (Ernst).
16. Klageschrift, January 5, 1948, Spruchkammerakte Fehrle.
17. Ibid.
18. Ibid.
19. Ibid.
20. Affidavit, Friedrich Panzer, January 16, 1948, Spruchkammerakte Fehrle.
21. Affidavit, Martin Dibelius, December 20, 1946, Spruchkammerakte Fehrle.
22. Affidavit, Paul Schmitthenner, January 1, 1948, Spruchkammerakte Fehrle.
23. Karl Jaspers to Spruchkammer Heidelberg, February 28, 1948, Spruchkammerakte Fehrle.
24. Protokoll, March 3, 1948, Spruchkammerakte Fehrle.
25. Spruch, March 3, 1948, Spruchkammerakte Fehrle.
26. Spruch, Berufungskammer IX Karlsruhe, October 2, 1948, Spruchkammerakte Fehrle.
27. Ministerium für politische Befreiung Württemberg-Baden to Berufungskammer Karlsruhe, March 2, 1949, Spruchkammerakte Fehrle.
28. Spruch, Berufungskammer IX Karlsruhe, December 29, 1948, Spruchkammerakte Fehrle.
29. Spruch, July 11, 1949, Spruchkammerakte Fehrle.
30. Spruch, January 16, 1950, Spruchkammerakte Fehrle.
31. Peter Assion, "Eugen Fehrle and 'The Mythos of Our Folk,'" in James R. Dow and Hannjost Lixfeld, eds., *The Nazification of an Academic Discipline: Folklore in the Third Reich* (Bloomington: Indiana University Press, 1994), p. 130.
32. Fritz Ernst to Spruchkammer Heidelberg, September 9, 1946, Spruchkammerakte Fritz Ernst, GLAK, 465a/59/5/4876.
33. Heinrich Dannenbauer, sworn affidavit, August 1, 1946, GLAK, 465a/59/5/4876.
34. Heinrich Dannenbauer to Württemberg Culture Ministry, Stuttgart, May 7, 1934, UAH PA, 3691 (Ernst).
35. Spruch, September 13, 1946, Spruchkammerakte Ernst.

36. Meldebogen, Willy Andreas, May 15, 1946, Spruchkammerakte Willy Andreas, GLAK, 465a/59/5/7298.
37. Klageschrift, September 2, 1946, Spruchkammerakte Andreas.
38. CIC Statement, October 31, 1945, Spruchkammerakte Andreas.
39. Willy Andreas to Spruchkammer Heidelberg, Spruchkammerakte Andreas.
40. Spruch, March 28, 1947, Spruchkammerakte Andreas.
41. Sellin, "Die Universität Heidelberg im Jahre 1945," p. 102.
42. Otto Regenbogen to Spruchkammer Heidelberg, March 17, 1947, Spruchkammerakte Andreas.
43. Klageschrift, January 15, 1948, Spruchkammerakte Wolfgang Panzer, GLAK 465a/59/2/11822–25869.
44. Wolfgang Panzer to Spruchkammer Heidelberg, October 10, 1947, Spruchkammerakte Panzer.
45. Ibid.
46. Ibid.
47. Ibid.
48. Ibid.
49. Spruch, March 10, 1948, Spruchkammerakte Panzer.
50. Klageschrift, Spruchkammerakte Ernst Forsthoff, GLAK, 465a/59/1/10807–7472.
51. Ibid.
52. Ibid.
53. Ernst Forsthoff to Spruchkammer Heidelberg, UAH PA, 3789 (Forsthoff).
54. Ibid.
55. Ibid.
56. Ibid.
57. Documents pertaining to the final disposition of Forsthoff's Spruchkammer process are missing from the relevant files in Karlsruhe, but see Jerry Muller, *The Other God That Failed: Hans Freyer and the Deradicalization of German Conservatism* (Princeton: Princeton University Press, 1987), pp. 394–395.
58. Eugen Ulmer to Rector, November 15, 1951, UAH PA, 3787 (Forsthoff). On Article 131, see Norbert Frei, *Vergangenheitspolitik: die Anfänge der Bundesrepublik und die NS-Vergangenheit* (Munich: Beck, 1996).
59. Karl Heinrich Bauer to Johannes Hoops, June 18, 1945, UAH PA, 885 (Duken).
60. Spruch, January 8, 1948, Spruchkammerakte Johann Duken, GLAK, 465a/61/13/503.
61. Ibid.
62. Duken, "A Defense of Professor Dr. Johann Duken concerning His Membership in the NSDAP and Its Organizations," October 15, 1947, Spruchkammerakte Duken.
63. Ibid.

64. Protokoll, Spruchkammer Sinsheim/Elsenz, January 28, 1948, Spruchkammerakte Duken.
65. Spruch, January 29, 1948, Spruchkammerakte Duken.
66. "Über der Belastung lag der Nebel," *Rhein-Neckar Zeitung*, February 14, 1948.
67. "Zum Fall Duken," *Rhein-Neckar Zeitung*, February 17, 1948.
68. "Noch einmal Fall Duken," *Rhein-Neckar Zeitung*, February 19, 1948.
69. Spruchkammerakte Duken.
70. Öffentlicher Kläger der Spruchkammer Sinsheim an die Berufungskammer Karlsruhe, April 5, 1948, Spruchkammerakte Duken.
71. Protokoll, Spruchkammer Sinsheim, November 24, 1948, Spruchkammerakte Duken.
72. Spruch, November 24, 1948, Spruchkammerakte Duken.
73. Karl Geiler to Karl Müller, March 8, 1949, UAH PA, 885 (Duken).
74. Faculty chairman to Johann Duken, July 8, 1954, UAH PA, 885 (Duken).
75. Memorandum for the Officer in Charge, April 13, 1945, reprinted in Hess et al., eds., *Heidelberg 1945*, p. 403.
76. Ibid., p. 413.
77. Spruchkammerakte Hans Runge, GLAK, 465a/59/6/8663–1885.
78. Hans Runge to Spruchkammer Heidelberg, November 18, 1946, Spruchkammerakte Runge.
79. Ibid.
80. Spruch, April 29, 1947, Spruchkammerakte Runge.
81. Michael Kater, *Doctors under Hitler* (Chapel Hill: University of North Carolina Press, 1999), p. 2.
82. Ralph M. Osborne to Ernst Rodenwaldt, May 25, 1946, Spruchkammerakte Ernst Rodenwaldt, GLAK, 465a/59/2/6458–2334.
83. Ernst Rodenwaldt (senior author), *FIAT Review of German Science, Hygiene* (Office of Military Government for Germany, Field Information Agencies Technical, British, French, U.S., 1948). The study contains no references to "racial hygiene."
84. Affidavit, Der Präsident der Landesverwaltung Baden, Abteilung Innere Verwaltung, March 3, 1946, Spruchkammerakte Rodenwaldt.
85. Meldebogen, Ernst Rodenwaldt, April 24, 1946, Spruchkammerakte Rodenwaldt.
86. Klageschrift, Spruchkammer Heidelberg, October 2, 1946, Spruchkammerakte Rodenwaldt.
87. Spruch, May 5, 1947, Spruchkammerakte Rodenwaldt.
88. Ernst Rodenwaldt to Military Government through the Dean of the Medical Faculty, n.d. (summer 1946), Spruchkammerakte Rodenwaldt.
89. Ibid.
90. Ibid.
91. Heidelberg Medical Faculty to Spruchkammer Heidelberg, April 25, 1947, Spruchkammerakte Rodenwaldt.

92. Friedrich Pietrusky to Spruchkammer Heidelberg, Spruchkammerakte Rodenwaldt.
93. Spruch, March 25, 1948, Spruchkammerakte Rodenwaldt.
94. Samuel Goudsmit, *Alsos* (New York: H. Schuman, 1947).
95. Ludwig Wesch, Schriftliche Erklärung, March 14, 1947, Spruchkammerakte Ludwig Wesch, GLAK, 465a/IN/2/79.
96. Affidavit, Philipp Lenard, April 29, 1947, Spruchkammerakte Wesch.
97. Rudolf Tomaschek to Spruchkammer Karlsruhe, July 3, 1947, Spruchkammerakte Wesch.
98. Protokoll, Spruchkammer I Karlsruhe, July 2, 1947, Spruchkammerakte Wesch.
99. Ludwig Rüger to Rector, May 22, 1947, Spruchkammerakte Wesch.
100. Protokoll, Spruchkammer Heidelberg, July 7, 1948, Spruchkammerakte Wesch.
101. This was a defense also employed by Maurice Papon, an official in Vichy France involved in the rounding up of French Jews for deportation to German death camps who was tried in France in 1998 for complicity in crimes against humanity. See Robert O. Paxton, "The Trial of Maurice Papon," *The New York Review of Books,* December 16, 1999.
102. Quoted in Michael Marrus, ed., *The Nuremberg War Crimes Trial, 1945–1946: A Documentary History* (Boston: Bedford Books, 1997), pp. 211, 213.
103. See Siegfried Matlok's interview with Best in Siegfried Matlok, ed., *Dänemark in Hitlers Hand. Der Bericht des Reichsbevollmächtigten Werner Best über seine Besatzungspolitik in Dänemark mit Studien über Hitler, Goering, Himmler, Heydrich, Ribbentrop, Canaris u.a.* (Husum: Husum Verlag, 1988), pp. 187–207.
104. Jeffrey Herf, *Divided Memory: The Nazi Past in the Two Germanys* (Cambridge: Harvard University Press, 1997), pp. 289–290. On Globke's role in crafting the Nuremberg race laws, see Saul Friedländer, *Nazi Germany and the Jews,* vol. 1: *The Years of Persecution, 1933–1939* (New York: HarperCollins, 1997), pp. 152, 159, 254–255.
105. See Frank Stern, *Jews in the Minds of Germans in the Postwar Period* (Bloomington: The Robert A. and Sandra S. Borns Jewish Studies Program, Indiana University, 1993), pp. 10–12.
106. See Weber's affidavits in the Spruchkammer cases of Schuster and Jecht, UAH PA, 641 (Schuster), and Spruchkammerakte Horst Jecht, GLAK, 465a/59/1/11154, respectively.
107. See Muller, *The Other God That Failed;* Dirk van Laak, *Gespräche in der Sicherheit des Schweigens* (Berlin: Akademie Verlag, 1993); and Eberhard Demm, "Alfred Weber und die Nationalsozialisten," *Zeitschrift für Geschichtswissenschaft,* 47, no. 3 (1999), 211–236.
108. Herbert Lehmann, "Wolfgang Panzer. Versuch einer vorläufigen Porträtskizze," in Dietrich Hafemann et al., eds., *Mainzer Geographische Studien.*

Festgabe zum 65. Geburtstag Professor Wolfgang Panzers am 16. Juli 1961 überreicht von seinen Schülern (Brunswick: Georg Westermann Verlag, 1961), p. 9.

109. Wolfgang Meid, "Hermann Güntert: Leben und Werk," in Manfred Mayrhofer and Hermann Güntert, eds., *Antiquitates Indogermanicae. Gedenkschrift für Hermann Güntert* (Innsbruck: Innsbrucker Beiträge zur Sprachwissenschaft, 1974), pp. 517–522.
110. See Assion, "Eugen Fehrle and the 'Mythos of Our Folk,'" and James R. Dow and Hannjost Lixfeld, "Epilogue: Overcoming the Past of National Socialist Folklore," both in Dow and Lixfeld, eds., *The Nazification of an Academic Discipline,* pp. 129–130 and 264–296, respectively. Also see Lily Weiser-Aall, "Eugen Fehrle, 1880–1957," *Hessische Blätter für Volkskunde,* 49–50, (1959), 9–10.
111. The essay is in Diethard Aschoff, *Fritz Ernst. Im Schatten des Diktators. Rückblick eines Heidelberger Historikers auf die NS-Zeit* (Heidelberg: Manutius Verlag, 1996).
112. Fritz Ernst, *Die Deutschen und Ihre Jüngsten Geschichte* (Stuttgart: W. Kohlhammer, 1963) and translated as *The Germans and Their Modern History* (New York: Columbia University Press, 1966).
113. Ernst, *The Germans and Their Modern History,* pp. 103–104.
114. Ibid., pp. 104–105.
115. Ibid., pp. 118–119.
116. Ibid., pp. 122–123.
117. Ibid., p. 127.
118. Ibid., pp. 130–131.
119. Ernst Rodenwaldt, *Ein Tropenarzt erzählt sein Leben* (Stuttgart: F. Enke, 1957).
120. Ibid., p. 399.
121. Ibid., pp. 467–468.
122. Spruchkammerakte Walter Mönch, GLAK, 465a/59/38/2847.
123. Quoted in Frank Rutger-Hausmann, *"Aus dem Reich der seelischen Hungersnot." Briefe und Dokumente zur romanistischen Fachgeschichte im Dritten Reich* (Würzburg: Königshausen und Neumann, 1993), p. 12. Other memoirs include Heinz-Dietrich Wendland, *Wege und Umwege: 50 Jahre erlebter Theologie: 1919–1950* (Gütersloh: Gütersloher Verlagshaus Mohn, 1977); Fritz Schachermeyr, *Ein Leben zwischen Wissenschaft und Kunst* (Vienna: H. Böhlaus, 1984); Ernst Wahle, *Und es ging mit ihm seinen Weg* (Heidelberg: self-published, 1980); and Hermann Glockner, *Heidelberger Bilderbuch. Erinnerungen* (Bonn: H. Bouvier, 1969).
124. The literature on this subject is extensive, but see in particular Herf, *Divided Memory,* chaps. 7–9; Muller, *The Other God That Failed,* chap. 10 and Jean Solchany, *Comprendre le nazisme dans l'Allemagne des annees zero (1945–1949)* (Paris: Presses Universitaires de France, 1997), pp. 213–255.

125. Quoted in Peter Jehle, *Werner Krauss und die Romanistik im NS-Staat* (Hamburg: Argument-Verlag, 1996), p. 135.
126. Compare Bäumler's "Meine politische Entwicklung," May 26, 1948, with his March 24, 1950, letter to Manfred Schröter, both published in Marianne Bäumler, Hubert Brunträger, and Hermann Kurzke, eds., *Thomas Mann und Alfred Bäumler. Eine Dokumentation* (Würzburg: Königshausen und Neumann, 1989), pp. 293–201 and 203–212, respectively.
127. Theodore Litt, "The National-Socialist Use of Moral Tendencies in Germany," in Internaional Council for Philosophy and Humanistic Studies, *The Third Reich* (New York: H. Fertig, 1975), pp. 438–455.
128. *Die Gegenwart*, December 24, 1945, pp. 23–26.
129. Ibid.
130. Hannah Arendt, "The Image of Hell," *Commentary*, 2 (September 1946), 294.
131. Max Weinrich, *Hitler's Professors: The Part of Scholarship in Germany's Crimes against the Jewish People* (New York: Yiddish Scientific Institute-YIVO, 1946), and Arendt, "The Image of Hell," p. 203.
132. This point is made by Muller regarding Hans Freyer and other "radical conservatives" in *The Other God That Failed*, p. 316.
133. Figures cited in Hermann Weisert, *Die Verfassung der Universität Heidelberg: Überblick, 1386–1952* (Heidelberg: Winter, 1974), p. 151.
134. Rolf Seeliger, *Braune Universität. Deutsche Hochschullehrer Gestern und Heute* (Munich: Verlag Rolf Seeliger, 1968), pp. 54–56.
135. See Verzeichnis der seit Oktober 1945 auf Anordnung der amerikanischen Militärregierung entlassenen Professoren, Beamten und Angestellten, March 13, 1946, GLAK, 235/29831, and *Kürschners Deutscher Gelehrten-Kalender* (Berlin: Walter de Gruyter, 1950, 1954, 1961).

7. A Culture of Forgetting

1. On the history of West Germany in the 1950s, see Axel Schildt and Arnold Sywottek, eds., *Modernisierung im Wiederaufbau. Die westdeutsche Gesellschaft der 50er Jahre* (Bonn: J. H. W. Dietz, 1998), and Robert Moeller, ed., *West Germany under Construction: Politics, Society, and Culture in the Adenauer Era* (Ann Arbor: University of Michigan Press, 1997). On West German political culture and the memory of National Socialism, see Jeffrey Herf, *Divided Memory: The Nazi Past in the Two Germanys* (Cambridge: Harvard University Press, 1997), pp. 267–333.
2. Volker Sellin, "Die Universität Heidelberg in der Geschichte der Gegenwart, 1945—1985," in *Die Geschichte der Universität Heidelberg: Vorträge im Wintersemester 1985/86* (Heidelberg: HVA, 1986), pp. 217–235.
3. Figures cited in Hermann Weisert, *Die Verfassung der Universität Heidelberg: Überblick, 1386–1952* (Heidelberg: Winter, 1974), pp. 150–162.

4. Eike Wolgast, *Die Universität Heidelberg, 1386–1986* (Berlin: Springer-Verlag, 1986), pp. 178–179.
5. This phenomenon was common in immediate postwar Germany; see Dirk van Laak, *Gespräche in der Sicherheit des Schweigens* (Berlin: Akademie Verlag, 1993), pp. 42–52. For Heidelberg, see Hubert Treiber, "Salon-Geselligkeit und Vortragskultur im Nachkriegs-Heidelberg—oder: Über die Rückkehr der 'letzten Bildungsbürger,'" in Jürgen Hess, Hartmut Lehmann, and Volker Sellin, eds., *Heidelberg 1945* (Stuttgart: Franz Steiner Verlag, 1996), pp. 255–269. Also see Jörg Thierfelder's, Heide-Marie Lauterer's, and Günther Roth's contributions to the same volume.
6. On "Free Socialism," see Alfred Weber and Alexander Mitscherlich, *Freier Sozialismus* (Heidelberg: Lambert Schneider, 1946). Also see Eberhard Demm, "Alfred Weber's 'Freier Sozialismus'," in Hess et al., eds., *Heidelberg 1945*, pp. 329–347. For a skeptical view of the health of postwar Heidelberg's intellectual life, see Jerry Muller, "How Vital Was the *Geist* in Heidelberg in 1945? Some Skeptical Reflections," in Hess et al., eds., *Heidelberg 1945*, pp. 197–200.
7. Klaus von Beyme, "Karl Jaspers—Vom philosophischen Aussenseiter zum *Praeceptor Germaniae*," in Hess et al., eds., *Heidelberg 1945*, pp. 130–148.
8. See the admiring account of this group's activities by Delbert Clark in the *New York Times,* July 6, 1947.
9. See Birgit Pape, "Vorschule der Demokratie in Deutschland, *Frankfurter Allgemeine Zeitung,* December 11, 1999.
10. Karl Jaspers, *Die Schuldfrage* (Heidelberg: L. Schneider, 1946).
11. Von Beyme, "Karl Jaspers—Vom philosophischen Aussenseiter zum *Praeceptor Germaniae.*"
12. For Jaspers's own account of his departure from Heidelberg, see Hans Saner, ed., *Schicksal und Wille. Autobiographische Schriften* (Munich: R. Piper & Co. Verlag, 1967), pp. 164–183. Also see von Beyme, "Karl Jaspers—Vom philosophischen Aussenseiter zum *Praeceptor Germaniae,*" pp. 135–143.
13. On Kuhn, see Max Weinreich, *Hitler's Professors: The Part of Scholarship in Germany's Crimes against the Jewish People* (New York: Yiddish Scientific Institute-YIVO, 1946), pp. 40, 48, 50, 51, 56.
14. Spruch, Spruchkammer 7 Stuttgart-Feuerbach, September 21, 1948, and Spruch, Staatskommissariat für die politische Säuberung Tübingen-Lustnau, Spruchkammer für den Lehrkörper der Universität Tübingen, October 18, 1948, both in Universitätsarchiv Heidelberg (herafter cited as UAH) Personalakte (hereafter cited as PA), 4714 (Kuhn).
15. Theology Faculty to Ministry of Culture, Baden-Württemberg, March 1, 1954, UAH PA, 4715 (Kuhn).
16. Karl Jaspers to Hannah Arendt, August 19, 1950, in Lotte Kohler and Hans Saner, eds., *Hannah Arendt / Karl Jaspers Correspondence, 1926–1969* (New York: Harcourt Brace Jovanovich, 1992), pp. 154, 155.

17. See van Laak, *Gespräche in der Sicherheit des Schweigens,* and Jerry Muller, *The Other God That Failed: Hans Freyer and the Deradicaliazation of German Conservatism* (Princeton: Princeton University Press, 1987), pp. 316–402.
18. Van Laak, *Gespräche in der Sicherheit des Schweigens,* pp. 52–69, 200–208, and 240–246.
19. Spruchkammerakte Eduard Wahl, Generallandesarchiv Karlsruhe, 465a/59/13/7379.
20. On the Juristenkreis, see Frank M. Buscher, *The U.S. War Crimes Trial Program in Germany, 1946–1955* (Westport, Conn.: Greenwood Press, 1989), pp. 99–104, and Norbert Frei, *Vergangenheitspolitik. Die Anfänge der Bundesrepublik und die NS-Vergangenheit* (Munich: C. H. Beck, 1996), pp. 133–306.
21. Buscher, *The U.S. War Crimes Trial Program in Germany,* pp. 91–113 and 159–164.
22. Delbert Clark, "Heidelberg Held Failure in Policy: Reactionary Elements Have Taken over Old University, Some Critics Declare," *New York Times,* December 16, 1947. Also see Fred Hechinger, "Nationalism in 'New' German Universities: Faculties in U.S. Zone Persist in Reactionary Ways That Paved Hitler's Path; Liberal Anti-Nazi Professors Are still Ostracized," *New York Herald Tribune,* December 31, 1947.
23. Delbert Clark, *Again the Goose Step: The Lost Fruits of Victory* (Indianapolis: Bobbs-Merrill, 1949).
24. Clark, "Heidelberg Held Failure in Policy."
25. Delbert Clark to Alfred Weber, January 23, 1948, UAH, B-1015/7.
26. Notes taken by Heinrich Kranz, Privatdozent on the Medical Faculty, "Allgemeine Dozentenversammlung am 13.2.1948," UAH, B-1015/7.
27. Wolfgang Kunkel to Ministry of Culture, Stuttgart, January 28, 1947, UAH, B-1015/7.
28. Karl Heinrich Bauer to the *New York Times,* April 19, 1948.
29. Alfred Weber to Delbert Clark, December 30, 1947, UAH B-1015/6.
30. Alexander Mitscherlich, *Ein Leben für die Psychoanalyse. Anmerkungen zu meiner Zeit* (Frankfurt: Suhrkamp, 1980), pp. 144–215.
31. Telford Taylor, Opening Statement of the Prosecution, December 9, 1946, quoted in George J. Annas and Michael A. Grodin, eds., *The Nazi Doctors and the Nuremberg Code: Human Rights in Human Experimentation* (New York: Oxford University Press, 1992), p. 67.
32. Alexander Mitscherlich and Fred Mielke, *Das Diktat der Menschenverachtung: Eine Dokumentation* (Heidelberg: L. Schneider, 1947). An English-language edition was published in 1949 as *Doctors of Infamy: The Story of the Nazi Medical Crimes* (New York: Henry Schuman).
33. Mitscherlich and Mielke, pp. 150, 152, 154–155.
34. Mitscherlich, *Ein Leben für die Psychoanalyse,* p. 146.
35. See Christian Pross, "Nazi Doctors, German Medicine, and Historical

Truth," in Annas and Grodin, eds., *The Nazi Doctors and the Nuremberg Code,* pp. 32–52. Also see Michael Kater, "The Burden of the Past: Problems of a Modern Historiography of Physicians and Medicine in Nazi Germany," *German Studies Review,* 10, no. 1 (1987), 31–56.

36. See the correspondence and documents in UAH PA, 1079 (Mitscherlich).
37. Karl Jaspers to Alaxander Mitscherlich, May 9, 1947, Alfred Weber to Alexander Mitscherlich, May 8, 1947, and memorandum, Gustav Radbruch, May 9, 1947, all in UAH PA, 5032 (Mitscherlich).
38. Alfred Weber, "Haben wir Deutschen seit 1945 Versagt?" *Die Wandlung,* 4 (December 1949),735–747.
39. See Karl-Siegbert Rehberg, "Verdrängung und Neuanfang: Die Soziologie nach 1945 als 'Normalfall' westdeutscher Geschichtserledigung," in Wilfried Loth and Bernd-A. Rusinek, eds., *Verwandlungspolitik. NS-Eliten in der Westdeutschen Nachkriegsgesellschaft* (Frankfurt: Campus Verlag, 1998), pp. 259–284.
40. These developments are described in detail in Eberhard Demm, "Alfred Weber und die Nationalsozialisten," *Zeitschrift für Geschichtswissenschaft,* 47, no. 3 (1999), 211–236, esp. pp. 229–236.
41. See Susanne Heim, *Ein Berater der Macht: Helmut Meinhold oder der Zusammenhang zwischen Sozialpolitik und Judenvernichtung* (Hamburg: Hamburger Institut für Sozialforschung, 1986).
42. By the 1957–58 academic year, twenty of ninety-seven full professors (20 percent) had been teaching until 1945 in what would become the Soviet occupation zone–German Democratic Republis or taught in the universities there in the immediate postwar years. Of the twenty, nine were on the Philosophy Faculty.
43. Victor Klemperer, *I Will Bear Witness: A Diary of the Nazi Years, 1933–1941* (New York: Random House, 1998), vol. 1, p. 184.
44. See Johannes Kühn, *Über den Sinn des Gegenwärtigen Krieges* (Heidelberg: Kurt Vowinckel Verlag, 1940), and "Der Sinn des gegenwärtigen Krieges," *Zeitschrift für Geopolitik,* 20 (1943), 252–256.
45. On Conze's and Schieder's engagement with National Socialism see Götz Aly, "Theodor Schieder, Werner Conze oder Die Vorstufen der physischen Vernichtung," and Hans-Ulrich Wehler, "Nationalsozialismus und Historiker," both in Winfried Schulze and Otto Gerhard Oexle, eds., *Deutsche Historiker im Nationalsozialismus* (Frankfurt: Fischer Taschenbuch Verlag, 1999), pp. 163–182 and 306–339, respectively.
46. On Maschke, see Michael Burleigh, *Germany Turns Eastward: A Study of Ostforschung in the Third Reich* (Cambridge: Cambridge University Press, 1988), pp. 57–59 and 199–200.
47. See Muller, *The Other God That Failed,* pp. 316–402, and Richard Wolin, "Untruth and Method: Nazism and the Complicities of Hans-Georg Gadamer," *The New Republic,* May 15, 2000, pp. 36–45.
48. Wolin, "Untruth and Method." Also see Teresa Orozco, *Platonische Ge-*

walt: Gadamers politische Hermeneutik des NS-Zeit (Hamburg: Argument-Verlag, 1995).

49. See Eugen Fehrle, *Sagen aus Deutschland* (Vienna: C. Überreuter, 1952), and *Feste und Volksbräuche im Jahreslauf europäische Völker* (Kassel: J. P. Hinnenthal, 1955). Also see Peter Assion, "Eugen Fehrle and 'The Mythos of Our Folk,'" in James R. Dow and Hannjost Lixfeld, eds., *The Nazification of an Academic Discipline: Folklore in the Third Reich* (Bloomington: Indiana University Press, 1994), pp. 130, 134.

50. Frank-Rutger Hausmann, *"Vom Strudel der Ereignisse verschlungen." Deutsche Romanistik im "Dritten Reich"* (Frankfurt am Main: Vittorio Klostermann, 2000), pp. 563–564.

51. See Conze's own account of the institute's founding, "Die Gründung des Arbeitskreises für moderne Sozialgeschichte," *Hamburger Jahrbuch für Wirtschafts- und Gesellschaftspolitik,* 24 (1979), 23–32. Also see Winfried Schulze, "German Historiography from the 1930s to the 1950s," in Hartmut Lehmann and James Van Horn Melton, eds., *Paths of Continuity: Central European Historiography from the 1930s to the 1950s* (Cambridge: Cambridge University Press, 1994), pp. 19–42.

52. Compare Muller's assessment of Forsthoff in *The Other God That Failed,* pp. 391–402, with Peter Caldwell, "Ernst Forsthoff and the Legacy of Radical Conservative State Theory in the Federal Republic of Germany," *History of Political Thought,* 15, no. 4 (1994), 615–641. On technological pessimism in conservative German thought, see Jeffrey Herf, "Technology and Twentieth-Century German Conservative Intellectuals," in Yaron Ezrahi, Everett Mendelsohn, and Howard Segal, eds., *Technology, Pessimism, and Postmodernism* (Dordrecht: Kluwer Academic Publishers, 1994), pp. 115–136.

53. Herf, *Divided Memory,* pp. 334–348.

54. The most notable of these efforts was Rolf Seeliger's six-volume study, *Braune Universität. Dokumentation mit Stellungnahmen. Dokumentenreihe* (Munich: Verlag Rolf Seeliger, 1964), and Hans Peter Bleuel, *Deutschlands Bekenner. Professoren zwischen Kaiserreich und Diktatur* (Bern: Scherz Verlag, 1967). The connections between the student protest movements of the 1960s and the memory of National Socialism has yet to be examined closely by scholars, but see Eckart Krause, "Auch der unbequemen Wahrheit verpflichtet. Der lange Weg der Universität Hamburg zu ihrer Geschichte im 'Dritten Reich,'" in Peter Reichel, ed., *Das Gedächtnis der Stadt. Hamburg im Umgang mit seiner nationalsozialistischen Vergangenheit* (Hamburg: Dölling und Galitz Verlag GmbH, 1997), pp. 187–217.

55. Bernd Laufs, "Vom Umgang der Medizin mit ihrer Geschichte," in Gerrit Hohendorf and Achim Magull-Seltenreich, eds., *Von der Heilkunde zur Massentötung. Medizin im Nationalsozialismus* (Heidelberg: Wunderhorn, 1990), pp. 233–257, esp. pp. 237–241.

56. Wilhelm Doerr, ed., *Semper Apertus: Sechshundert Jahre Ruprecht-Karls-*

Universität Heidelberg, 1386–1986, 3 vols. (Berlin: Springer Verlag, 1985), and Wolgast, *Die Universität Heidelberg, 1386–1986.*
57. Karin Buselmeier, Dietrich Harth, and Christian Jansen, eds., *Auch eine Geschichte der Universität Heidelberg* (Mannheim: Edition Quadrat, 1985).
58. Seeliger, *Braune Universität,* vol. 6, p. 26.
59. Quoted in van Laak, *Gespräche in der Sicherheit des Schweigens,* p. 205.
60. Quoted in Wulf Kansteiner, "Mandarins in the Public Sphere: *Vergangenheitsbewältigung* and the Paradigm of Social History in the Federal Republic of Germany," *German Politics and Society,* 17, no. 3 (1999), 107.

Conclusion

1. Fritz Ringer, *The Decline of the German Mandarins: The German Academic Community, 1890–1933* (Cambridge: Harvard University Press, 1969).
2. George Mosse, *Toward the Final Solution: A History of European Racism* (Madison: University of Wisconsin Press, 1985).
3. See, for example, Tom Bower, *Blind Eye to Murder: Britain, America, and the Purging of Nazi Germany—a Pledge Betrayed* (London: A. Deutsch, 1981).
4. Alan Beyerchen, *Scientists under Hitler: Politics and the Physics Community in the Third Reich* (New Haven: Yale University Press, 1977).
5. Dirk van Laak, *Gespräche in der Sicherheit des Schweigens* (Berlin: Akademie Verlag, 1993).

Appendix A

1. For an overview of the traditional structure of the pre-1933 German university, see R. H. Samuel and R. Hinton Thomas, *Education and Society in Modern Germany* (London: Routledge & Kegan Paul, 1949), pp. 111–134.

Appendix B

1. This list is from "Bei Herrn Staatsminister Prof. Dr. Paul Schmitthenner angefertigte Dissertationen," n.d., but probably 1941, Universitätsarchiv Heidelberg, Rep. 26/18.

Index

Aachen, 148
Abendroth, Rudolf, 132, 134
Academia Moralis, 223
Achelis, Johann Daniel, 45, 89, 296; wartime teaching, 95; denazification, 137, 156–157
Adenauer, Konrad, 151, 207, 218
Adler, Hans Hermann, 40; on universities in the National Socialist state, 34; wartime teaching, 96
"Aktion Ritterbusch," 96–97
Alewyn, Richard, 38
Ancestral Heritage project (Ahnenerbe), 31, 75, 76
Andreas, Willy, 38, 136–137, 184; as Rector (1933–1934), 14, 19–20, 21; responds to National Socialism, 23, 24, 236; on universities in the National Socialist state, 33; wartime teaching, 96; denazification, 163–164; Spruchkammer trial, 180–181, 187–189
Anniversary celebration (550th, 1936), 50–51, 52, 57; as propaganda, 51, 57–58; controversy with British universities, 54–57; foreign representatives attending, 58, honorary degrees granted, 63–66
Anschütz, Gerhard, 21, 42, 142; responds to National Socialism, 28
Anti-Semitism: in Weimar-era academic culture, 10–11; of Heidelberg professors, 25, 27–28, 36, 52–53, 71–72, 78, 80–81, 83, 87, 91–92, 99–100, 103, 175, 239
Arendt, Hannah, 216
Article 131 (of the Basic Law), 194, 206, 216, 218, 222, 232, 245
"Aryan physics," 46, 52–54, 59, 107, 204, 205, 236, 244

Basel, University of, 221
Bauer, Karl Heinrich, 87, 88–90, 114, 147, 161, 220, 225, 227, 231–232, 240, 241–242, 243; wartime teaching, 95; reopening of university, 118–120, 121, 123–124, 130, 139, 141; interpretation of National Socialism, 123, 134–138; denazification, 134, 155–158, 164–166, 168, 169, 173–174, 194, 199, 200
Baum, Marie, 142, 145, 220
Bäumler, Alfred, 31, 154, 214
Becker, August, 46, 55, 92, 94–95
Becksmann, Ernst, wartime teaching, 96
Beer, Georg, 36
Bergsträsser, Arnold, 24, 26–27, 41
Berlin, University of, 16
Best, Werner, 207
Bilfinger, Carl, 43, 93, 104, 105, 107; wartime publications, 97
Bobtschev, Konstantin, 105
Böckmann, Paul, 93; wartime publications, 97, 101
Borch, Herbert von, 227

Bothe, Walter, 20, 54, 118, 205
Bötticher, Eduard, 61
Boyle, Marvin, 173
Brinkmann, Carl, 41, 42, 63–64, 104–105; responds to National Socialism, 26, 29–30; on the universities in the National Socialist state, 34–35; wartime teaching, 96; wartime publications, 97
Broemser, Philipp, 24
Browning, Gordon, 173
Brunner, Otto, 230

Chateaubriant, Alphonse de, 78
Chelius, Goetz von, 15
Christian Democratic Union (CDU), 178
Clark, Delbert, 224–225
Classen, Wilhelm, 58, 133; wartime teaching, 95–96
Clay, Lucius D., 127, 148, 150, 178, 224, 242
Cohn, Ernst, 17
Committee of Thirteen, 118–120
Conze, Werner, 221, 228–229, 230, 244
Coordination (Gleichschaltung), 12–15, 16, 48
Copland, Douglas B., 64
Counter Intelligence Corps (CIC), 117–118, 125–126, 127–128, 131, 146, 149, 156–157, 159, 168–169, 170–172, 175, 187–188, 195, 197–198, 199–200, 242
Crum, Earl, 158, 159–160; and denazification, 160–161, 168–171, 172

Dahm, Georg, 26, 42, 43
Dannenbauer, Heinrich, 185–186
Denazification, 131–138; "Law Number 8" (1945), 148–149; German émigré officers' views on, 149–151, 174–175; German public views on, 151, 216; Heidelberg professors' views of, 216–217; impact on Heidelberg University, 216–217. See also Spruchkammer
Dibelius, Martin, 36–37, 110, 111, 183, 188; responds to National Socialism, 24–25, 28; wartime publications, 97–98; and reopening of university, 118–120, 133–134; on denazification, 152
Dittmar, Otto, 45, 157, 165
Döblin, Alfred, 127
Dodd, William, 125
Dolmetscher Institute, 93–94, 96, 106

Dorn, Walter, 172
Duhm, Andreas, 23, 36, 133
Duken, Johann, 45, 118, 132, 134; Spruchkammer trial, 180–181, 194–197
Dulckeit, Georg, 43, 91–92
Dunelm, Herbert, 56

Ebbinghaus, Julius, 132
Ebrach seminars, 223
Eckard, Hans von, 40, 111–112, 142, 145, 220; responds to National Socialism, 28–29; on denazification, 138
Eckhard, Waltraud, 133
Eichholtz, Fritz, 94, 157, 221; wartime teaching, 95
Emmet, Thomas, 157, 159, 163, 187–188
Endemann, Friedrich, 30, 42
Engelking, Ernst: reopening of university, 118–119; on denazification, 134, 156, 168, 174
Engisch, Karl, 63, 115, 158
Erdmannsdörfer, Otto, 23–24, 46
Erixson, Sigurd, 63
Erlangen, University of, 165, 173
Ernst, Fritz, 68, 69–70, 117, 147, 161, 189, 191, 220; wartime teaching, 96; wartime publications, 100, 113–114; reopening of university, 118–120, 121, 136; and denazification, 152–153, 168, 174; Spruchkammer trial, 180–181, 185–187, 211–212; assessment of National Socialism, 210–213
"Euthanasia," 43, 74; related research at Heidelberg University, 43, 107–110. See also Schneider, Carl

Fehrle, Eugen, 13, 16, 30, 39, 60, 68, 115, 132, 133, 210, 229, 239, 241; wartime teaching, 96; wartime publications, 97, 98, 101; Spruchkammer trial, 180–185
Festschrifts, 209–210
Feuchtwanger, Lion, 127
Field Information Agency, Technical (FIAT), 200, 244
Fischer, Eugen, 73
Folk and Cultural-Political Institute (Volks- und kulturpolitischen Institut), 72
Forsthoff, Ernst, 43, 87–88, 158–159, 222–223, 230–231, 232, 233, 244; Spruchkammer trial, 180–181, 191–194
Four Year Plan, 51, 59

Franges, Otto von, 64
Frank, Bruno, 127
Frankfurt, University of, 16, 172, 173
Franz, Günther, 39, 41, 67
"Free Socialism," 220
Freiburg, University of, 154–155
Freudenberg, Karl, 63, 86, 95, 191; reopening of university, 122; on denazification, 132, 157, 205
Freyer, Hans, 3, 31, 228, 230
Frommel, Otto, 36–37
Fuchs, Walter Peter, 68

Gadamer, Hans-Georg, 17, 229
Ganser, Wilhelm: wartime teaching, 95; and denazification, 133
Gehlen, Arnold, 230
Geiler, Karl, 80, 142
Gentner, Wolfgang: reopening of university, 118–119, 121; and denazification, 174
"German Christians," 36
"German Civil Servants Law" (1937), 80–82. *See also* "Law for the Restoration of the Professional Civil Service"; Purges
German Institute for Foreign Policy Research (Deutsches Institut für Aussenpolitische Forschung), 97, 110
German Research Society (Deutsche Forschungsgemeinschaft, DFG), 59, 96
German Scientific Institutes (Deutsche Wissenschaftliche Institute, DWI), 86, 90, 98–99
Giessen, University of, 194, 196, 197
Gilbert, Felix, 120, 121, 152–153
Gladenbeck, Johann Friedrich, 107
Glässer, Edgar, 78, 79, 214; wartime publications, 97
Globke, Hans, 207
Glockner, Hermann: on the universities in the National Socialist state, 33–34; wartime publications, 97
Goebbels, Joseph, 57, 92–93
Goethe, Johann Wolfgang von, 101
Görttler, Curt, 157, 196
Goudsmit, Samuel, 118
Greeven, Heinrich, and denazification, 159–160
Greifswald, University of, 198
Griesebach, August, 38, 80, 142, 143
Griffith, William, 148–149
Groh, William, 16, 42, 80–81, 187; as Rector (1934–1936), 14–15, 57, 85

Gumbel, Emil J., 10–11, 142, 235–236
Gundert, Hermann, wartime publications, 97
Gundolf, Friedrich, 50
Güntert, Hermann, 38, 209–210; responds to National Socialism, 27, 28, 60–61, 63, 75–76

Hamburg, University of, 201
Hampe, Karl, 29. 38
Hartshorne, Edward Y., 111, 128; on reopening the universities, 128–130; on denazification, 129–130, 131–132, 134, 136–137, 138, 145, 155–156, 172–173, 197, 241, 242; murdered, 141
Haubach, Theodor, 110
Heidegger, Martin, 2, 3, 13, 14, 15, 154–155, 216; on the universities in the National Socialist state, 31
Heidelberg, University of: in Weimar Republic, 7–11, 30, 36, 235–236; "coordination" of after 1933, 12–22, 236; purges at (1933–1937), 16–19, 80–82; reconstruction of faculties after 1933, 35–48; anniversary celebration (1936), 50–51, 54–58; war-related research and teaching conducted at, 93–114, 237–238; occupation of, 117–118; reopening of (1945–1946), 124–130, 240; denazification at, 131–141, 146–147, 151–172, 174–176, 241–244; postwar growth of, 219–220; former Nazis at, 221–229
Heidelberg Action Group for Democracy and Free Socialism, 220
Heidelberg Committee on Regional Research (Arbeitsgemeinschaft für Raumforschung), 106
Heidelberger Jurists Circle (Heidelberger Juristenkreis), 223
Hellpach, Willy, 183, 191, 203; responds to National Socialism, 30
Henk, Emil, 110, 118, 186
Herbig, Reinhard, 221, wartime publications, 97, 99–100
Herder, Gottfried von, 101, 229
Hess, Gerhard, wartime publications, 97
Heuss, Theodor, 188
Heydrich, Reinhard, 52
Heym, Stefan, 150–151, 174
Hildebrandt, Heinz, 24, 26, 42, 43

Himmel, Hans, 132
Himmler, Heinrich, 195
Hitler, Adolf, 5, 11, 12, 22, 30, 50, 51, 57, 83, 86, 89, 100
Hoelscher, Gustav, 36, 37–38, 111, 112; reopening of university, 133–134; and denazification, 159, 168
Hoepke, Hermann, 142
Hoffmann, Ernst, 10, 38, 111, 142
Höhn, Reinhard, 26, 41, 42, 43
Hoops, Johannes, 38, 114, 132, 191; wartime publications, 97
Höpke, Heinrich, 80
Horstmann, Ernst, 132, 134
Hupfeld, Renatus, 36, 111; reopening of university, 118

Ibrahim, Jussef, 195
Institute for Air Defense Research (Institut für Luftfahrtforschung), 106
Institute for Frankish-Pfalz History and Regional Studies (Institut für Fränkisch-Pfälzische Geschichte und Landeskunde), 39, 67–69, 70
Institute for International Post and News Broadcasting (Institut für Weltpost- und Weltnachrichtenwesen), 107
Institute for Political Economy and Statistics (Institut für Volkswirtschaftslehre und Statistik), 106
Institute for Regional Economic Research (Institut für Grossraumwirtschaft), 101–106
Institute for Social and Political Sciences (Institut für Sozial- und Staatswissenschaften, Insosta), 9, 39–42, 219, 236
Institute for the Study and Eradication of Jewish Influence in German Church Life (Institut zur Erforschung und Beseitigung des jüdischen Einflusses auf das deutsche kirchliche Leben), 36, 221, 222
Institute for the Study of Journalism (Institut für Zeitungswesen), 40, 94, 96, 145

Jaffe, Elsa, 118
Jansen, Barend C. P., 65
Janssen, Henry, 64
Jaspers, Karl, 21–22, 29, 111, 115, 129, 142, 183, 220, 227, 245; responds to National Socialism, 31–32, fired from Heidelberg, 38, 80–82; reopening of university, 118–120, 122, 124, 139–140; on National Socialism and scholarship, 139; on denazification, 140, 154–155, 161, 168; leaves Heidelberg, 221, 222, 224
Jecht, Horst, 103, 160
Jelke, Robert, 30, 36, 37–38, 133
Jellinek, Walter, 17, 30, 42, 142, 188; responds to National Socialism, 23, 25–26, 28; reopening of university, 118–120; on denazification, 153–154, 158
Jena, University of, 195
Jensen, Harro, 93; wartime publications, 97

Kaiser Wilhelm Institute, 86, 94
Kiefer, Ernst, 36, 133
Kiel, University of, 201
Kienle, Richard von, 69, 76, 185
Kirschner, Martin, wartime teaching, 95
Klein, Hans, 221
Kleine, Hugo, 134
Klemperer, Victor, 17, 82, 228
Klumberg, Wilhelm, 63
Knight, Frank, 64
Köhler, Walter, wartime publications, 101
Komppa, Gustav, 63
Königsberg, University of, 192, 193, 228
Krause, Hermann, 158, 159
Krieck, Ernst, 32–33, 41, 66–67, 72, 83, 115, 118, 132, 133, 180, 183, 184, 239, 241; on the universities in the National Socialist state, 31; as Rector (1937), 38, 79–80, 81; on scholarship in the National Socialist state, 53, 55, 57, 60; on the war, 90; wartime teaching, 96
Krüger, Herbert, 43, 91
Krüger, Paul, 72; wartime teaching, 95
Kubach, Fritz, 15
Kühn, Johannes, 221, 227, 228
Kuhn, Karl Georg, 217, 221–222
Kunkel, Wolfgang, 225
Kunstmann, Heinrich, 16
Kutscher, Waldemar, wartime teaching, 95

Lamartine, Alphonse de, 78
Landfried, Fritz, 102, 104, 106, 114
Laughlin, Harry Hamilton, 65
Law Faculty, 42–43, 96, 158–159, 191, 193–194, 219–220, 222–223

"Law for the Liberation from National Socialism and Militarism" (1946), 178–179. *See also* Spruchkammer
"Law for the Prevention of Genetically Diseased Offspring" (1933), 44, 198. *See also* Sterilization
"Law for the Restoration of the Professional Civil Service" (1933), 16. *See also* Purges
Lederer, Emil, 9
Leipzig, University of, 162–163
Lenard, Philipp, 30, 46, 107, 118, 180, 204–205, 236
Lenz, Friedrich, 73, 75
Levy, Ernst, 42
Lichnowsky, Leonore, 227
Liebmann, Heinrich, 47
Litt, Theodor, 162, 215
Loewenstein, Karl, 149, 172, 174, 179
Löwith, Karl
Ludwig, Emil, 127
Lundborg, Herman, 65

Maas, Hermann, 110
Mainz, University of, 191, 214
Mann, Otto, response to National Socialism, 28
Mann, Thomas, 57, 127
Marburg, University of, 132, 137, 141
Markmann, Heinz, 227
Maschke, Erich, 221, 228, 229
Medical Faculty, 43–46, 93, 94, 95, 137–138, 139, 141, 151–152, 156–158, 194, 196, 197, 199, 203, 220, 236
Mehls, Walter, wartime teaching, 96
Meinecke, Friedrich, 188, 215
Meinhold, Helmut, 221, 227, 228
Meister, Karl, 183
Mennecke, Friedrich, 108
Metz, Friedrich, wartime publications, 101
Mielke, Fred, 226
Mierendorff, Carlo, 110
Mitscherlich, Alexander: reopening of university, 118, 119, 121; on denazification, 152, 156–157; investigates German medical profession, 226–227
Mitteis, Heinrich, 42
Moldaenke, Günther: wartime teaching, 96; and denazification, 159–160
Mollier, Georg, 132, 134
Mönch, Walter, 76–78, 229–230; wartime publications, 97, 98–99; on denazification, 213–214
Montaigne, Michel de, 77
Moskowitz, Moses, 149–150, 174
Muccio, John, 130
Munich, University of, 46, 54, 172, 173, 201
Murphy, Robert, 126

Nägeli, Otto, 66
National Socialist German Workers' Party (Nazi Party, NSDAP): and universities, 4, 5–7, 12–13, 22; professors and, 22, 70, 238. *See also* Denazification
National Socialist University Instructors League (NSDDB), 13
Natural Sciences Faculty, 46–48, 93, 94–95, 96, 151–152, 205, 220
Neumann, Franz, 127, 172, 176
Nieland, Hans, 30
Niemöller, Martin, 124
November pogrom (1938), 82–83
Nuremberg Medical trial (1946), 226. *See also* Mitscherlich, Alexander
Nuremberg race laws, 51. *See also* Purges

Odenwald, Theodor, 36, 37, 118, 133
Oehme, Curt, 118–119, 136; and denazification, 156
Oeschle, Richard, 15, 37
Office of Strategic Services (OSS), 119, 127, 149, 150
Ohnesorge, Wilhelm, 107
Olschki, Leonardo, 38, 143
"Operation T-4." *See* "Euthanasia"

Paatz, Walter, 143
Panzer, Friedrich, 38, 50, 68, 183; wartime publications, 97, 100–101
Panzer, Wolfgang, 42, 68–69, 209; wartime teaching: 95, 96; Spruchkammer trial, 180–181, 189–191
Paret, Rudi, 36
Parsons, Talcott, 10
Patton, George S., 148
Penham, Daniel F., 146–147, 159, 160, 174, 175, 188, 242–243; background, 161–163; investigation of Heidelberg professors, 163–167; and Karl Heinrich Bauer, 164–166, 168, 169; and Karl Jaspers, 167, 169–170; denounced by Heidelberg University Senate, 168–169

Perels, Leonard, 142
Philipp Lenard Institute, 52–54, 62, 93, 94–95
Philosophy Faculty, 38–39, 93, 122, 132–133, 151–152, 181, 183–184, 188–189, 219, 221, 227–229
Pietrusky, Friedrich, 203
Purges (1933–1937), 16; fate of purged scholars, 16–17, 141–145; response of Jewish scholars to, 17–19; response of non-Jewish scholars to, 17–22, 28–29

Race: in nonmedical scholarly areas, 71, 74–79, 236–237; in medical sciences, 72–74, 88–89, 199–201, 202–203, 237
Radbruch, Gustav, 9, 21, 42, 138, 142, 188, 221, 227; reopening of university, 118–120; on denazification, 153–154, 158, 168
Ranke, Hermann, 38, 80, 142
Rauch, Joachim, 109, 221
Rauchhaupt, Friedrich Wilhelm von, 42; wartime teaching, 95
Raumer, Kurt von: response to National Socialism, 27, 28, 68
Regenbogen, Otto, 111, 142, 183–184, 189; on the universities in the National Socialist state, 34; fired from Heidelberg, 80; reopening of university, 118–119, 122, 132–133; on denazification, 155, 168
Reich Education Ministry (Reichserziehungsministerium, REM), 13. *See also* Rust, Bernhard
Reich Institute for the History of the New Germany (Reichsinstitut für Geschichte des neuen Deutschlands), 30–31, 221
Rein, Adolf, 31
Richter, Werner, 126–127
Rickert, Heinrich, 38
Ritter, Gerhard, 2, 183, 215–216
Ritterbusch, Paul, 96
Ritzert, Alex, 118
Robertson, Charles Grant, 56
Rodenwaldt, Ernst, 45–46, 64–65, 72, 73–74, 221; wartime teaching, 95; wartime publications, 97; Spruchkammer trial, 180–181, 199–203; on denazification, 213; memoirs of, 213
Roelcke, Karl, 118
Rosenberg, Alfred, 192, 193, 207

Rosenkranz, Gerhard, 74–75; wartime teaching, 96
Rosenthal, Arthur, 16–17, 47, 143–144
Rüdin, Ernst, 73
Rudolph, Herbert, wartime publications, 101
Rüger, Ludwig, 205
Rukop, Hans, 53
Runge, Hans, 45, 94, 138, 157, 221; Spruchkammer trial, 180–181, 197–199
Rust, Bernhard, 13, 14, 79–80, 89; on scholarship in the National Socialist state, 58–59

Salin, Edgar, 224
Sandig, Carl, 104
Schachermeyr, Fritz, 74
Schäffer, Fritz, 148
Scheel, Gustav Adolf, 15, 163
Scherberger, Richard, 69, 70
Schieder, Theodor, 228, 230
Schirach, Baldur von, 193
Schlüter, Hermann, 132, 134
Schmidhuber, Karl, 37, 88, 118, 156, 157, 180
Schmincke, Alexander, 95
Schmitt, Carl, 2, 3, 154, 222–223
Schmitthenner, Paul, 30, 38–39, 104, 114, 115, 118, 132, 133, 175, 180, 183, 184, 237, 239, 241; on the university in the National Socialist state, 33; on military sciences, 61–62, 66–67; as Rector (1938–1945), 79, 80, 83–84, 85; on the war, 90–91; wartime teaching, 95, 96; wartime publications, 97, 100–101
Schneider, Carl, 41, 43–45, 62–63, 64–65, 72–73, 114, 118, 132, 134, 138–139, 180, 196, 221, 236; wartime teaching, 95; as "euthanasia" researcher, 107–110
Schneider, Lambert, 220
Schneider, Monika, 109
Schönfeld, Walther, 156
Schrade, Hubert, 38, 93, 97
Schurman, Jacob Gould, 10, 58
Schuster, Ernst, 16, 41, 42, 91, 104, 106, 160
Schweitzer, Bernhard, 162–163
Security Service (Sicherheitsdienst, SD), Heidelberg professors as informants for, 13
Seeliger, Rolf, 217, 232

Seifert, Herbert, 47, 143, 168
Seiffert, Alfred, 156
Seybold, August, 55–56, 72, 205; on scholarship in the National Socialist state, 53; wartime teaching, 95
Siebeck, Richard, 18; wartime teaching, 95
Sieber, Eugen, 104
Six, Franz Alfred, 15, 16, 29, 41
Snijder, G. A. S., 63
Social Democratic Party of Germany (SPD), 178
Söllner, Otto, 132, 133
Sombart Corinna, 220
Spitzer, Leo, 17–18
Spruchkammer, 174, 175, 177–180, 206, 216–217, 232, 243–244, 245
Srbik, Heinrich Ritter von, 63
Stain, Johannes, 33, 62; on scholarship in the National Socialist state, 53
Stannard, Harold, 56–57
Stark, Johannes, 54
State and Economic Sciences Faculty, 40–42, 61, 70–72, 93, 94, 103–104, 236; dissolved (1945), 122
Stayer, Morrison, 128, 129
Steiner, John, 171
Sterilization, 43–44, 89; practiced at Heidelberg University, 45, 199
Sternberger, Dolf, 220
Stone, Shepard, 10, 124
Students: Nazi, 15–16, 20, 22, 59; postwar, 123–124
Sultan, Herbert, 29, 41, 145

Täubler, Eugen, 38; responds to National Socialism, 29
Tellenbach, Gerd, 14; on the university in the National Socialist state, 33
Tomaschek, Rudolf, 205
Theology faculty, 35–38, 96, 133–134, 141, 159–160, 221–222
Thoms, Walter, 41–42, 71–72, 93–94, 97, 102–103, 104, 105–106, 118
Threlfall, Wilhelm, 143
Thun, Ferdinand, 64
Timm, Kurt, 107
Tübingen, University of, 69, 210, 222

Ubisch, Gerta von, 18–19, 144, 239
Ulmer, Eugen, 158
United States of America: occupation policy, 124–125; policy toward postwar universities, 125–130. *See also* Denazification
Urbach, Rudolf, 173

Vienna, University of, 193
Vogt, Heinrich, 46, 47, 157

Wacker, Otto, 13
Wagenknecht, Willy, 96
Wagner, Robert, 80
Wahl, Eduard, 223
Wahle, Ernst, 30, 41, 68
Waldecker, Ludwig, 17
Waldkirch, Wilhelm, 34
Wandlung, Die (Metamorphosis), 220, 221
Wallach, Frederick, 164–165, 175
Wandruszka, Mario von, 97
"War Lectures" (Kriegsvorträge), 90–92
Weber, Alfred, 9, 110, 111, 144–145, 220, 221, 225, 227, 245; responds to National Socialism, 21, 22, 29, 40; reopening of university, 118–120, 122, 130; on denazification, 138, 160
Weber, Marianne, 9; salon circle, 20–21, 22, 29, 110–113, 114–115, 220
Wegner, Udo, 47, 106, 107
Weimar Republic, and Heidelberg University, 7–11, 30, 36, 235–236
Weinreich, Max, 2–3, 216
Weizäcker, Viktor von, 74, 138, 290, 221
Wendland, Heinz-Dietrich, 37
Wendt, Karl Friedrich, 109, 221
Wesch, Ludwig, 20, 46, 62, 107, 118, 132; Spruchkammer trial, 180–181, 204–206
"Westforschung," 67–68, 100–101
Wilmanns, Karl, 43, 142
Wilser, Julius, 95, 96
Working Group for Modern Social History, 230
Wunderlich, Frieda, 125
Wüst, Walther, 75

Zehrer, Hans, 230
Zimmer, Heinrich, 80, 82

ST. JOSEPH'S COLLEGE CALLAHAN LIBRARY

3 1960 02438 889

CALLAHAN LIBRARY
ST. JOSEPH'S COLLEGE
25 Audubon Avenue
Patchogue, NY 11772-2327